SIR HENRY NEVILLE
WAS SHAKESPEARE

SIR HENRY NEVILLE WAS SHAKESPEARE

The Evidence

John Casson and William D. Rubinstein

AMBERLEY

Dedicated to Brenda James, who discovered that Henry Neville was the writer Shakespeare, and without whom we would not have made these discoveries.

The 1596 portrait of Sir Henry Neville on the front cover is reproduced courtesy of the Neville family. It is the earliest of three portraits, the other two being at Audley End House and dated 1599. These were all painted in Neville's lifetime, unlike the existing pictures of William Shakspere from Stratford. In contrast, they were created after his death, and all of these pictures are disputed, fake or questionable.

First published 2016

Amberley Publishing
The Hill, Stroud
Gloucestershire, GL5 4EP

www.amberley-books.com

Copyright © John Casson and William D. Rubinstein, 2016

The right of John Casson and William D. Rubinstein to be identified as the Author
of this work has been asserted in accordance with the Copyrights, Designs and Patents Act 1988.

British Library Cataloguing in Publication Data.
A catalogue record for this book is available from the British Library.

ISBN 978 1 4456 5466 9 (paperback)
ISBN 978 1 4456 5467 6 (ebook)

Typesetting and Origination by Amberley Publishing.
Printed in Great Britain.

Contents

Introduction

How is this justified?

All's Well That Ends Well: 4.3.54

Is yet another book on the Authorship Question and Henry Neville in particular (there are now eight) justified? Our answer is yes. The reason we suggest it is justified is the emergence of new and telling evidence: hence our title. In contrast there is a growing body of negative evidence against William from Stratford. Many researchers are now able to show again and again that he lacked not only the knowledge and experience to have written the plays but also left no clear evidence of having been a playwright at all. We will focus this book on extant evidence rather than speculation or belief. We aim to show that William from Stratford not only *was not* the author of the Shakespeare canon but also that he *could not* have been.

For over 150 years, highly intelligent and well-informed people have questioned whether William Shakspere wrote the works attributed to him. In recent years these doubts have grown and are in the mainstream, in the sense that serious academics now pose the same question. At least two universities, Brunel in Uxbridge, Middlesex, UK and Concordia in Portland, Oregon, USA, have offered advanced and objective courses in the 'Shakespeare Authorship Question' which dispassionately assess the evidence surrounding this matter. Numerous learned societies debate the authorship and conferences are held to discuss the issue. Those who question the orthodox belief in William from Stratford are known as 'Anti-Stratfordians'. While some of these are eccentric and highly imaginative in their approach, most are intelligent, rational people who are simply bewildered by the enormous gap between the magnitude of Shakespeare's achievement and the meagre background of the man from Stratford.

The Authorship Question can be defined as the reasonable doubt that the works of Shakespeare were written by a man who left no letters, manuscripts or traces of his literary life; whose daughters were illiterate; whose family owned no copies of his works and never referred to him as a writer; who never travelled outside England yet set many plays in other countries; whose life, and the documents of that life, do not offer any explanation as to how he became such a great writer (see Chapter 1). The Authorship Question arises from this: if not the man from Stratford, who was the writer? Various names have been suggested in answer to this question but most of these were guesses unsupported by evidence that can withstand careful scrutiny (see Chapter 2). Among the candidates for the authorship of the Shakespeare canon

Henry Neville stands out because of the wealth of documentary and other evidence linking him intimately with the works. This book surveys the evidence which has emerged since his authorship was first identified by Brenda James. It has been startling to find more and more evidence for Henry Neville as we have examined letters, manuscript documents and annotated books. His life story has also slowly revealed more and more relevant experience that enabled him to write the canon and explains why he would have concealed his authorship. Many writers have used pen names and hidden their identity for a variety of reasons. For example, 'Walpole initially claimed that *The Castle of Otranto* was a translation of an earlier manuscript from 1529. The novel employs an archaic style of writing to further reinforce this subterfuge. It was only in the second edition that Walpole admitted authorship – fiction generally being considered a waste of a gentleman's time in the 1760s.[1] Writers living under oppressive regimes today are using pen names and hiding their identities so they are free to write what they wish: failure to hide your identity can cost your freedom, physical safety and even your life. It was so in Shakespeare's day when the written word was readily interpreted as evidence of treason. We examine Neville's reasons for secrecy in Chapter 2.

The accuracy of our claim that Sir Henry Neville (*c.* 1562–1615) wrote Shakespeare's works depends in part upon the orthodox dating of the plays being mostly accurate. We generally accept this dating and our identification of Neville as the author depends upon the accepted chronology being accurate, given the close match with his life and the relative lack of a mesh with the life of Shakspere or of any other authorship candidate. The chapters in this book follow the development of Shakespeare's writing through the plays in chronological order. There is one exception to this. We make a case that *The Merry Wives of Windsor* was written in 1599–1600 and not in 1597 as has previously been suggested. A number of orthodox scholars agree with this change of date, which was proposed before we found reason to question the earlier date. In Chapter 6 we treat *The Merry Wives of Windsor* as a test case for Neville's authorship.

Finally in our last chapter we survey the different categories of evidence with reflections on Neville's psychology as far as we can gauge it from his life, letters and library books. Time and again Neville fits the profile of the Bard, whereas the evidence for William from Stratford remains too scant and inconclusive to justify the belief in his authorship. The unusual vocabulary used in Neville's letters shows a parallel evolution to that of Shakespeare far too often to be explained as coincidence. Neville's library is preserved at Audley End House near Cambridge and contains books that were source works for Shakespeare, many of which are annotated.[2] An extensive collection of books at the time was both rare and extremely expensive. This makes it highly unlikely that someone with borrowing access would feel free to annotate the texts. From this it is reasonable to infer that the annotator must have been a Neville family member. It is evident that Neville both read these source texts and used the annotations to aid his reading and writing even if it cannot be proven conclusively that he wrote every note. The one reason to doubt that Neville wrote all the annotations is because the handwriting varies. However, the annotator's habits of abbreviation and transposing letters occurs frequently across the hands and it can be argued that a variation of handwriting between a young student and a mature adult is to be expected. Also, the writing implements and inks varied and the use of different scripts by those educated at the time was common.[3] In the absence of evidence to the contrary, it is reasonable to presume that Neville himself made most of the annotations on the source material held in his library.

Among the books in the Neville library are two volumes on Roman history by Appian and Dionysius of Halicarnassus: both have been acknowledged as sources for Shakespeare's Roman plays. Some confusion may arise in the fact that the Appian volume also contains another copy of Dionysius's work so when referring to this we will list it as Appian (Dionysius section) whereas when illustrating the annotations in the Dionysius volume we will refer to that as Dionysius of Halicarnassus. Neville annotated this latter volume as far as page 89 but made notes in the margins of the entire Appian and its Dionysius section, reading hundreds of pages of Greek: he was indeed a scholar. Most of the photographed images of Neville manuscripts and annotations that we have included throughout this book are exactly as they were taken. A few have had the contrast increased to highlight very faint annotations. This work was done with great care not to alter the content while ensuring that the image is as clear as possible.

We conclude our book with an appendix offering the result of groundbreaking research by David Ewald and John Casson into the sonnets.

We identify quotations from Shakespeare by putting the act, scene and line in brackets after the quotation. We mostly use the Arden editions of the plays but have also used the Oxford and Cambridge editions among others. This can lead to some confusion as editors vary and so the line numbers can be different. Readers may need to search a little in their editions, if lines are different, to find the passage.

We have modernised the dates of letters of the period. The Elizabethan year ended in March, not in December, so a letter that Neville dated 5 March 1600 was written on 5 March 1601 in the modern calendar.

What's in a Name?

In this book we propose that 'William Shakespeare' was two different men: the actual author, Sir Henry Neville, and the actor/manager in the theatre, William Shakspere. To distinguish between the two men we will use the spelling Shakspere for William from Stratford and Shakespeare for the poet-playwright, except when quoting other scholars' works, when we retain these authors' original spelling. (See Chapter 1 for more detailed examination of the question of spelling these names.) We also refer to the poet-playwright as the Bard.

Confusion may arise because Neville's father, son, grandson and cousin were all called Henry Neville. When referring to our subject we generally name him Neville, whereas when referring to his father we use his full name, Sir Henry Neville, and definitively identify anyone else of this name by qualifying their identity.

Acknowledgements

We are grateful to Vian Smith for his invaluable help editing the text and enhancing some of the illustrations. We wish to thank Mark Bradbeer for his help on the History Plays;

Dr John O'Donnell for his help with Chapters 2 and 7; L. S. Deas for his translation of the Latin poem by John Chamber; David Ewald for the paper we present in the appendix and other research including Neville's monopoly of the export of iron guns and also for proofreading; Hilary Elstone researched Neville's son William and shared her findings with us so we have been able to include some of what she found in Chapter 2. We are grateful to Tony Minchin, John O'Donnell and John Leigh who helped with proofreading. Without all their help this book would have been much the poorer.

Permissions

1) The Hollar engraving of the Holy Trinity Stratford-upon-Avon Shakespeare Monument is published with the permission of the Thomas Fisher Rare Book Library, University of Toronto.
2) Today's monument at Stratford is published with the permission from Holy Trinity Church, Stratford-upon-Avon. The image was taken from the web: http://commons.wikimedia.org/wiki/File:ShakespeareMonument_cropped.jpg#/media/File:ShakespeareMonument_cropped.jpg. The original, cropped from Image:ShakespeareMonument.JPG was released to PD by Tom Reedy. Licensed under Public Domain via Wikimedia Commons.
3) The images of the annotated Hall's *Chronicle* are published with the permission of the owners.
4) Reproduction of the miniature Nicholas Hilliard portrait of Henry Wriothesley, 3rd Earl of Southampton (Accession number: 3856) is © The Fitzwilliam Museum, Cambridge.
5) Images from the inscription at the end of *A Lover's Complaint* in the John Rylands copy of the 1609 *Shake-speares Sonnets* are copyright of the University of Manchester.
6) Images from Neville's draft letter of 1603/4 are published with the permission of the Berkshire Record Office, Reading.
7) The photograph of Neville's name in the 1538 *Ptolemiæi Astronomi*, 32.A.4, at Merton College Library is published with the permission of the Warden and Fellows of Merton College, Oxford.
8) Images from the Northumberland Manuscript are reproduced with the permission of the Archives of the Duke of Northumberland at Alnwick Castle (DNP: MS 525).
9) Images of Neville's draft 1603-4 letter, CP94/90 in the Salisbury manuscript collection at Hatfield House, are published by courtesy of the Marquess of Salisbury, Hatfield House.
10) The illustrations from the Worsley Manuscripts are published with the permission of the 8th Earl of Yarborough and Lincolnshire Archives.
11) Images from the following manuscripts are © The British Library Board:
Harley MS7368 folios 8, 9 and watermark (Hand D of *Sir Thomas More*);
Cotton MSS Caligula EX folio 21 and 21V: Neville's letter of 19 February 1601;
Stowe 174 folio 116: Neville's letter of 16 July 1613.
12) Images of books possibly annotated by Henry Neville are published with the permission of the owners: Private Collection.

1

Why Question the Authorship? Shakespeare or Shakspere?

What's in a name?

Romeo and Juliet, 2.2.43

Why does anyone question whether 'William Shakespeare', who was born in Stratford-upon-Avon in Warwickshire in 1564 and who died there in 1616, wrote the plays and poems attributed to him? His name is apparently on the title page of most of his works, and a splendid memorial collection of his plays, edited and with an introduction by Ben Jonson, known as the First Folio, was published in 1623. Why question his authorship, when no one doubts that John Milton, William Wordsworth, Jane Austen, Thomas Hardy, or many other famous authors, wrote the works attributed to them? In fact there are many reasons, so many and so puzzling that during the past 200 years many people have questioned whether the William from Stratford was the actual author. We will now set out some of the most important reasons for questioning whether this was the man who wrote the plays and poems published under the name of 'William Shakespeare'.

Spelling Shakespeare

There is a major anomaly in the spelling and use of William Shakespeare's name.[1] Briefly put, all official documents and records from his lifetime which mention him, except two, spell his name as 'Shakspere' or something very similar, not as Shakespeare, the name by which the Bard is universally known.[2] In complete contrast, all of the published editions of his plays and poems which appeared in his lifetime or soon afterwards, like the First Folio of 1623, spell his name in the commonly accepted way, William Shakespeare. This difference may appear trivial, but this discrepancy may well conceal something fundamental about the author's identity. The Stratford man's surname is spelled 'Shakspere' (not 'Shakespeare') in the record of his christening and those of his sisters Joan (September 1558) and Margaret (December 1562 and again in April 1563), his brother Gilbert (October 1566), and for all other relatives baptised at Stratford-upon-Avon. His own baptismal record (26 April 1564) describes him as 'Guilielmus filius Johannes Shakspere' and he was buried (26 April 1616) as 'Will. Shakspere, gent.' The two existing marriage licences (both in November 1582, to 'Anne Whately' and 'Anne Hathwey') spell his surname, respectively, as 'Shaxpere' and 'Shagspere'. On the baptismal record of his daughter Susanna (May 1583) it is 'Shakspere', as it is on the baptismal record of his twins Hamnet and Judith (February 1585).[3] On the six authentic signatures of the Stratford man, although they are blotted and partly illegible, the name is apparently 'Shaksper'.[4]

In complete contrast, the name of the author of the poems and plays stated on their title page is 'William Shakespeare' or a hyphenated version of this name: 'Shake-speare'. It is never 'Shakspere'. William from Stratford never spelt his name with a hyphen, which strongly suggests it was a pseudonym. The earliest use of the hyphen was in the anonymous *Willobie His Avisa* published in 1594, where we find the statement, 'And Shake-speare paints poor Lucrece rape'. The hyphen then appeared on the title page of the second quartos of *Richard III* and *Richard II* in 1598, the first plays to identify Shakespeare as their creator.[5] The hyphen was again used in the 1599 second quarto of *Henry IV: Part I*; in 1601 at the end of *The Phoenix and the Turtle*; in 1603 on the frontispiece of the first quarto of *Hamlet*; in 1608 on the first quarto of *King Lear* and again in 1619; in 1609 when *Shake-speares Sonnets* were published (without any William); on the third quarto of *Henry VI: Parts II and III* published together in 1619; on the fourth variant and fifth quartos of *Romeo and Juliet* in 1622 and 1637 (all previous quartos of this play had been anonymous); on the third quarto of *The Merry Wives of Windsor* printed in 1630. Furthermore in 1611 John Davies used the hyphen in his *Scourge of Folly*: 'To our English Terence, Mr. Will Shake-speare.' Terence was a Roman actor who passed off other people's plays as his own.[6] Ben Jonson used the name 'Will. Shake-speare' when listing the actors in *Sejanus* in the 1616 folio edition of the play, which had been performed in 1603. In 1616 Shakspere was dead.

So, if the Stratford man's name was actually 'Shakspere' (or the like), why aren't his works known as by 'William Shakspere' rather than 'Shakespeare'? We do not know whether the two men, actor and author, co-operated. We could speculate that the actual author, who perhaps was using the Stratford actor and theatre-sharer as his producer-director, wished to distinguish between them. Possibly this was the only basis on which the Stratford man would agree to co-operate in the scheme, which entailed his taking apparent credit for many controversial works, some of which could have led to him being charged with treason, imprisoned and tortured (as happened to some of his fellow playwrights). To do this and keep intact the fiction that the Stratford man wrote the works attributed to him, the real author adopted a somewhat more phonetic spelling of the actor's name, close enough for the two to be confused, but different enough to retain the identity and autonomy of the actor. If this was not so, why was the purported author's name never spelled 'Shakspere' on the title page of his works, not even once? Didn't the Stratford man want to see his own name in print?

Books in the Running Brooks

There is no evidence that William Shakspere ever went to school. He had the right as a burgess's son to go to Stratford Grammar School and might have attended between about 1571, when he was seven, until about 1579, when he was fifteen.[7] This is uncertain because the records of Stratford Grammar School for that period no longer exist. The upward age limit given here may also be in some doubt because William's father, John, appears to have run into considerable financial difficulty around 1576–7 and might have considered the payment of his son's school fees an unnecessary expense. Many commentators have stressed the apparently difficult curriculum of the school, consisting of endless hours of memorising Latin texts, which, according to them, gave the young Shakspere all the erudition he needed to write his plays. But the exact curriculum employed at Stratford Grammar School is unknown to us. The known syllabus of other grammar schools of the time varied very considerably, with some being quite superficial.[8] As Park Honan noted, 'the narrow focus upon Latin could be stultifying. Grammar school boys were taught nothing about modern history, society, politics, the life of their town or country or nation, almost nothing about the crafts, the trades, agriculture, the human body, or any other topic likely to be useful to them.'[9] Nor, it might be added, any other foreign language, whether ancient (Greek or Hebrew) or modern (like French, Italian, or Spanish); nor, for that matter, either how to write a cogent sentence or paragraph in English, or anything about the body of English literature such as it was by the 1570s (such as Chaucer, Gower and Lydgate) or any recent foreign literature; nor about astronomy, medicine, the law, sailing at sea, court life, or any other of the many subjects of which Shakespeare apparently had considerable knowledge. Finally, it might be pointed out that among the main purposes of education at any English grammar school at that time was to enforce political and religious conformity in a country which had, within the previous century, changed dynasty and religion, whose ruling regime sought stability and loyalty above all and severely punished dissenters and would-be traitors. Yet Shakespeare's works are the epitome of the liberated imagination and often sail close to the wind in terms of their depictions of political disloyalty.

Whatever its content, it is clear that Shakspere's formal education ceased by the time he was fifteen, possibly by thirteen. William Shakspere had no further formal education. He certainly did not attend either of the two universities that existed at the time in England, Oxford and Cambridge. We know this because both universities have complete records of matriculants. As Shakspere married aged eighteen in November 1582, and university undergraduates had to be unmarried, he could not have attended a university in any case. We also know that he did not he attend any law training such as the Inns of Court in London.

It is also clear that William Shakspere's educational profile was quite different from that of most leading playwrights of the time. Examining a list of the thirty-one most prominent English playwrights active at the same time (*c.* 1590–1612) reveals that seventeen (55 per cent) attended Oxford or Cambridge Universities, and two others one of the Inns of Court.[10] Of the twelve men who apparently did not have any higher education, there is usually a good explanation of how they acquired their erudition and literary skills. The best-known of these was Ben Jonson and there is no mystery about his education and ability to write. Jonson attended Westminster School where he was taught by William Camden, the great scholar, whom he later acknowledged as the source of 'all that I am in arts, all that I know'.[11] At Westminster School, Jonson also 'benefited deeply from the school's traditions of rhetorical and classical training, and in particular, from the exercise of rendering Greek and Latin verse and prose into their equivalent English forms. Camden, who had a good knowledge of earlier English poetry, seems also to have encouraged his boys to write verses of their own in English.[12] Jonson is also known to have used extensively the 'superlative collection of books and manuscripts' assembled by his classmate Robert Cotton.[13]

Another contemporary playwright who was not a university man, Anthony Munday (1560–1633), apparently studied with Claudius Hollyband, a London Huguenot, who taught him Latin, French, and Italian, and then travelled to France and to Italy where he attended the English School in Rome.[14] A third non-university playwright, Cyril Tourneur (d. 1626), was probably the son of a barrister of the Middle Temple.[15] The majority of well-known playwrights who were Shakespeare's contemporaries, it should be stressed, were university men: Marlowe, Lyly, Middleton, Heywood, Massinger, Beaumont and Fletcher among others.

In complete contrast, there is no evidence which explains how or where William Shakspere acquired the remarkable erudition or ability to express himself so uniquely, and no clue where he obtained the plethora of books he used as the basis of his plays and poems. Despite Jonson's lines about the Stratford man having 'small Latin and less Greek', the author of the plays was in fact quite extraordinarily learned. Shakespeare's plays and poems apparently used as their sources the works of no fewer than 140 different authors, both ancient and modern. (*Notes and Queries* and other scholarly journals constantly report previously unsuspected sources which Shakespeare used in his works.) He apparently knew Latin, Greek, French, Italian and Spanish, since he used sources in these languages that had not been translated into English.[16] For example:

> In four instances in which Shakespeare's important characters deviate from [Arthur] Brooke's poem [*The Tragicall Historye of Romeus and Juliet*, written in 1562], *Romeo and Juliet* agrees with the original version [in Italian] of Luigi da Porta of which no known English or French translation was in existence ... Shakespeare's reliance on *Il Pecorone* in the original Italian for *The Merchant of Venice* illustrates the problem [of Shakespeare's knowledge of foreign languages] perfectly. *Il Pecorone* was published in Milan in 1554 but not translated into English in Shakespeare's time.[17]

Shakespeare appears to have been able to read ancient Greek and had an extensive knowledge of classical Greek sources. For example, the final two sonnets (153 and 154) are apparently based on *The Greek Anthology*, a Byzantine compendium of Greek epigrams (see Chapter 10).[18]

Orthodox biographers consistently ignore or downplay the overwhelming evidence of Shakespeare's extraordinary erudition, because the eight years (at the very most) spent at Stratford Grammar School, and the lack of education beyond the age of fifteen, is incapable of explaining it. They also ignore another problem just as significant and puzzling: just where did Shakspere obtain and read the countless sources which he clearly incorporated in his works? There were, of course, no public libraries in his time; there was no university in London until the 1820s, and the Stratford man had no access to the libraries at Oxford or Cambridge. Shakspere would have needed a truly extensive private library, one which would have presumably cost him a fortune. At the time he had no known permanent address in London and was perhaps travelling several times a year back and forth to Stratford. There is no evidence to suggest he had such a library and there are no Shakespeare source books with his name written in them identifying them as his property which are not considered doubtful or forgeries. There is also no evidence that he had access to someone else's extensive private library. Two such candidates have been suggested by orthodox scholars who have addressed this question. First, the say that Shakspere may have had access to the private library of a nobleman like Lord Burghley or the 3rd Earl of Southampton. However, this is speculation without evidence, just as there is no evidence that the Stratford man knew any noblemen, even Southampton, his supposed patron. Secondly, it has been suggested that Richard Field (*c.* 1561–1624), Shakspere's contemporary from Stratford-upon-Avon, who became a leading publisher in London and published Shakespeare's two long poems of 1593 and 1594, as well as *Love's Martyr* (1601), which contained *The Phoenix and the Turtle,* may have provided him with access to the necessary library.[19] However, there is no evidence that Field maintained a library of obscure literary sources in many languages: he was simply a skilled London printer. There is also no evidence that Field had any continuing connection of any kind with Shakspere. Apart from *The Phoenix and the Turtle,* which appeared as part of a longer collection edited by Robert Chester, Field printed or published none of Shakespeare's works after 1594. He had no connection with any of the many quarto editions of the plays or with the First Folio of 1623. He was not mentioned in Shakspere's will, although he survived his former townsman by eight years.

Shakespeare and Warwickshire

A number of points about Warwickshire are regularly made as evidence that the Stratford man wrote the works attributed to him. One seemingly telling point is that he used 'Warwickshire dialect' words and 'localisms' in several of his plays. Because these dialect words would only be known to persons living there, and nowhere else in Britain, the author of Shakespeare's works must have been very familiar with Warwickshire and, in all likelihood, to have grown up there. According to David Kathman, 'Shakespeare's works are peppered with dialect words from Warwickshire and the West Midlands.' These words include 'batlet' for a paddle used to beat laundry (*As You Like It* 2.4.46); 'ballow' for cudgel and 'gallow' for terrify (*King Lear* 4.6.238; 3.2.44); 'unwappered' for unfatigued or fresh (*The Two Noble Kinsmen* 5.6.10).[20]

Before discussing any specific examples, two general points should be made. First, and despite the claims made by advocates of this viewpoint, we simply have no idea what words were unique to Warwickshire in the late sixteenth century when William Shakspere lived there. Our knowledge of what words and usages were 'dialect words' and 'localisms', employed in the speech of one distinct part of Britain derives from Joseph Wright's six-volume *English Dialect Dictionary,* which was published between 1898 and 1905.[21] The project to compile this work was begun in 1873 by Professor W. W. Skeat, who had founded the English Dialect Society in that year. Obviously neither Skeat nor Wright could record any words spoken in one distinct part of Britain three centuries before any living dialect speaker was interviewed for the project. The oldest dialect speakers would have been children over 200 years after Shakespeare's lifetime. Claims about 'Warwickshire dialect words' are thus based exclusively upon their appearance in a dictionary whose first volume appeared 282 years after Shakspere died, and more than 300 years after he was a child in Stratford-upon-Avon. There are no earlier dialect dictionaries, and so absolutely no way of knowing whether a word or usage described as exclusive to Warwickshire was actually spoken exclusively in or near Warwickshire (or anywhere else) in 1580. Claims about Shakespeare's use of Warwickshire words and usages are thus *ipso facto* dubious, and based upon inadequate or even misleading evidence. Moreover, Wright apparently classified some words as specific to Warwickshire because they appeared in Shakespeare's plays, so providing an egregious example of circular reasoning.[22]

There is also a second general reason why the attribution of words or usages in Shakespeare's plays as 'dialect words' specific to Warwickshire is *a priori* implausible. Shakespeare was writing for the London stage and for an audience of whom only a tiny percentage came from Warwickshire. Why, then, would he deliberately use words in his plays that could be understood by only a handful of theatregoers? Perhaps, if Shakspere of Stratford wrote the plays, he would be simply unaware that these words were local provincialisms? But surely the actors in the Lord Chamberlain's Men/King's Men would not have understood them and so would have asked him to substitute words in common usage. In fact, the popular success of the plays makes it more credible that the 'dialect words' in Shakespeare's plays were actually in common use in London at the time and would have been understood by most of the audience.

There are many specific reasons for rejecting the view that the author's Warwickshire origins are proved by his use of alleged local 'dialect words'. For instance, C. T. Onions claimed in 1911, in his *Shakespeare Glossary,* to have identified twenty-four Warwickshire words in the plays, but his contention was false and was withdrawn from revised editions of the book.[23] At least twenty-five words or terms in Shakespeare's works that have been claimed to provide examples of 'Warwickshire dialect' can be shown to have been in common use elsewhere.[24] For example, the entry for 'batlet' (see above) in Wright's *English Dialect Dictionary* actually reads: 'Yorkshire, also Warwickshire', with the additional comment: 'Obs[olete]? Not known to our correspondents in War[wickshire]'.[25] The only connection of 'batlet' with Warwickshire, in fact, is that it appears in *As You Like It,* by the circular reasoning that it must be a Warwickshire dialect word because Shakspere came from Warwickshire, and the Stratford man wrote the plays. In addition, 'dialect words' from all parts of Britain are found in Shakespeare's plays. Indeed, as A. J. Pointon notes, 'of all the regions of Britain, Warwickshire … has had the least influence on Shakespeare's language'.[26] There is simply no real evidence that Shakespeare employed Warwickshire 'dialect words'.

The second major point about Warwickshire made by many orthodox supporters of the Stratfordian view is that the plays contain references to specific places and persons near Stratford-upon-Avon. These claims also lack real evidence and strain credibility. For example, *The Taming of the Shrew* refers to 'Marian Hacket, the fat alewife of Wincot'. According to David Kathman, 'Wincot is a village four miles from Stratford where a real Hacket family was living in 1591, although the name also suggests Wilmcote, the hometown of Shakespeare's mother Mary Arden'.[27] Sidney Lee, the famous Victorian/Edwardian scholar and author of the entry on Shakespeare in the original *Dictionary of National Biography,* disagreed.

Wincot was the familiar designation of three small Warwickshire villages ... There is a very small hamlet named Wincot within four miles [of Stratford] now consisting of a single farmhouse which was once an Elizabethan mansion; it is situated on what was doubtless in Shakespeare's day, before the land there was enclosed, an open heath. This Wincot forms part of the parish of Quinton, where, according to the parochial registers, a Hacket family resided in Shakespeare's day ... Yet by Warwickshire contemporaries the Wincot of *The Taming of the Shrew* was unhesitatingly identified with Wilnecote, near Tamworth on the Staffordshire border of Warwickshire, at some distance away. [Actually, it is about fifty miles from Stratford.] This village, whose name was pronounced 'Wincot', was celebrated for its ale in the seventeenth century, a distinction which is not shown by contemporary evidence to have belonged to any place of like name.[28]

Similarly reliant on selective supposition is Kathman's statement that 'Christopher Sly calls himself old Sly's son of Burton Heath, referring to Barton-on-Heath, a village sixteen miles south of Stratford where Shakespeare's aunt Joan Lambert lived'.[29] This is just as likely to be a reference to Burton-upon-Trent in Staffordshire, also famous for its beer, and situated about ten miles north of Tamworth/Wilnecote, on the 'wrong' side of Stratford-upon-Avon. The other alleged references to places and persons near Stratford are similar, and equally debatable and dubious. Stratford-upon-Avon itself is never mentioned by the Bard. The only Stratford in the plays is 'Stony-Stratford' in *Richard III*, when the Archbishop of York reports on the whereabouts of the young Princes soon to be murdered in the Tower (2.4.1). The two Stratfords are fifty miles apart. The only play set in a provincial town is *The Merry Wives of Windsor* (see Chapter 6).

Shakespeare in Italy

Thirteen of Shakespeare's plays are set in whole or in part in Italy. Many contain minor details of geography or description of local places and sites which do not appear in any printed work likely to be known to William Shakspere. These details and descriptions could only be known to a visitor to the settings in Italy. There is no evidence that William Shakspere, the Stratford man, ever left England. For this reason, many non-Stratfordian commentators have suggested that the real author of Shakespeare's plays must have travelled to Italy. An example of detail that could not be guessed occurs in *Romeo and Juliet*, when Benvolio describes a sycamore grove to the west of Verona:

Madam, an hour before the worshipp'd sun
Peer'd forth the golden window of the East,
A troubled mind drave me to walk abroad
Where, underneath the grove of sycamore
That westward rooteth from the city's side,
So early walking did I see your son. (1.1.116)

Shakespeare's *Romeo and Juliet* is derived from previous versions of the story in Italian by Luigi da Porta and later Matteo Bandello, in French by Pierre Boaistuau, and later, in

English, by Arthur Brooke. None of these sources mentions a grove of sycamore. Yet, even today, a grove of sycamores still exists outside of Verona's west wall.[30] This detail could only have been known to an eyewitness visitor to Italy. There are dozens of similar minor details of the scenery and geography of Italy, and especially of the scenery and geography of the north-eastern corner of Italy from Milan and Mantua, to Verona, Padua and Venice, to be found in Shakespeare's plays.

It is just possible that Shakspere travelled to Italy during the 'lost years' of the 1580s, although no record that he did exists, and any such trip would have been expensive and needed government permission. The Stratford man was married and the father of children from 1582–3, when he was still a teenager, and had his way to make in the world. None of the accounts of Shakspere's life compiled in the seventeenth and eighteenth centuries claim that he had travelled abroad, although this would surely have been noted by some early biographer if it were true. It is sometimes suggested that he travelled to Italy in the entourage of an English nobleman such as the Earl of Southampton, but, again, there is no evidence that he did, nor, indeed, that he ever spoke to Southampton or any other nobleman. In fact, Southampton never visited Italy, and neither, it seems, did Ferdinando Stanley, 5th Earl of Derby (*c.* 1559–94), the 'Lord Strange' whose acting company, Lord Strange's Men, is thought to have employed the young Shakspere (again there is no evidence of any such employment). There is no hard evidence that begins to explain how the Stratford man could have known these details about Italy that appear in the canon.

Given that there is no evidence that Shakspere ever left England, most orthodox commentators have been reduced to claiming that his knowledge of Italy was actually superficial and slight, and that he could easily have learned about the country from Italian visitors or nationals in London, although, again, there is no evidence that he ever spoke to any Italian visitors or residents in London. He would have had to have asked them about innumerable minor details of geography used in his plays and received reliable answers. It is sometimes suggested that the linguist and author John Florio (1553–1625) might have been the source of these details. But Florio, whose writings and translations certainly influenced Shakespeare, never set foot in Italy.[31] Orthodox scholars consistently deny that Shakespeare had necessarily to have visited Italy to have used its local geography in his plays. He 'could and would have talked to travellers, seen paintings, read accounts' of Italy and other European sites.[32] But other scholars and researchers have concluded that the level of detail shown in his plays makes this highly improbable. Several scholars who hold this view are Italians who were familiar with the Italian settings at first hand.[33] Richard Paul Roe compiled a detailed description of the Italian sites in Shakespeare's plays, showing their consistent accuracy. These claims of remarkable accuracy are much better informed than the superficial and inaccurate orthodox view.

> Let us take, for example, the seeming trifle of St. Peter's in Verona, a church mentioned three times by Shakespeare in *Romeo and Juliet*. Stratfordian John Doherty has this to say about it: 'There has never been a Saint Peter's church in Verona. There is a San Tomaso's, a San Stefano's, etc … However, St. Peter's was as good a name for a church as any other for Shakespeare.' … the non-Stratfordian rolls up his sleeves, gets himself to Verona … not in order to discover if there is a church in Verona called St. Peter's, but

to establish which of the *four* churches of that name ... Shakespeare had in mind. By a process of elimination ... Richard Paul Roe was able to confirm Shakespeare's precise eye for detail by identifying the place of Juliet's proposed marriage to Paris as *San Pietro Incarnario* in the Via San Pietro Incarnario.[34]

Doherty made the simple mistake of not realising that St Peter is San Pietro in Italian. It thus seems overwhelmingly likely that the author of Shakespeare's plays, whoever he was, must have visited Italy, and particularly the towns in its north-east corner which figure so largely in his plays.

It is not credible that the author of Shakespeare's plays could have learned the dozens of eyewitness details about Italy by casually speaking to travellers in London pubs. Rather, it is necessary that the author had personally visited an extensive range of settings. This would have been expensive and, because it required government permission, is highly likely to have been recorded. Shakespeare used Italy as the scene of many of his early plays, rather than his later ones. It therefore seems likely that the Bard had visited Italy before he began writing.

The Rest Is Silence

Virtually everything we seemingly know about the supposed life and career of William Shakspere is based upon anecdotes and apocryphal stories written down many years after his death. The evidence which dates from Shakspere's lifetime is extraordinarily slight. For instance, in *Contested Will* (2010), James Shapiro discussed the evidence that Shakspere wrote the works attributed to him, trying to find convincing reasons why he did. He noted that George Buc (or Buck), Master of the Revels from 1610 to 1622, inquired about the authorship of a play published in 1599, *George a Greene, a Pinner of Wakefield* (a pinner is a dogcatcher). On the title page of the quarto edition of the play Buc wrote, 'Written by ... a Minister, who act[ed] the pinners part in it himself. *Teste* [Attested by] W. Shakespea[re].' The implication is that Buc met Shakspere and asked him about the authorship of the play.[35] As Shakspere was an actor and a sharer in the Lord Chamberlain's Men, this is not remarkable, but it tells us nothing whatever about whether Shakspere wrote *Hamlet*. Moreover, *George a Greene* is universally regarded as having been written by Robert Greene (1558–92), notorious for his dissolute lifestyle, who allegedly attacked Shakspere in *Greenes Groatsworth of Wit*. Shakspere appears either to have been ill-informed or have been deliberately misleading Buc. That Shapiro used this dubious anecdote as evidence that Shakspere was a playwright, despite the fact that it shows nothing of the kind, is indicative of the lack of contemporary evidence about his life, which frequently obliges those seeking to prove Shakspere's authorship to clutch at straws.

Much of the standard biographical lore about Shakspere's life was the product of two men, Revd John Ward (1629–81), who was Vicar of Stratford from 1662 until 1681, and Nicholas Rowe (1674–1718), the first critical editor of Shakespeare's works, who, in his 1709 edition of the plays, included the first brief biography of 'William Shakespeare' ever to appear in a published work. The dates here are significant: Ward became Vicar of Stratford forty-six years after Shakspere died and eighty years or so after he had left Stratford for London. Ward's remarks on Shakespeare were written in his *Notebooks* in 1662–3, and take up only twenty lines or so. Ward wrote an aide-memoire: 'Remember to peruse Shakespeare's plays ... that I be not ignorant of them.' About Shakespeare, Ward claimed that in writing his plays he 'had an allowance so large, that he spent at the rate of £1000 a year, as I have heard'.[36] (Modernised spelling.) Ward does not say where he heard this, or where this allowance came from. Presumably he meant it was from the Lord Chamberlain's Men/King's Men. The figure of £1,000 a year, the equivalent of £1 million today, is impossibly large. If Shakspere had received £25 for a play, this would have been generous. Ward's *Notebook* is also the source for the claim that 'Shakespeare, [Michael] Drayton and Ben Jonson had a merry meeting, and it seems drank too hard, for Shakespeare died of a fever there contracted'. Needless to say, there is no independent confirmation for this account.

Rowe's biography of Shakespeare appeared nearly a century after the Stratford man died, and is the source of the claim that Shakspere fled to London 'after robbing a park belonging to Sir Henry Lucy'; that as an actor he played the ghost in *Hamlet,* and that Lord Southampton 'at one time gave him a thousand pounds to enable him to go through with a purchase he had a mind to'.[37] This claim, apart from being *a priori* improbable, was described by Shakespeare's recent biographer as a myth, probably invented by Sir William Davenant, who claimed to be Shakespeare's illegitimate son. In early life, Southampton, who was living on a moderate allowance, inherited lands worth £1,097 per annum in total, and spent so lavishly that he had to sell off five manors.[38] There is no evidence that Southampton ever set eyes on Shakspere or that he ever saw him act in any play. Rowe's account is also inaccurate in other ways, for example he stated that Shakspere had three daughters (when in fact he had two). Ward and Rowe had no written sources from which to base a life of Shakspere, and no surviving letters, diaries, accounts by friends or colleagues, nor any newspaper clippings or obituaries: nothing whatever of the kind which would be used routinely today by any biographer of a writer. Both lived so long after Shakspere that virtually no one remained alive who knew him, in Rowe's case no one at all. They apparently relied on third-hand rumours and apocryphal tales invented or exaggerated many years later, some demonstrably false. Similarly, *Brief Lives* by John Aubrey (1626–97) contains an account of Shakspere's life which states that 'he understood Latin pretty well: for he had been in his younger days a schoolmaster in the country'.[39] Aubrey's biographical sketches were collected between 1680 and 1693, a century after Shakspere would have served as a 'schoolmaster in the country'.[40] Since schoolmasters, in the country or city, were almost invariably Oxbridge graduates (as were all of the schoolmasters at Stratford Grammar School in Shakspere's lifetime), and as Shakspere never attended a university, this claim is almost certainly false, and, in over 300 years of research, no one has ever identified the school where Shakspere was allegedly a schoolmaster. Similarly inaccurate is Aubrey's claim that Shakspere's father was a butcher, and that the young William 'exercised his father's trade, but when he killed a calf, he would do it in high style and make a speech'.[41] John Shakspere, the supposed Bard's father, was a glove-maker and wool dealer, not a butcher, and no one could possibly have remembered, a century later, how the young Shakspere 'killed a calf'. It may well be the case that not a single anecdote about the purported life of William Shakespeare/Shakspere, written in the century or so after his death, is accurate.

Indeed, to an extent which may seem astonishing today, little or nothing of an accurate and factual basis about William Shakspere's life was researched by scholars until the eighteenth century or even later. Perhaps the most striking example of this is that no one, literally no one, bothered to read Shakspere's will, with its celebrated legacy of the 'second-best bed' to his wife, until 1747, when Revd Joseph Greene (1712–90) did so; it was not published anywhere until 1763. No one made an attempt to determine the order in which the plays were written, absolutely central to understanding Shakespeare's evolution as a writer, until 1778, when the great scholar Edmond Malone (1741–1812) published his *Attempt to Ascertain the Order in Which the Plays of Shakespeare Were Written*.

The almost complete absence of contemporary evidence about Shakspere the man has meant that the flimsiest evidence about him has been expanded by orthodox biographers in almost astronomic fashion, and in a way which would surely be regarded as unacceptable and improper for the biographers of any other famous person. For example, in the 1920s it was discovered that the will of a Catholic landowner in rural Lancashire, Alexander de Hoghton, written in August 1581, requested that his friend Sir Thomas Hesketh, another Lancashire landowner, 'be friendly unto Fokke Gwyllim and William Shakeshafte [*sic*] now dwelling with me' and either take them into service or find them 'some good master'.[42] From this obscure clause in a Lancashire will concerning a 'William Shakeshafte' has grown a considerable industry of 'biographical' works claiming that this was actually the young William Shakespeare. Apparently de Hoghton did not know the actual name of someone he liked so much that he mentioned him in his will, who was employed as a kind of tutor or entertainer in this Catholic household in Lancashire (although what Shakeshafte was employed to do is quite unclear) and therefore Shakspere must himself have been a secret Roman Catholic. There is no evidence that Shakspere ever set foot in Lancashire (the early anecdotal accounts, of course, claim that he poached deer illegally near Stratford and bolted to London) or that he was a Roman Catholic. The Stratford man was baptised, married, and buried as a conforming Anglican. If he had been a secret Catholic, he would surely have taken pains to have his two daughters marry Catholic men, but neither did. His daughter Susanna married Dr John Hall (1575–1635), a prominent Puritan who would have been fiercely opposed to the Catholic Church.

That so little is known about Shakspere the man must be placed in the context of him being arguably the most intensely studied human being in history. Literally every scrap of paper from his lifetime has been examined for any reference to the Bard of Avon, especially his life as a writer. But *nothing* – quite literally *nothing* – ever turns up, regardless of how intensively researchers scour the archives. The Bellott–Mountjoy Lawsuit, the most important new documentary evidence relating to Shakspere, was found in 1910 in the Public Record Office in London by the American researchers William and Hulda Wallace. In 1612 William Shakspere briefly gave evidence about the alleged failure of a Huguenot family in London, with whom he had lodged in 1604, to provide a promised marriage dowry to their former apprentice. Shakspere stated that he could remember nothing about the matter. He signed the deposition with his very first signature, as 'William Shackp' (unless this is the hand of a legal clerk signing on his behalf).[43] The lawsuit sheds no light on Shakspere's career as a writer or even if he was a writer, as opposed to an actor and part-owner of an acting company, but has become world-famous in the absence of anything else. Precisely *nothing* relating to Shakspere's alleged career as an actor or a writer has been found by any researcher or scholar in modern times. The complete absence of a paper trail relating to William Shakspere contrasts markedly with what is known about most other well-known writers of his time, as has been shown by Diana Price.[44] This is especially striking in that certainly a thousand times more archival and original research had been undertaken about William Shakspere, and especially his supposed career as a writer, than about any of his contemporaries. One obvious inference is that this is because no evidence of his authorship exists.

In his will Shakspere left twenty-six shillings and eight pence each to three of his fellow actors in the King's Men ('John Hemynge, Richard Burbage & Henry Condell') 'to buy them rings'. However, these gifts seem to have been afterthoughts as they are inserted above one line in the will. The will does not mention anything concerning books or manuscripts. Shakspere did not leave legacies to any literary figure that one might expect a leading playwright to remember in his will: nothing, for instance, to John Fletcher, with whom he had recently collaborated on three last plays; to Ben Jonson, who was to edit the First Folio; to Michael Drayton, the playwright with whom Shakspere allegedly had a 'merry meeting' just before his death; or to Richard Field, the Stratford-born London printer who had published Shakespeare's two long poems; nor to anyone else: no, not a single person in the London literary world.

'Thy Stratford Moniment'

One of the more curious but telling points about the Stratford man as the supposed author of the plays concerns his memorial in Holy Trinity Church, Stratford-upon-Avon. Every year, tens of thousands of tourists in Shakspere's home town visit his grave and look at his funerary monument.[45] There they see the coloured bust of the head and upper body of a portly, balding man with a moustache and goatee beard, staring straight ahead. He is clearly holding a quill pen in his right hand, while his left hand holds down a blank piece of paper, itself resting on a cushion on a writing table. The problem with this statuary is that, almost certainly until the early eighteenth century, Shakspere's bust in Holy Trinity Church looked nothing like it does today. Instead, it depicted a thin, dour man, both of his hands resting on a large sack, presumably of wool. Most importantly, there was no sign of this man holding a pen or a piece of paper. One might guess that the man in the original depiction was a local tradesman, a kind of provincial Elizabethan version of the man depicted in Grant Wood's famous painting *American Gothic*. Many other details of the original monument also apparently differ from those there now. For instance, in the original depiction there were two cherubs at the top of the statuary who were holding, respectively, what appears to be a shovel and an hourglass, presumably symbols of death and mortality. Today, the postures of the cherubs have been changed, the shovel and hourglass have vanished.

Above left: The Hollar engraving of 1656.

Above right: Today's monument in Holy Trinity Church, Stratford-upon-Avon.

There is not the slightest doubt that the original appearance of the monument differed significantly, perhaps comprehensively, from the one we know today. The original monument was sketched in Stratford Church in 1634 by Sir William Dugdale (1605–86); his sketch still survives.[46] It was then redrawn by the illustrator Wenceslaus Hollar (1607–77), who is best known for his *Long View of London*, drawn about 1637, which depicts the Globe Theatre. Hollar's engraving was published in Dugdale's *Antiquities of Warwickshire* in 1656, and continued to appear in further editions of that work down to 1765. It was the basis for the illustration in Rowe's 1709 *Works of William Shakespeare* but by 1725, when Pope published his edition of Shakespeare, the monument had changed considerably to more or less what we have today: the portly man with his quill. Thus for the first 100 years of its existence the monument was quite different. Although the Dugdale/Hollar depiction is well known, orthodox biographers of Shakespeare have been extremely reluctant to discuss it or even mention it. When they do, the gross differences between the two have often been explained by claiming that Dugdale drew it inaccurately by dim light, but he is hardly likely to have missed the quill pen and writing paper. According to David Kathman, 'Dugdale's original 1634 sketch of the Shakespeare monument is significantly closer to the monument we see today, proving that Wenceslaus Hollar introduced errors into his engravings'.[47] As anyone can plainly see, however, this is simply nonsense: Dugdale's original is entirely different from today's monument in crucial respects, above all in the absence of pen and paper. Usually, however, the original monument is simply ignored by orthodox biographers, presumably because the anomaly is so glaring that it would have to be accounted for, a difficult task indeed. An example of how the problem is simply ignored is that the book accompanying the much-publicised exhibition held at the

National Portrait Gallery in London in 2006 did include a photograph of Shakespeare's plaster effigy as it is today at Holy Trinity Church, but its text said absolutely nothing about the original Dugdale/Hollar illustration, nor was it included in this book.[48] There was no mention about the original illustration differing substantially from the bust there today. This is especially curious, since the National Portrait Gallery's exhibition was *about* visual depictions of Shakespeare and his world. The exhibition and its accompanying book included many alleged portraits of Shakespeare which are almost certainly not of him, but it failed to include the Dugdale/Hollar drawings which, after the portrait frontispiece in the 1623 First Folio, are actually the oldest existing depictions of the Stratford man, or what purports to be him. Beyond this, virtually every recent Stratfordian biography of Shakespeare has either glossed over the issue or simply ignored it.[49]

Because the original funerary monument is so different from that seen today, it is often suggested that the former monument is actually a bust of someone else. The most obvious candidate, and he is regularly proposed, is John Shakspere (d. 1601), William's father, who was a local tradesman, a glove-maker and dealer in wool, and who served as Bailiff (the equivalent of Mayor) of Stratford and as a local Justice of the Peace (JP), meaning that a memorial of him in the local church would have been fully appropriate. By 1601, his son was almost certainly wealthy enough to have commissioned a suitable memorial of this kind. Strikingly, there is no other monument or memorial to John Shakspere, despite his local prominence. The sack of wool in the original depiction would be appropriate for a monument to a local wool dealer. According to Sir William Dugdale's *Diary* of 1653, the Stratford Church monument was made by Gheerart Janssen (who anglicised his name to Gerard Johnson), of the prominent family of stonemasons and sculptors, originally from Amsterdam, whose premises were on Bankside in London near the Globe Theatre. It would have been simple for William to have commissioned Janssen to produce the monument to his father who died in 1601. The dates, however, do not match: why would William wait a decade to commission a bust of his father from a sculptor who was only active from 1612 to 1623?[50] The implication is that the bust is of William himself, showing him with his hands on a sack of grain: William hoarded grain in the famine of 1598.

It appears that the present altered version of the monument, showing William Shakspere with pen and paper, dates from the second decade of the eighteenth century. As late as 1709 Nicholas Rowe, in his edition of Shakespeare's works, included the Dugdale/Hollar depiction.[51] The first published picture of the monument with pen and paper appeared in George Vertue's engraving in Alexander Pope's 1725 edition of Shakespeare's works.[52] Why and by whom the substitution was made is unclear. Numerous repairs were carried out on the monument in the eighteenth century, especially when Revd Joseph Greene (1712–90) became curate of the church and Master of Stratford Grammar School.[53] The actual sequence of events about the major alteration of the monument probably cannot be reconstructed today, but it is clear that the bust is not authentic nor the original. It is obviously difficult not to believe that the alterations were undertaken to make it seem that Shakspere was a writer, a claim strikingly absent from the original memorial. Below the bust is a strange inscription, with two lines in Latin and six lines in English. The first words of the Latin inscription (although not the rest) were drawn in Dugdale's 1634 sketch, and therefore must date from soon after Shakspere's burial. The Latin reads:

Judicio Pylium. Genio Socratem. Arte Maronem.
Terra Tegit. Populus Maeret. Olympus Habet.

This is usually translated as: 'In judgment a Nestor, in genius a Socrates, in art a Virgil. The earth covers him, the people mourn him, Olympus has him.' This Latin inscription is most curious. Omitting the fact that neither Socrates nor Virgil wrote plays, Nestor was a king in *The Iliad* who is seen as an elder statesman and was known for his wisdom. Yet his advice was frequently not taken and ineffective.[54] This supposed comparison between William Shakspere and Nestor seems to be wholly inappropriate. Shakspere held no political office of any kind, despite him being a relatively wealthy gentleman with a coat of arms and his father having held several local offices. William Shakspere expressed no political views of any kind, and gave no political advice, wise or not. He was not an elder statesman and had no known connection with any political figure. The most notable fact about Shakspere's death and burial is that no one took the slightest notice of it: the people most emphatically did not mourn him until much later. It is unclear who wrote the inscription, and the number of people in Stratford with the erudition to have written it was limited, especially as its author was commemorating a playwright whose texts frequently sailed close to the political wind. Perhaps it was the handiwork of Ben Jonson, who certainly had a role in both asserting and confusing the Shakespeare authorship in his cryptic verses in the First Folio. The final lines (in English) of the Stratford monument read:

Stay, Passenger, why goest thou by so fast?
read if thou canst, whom envious Death hath plast
with in this monument Shakespeare: with whome,
quick nature dide [*sic*]: whose name doth deck yt Tombe,
Far more than cost: sieh [*sic*] all, yt He hath writt,
Leaves living art, but page, to serve his witt.
Obiit ano do 1616/ Aetatis 53 die 23 apr.

This inscription sounds very much like Ben Jonson.[55] That Shakespeare's body was not 'plast with in this monument' but supposedly buried a few feet away below the floor of the church, in a grave that does not name him, strongly suggests that the author of the inscription was unfamiliar with the church and perhaps never visited it. The wording is very odd indeed and does not give one confidence that this is unequivocally the monument of the great poet-playwright. The baffling words 'all, yt He hath writt, Leaves living art, but page, to serve his witt' could be taken to mean, 'As for leaving us anything of living art, he wrote nothing but an empty page – such was his talent'.[56] This does chime with Jonson's puzzling ambiguity in the First Folio dedications.

These Vacant Leaves Thy Mind's Imprint Will Bear[57]

Both of William Shakspere's parents were illiterate, as is proved by them having signed various documents with their mark rather than with a signature. This fact strongly implies that

William Shakspere had no books in his childhood home. While not an insuperable obstacle to becoming the world's greatest writer, the lack of an appropriate home environment flies in the face of modern theories of cognitive and creative development, which emphasise parental encouragement, an appropriately stimulating environment, and opportunities for play and learning.[58] Innate genius is important, but it cannot flourish without realistic opportunities for its development. Mozart was certainly a child prodigy and a composer of assured greatness, but his father was not an Austrian peasant but a court musician in Salzburg and a minor composer in his own right who deliberately set out to nurture and encourage his son's talents. The father of Albert Einstein was an engineer who manufactured electrical equipment and his son's educational career is well documented. In contrast, there is simply no evidence that William Shakspere had either the parental or the educational background to have written plays demonstrating extraordinary erudition in virtually every line.

Perhaps William Shakspere might have risen from a meagre background to write his plays. But it is much more difficult to explain why his two daughters were illiterate.[59] If the Stratford man actually wrote the works attributed to him, this fact is as extraordinary as it is bizarre: Shakspere's own daughters could not read the works their father, the greatest writer in history, had written. This is despite the fact that in his plays, Shakespeare, whoever he was, appears to have been centuries ahead of his time in creating strong, memorable, verbally skilled and assertive, educated female roles, such as Beatrice, Rosalind, Lady Macbeth and Portia, the latter being a highly intelligent and skillful lawyer, and possibly the most accomplished female depicted in English literature for many centuries. Shakspere's two daughters were also his direct heirs, as his only son Hamnet had died in childhood. They would have been responsible, along with their husbands, Dr John Hall and Thomas Quiney, for supervising the family inheritance. Any ordinary family of Jacobean property owners would have arranged for their only children, two daughters, to learn to read and write, so it is inexplicable that a man whose entire career was spent as both a writer and an increasingly wealthy businessman should neglect to do this.

The last of William Shakspere's direct descendants, Elizabeth Hall, later Lady Bernard (the wife of John Bernard, who was knighted by Charles II in 1661) died in 1670. She left no record of her grandfather. Shakspere, however, did have surviving collateral descendants: the offspring of his sister Joan (1569–1646), who married William Hart (d. 1616), a local hatter, in 1599, and whose family continued via their son Thomas Hart (d. 1634). No one could realistically expect any of Shakspere's collateral descendants to have inherited his transcendent genius in full measure, but the occupations and career patterns of these relatives are startling. Joan's great-grandson Shakspeare Hart (1666–1747) was a plumber in Stratford; his son William Shakspeare Hart (1695–1750) was a glazier there; his son Thomas Hart (1729–93) was a turner; and his son John Hart (1753–1800), who claimed to own William Shakespeare's family Bible, was a chair-maker. Despite William Shakspere's intelligence and all of the opportunities provided by the wealth he had accumulated, none of his collateral descendants rose above these working-class occupations: none rose into the middle classes to become solicitors, clergymen, doctors, public servants, schoolmasters or successful businessmen. Not one attended a university, or published a word. If the Stratford man was the actual author, this is so extraordinary as to be more than improbable.

Bestriding the World Like a Colossus

We must also wonder whether William Shakspere had the time to be both an actor and an author. As an actor, a member of the Lord Chamberlain's Men/King's Men, until at least 1604, he would have had to memorise, rehearse and perform in plays on the London stage several times a week, in an open-air theatre. He would also have gone on tours of the provinces with his acting company, and performed before the Royal Court. He was also a sharer (part-owner) of his acting company, possibly involved in its management. Shakspere presumably maintained two separate households, one in London and the other in Stratford, three days' travel time apart, with significant business interests in both, and went back and forth between the two several times a year on horseback or in a primitive carriage, on unmade English roads. He allegedly then wrote (at least) thirty-seven plays, two long poems and several shorter ones, more than 154 sonnets, all in less than twenty-five years. No other playwright of Shakespeare's time was *both* an actor and an author throughout his career. Ben Jonson, for instance, was an actor at the beginning of his career but not thereafter, when he was apparently a full-time writer. Nor has any famous playwright in more recent times been both an actor and an author throughout their careers: this would be just too exhausting and, if one can generate a sufficient income from writing alone, quite pointless. It is much more likely that the actual author was a man with the leisure and means, and a large library, to compose the plays.

The Lack of Any Life–Work Mesh

The orthodox chronology of Shakespeare's plays, which we accept, shows an unusually clear evolutionary trajectory. In the first part of the author's career, from around 1590 to around 1601, he wrote the Histories, the Italianate Comedies and two Tragedies. There was then a break in the author's career around 1601, after which he wrote the great Tragedies, beginning with *Hamlet* in 1601, followed by the 'problem plays' and the 'romances', before moving towards closure with *The Tempest* and the final plays co-written with Fletcher. This accords with little or nothing in the known life of William Shakspere, in particular the great break around 1601. Most scholars believe that Sonnet 107, which begins, 'The mortal moon has her eclipse endur'd', refers, with relief, to the death of Queen Elizabeth in 1603. But William Shakspere has no reason to be glad when the queen died (see Chapter 10). *The Tempest,* written around 1611, is clearly based in part on the Strachey letter of July 1610, which was only circulated confidentially to directors of the Second London Virginia Company, the company that had financed the expedition to Virginia and whose ship foundered at Bermuda. William Shakspere had no connection with the Second London Virginia Company and no possible access to its confidential documents. This provides further evidence that we are dealing with two different men: the actor, Shakspere, and the author, Shakespeare.

The Junius Test

The *Letters of Junius* were a series of contributions on politics published anonymously in the *Public Advertiser*, a London newspaper, between 1769 and 1772. Their actual author was unknown at the time and has remained unknown ever since. Many then and since have speculated over the identity of their actual author (now often thought to be Sir Philip Francis), but this question has never been settled definitively.

Supposing that Shakespeare's plays and poems had all been published anonymously (as many were, in quarto form), would anyone seriously suggest that they were actually written by William Shakspere, an actor and theatre-sharer from a small provincial town, with no known education; who left not a single piece of writing apart from six signatures on legal documents; whom no one else ever met or wrote of in their letters and diaries and whose daughters were illiterate? Of course not: no one would seriously suggest that the Stratford man wrote these erudite plays and poems, which show an apparently personal knowledge of court life, indeed a deep understanding of human interactions in the circles of power; a direct acquaintance with Italy and France; knowledge of many and varied topics such as falconry, forestry, astronomy and the law; a profound familiarity with historical texts including those in French, Italian, Spanish, Latin and Greek? They would be universally attributed to someone from the upper classes, most likely a university-educated man, with a large library and a direct knowledge of the inner workings of the English government. Anyone who suggested that William Shakspere from Stratford was the actual author of the plays and poems would be greeted with incredulity.

2

Why Sir Henry Neville?
The Authorship Test

Let there be some more test made of my metal,
Before so noble and so great a figure
Be stamp'd upon it.

Measure for Measure, 1.1.48

In weighing up the various claims to the authorship of the works of Shakespeare we invite readers to compare the evidence for Neville against that for the best-known of the other candidates. We will then apply a test to see how they measure up compared to Neville. We also provide a brief biography of Neville and compare what emerges from that with the life and experience of William Shakspere from Stratford.

Edward de Vere, 17th Earl of Oxford (1550–1604)

For many years the most popular alternative candidate for the authorship of Shakespeare's works has been Edward de Vere, 17th Earl of Oxford. Oxford was the senior earl in the English peerage; his mother, Margery Golding, was the half-sister of Arthur Golding, the translator of Ovid (a work considered essential to Shakespeare who admired Ovid above all). Oxford had a brief career at Cambridge University from the age of eight to nine, and was then tutored at home, later becoming a ward of Lord Burghley, whose daughter he married as his first wife.

Oxford was known for his extravagance, his violent temper, his luxurious and often effeminate dress. He may have been bisexual. He visited Italy and other places on the Continent. He wrote plays which were well regarded at the time, none of which survive. In his famous list of 1598, Francis Meres judged him the 'best for comedy'. A number of Oxford's poems do survive, showing him to have been a poet of some talent but limited range. Oxford also maintained his own acting company, Lord Oxford's Men, which had been founded by his father in *c.* 1547. No one suggested that Oxford had written Shakespeare's plays until 1920, when J. T. Looney (pronounced 'Loney') wrote a large-scale work, *Shakespeare Identified in Edward de Vere, Seventeenth Earl of Oxford*. Looney was a schoolteacher in Newcastle-upon-Tyne who was familiar with the anti-Stratfordian view that Sir Francis Bacon had written the works of Shakespeare. Looney produced a list of biographical points that, in his view, any actual author of Shakespeare's works must have experienced, and decided that Oxford best fitted all of these points. He also found that many characters, events, and situations in Shakespeare's plays were, in his view, based upon actual events in Oxford's life or the lives of persons close to him.

Looney's argument became known as the Oxfordian theory. It faded somewhat in popularity after the 1930s, then re-emerged in recent decades as the most widely known of the theories positing an alternative author for the canon. Several international societies, newsletters, journals, conferences and websites in America, Britain, Canada and Europe supporting his candidacy now exist and there have been a steady stream of books in support of his candidacy. There are, however, many critical objections to the argument that Oxford was the real author of Shakespeare's works. Above all, his dates, 1550–1604, simply do not fit. Shakespeare, whoever he was, wrote all of his works between about 1590, when Oxford was already forty, and about 1613, nine years after Oxford died. Oxfordians claim that he actually wrote many of Shakespeare's works earlier than the normal chronology, but there is no evidence to support this. Shakespeare's plays exhibit an unusually clear evolutionary trajectory, but Oxfordians have not established their own chronology for him as Shakespeare which is in any way plausible. Several of Shakespeare's plays, for example *Macbeth* and *The Tempest*, are generally accepted as having been based upon sources which can be dated to after Oxford's death in July 1604. In his 1598 list Francis Meres clearly referred to Oxford and Shakespeare as two different men. Perhaps most telling is the fact that Oxford's surviving poetry is unlike Shakespeare's, lacking all of the subtlety, multiplicity of meaning, and invention of new words associated with the Bard. Also if Oxford were the author, one is bound to wonder why Shakespeare's plays were not performed by Oxford's Men, his acting company, but by the Lord Chamberlain's Men/King's Men, with which Oxford had no known connection.

The case for Oxford has not always been helped by the zeal with which its proponents have promoted it. Some pro-Oxfordian writings go well beyond merely claiming that de Vere wrote Shakespeare's works, asserting that Oxford actually wrote most of the literature of his time, including the works attributed to Edmund Spenser and Christopher Marlowe. Some also claim that Oxford was the illegitimate son of Queen Elizabeth, or the lover of Queen Elizabeth and the father of the Earl of Southampton, Shakespeare's supposed patron. The recent film *Anonymous*, with its fantastic elements and historically inaccurate scenes, backfired. Although the Oxfordian theory has been around for nearly a century, and has attracted many supporters, no direct evidence of any kind showing that he wrote Shakespeare's works has ever been found.

Sir Francis Bacon (1561–1626)

The first and for many years the leading alternative contender for the authorship of the Shakespeare canon was Sir Francis Bacon, Lord Verulam and Viscount St Alban. Bacon was certainly a man of the highest accomplishments, a lawyer who became Lord Chancellor and a philosopher who was one of the first to argue that empirical, scientific reasoning is superior to the automatic acceptance of classical learning. The theory that Bacon wrote the works was first suggested in the mid-nineteenth century by his unrelated American namesake Delia Bacon and peaked in popularity in the late Victorian period, when it had become the subject of many books. The theory still has its supporters and several works have appeared in recent years supporting the contention that Bacon was the real Shakespeare.

There is some evidence in favour of the Baconian theory, although, as in the case for Oxford, there is no direct evidence of his authorship despite the theory having been around for over 150 years. Bacon wrote a lengthy series of manuscript notes, only published in 1883 and known as *Promus,* which consists of 1655 pithy sayings, phrases, and biblical texts, apparently written around 1595. Baconians claim that 1,400 of these can be found in Shakespeare's works. In 1985 workmen renovating an old inn in St Albans, Hertfordshire, where Bacon had his country house, found a wall painting behind more recent panelling. The painting illustrated the hunt in Shakespeare's *Venus and Adonis.* There is nothing to connect the Stratford man with St Albans, and it is difficult to explain why the painting is there if unconnected with Bacon. Perhaps the best evidence of all is the fact that the name Francis Bacon was written adjacent to William Shakespeare on the Northumberland Manuscript (which has been dated to 1596-7).

There are, however, also many points against his candidacy. His pompous and convoluted prose style is nothing like Shakespeare's. Bacon never visited Italy. Bacon's politics do not mirror those of the Bard: he was on the wrong side in the Essex rebellion, and served as a prosecutor of the Essex conspirators, including Neville. Bacon died in 1626, thirteen years after the last Shakespeare play was apparently written, which begs the question why he would have stopped writing while he was still in his prime. Bacon's life cannot be readily matched with the evolutionary trajectory of Shakespeare's plays. Finally Bacon did not keep his authorship of essays secret: they first appeared in print in 1597, proudly proclaiming their author to be Sir Francis Bacon. The credibility of the Baconian theory has been marred by the finding of implausible codes that supposedly contain Bacon's name in Shakespeare's works.

William Stanley, 6th Earl of Derby (1561–1642)

Recently, the candidacy of William Stanley, 6th Earl of Derby, first proposed by French author Abel Lefranc in 1919, has been revived. Derby did have an acting company of his own, Derby's Men, and he is known to have written comedies for the London stage, none of which survive. He certainly had theatre contacts, financing and possibly writing for the Children of Paul's acting company in 1599. He was well educated and widely travelled. He was in France in 1582 and so could have witnessed events that underlie *Love's Labour's Lost* and *Measure for Measure.*[1] Rollett provided some evidence that Derby's handwriting in his extant letters had similarities to what might be expected of Shakespeare's.[2] Titherley showed that Derby's handwriting matched Hands D and E in the manuscript of *Sir Thomas More.*[3] Hand E has subsequently been shown to be by Thomas Dekker.[4]

Derby's candidacy has many deficiencies. There is nothing whatever to connect him with Shakspere/Shakespeare. It has been suggested, though without any evidence, that

William Shakspere began his career as an actor with Lord Strange's Men, a company organised by Derby's brother. However when Lord Strange died in 1594, Derby did not continue his patronage of that company and there is no evidence that Shakespeare the writer had any connection with Derby's Men. In addition, Derby lived too long: one has to explain why he stopped writing plays twenty-nine years before he died.[5] Derby had no connection with Essex or his circle, and was not a shareholder or a director of the Second London Virginia Company, so could not have read the Strachey letter, one of the main sources of *The Tempest*.

Other Candidates and the Authorship Test

Many others have been put forward as the real author of Shakespeare's works. These include Christopher Marlowe (1561–1593), despite his early death in a tavern brawl; Roger Manners, 5th Earl of Rutland (1576–1612), who would have been a teenager when the first Shakespeare plays were written and died a year before the last play was written; Mary Sidney (1561–1621); Amelia Lanier (1569–1645) and many other, less credible, candidates. We suggest that all these contenders should be checked against the following Authorship Test which offers fifteen evidential requirements that any candidate would fulfil if he/she were to satisfactorily answer the Authorship Question.[6] In the test, the distinction between 'must' and 'should' is that the first is essential, the second highly desirable. Where evidence for two candidates meets all essential requirements, the highly desirable evidence would provide a tie-breaker. First we offer ten criteria that any authorship candidate might reasonably be expected to fulfil.

1. The authorship candidate's life span must be contemporary with that of William Shakspere and the works written under the name Shakespeare. The known facts of this person's life and career must fit the generally accepted order and chronology of the plays. Biographical details should mesh with and illuminate the motivation and meaning of the plays.
2. There must be evidence of a friendship between this person and Henry Wriothesley, the Earl of Southampton, who should be a patron of the candidate.
3. There must be manuscript evidence of a similarity between the person's handwriting and the Hand D section of *Sir Thomas More*.
4. There should be some writing, such as letters or other documents, that show evidence of shared vocabulary between the candidate and Shakespeare.
5. To enable the candidate to read known Shakespeare sources that were not translated into English there must be evidence the person could read/write French, Spanish, Italian, Latin and Greek.
6. The candidate must have visited some of the places such as Padua, Venice, Florence, Vienna and Scotland, which appear in the plays.
7. The candidate must be a known supporter of Robert Devereux, the 2nd Earl of Essex, and have connections with William and Philip Herbert, the 3rd and 4th Earls of Pembroke, to whom the First Folio was dedicated in 1623.

8. The candidate must have had access to the Strachey letter (a source for *The Tempest*).
9. There must be some connection between the candidate and John Fletcher with whom Shakespeare wrote the last plays.
10. There should be handwritten notes, either in books or manuscript notebooks, belonging to the candidate that relate to the Shakespeare plays.

We now add a further five criteria which have emerged from our Neville research to see whether there is comparable evidence for other authorship candidates:

11. There should be at least one contemporary document that connects the candidate with the name 'William Shakespeare' and mentions a work known to have been written by the Bard.
12. There should be at least one extant autographed poem that proves the candidate could write poetry.
13. The real surname of this candidate and members of their ancestral family should appear in the history plays.
14. At least one contemporary relative should refer to Shakespeare and at least one relative should be known to have owned a manuscript of a poem or play by Shakespeare.
15. At least one descendent of the candidate should have been a writer and other relatives should have been involved in theatre.

The only candidate who meets all the essential requirements for authorship listed above is Henry Neville. Remarkably he also meets all those requirements listed as highly desirable. We now offer evidence that Henry Neville (*c.* 1562–1615) was the actual author of the works of William Shakespeare by giving examples of how he meets each of the Authorship Test requirements one at a time, comparing these with the evidence for other candidates. The rest of this book expands on this evidence.

1) Contemporary Life Span, Chronological Fit and Illumination of the Plays

Throughout this book, we give examples of how Neville's life and experiences precisely match the evolution of Shakespeare's works and invariably explain why Shakespeare wrote what he did at that time. In particular, Neville's catastrophic experience of arrest, trial and imprisonment after the Essex rebellion explains the great break in Shakespeare's oeuvre in 1601, when he worked on *Hamlet* and then wrote the other great tragedies. Neville's dates (1562/4–1615) fit the accepted chronology of the plays. None of the other candidates fulfil this test, either dying too soon or living too long and not fitting the psychological trajectory suggested by the plays. For example William Stanley lived until 1642 but Shakespeare stopped writing in 1613.[7] Walkley published the first quarto of *Othello* in 1622 and stated in an epistle that the author was dead.

2) Friendship with Henry Wriothesley, 3rd Earl of Southampton

There is documentary evidence associating Henry Neville with the Earl of Southampton over thirty years. The following sequence of documents and events tie Neville, Southampton and Shakespeare together:

1583–5: Neville met Henry Wriothesley, 3rd Earl of Southampton, when the latter was a boy and a ward of William Cecil, Lord Burghley. Both had attended Burghley's private school as boys, though at different times.

1591–5: *Romeo and Juliet* was written by Shakespeare. Romeo is a Montague and Southampton was related, on his mother's side, to Anthony Browne, 1st Viscount Montague. Romeo's name is also likened to a rose (Wriothesley was pronounced Rosely).

1593: *Venus and Adonis* was dedicated to Southampton by Shakespeare.

1594: *The Rape of Lucrece* was dedicated to Southampton by Shakespeare. *The Comedy of Errors* was first performed at Gray's Inn during the Christmas celebrations of 1594. Henry Wriothesley, Earl of Southampton, was in the audience. On the Northumberland Manuscript Neville listed 'Orations at Graies Inne revells by Mr. Francis Bacon' which may have been delivered the evening of the Night of Errors when Shakespeare's play was performed.

1601: Neville met Southampton during the build-up to the Essex rebellion.

1601–1603: Neville and Southampton were both imprisoned in the Tower of London.

1603: Southampton dedicated his copy of *The Encomium* on Richard III to Henry Neville.

1604: Neville and Southampton were arrested and spent a night in prison due to unfounded rumours of a plot.[8]

1605: Southampton staged *Love's Labour's Lost* for Queen Anne.[9] James I and Southampton were in Oxford when Henry Neville was awarded an MA.

1609: The Second London Virginia Company was founded: Neville and Southampton were investors and members of the council. The dedication to *Shake-speares Sonnets* encodes the names of Henry Wriothesley (Southampton) and Henry Neville (see Chapter 10).

1611: Southampton and Neville, as members of the Virginia Company, would have had access to the Strachey letter that is a recognised source for Shakespeare's *Tempest*.

1612–13: Southampton supported Neville's candidacy to be Secretary of State. Southampton was identified as Neville's 'great patron' by Chamberlain in 1613.

1613: Frederick, the Elector Palatine, and his new wife, Princess Elizabeth, left England in April, arriving in Heidelberg in June. On 6 July William Trumbull (English ambassador to Brussels) wrote that Neville was in Brussels.[10] Southampton was also in the Netherlands that summer, intending to visit Brussels 'very privately' (according to a letter from Sir John Throckmorton to Trumbull) and he returned to England in August.[11] They may both have accompanied the royal party. In a letter dated 6 August 1613 Southampton wrote about Neville.[12]

While a few of the above require plausible inference, enough documented facts exist to show a pattern interweaving Southampton, Neville and Shakespeare. By contrast there is no evidence whatsoever linking William Shakspere from Stratford with the Earl of Southampton. Similarly no other authorship candidate has been shown to have such a continuous relationship with Southampton.

3) Evidence of Similarity Between the Candidate's Handwriting and Hand D

The Hand D section of *Sir Thomas More*, a manuscript of a play co-written by several writers and revised in 1603–4, is generally accepted as having been written by Shakespeare because of its style and the vocabulary used. The handwriting has been identified as that of William Shakspere based on a comparison with the six extant signatures, using especially two features: a spurred 'a' in just one signature and long descenders from 'm' and 'W' in the final signature on William's Stratford will. However, the signatures are so varied that no one can be confident that any or all them were written by Shakspere and not by legal clerks. In Chapter 8 we show how Neville's handwriting and spelling matches Hand D far more comprehensively than any of these six poor Shakspere signatures. The scene in the Hand D section shows More persuading the rabble to give up their rebellion, submit to the authorities and ask for pardon. This content has parallels with Neville's experience at that time when he had been asking Cecil to procure his pardon from Elizabeth (see Chapter 8).

There is some evidence that Derby's handwriting is similar to Hand D: Titherley claimed it was identical, although, given he was unable to provide sufficient photographs of the script but used drawings for his examples, it is difficult to agree with his conclusion.[13] No other authorship candidate's handwriting has been found to have significant similarities to Hand D.

4) Letters: There Should Be Some Writing That Shows Evidence of Shared Vocabulary

Throughout this book we give examples of how Neville's vocabulary in his notebooks and letters anticipated rare vocabulary used by Shakespeare. We especially pay attention to hapax legomena, words which Shakespeare only used once in his entire canon, because when we find Neville regularly using these words either before Shakespeare or contemporaneously, we see this as evidence of his authorship. William Shakspere left no letters so no comparison with his private vocabulary is possible.

Scholars have found some overlap of vocabulary between Oxford and Shakespeare, although this is random and weak.[14] There is a greater degree of shared vocabulary between Bacon and the Bard. Bacon's relative closeness to Shakespeare in vocabulary may be explained by the fact that Neville was related to Bacon and interested in his writing, collecting his essays in the Northumberland Manuscript folder (see item 10). This means that Neville would have been familiar with Bacon's vocabulary and may have adopted words and phrases.

5) French, Spanish, Italian, Latin and Greek

Neville was fluent in French and Latin. He had a working knowledge of Greek, Italian and Spanish, being able to read works in those languages, as is evident from the books in his library. In his letters he used Latin, French, Italian and Spanish. He annotated books in Latin and Greek. Many of these books are annotated with ideas, words, phrases and incidents we later see in the plays. We give examples throughout the book (see item 11).

There is no evidence that William Shakspere could read or speak any foreign language. Oxford, Bacon, Derby, Rutland and Mary Sidney all had foreign languages but no books owned by them with handwritten annotations relevant to the Shakespeare plays have been found.

6) Travel to Padua, Venice, Florence, Vienna and Scotland

In 1581 Neville travelled through Northern Italy and visited Padua, Venice and Florence. On the way he had passed through Vienna. In 1583 he travelled to Scotland. (See Chapter 3 for further evidence of Neville's travels in Italy.)

William Shakspere never left England: indeed there is no evidence of him ever having been anywhere except Stratford and London. By contrast some of the other candidates are known to have travelled. Marlowe was arrested in the Netherlands; Oxford visited Italy; Bacon went as far as France; Derby travelled widely, indeed possibly as far as Egypt, Anatolia, Moscow and Greenland. Incidents in *Love's Labour's Lost* and *Measure for Measure* have been traced to France in 1578 and 1582 respectively. Derby was in France in 1582.[15] Neville had travelled through France in both 1578 and 1582.

7) The Earl of Essex and William Herbert, 3rd Earl of Pembroke

Neville first met Robert Devereux, 2nd Earl of Essex, in 1583 when they travelled to Scotland together on a diplomatic mission with Walsingham. Despite his reluctance Neville accepted Essex's encouragement to take up the role of ambassador in France and showed his interest in Essex by many enquiries to Cecil in letters of 1599–1600 asking how the earl was progressing in Ireland. While he was very careful to keep his distance, being also dependent on Cecil and sceptical about what Essex was planning, Neville nevertheless could not bring himself to report to Cecil what he knew in the lead up to the Essex rebellion. Essex had hinted to Neville that he might replace Cecil as Secretary of State so perhaps Neville's own ambitions made him silently collude. Several associates and friends, including Savile and Cuffe, were supporters of Essex. Of the other authorship candidates only Roger Manners, 5th Earl of Rutland, was a supporter of Essex. He was imprisoned and heavily fined for his role in the rebellion. Francis Bacon had been close to Essex in the early 1590s but then distanced himself and in 1601 he became a member of the prosecution team at Essex's treason trial.

William Herbert, 3rd Earl of Pembroke, was Neville's chief backer in the Privy Council during his last years as an MP trying to negotiate with James I. In 1614 Neville was supported in Parliament by the earl's cousin, Sir William Herbert. The famous brothers William and Philip Herbert, 3rd and 4th Earls of Pembroke respectively and patrons of the First Folio, became patrons and mentors of Henry Neville's oldest son Henry and grandson Richard. William Herbert, 3rd Earl of Pembroke, 'was stoutly Protestant, and in December 1628 his brother, the Earl of Montgomery (Sir Philip Herbert), appointed Neville a gentleman of the privy chamber in extraordinary. Moreover, following Neville's death, Pembroke purchased the wardship of Neville's son, and his secretary, Sir John Thoroughgood, subsequently married Neville's widow and acquired the wardship himself'.[16] This shows how Neville's friends, political supporters and patrons were Shakespeare's dedicatees, Southampton, Pembroke and Montgomery. William and Philip Herbert were the sons of Mary Sidney (1561–1621) who was the sister of Philip and Robert Sidney. Neville knew the Sidneys. Mary was a friend of Neville's mother and mother-in-law. Mary Sidney is also an authorship candidate although she was not a supporter of Essex.[17]

8) The Strachey Letter (a Source for *The Tempest*)

Neville, as a member of the Second Virginia Company, would have had access to the confidential Strachey letter that is a recognised source for Shakespeare's *The Tempest* (see Chapter 10). Oxford was already dead by the time the letter was written. Bacon was on the list of subscribers and so could have had access. Other authorship candidates were not.[18] Given that the list of subscribers includes grocers, fishmongers, shoemakers and ironmongers it is worth noting that Shakspere from Stratford did not subscribe.

9) A Connection with John Fletcher

With Francis Beaumont, John Fletcher wrote a political play, *A King and No King*, which was first performed in 1611 in the same season as *The Tempest*. When *A King and No King* was first printed in 1619, Walkley's dedicatory epistle to Sir Henry Neville introduced the play. In it he said that Neville had encouraged the writers.[19] Whether this epistle was addressed to Neville (who died in 1615) or his son (who shared his name and lived 1588–1629), it is documentary proof of a relationship between Fletcher and the Nevilles. We hypothesise that the elder Neville (the playwright) had originally received the play from Fletcher, and that his son later offered it for publication. It is far more likely that Walkley is referring to Neville rather than his son because Beaumont retired in 1612 (when Fletcher began to co-write with Shakespeare, see Chapter 11), therefore for Neville to have 'encouraged the writers' he would have had to do so before then, when his son and namesake would have been in his early twenties. John Fletcher and Henry Neville both attended the Mermaid Club. No other authorship candidate, including William Shakspere, had any documented relationship with Fletcher.

10) Handwritten Notes That Relate to the Shakespeare plays

Neville left several notebooks and many annotated books. Of these, three of the most important contain material later found in the history plays. These are his 1584–5 manuscript copy of *Leicester's Commonwealth*, Worsley MSS 47; the handwritten marginalia in the annotated copy of Hall's *Chronicle* which have been dated 1586–98; and the 1602–3 Tower notebook. [20] Between them these cover material to be found in all the history plays. [21] Neville's library was moved from Billingbear to Audley End House some time before 1916 and so many of his books are now preserved there. These volumes contain handwritten marginal notes that pertain to *The Comedy of Errors*, *Love's Labour's Lost*, *Venus and Adonis*, *Titus Andronicus*, *The Rape of Lucrece*, *Much Ado About Nothing*, *Julius Caesar*, *Henry V*, *Hamlet*, *Macbeth*, *Coriolanus*, and *Antony and Cleopatra*. Other unmarked books in the Neville library are sources for *The Two Gentlemen of Verona*, *A Midsummer Night's Dream*, *As You Like It* and *The Winter's Tale*. We give examples of these throughout the book.

After careful study of the actual volume we have accepted that the notes in the annotated Hall's *Chronicle* were by Neville. [22] Keen and Lubbock tried very hard to establish a link between the annotations and Shakspere from Stratford but were unable to make a convincing case. [23] They modernised the spellings of the annotations and missed vital evidence as a result. The person who annotated Hall's *Chronicle* had the following characteristic habits:

1) he abbreviated words beginning with 'pro' such as 'pmotyd' instead of promoted;
2) he substituted the symbol '&' for 'and';
3) he used õ to symbolise an abbreviated m as in 'cõpanions' instead of companions;
4) he used 'X' (the Greek letter χ) as in Xmas for Christmas;
5) he used Roman numerals;
6) he used 'au' instead of 'a' as in 'Fraunce';
7) he drew little hands pointing to text;
8) he used '#' marks to highlight text;
9) he systematically numbered points in the margin;
10) he used characteristic spellings such as 'rebells' with a double 'l' and 'howse' with a 'w'.
11) he misplaced 'in' to read 'ni', such as 'knig';
12) he used miniscules such as 'S^r' for Sir and 'wth' for with.

Neville showed all of these twelve habits in his copy of *Leicester's Commonwealth*, and in his extant manuscript letters and other documents. [24] Needless to say there is no instance of William Shakspere from Stratford using any of these devices unless it be in his second signature on the 1612 Blackfriars mortgage document when he signed his name as: *Wm Shakspe^a*. Furthermore, one early annotation in Hall reads, 'duke of Norfolk (dy)ed at venice'. [25] This piece of information about Thomas de Mowbray is in Hall's text and in *Richard II* (4.1.97). Neville and his father had both visited Venice. A hash mark, #, is placed in the margin next to a passage that includes mention of Windsor. In a later annotation he specifically notes 'henry the kynge of england his sonne borne at Windsor'. [26] Neville's home was at Billingbear near Windsor. Also, the annotator notes 'a justinge [jousting] at Oxford'.[27] Neville studied at Oxford. Paris is also noted several times.[28] Neville had travelled there as a young man in 1578 and 1582 and would later be ambassador in Paris. These place names, Venice, Windsor, Oxford and Paris, all have Neville connections which might explain why the annotator made a note of them.[29]

No other authorship candidate has been linked to such a range of relevant, annotated source materials. Just one 1568 law book contains an uncertain signature of W[m] Shakspr.[30]

Now the additional five criteria which emerged from our research into Neville's authorship.

11) A Contemporary Document Connecting the Candidate with William Shakespeare and His Works

The Northumberland Manuscript (NHMS) is a faded, charred, fragile folio of papers housed at Alnwick Castle. On the front cover someone has repeatedly written the name 'William Shakespeare'. The NHMS was owned by Henry Neville.[31] The name 'Nevill' is visible, with the family motto, 'Ne Vile Velis', at the top left of the front page. The NHMS is the earliest manuscript reference to William Shakespeare as a playwright. The NHMS has been dated to 1596–7,[32] just over three years after the appearance of *Venus and Adonis*.[33] The seven examples of the name 'William Shakespeare' on the NHMS could have been written earlier but were certainly penned before 1597. The plays *Rychard the second* and *Rychard the third* are listed on the front cover of NHMS, just below the name 'William Shakespeare'. The fact that they are listed with other works that are contained in the NHMS folios suggests that they were manuscripts of the plays. In 1597 no play had been identified as by Shakespeare. No play was published as the work of Shakespeare until 1598. *Richard III* and *Richard II* were first printed in 1597 without any author being named. The second quartos of both plays were published as written by 'William Shake-speare' in 1598.[34] This is the same spelling, with the hyphen, as used on the 1609 volume of sonnets (see Chapter 10). That same year the first quarto of *Love's Labour's Lost* appeared with the author named as 'W. Shakespere'. This means that the NHMS, which refers directly or indirectly to all three plays, was written during the anonymous period before Shakespeare was identified as the playwright. Only the year after the NHMS received its last scribbles did the name of that author appear in print on any play. Neville was thus the very first person to record any knowledge that William Shakespeare had written these plays or indeed any play. An alternative possibility is that Neville was indeed the playwright.

The word 'honorificabiletudine' is written on the front cover of the NHMS. This is a shortened version of 'honorificabilitudinitatibus' which Costard uses in *Love's Labour's Lost* (5.1.40). The word 'honorificabilitudinitatibus' occurs on page 662 of the *Adagia* of Erasmus, a copy of which, dated 1558, is in Neville's library.[35] The play dates from 1594–6 and was printed in 1598. The title page of the quarto states it was performed during 'this last Christmas', which would be 1597. The writer of the Northumberland Manuscript must therefore have had access to a manuscript of *Love's Labour's Lost* or seen the play and remembered this long word before the court performance. That the word is misquoted may be due to misremembering it, simply misspelling such a long word, having seen an earlier version of the script, or indeed the poet noting the word for use: the NHMS covers the entire period during which the play would have been written. Also on the NHMS is a quotation from *The Rape of Lucrece*: 'revealing day through every crany peepes and see ...' which is a misquotation of stanza 156, or might represent an earlier version that the poet later revised.

On the verso of the front page there are what seem to be random words including 'Thomas', 'Imprisonm', 'Imitatio' and 'Anthonie ffitzherbert'. When we put Neville and his secret authorship into the picture some sense emerges. Thomas Nashe (whose name occurs on the front page) was threatened with imprisonment for his part in writing *The Isle of Dogs*. 'Imitatio', as Bate elucidated, was the rhetorical and creative method which Shakespeare used, imitating Ovid, Plautus, Virgil and other writers while also varying, embellishing and diverging from these models.[36] Shakespeare refers to 'imitari' in *Love's Labour's Lost* (4.2.125). Scholars have long remarked on Shakespeare's knowledge of the law. Neville, in referring to Sir Antony Fitzherbert (1470–1538) shows his awareness of one of the most important legal authorities of the previous reign. Fitzherbert wrote the first systematic attempt to summarise English Law: *Le Graunde Abridgement*.[37] Neville had referred to John Rastell's three-volume legal encyclopedia, the *Graunde Abridgement*, in his Worsley MS47 copy of *Leicester's Commonwealth*.[38] From 1583 Neville was involved in legal cases as a Justice of the Peace and from 1584, as a Member of Parliament, he would also have been involved in lawmaking.

There are only two Shakespeare play manuscripts from the writer's lifetime: the Hand D section of *Sir Thomas More*, 1603–4, and the Dering MS of *Henry IV*, c. 1613 (the latter being in the handwriting of Edward Dering, copied from the printed quartos). This means that in 1596 Henry Neville was the first individual who owned two lost Shakespeare manuscripts: *Richard II* and *Richard III*. Indeed before the editors of the First Folio worked from play manuscripts Neville is the only person known to have owned a Shakespeare play manuscript and he did so before anyone else.

The NHMS is proof that Neville was interested in courtly entertainments such as speeches by the earls of Essex and Sussex at tilts (jousting tournaments), in theatre, indeed radical political theatre and radical political argument and controversy (*The Isle of Dogs* and *Leicester's Commonwealth* and the letters to Elizabeth I by Philip Sidney and the Earl of Arundel). He knew *The Rape of Lucrece* and was the first person to quote from that poem.

Of the other authorship candidates Bacon is named on the NHMS and his essays and speeches (including 'Orations at Graies Inne revells' performed a month after 'The Night of Errors' before Elizabeth I in 1595) are listed and copied out. The early Baconians claimed the NHMS proved their case. No other authorship candidate is listed on the NHMS, although Titherley claimed that Derby was referred to by a capital letter D and constructed an elaborate fantasy that he might have been present when the manuscript was written.

12) One Extant Autographed Poem

Neville was praised in two Latin poems of 1600 and 1603 for being inspired by the Muses (see Chapter 6). Having decided to keep his authorship secret it is not surprising that there are no published poems by him. However, Casson discovered one small poem written in France in 1599 and autographed by a jovial, carefree Neville who perhaps felt safe to own this miniature piece because he was abroad. The poem is analysed in Chapter 6 and shown to have Shakespearean qualities and links to contemporary works despite being very short and slight.

Of the other candidates Oxford wrote poetry but it is not of Shakespearean quality and Francis Meres listed Shakespeare and Oxford separately in the same list so he must have believed them to be two different poets. Bacon wrote speeches for court entertainments, some of which Neville had copied out in his NHMS folder. Bacon wrote a great deal but not Shakespearean poetry. There is not a single autographed poem by William Shakspere.[39]

13) The Writer's Real Surname in the History Plays

The name 'Nevil' is found eight times in the first quarto of *Henry VI: Part II*. The name Nevil (Nevils, Nevil's) occurs five times in First Folio version of *Henry VI: Part II*. There are many members of the Neville family mentioned in the history plays who are identified only by their titles such as the earls of Westmoreland, Warwick and Salisbury. Other minor characters were also related to the Neville family. See chapters 4, 5 and 11 for the half-hidden members of the Neville family in the plays.[40] Earls of Oxford are repeatedly named in *Richard II, Henry VI: Part III* and *Richard III*. An Earl of Oxford is executed in *Richard II*. However only once does the name 'Vere' occur, when Oxford says, in *Henry VI: Part III*, 'My older brother, the Lord Aubrey Vere was done to death' (3.3.102). The names Stanley and Derby occur in *Henry VI: Part I* and *Part III*, *Richard II* and *Richard III*.

By contrast no one called Bacon or Shakspere/Shakespeare is to be found in any play.

14) One Contemporary Relative Should Refer to Shakespeare, One Relative Own a Manuscript of a Poem or Play by Shakespeare

The first person to state in print that 'Shake-speare' was a pseudonym was Neville's son-in-law, (Revd) Thomas Vicars (1589–1638). After some years at Oxford (from 1607) where he was recognised as a gifted theologian, Vicars entered the household of George Carleton, Bishop of Chichester. Carleton had married Neville's widow, Anne. In 1620 Vicars dedicated one of his published works to Anne: a translation of a theological text.[41] Later he married her daughter, Anne Neville (b. 1610). So Vicars knew Neville's wife, his close friend, Carleton, and daughter, and it seems that he was let into the family secret. In 1628, the year Carleton died, Vicars published the third edition of his book on Rhetoric.[42] In this edition he added to the Latin text where he named several English poets and referred to Shakespeare indirectly: 'to these I believe should be added the famous poet who takes his name from shaking and spear'. In Latin the words are 'quassatione & hasta'.[43] This phrase is highly suggestive of inside knowledge that the name 'Shake-speare' was a pseudonym.

Robert Killigrew was an MP and an investor in the Second London Virginia Company who owned a copy of Shakespeare's second sonnet that is now in the British Library. Killigrew was Neville's wife's cousin (see Chapter 10).

No relative of any other authorship candidate wrote about or hinted at their authorship. It is one of the strangest aspects of the myth of William Shakspere's authorship that no one in Stratford owned a First Folio or even a single quarto edition of a play or had a copy of the sonnets. Shakspere did not give his wife or daughters a single poem.

15) One Descendent of the Candidate Be a Writer and Other Relatives Involved in Theatre

Neville's grandfather, Edward, was involved in court masques and dramatic entertainments. His uncle owned a theatre company, Lord Abergavenny's Men. Neville's grandson, Henry Neville (1620–94) was a writer. Especially interesting is his *Isle of Pines*, a satirical work published in 1668. It is a story reminiscent of *The Tempest* in which a man, George Pines, and four women are castaways, marooned on an island. Spiced up with sexual license, the book is a utopia that goes sour, offering reflections on culture, governance, religion and politics. This Henry Neville also wrote other works on the nature of government as a Cromwellian radical later turned monarchist, and has a lengthy entry in the *Oxford Dictionary of National Biography*.[44]

Neville's wife was Anne, *née* Killigrew. Her cousin was Robert Killigrew and his sons William, Thomas and Henry became playwrights. Henry was father of the poet Anne Killigrew. In 1669 a royal warrant gave the King's Players, the company established by Thomas Killigrew and Sir William Davenant, the exclusive right to perform twenty of Shakespeare's plays.[45] Thomas built the Drury Lane Theatre in London.

None of William Shakspere's relatives or descendants were writers. His brother, Edmund, 'a player', died aged twenty-seven in December 1607 and was buried at St Mary Overy, Southwark. No other authorship candidates had significant poets or theatre creators among their descendants.

A Brief Biography

Henry Neville was baptised in May 1564 and this is taken as evidence that he was born that year but this is almost certainly not the case. When Neville matriculated at Merton College, Oxford on 20 December 1577, his age was given as fifteen, meaning that he was born between December 1561 and December 1562.[46] On his 1599 portrait at Audley End House, his age is stated as thirty-six which would mean he was born in 1562–3. If he was born in June of 1562 he would have been thirty-six in April of 1599 when the portrait may have been completed before he left for France. Neville's parents' marriage settlement was not ratified until 1567, so keeping his own birth date obscure might have been intended to avoid questions of his legitimacy.[47] Weighing the evidence, we suggest that 1562 is the most likely year for his birth, the delayed baptism being a consequence of his parents' uncertain marital status. Neville's father had an earlier wife, Winifred Loss, who disappeared from the record about 1561. The simplest explanation for her disappearance is that she died. She had no children.

Neville was the eldest son of Sir Henry Neville (*c.* 1520–93). His paternal ancestors came from the illustrious and previously powerful Neville family, which Neville celebrated on his father's tomb.[48] Neville's father, a godson of Henry VIII and a signatory of that king's will, was a prominent courtier and leading figure in Berkshire local government, holding, among other offices, that of the Keeper of Windsor Forest. His country house, where Neville lived for much of his life, Billingbear Park, was adjacent to Windsor Forest and about 5 miles from Windsor. The house remained in the family until the 1920s, when it burned to the ground and the remains were demolished. Paintings of Billingbear House and Park may be seen at Audley End House, Saffron Walden, near Cambridge.

Neville's mother, Elizabeth, was the daughter of John Gresham (d. 1560), a wealthy London merchant, and the niece of the celebrated Sir Thomas Gresham (*c.* 1518–79), the founder of the Royal Exchange and of Gresham College in London. The senior Sir Henry Neville was the Chief Mourner at Sir Thomas's funeral and his closest male heir. Neville's mother borrowed, or was given, a rare manuscript of John Lydgate's *Fall of Princes* that was from the library of Mary Sidney. This was a possible source for *The Rape of Lucrece*.[49] Neville's father counted Henry Sidney as his best friend. After the death of his wife Elizabeth in 1573, Sir Henry Neville married Elizabeth Bacon (*c.* 1541–1621), the half-sister of Sir Francis Bacon. This shows how closely Neville and Bacon were related.

Neville was between ten and eleven years old when his mother died. As a boy he attended a private school run by William Cecil, Lord Burghley. The curriculum is known to have included French, Latin, cosmography and dancing. He then went to Merton College, Oxford in 1577. He became a student of the great classics scholar Sir Henry Savile. Neville was a member of a group headed by Savile that travelled through Europe from 1578 to 82, visiting France, the Low Countries, Germany, Poland and Italy.[50] They visited leading scholars and astronomers and were searching for and collecting rare Greek and Latin manuscripts. Neville became Savile's lifelong friend. Neville was especially interested in history, astronomy and mathematics; he bought books while on the European tour on subjects as varied as language, military and political history, poetry and fiction. These were added to the library at Billingbear which already contained books in Italian bought by his father when he had been in Italy as a Marian exile. Neville, fluent in Latin and Greek, learned French and Italian. Henry Neville certainly owned an extensive private library, some of which survives today at Audley End House. He would have had access to other libraries and private book collections, as well as to the published and unpublished holdings of Oxford University and its scholars and his circle of friends. Posit Neville as the real author and there is no mystery to explain as regards either Shakespeare's erudition or his access to sources.

In 1584 Neville married Anne Killigrew (d. 1632), the daughter of Sir Henry Killigrew (*c.* 1525–1603), who was a court insider and diplomat. Anne's mother was Katherine Cooke, one of the illustrious Cooke sisters, the most educated women of their generation. Between 1586 and 1610 Neville and Anne had fifteen children, at least three of whom died in infancy. His first son he named Henry. His second son, born in 1596, he called

William. His third son was born when Neville was in the Tower of London, and where his grandfather Edward was buried. He named this boy Edward. His last child, born in 1610, he named Elizabeth, perhaps after his own mother.

From 1584, Neville was a Member of Parliament. He sat in Parliament for the whole of his adult life apart from three years after 1601 when he was imprisoned in the Tower for his role in the Essex rebellion. Neville was appointed ambassador to France in 1598, arriving in Paris in May 1599. The appointment was apparently the result of influence having been brought to bear by his father-in-law and Robert Devereux, the 2nd Earl of Essex. After serving there for more than a year in difficult negotiations with the French government, Neville temporarily returned to England, where he was secretly drawn into the Essex conspiracy before the rebellion. Upon his return to England, Neville met with Essex and his key associates, including Henry Cuffe, Essex's secretary, whom he would have known from their time at Oxford. Cuffe promised Neville the post of Secretary of State if the rebellion succeeded and Essex replaced the Cecil hegemony with his own men. Neville's previously unsuspected role in the rebellion was mentioned for the first time in the trials of Essex and Southampton, the latter being one of Essex's key supporters. As a result, Neville was arrested and, after a trial, sentenced to spend an indefinite period in the Tower of London until he paid off a fine of £10,000 (later reduced to £5,000), an astronomical sum at the time. He spent the next two years in the Tower along with Southampton. Neither was in 'close confinement' and Neville occupied some of his time with historical research.[51] During this time he was ill and traumatised by the events and his imprisonment. He was also very worried for his wife's physical health and sanity. He wrote letters begging for a pardon and negotiating how to pay the large fine imposed on him.

Neville and Southampton were released from the Tower by James I shortly after he came to the throne in early 1603. After more than four years away from home and his normal pursuits, first as ambassador and then as a prisoner in the Tower, Neville had to attend to his personal affairs and depleted finances. He also had to secure his re-election to Parliament, which he did in 1604. In 1605 he was awarded his MA at Oxford in the presence of the king and Southampton. King James, however, apparently took an immediate dislike to Neville, and never gave him the offices or perquisites that he, and many others, expected that he would receive. This contrasts with the king's generous treatment of Southampton. As a result, Neville, who had lost a great deal of money as ambassador (he had to pay his expenses out of his own pocket), and as a prisoner in the Tower, was never able to recover the wealth he had lost. By 1608 he was having financial difficulties. Early in 1609 he pleaded with Cecil for help as he feared he would 'sink beneath the burden of his debts'.[52] In May 1609 Neville's fortunes, it seemed, had at last changed for the better. His eldest son, Henry, married the niece of Sir John Smyth, a very wealthy London merchant and (in effect) the managing director of the Second London Virginia Company. Neville, a director of the company, expected that his wealth would be restored. However, instant wealth was not forthcoming.

By that time Neville had become much more active in Parliament, serving on a number of committees, including one on illegitimate children. He became increasingly identified with the 'popular party', standing with the opposition on the issues of free trade, religion and foreign policy. He was involved in the negotiations for the Union of Scotland and England, fiercely opposing it if the Scots continued their alliance with France. He continued to support Cecil, who in 1604 had become godfather to his son Edward. Looking for ways to increase the king's income he proposed a fee for exemption from jury service which he thought would raise £80,000. The scheme was accepted by James I in 1608 but failed to bring in the expected revenue. James continued to increase his spending and demanded more money from Parliament. Neville was part of secret negotiations with the government in attempts to establish a 'great contract' but the House of Commons became suspicious of his efforts. James singled out Neville to speak on the crucial issues in a special meeting of selected MPs in 1610 and Neville was fearless in speaking truth to power. Not satisfied by the MPs, James contemptuously dismissed them as dogs.[53]

Neville was disappointed in his Parliamentary career (perhaps all political careers end in failure). He tried to use his connections with Sir Thomas Overbury and Robert Carr, the king's favourite and Viscount Rochester, to gain political influence. Neville was also allied to William Herbert, 3rd Earl of Pembroke.[54] In May 1612 Cecil died, and Neville became a leading candidate to become Secretary of State. He was supported by the Earl of Southampton and Robert Sidney. Neville tried in vain to reconcile king and commons, having secret meetings with James I while they were hunting in the Windsor forest in July 1610. He wrote papers encouraging the king to compromise with Parliament. He made a number of reasonable proposals and continued to negotiate until 1612. He tried to manage the commons for the king but was exposed and even attacked as an 'undertaker'. He admitted he was the author of a secret memorandum on these matters in 1614.[55] Ultimately Neville's political ambitions were frustrated and, perhaps on his recommendation, or on his own merits, Ralph Winwood, who had been his secretary in Paris, was appointed Secretary of State in April 1614. By that winter Neville was ill with a combination of jaundice, scurvy and dropsy which led to his death.[56] He died on Monday 10 July 1615.[57] James Whitelocke summed up his character and political career by writing, 'He was the most sufficient man for understanding of state business that was in this kingdom … and a very good scholar and a stout man, but was as ignobly and unworthily handled as ever a gentleman was.'[58]

Neville, Shakespeare and Shakspere

The reader will have noticed times in this brief biography when the events and experiences of Neville's life have coincided with those we might reasonably expect the author of the Shakespeare canon to have had. We now sketch some of these Shakespeare–Neville connections that are explored in more detail in the following chapters. We also consider some possible links between Neville and William Shakspere, the man from Stratford.

As a young man Neville attended Lord Burghley's school. In questioning where Shakespeare gained his considerable medical and alchemical knowledge, Showerman[59] pointed out that Burghley 'had a magnificent library with nearly 200 editions on alchemy and medical topics from all over Europe.'[60] During Neville's travels with Savile in Europe they met Tadeáš Hájek, the imperial physician in Prague.[61] In 1612, when meeting James

I, Neville used a medical metaphor: 'Some <u>medicines</u> ... do rather take away the sense of pain for the present than <u>cure</u> the <u>grief</u> for which they are applied'.[62] In *Macbeth* Malcolm says, 'Let's make us <u>medicines</u> of our great revenge to <u>cure</u> this deadly <u>grief</u>' (4.3.214). Neville follows Shakespeare here with the three key words in the same order.

Neville's experience of Burghley's school would also explain Shakespeare's ability to parody Burghley's advice to his son, in Polonius's precepts for Laertes.[63] In the first quarto Polonius was called Corambis: a not entirely respectful pun on Burghley's motto.[64] The change to Polonius in later editions may have been self-censorship. The name refers to Poland. From Prague, Neville and Savile had travelled to Wrocław in Poland, so Neville knew how the Polish lived and behaved. Furthermore these travels included meeting astronomers. Savile was an astronomer and Neville owned a book on Ptolemaic astronomy.[65] In Sonnet 14 Shakespeare wrote, 'I have astronomy.'

Scholars are increasingly confident, indeed certain, that Shakespeare travelled to Italy. There is good evidence that Neville travelled to cities that are featured in the Shakespeare plays: Verona, Padua, Venice, Florence (see Chapter 3).

In 1593 Neville's father died. It is in 1593 that the name William Shakespeare first appears as the author of *Venus and Adonis*. One plausible explanation of this timing is that Neville felt free to publish his work under a pseudonym after his father's death. In 1596 Neville named his second son William.[66] This is the date of the Northumberland Manuscript on which Neville repeatedly wrote the name William Shakespeare and this was before that name had appeared on any play. In Shakespeare's late play, *Henry VIII*, on stage in 1613, we see the christening of a Princess Elizabeth. Neville's daughter Elizabeth was christened in November 1610.

Neville inherited an ordnance manufacturing business from his mother's uncle. This would explain Shakespeare's knowledge of furnaces, iron and cannon. Neville sold the business before he went to France as ambassador. *King John* has more references to cannon than any other play and was written before the business was sold. Neville went to France at least three times, in 1578, 1582 and 1599. With Neville as author, Shakespeare's knowledge of France and his ability to write in French are explained. Similarly Neville's parliamentary and diplomatic career, and the long experience of his ancestors in government, would explain Shakespeare's interest in politics and history (see chapters 4, 5, 8 and 9). There are many members of the Neville family on stage in the history plays, arguably too many to be explained away as mere coincidence.[67]

The central debacle of the Essex rebellion and Neville's imprisonment marked a crucial turning point in Neville's life. We trace the effects of this experience and how it is manifest in Shakespeare's works throughout the second half of this book. Neville was in London at the time of the performance by the Lord Chamberlain's Men of *Richard II* (a play about the deposition of an English king). This was immediately before the rebellion in 1601. Shakespeare's play was performed a few days after Neville met with Essex's allies. Incarcerated in the Tower of London for his role in the failed rebellion, we know that Neville studied and wrote. This coincides with the time that Shakespeare wrote his great tragedies, beginning with *Hamlet* in 1601 and *Othello* in 1602–03 (see Chapter 7). He also wrote sonnets, many of which are clearly addressed to Southampton, especially those forgiving someone who has done the author a serious wrong. Amongst these sonnets are those which bewail the author's 'outcast state' and the 'stain' he had received (see Chapter 10). While Neville's imprisonment could explain the changes in Shakespeare's writing, there is nothing in the life of William Shakspere that could account for such a dramatic shift.

The gap in the accepted chronology of Shakespeare's plays at the end of Neville's imprisonment, between *Troilus and Cressida* and *Measure for Measure* of 1604, is the longest in the canon, as one might expect if the author were released from imprisonment and busy rebuilding his personal life. When he started writing plays again *Measure for Measure* has scenes in prison and deals with the themes of the nature of guilt and forgiveness, which is as one might expect given Neville's recent experiences. The play has no known connection to anything in William Shakspere's life.

After 1603 Neville was increasingly busy seeking influence in Parliament as a leading Member of Parliament. This coincides with a reduction in Shakespeare's output. Before 1600 Shakespeare wrote on average two plays a year. After 1603 his average was a single play each year, among them such masterpieces as *Macbeth, King Lear* and *Antony and Cleopatra* (see Chapter 8).

In May 1609 Neville's eldest son Henry married; the Second London Virginia Company was formally granted its Charter by King James; and *Shake-speares Sonnets* was published. We suggest that these three events provide further evidence of Neville's authorship (see Chapter 10).

The mysterious dedication to the sonnets was, we propose, written by Neville himself (although signed 'T. T.' for Thomas Thorpe, the publisher) and dedicated to Southampton, 'Mr. W. H.', the reversed initials of Henry Wriothesley, Earl of Southampton. While in the Tower in 1601–3, Southampton had been stripped of his titles and was simply 'Mr. Henry Wriothesley' (see Chapter 10).

The shipwreck of one of the Second London Virginia Company's ships in Bermuda caused a sensation. The full story of the ill-fated voyage, known as the 'Strachey letter', was circulated to the directors of the London Virginia Company (who were forbidden to let others read it). The Strachey letter was a source for *The Tempest*, which was premiered in 1611. William from Stratford could not have had access to this confidential company document but it would have been available to Neville (see Chapter 10).

We do not know whether Neville ever met William Shakspere. The latter may not have known where the plays came from. This ignorance would have protected him had he ever been interrogated. However, there is some evidence linking the two men.[68] Through his mother, Mary Arden, William Shakspere, the actor and theatre sharer, was a distant relative of Henry Neville.[69] There is both textual and circumstantial evidence for an agreement, in Neville's lifetime and afterwards, between Neville, Ben Jonson and John Beaumont, to pass off Neville's works as those of William Shakspere. A poem apparently written by Beaumont to Jonson in 1615 states that:

… our heirs shall hear
Preachers apt to their auditors to show
How far sometimes a mortal man may go
By dim light of nature.

This is followed by what appears to be a description of Neville's funeral which had been held at Windsor shortly before.[70] Some have taken these lines to mean that Shakspere's lack of education did not prevent the flowering of his genius. Most authorities believe that Ben Jonson edited the First Folio of 1623, providing it with its introductory poem in which he stated that Shakespeare had 'small Latin and less Greek'. At the time when the First Folio was being edited, Jonson was employed at Gresham College, London, which had been founded by Neville's relatives and where the Neville family had legal rights of governance. It is plausible therefore that Jonson was employed there to edit the plays in a way that made their authorship by William Shakspere universally accepted, so concealing the real author's identity. At that time it was most uncommon to provide any biographical information about writers and Jonson did not do so. It is obvious that the real author of Shakespeare's works must have been a man of great erudition and education, which Neville indeed was.

Neville died less than a year before the death of William Shakspere. No plays were written between 1614 and 1616.

Neville's Need for Secrecy

If a convincing case showing that Neville was the real writer of the works of Shakespeare is to be made, we must now address the central question of why he chose lifelong secrecy and took such care to preserve his anonymity, so that it has taken 400 years for the truth to emerge. We offer the following evidence as a plausible explanation.

Neville was born into a family engaged in secret government work and diplomacy. His father was employed on highly sensitive government business including taking custody of the Duke of Norfolk between 1569 and 1570 and of Mary, Queen of Scots in from 1584 to 1585. In 1585, Sir Edmund Neville denounced William Parry for treason. The latter was executed but, despite his loyal service, Edmund was imprisoned for thirteen years. It was at this very time that the incendiary *Leicester's Commonwealth* was printed. Neville's father was a supporter of Robert Dudley, Earl of Leicester. For Neville to have owned three copies of a banned work attacking Leicester is extraordinary.[71] Secrecy would have been essential to avoid imprisonment, or worse, for owning such a dangerous political tract. Unless, that is, Neville had been authorised to hold them, in which case he would have been doing so with official sanction from Francis Walsingham, Elizabeth's spymaster and founder of the Queen's Men theatre company, or from William Cecil, Lord Burghley. Neville knew and worked with both. If Neville was commissioned by Walsingham to start writing plays for the Queen's Men then keeping his identity secret would be part of the plan to use theatre for Tudor establishment propaganda.[72] However, keeping his identity secret would also free Neville to write whatever he wanted without fear of prosecution.

Many of the history plays deal with the succession crises of the Plantagenet kings, and Neville, a young Member of Parliament from a family closely involved with these events, would not have wanted to be identified as the author because Elizabeth I had ruled that any discussion of the succession was treason. Using history as metaphor enabled Neville to discuss issues too delicate to be set in contemporary times and to hint at the importance of the Neville family, without exposing himself. Others were censored for addressing such matters more directly and, in 1579, John Stubbe had his hand cut off for writing a pamphlet that offended the queen.[73]

Neville had good reasons to conceal his Shakespeare authorship. On the Northumberland Manuscript he listed a play by Thomas Nashe: *The Isle of Dogs*. This play's satire was too pointed for the government and so it was immediately banned, copies were destroyed and Nashe's career effectively ended. It is possible that co-writing with George Peele and others also helped hide Neville's identity.

Price pointed out that there was no need for any conspiracy to keep the identity of a 'gentleman of rank' secret: social convention and state censorship would preclude people identifying themselves as a writer.[74] Men in Neville's social position preferred not to be identified as poets or playwrights. Neville's mentor Sir Henry Savile did not like 'wits' (as he called them), and might well have been scandalised if he knew that his favourite student was writing plays such as *Titus Andronicus* and *Romeo and Juliet*. Thomas Bodley refused to have plays in his famous Oxford library. Other writers of the time were similarly reticent about being identified. When Cornwallis's *Paradoxes* were published in 1616 Henry Olney wrote in his dedication that, 'The author hateth nothing more than coming in publick.' Cornwallis wrote in a letter to Sir John Hobart, who had commended them, that 'in keeping them secret, he had shown some little discretion.'[75]

In his own diplomatic career Neville used spies and codes in his letters. He was related to Anthony and Francis Bacon who, in the 1590s, were both working for the Earl of Essex. Anthony Bacon, Francis' elder brother, ran an intelligence network for Essex on the Continent. The name Anthony occurs on the front cover of the Northumberland Manuscript with a fragment of a verse, 'Multi annis iam transactis ...' which occurs in a 1597 letter to Anthony.[76] As Neville was Essex's preferred candidate to be ambassador to France, it would have been strange if Neville and Anthony were not in touch. That Neville had involvement with the secret services of the time is evidenced by the existence of a copy of a letter written by Francis Bacon (the original was signed by Walsingham) in the NHMS and Neville's own travels to Scotland with Walsingham and Essex in 1583.[77] As ambassador to France, Neville was involved with spies and intelligence gathering from 1599 to 1600. On 17 July 1600, Ralph Winwood wrote to Neville, 'At my being in England, I told Mr. *Cuff* of that speech which *Prentice*, Mr. *Anthony Bacon's* Man, had with the Lord *Weems*. Mr. *Cuff* informed Mr. *Bacon* of it ... he was desirous to know whether your Lordship had advertised it into *England*.'[78] Anthony Bacon and Cuffe were key figures in the intelligence-gathering service established by Essex. This letter proves that Neville was in touch with them.

Neville, whose first loyalty was owed to his close kinsman Robert Cecil, needed to be discreet to safeguard his delicate position between Cecil and Essex, the two major power figures of the late Elizabethan years. Indeed, Neville was known for his discretion. On trial for his life after the Essex rebellion Neville wrote in his declaration of 2 March 1601, 'My Lord Southampton ... began to break with me that my lord (Essex) had received by Mr. Cuffe so good a persuasion both of my love to him and of my honesty, <u>discretion, and secrecy</u>, that he had given him commission to reveal unto me a matter of great secrecy and importance ...'[79] (Italics in the original; our emphasis underlined.)

In his 1603 *Microcosmos* John Davies described Neville as 'the Noble, <u>discreete</u>, and wellbeloved *Knight Sir Henry Nevill*' (italics in the original, our emphasis underlined). Neville demonstrated his discretion by keeping his authorship of a 1614 parliamentary document secret until obliged by questions in the House of Commons to reveal his authorship. Even after his death this discretion lingered on. When the Earl of Southampton's *Encomium* on Richard III was printed in 1616 as one of Cornwallis's *Paradoxes* it did not include Southampton's dedication to Neville.[80] At about the same time George Carleton tried to bring out a second printing of his book *Heroici Characteres* which he had dedicated to Neville in 1603. In a letter dated 1617 he acknowledged that, 'Sir Henry Neville in his life tyme wished that the dedication had been altered, and the verses written to hym placed in som other part of the book, which may be done with little alteration.'[81] This indicates that Neville did not want Carleton's effusive dedication with its hints of his authorship re-printed (see Chapter 6).[82] Such secrecy was essential in the febrile political atmosphere of both Elizabeth's and James's courts. Towards the end of his life Neville had been under investigation by the Earl of Northampton. Whitelocke, whose eulogy of Neville we quoted above, stated that Neville was a most faithful friend who had supported him when Whitelocke was imprisoned, and that the Earl of Northampton 'durst not name him [Neville] playnly, although he aymed at him, and I had reason enough to conceal him.'[83]

There was a further, more personal reason why Neville may have felt deeply concerned to keep his writing secret. It seems he was born out of wedlock, or at least before his parents were formally married. His father's first wife disappeared and it was not until after Neville's birth that a marriage settlement between Sir Henry Neville and Elizabeth Gresham was formally concluded. Any suspicion of illegitimacy would have threatened Neville's inheritance, just as we see in *King John*, when Robert Falconbridge challenges his older brother Philip's legitimacy. If indeed Neville did harbour secret anxieties about his own legitimacy he would have had a clear motive for Shakespeare's recurring interest in bastards. Neville served on a Parliamentary committee on illegitimacy at the time Shakespeare wrote *King Lear*, with the most famous of his bastards, Edmund, demanding, 'Now gods, stand up for bastards!' (1.2.22)

Furthermore Neville was ashamed of his imprisonment and the failure of his diplomatic career. The word 'shame' is used 346 times in the canon. This is much higher than the usage of the other emotion words such as grief, anger, guilt, jealousy, envy, hurt or hate: only love has a higher occurrence. The highest number of uses of the word 'shame' in a single work is thirty-one in *The Rape of Lucrece*. The highest number in any play is *King John*, which boasts eighteen. Many of these are to do with the illegitimacy of the Philip Falconbridge (a Neville family name: Thomas, the Bastard of Fauconberg, was the illegitimate son of William Neville, Lord Fauconberg and Earl of Kent. He was beheaded in 1471. He is mentioned in Shakespeare's *Henry VI: Part III*). The word 'shame' is spread throughout *King John*: the conduct of King John, political betrayals and the plan to kill the innocent Arthur all being shameful. In other words shame is connected to illegitimacy, political betrayal and kings killing innocents: the constellation of Henry Neville, his hidden illegitimacy and his grandfather's execution. Shakespeare used the word 'shame' more in early works than later, though in three connected works there is a sudden upward spike in the graph: *Hamlet*, *Troilus and Cressida* and *Measure for Measure*, namely the three plays probably written in, or just after he left, the Tower of London, when Neville had been shamed by his trial and imprisonment. Ewan Fernie in *Shame in Shakespeare* seems to describe Neville's situation: 'For Shakespeare, shame is explicitly a form of not being, not being one's ideal self; or else it is an experience of hideous deformity, of being something horrifically other, somebody else.'[84] Furthermore he suggested that 'shame is connected with the established Shakespearean motif of concealment and disguise …'[85]

Neville was not his ideal self: he was not legitimate; he was unable successfully to play the role of ambassador; he failed to become Secretary of State; he could not be acknowledged as a poet. He was a man in hiding who used disguise and hid his true identity. We know of one incident when, as ambassador in Paris, he went in disguise to the king of Spain's obsequies. He would have wanted to protect the Neville name and his son from the shame he felt which explains why secrecy was essential throughout his career and after his death. Neville could not have guessed that it would take 400 years for his true identity to emerge.

The Discreet Mr William Shakspere

William Shakspere was never arrested, questioned nor punished for the content of the plays at a time when the Crown brooked no criticism, or discussion of the succession, including when *Richard II* was performed on the eve of the Essex rebellion. This implies that it was known that he was not the author. Nevertheless we must acknowledge that Shakspere was extraordinarily discreet about his supposed authorship. He never bragged, as Jonson did, of being a writer, nor did he leave any hint of his authorship in his will or in any document. This suggests that his discretion was not due to modesty but because he knew he was not the author! Perhaps he was well paid for his role because he died one of the richest men in Stratford.

It was exceptionally dangerous at this time to be identified as a writer of anything that could be regarded as seditious. As we have seen, John Stubbs had his hand cut off in 1579 for offending the queen with a pamphlet she regarded as seditious; in 1593 Kyd was tortured and revealed that Marlowe had given him a heretical pamphlet; Marlowe was eliminated; John Penry was executed on 29 May 1593 (just a day before Marlowe was killed) for an unpublished rough draft of a petition to the queen (but also probably because he printed the Marprelate pamphlets); in 1597 Jonson served time in prison for his part in writing *The Isle of Dogs* (two of the actors were also imprisoned). [86] At about the time Penry and Marlowe died *Venus and Adonis* was published.[87] This was the first occasion the name William Shakespeare appeared in print. At such a dangerous time for writers Neville needed the protection of a pseudonym. Casson suggested that he had previously used the pen-name 'Phaeton' on a dedicatory sonnet published in 1591 in John Florio's *Second Fruits*.[88] Such a mythological name however would not do: people were bound to ask, 'Who is Phaeton?' Neville needed a real name so that such questions would not be asked.

That William Shakspere was never arrested beggars belief if he had been believed to be the author of the plays. We wonder whether Neville was detained so long in the Tower after the Essex rebellion not only because Cecil felt betrayed by him (though he did save his life) but also because he knew that Neville had written *Richard II*. It is plausible to conjecture that Cecil knew it was Neville who had written the plays in which he was satirised and which suggested that a monarch could be de-throned and the regime changed.

A Timeline: Shakspere and Neville 1583–1623

The following timeline starts after Henry Neville's return from four years travelling round Europe with his tutor, Henry Savile. They returned in 1582. William Shakspere, aged eighteen, was in Stratford, having married in 1582. This start date dramatically illustrates the difference between the two men before Shakespeare began writing. One was a villager with no known education, possibly forced into a marriage with an older woman who was pregnant. The other was already an international figure; a friend of Sir Philip Sidney, the poet; educated at Oxford; having travelled to many of the locations of the Italian plays; a man who from childhood knew courtiers and diplomats. The timeline enables us to compare their lives and see which has more links to the themes and issues of the works of Shakespeare. We have included references to some of the early anonymous plays which we suggest may be by the young Shakespeare.[89] (Where a play title is listed we are suggesting that this was the earliest date of writing: if it is a publication date we write 'published/printed'.)

If we take the early references to William Shakspere between 1592 and 1600 we find just two that show he was definitely connected to the theatre as either an actor, a manager and/or a sharer.[90] Neither of these identify him as a writer. The majority of official records show him as concerned with money, whether as debtor/debt collector or dealer. During this period plays by Shakespeare were on stage and in print anonymously until the name first appeared on quartos in 1598. Whereas Shakspere at this time was concerned with sums of money the evidence shows that the writer Shakespeare was concerned with history, law and politics: Neville's main recorded activities are those of a politician. As Justice of the Peace and Deputy Lieutenant of Berkshire he had significant legal roles. The sale of his cannon factory in 1598 meshes with *King John* (1596) in which cannon are frequently and anachronistically mentioned. This sale was in preparation for his ambassadorship in France (1599). In *Henry V* (1599) Bardolph says, 'We must to France' (2.1.90).

TIMELINE 1583–1623: SHAKSPERE, SHAKESPEARE AND NEVILLE

Date	1583	1584	1585	1586	1587	1588
Shakspere, the actor from Stratford	Daughter Susana baptised in Stratford.		2 February, the twins, Hamnet and Judith, baptised in Stratford.			'Willielmo Shackespere' in a legal action over land.
Shakespeare, the writer						
Other works, possibly by the Bard		*Mucedorus (L/C references).*	**Look About You¹ (L/C references).*	*Arden of Faversham (L/C reference).*	*Locrine co-written with George Peele?* *The Famous Victories of Henry V co-written with Henry Evans?*	*Edmund Ironside.*
Events	Walsingham sets up the Queen's Men.	*Leicester's Commonwealth* (L/C) published. Neville copies L/C into Worsley MS 47.		Trial of Mary Queen of Scots. Philip Sidney dies.	Execution of Mary Queen of Scots.	The Spanish Armada defeated.
Neville's life and family	Neville travels to Scotland with Walsingham and Essex; becomes a J.P. Ambrose Dudley, 3rd Earl of Warwick, is sent to discipline Neville on his export of ordnance and this results in an argument.	Neville becomes an M.P.; marries Anne Killigrew; meets Henry Wriothesley (at some time 1583-85). Neville's father (with Ralph Sadler) has custody of Mary Queen of Scots.	Sir Edmund Neville, after denouncing William Parry, who is executed, is imprisoned for thirteen years.	Henry Neville 6th Baron of Bergavenny (Neville's father's cousin) is one of the peers who try Mary Queen of Scots.	Holinshed's *Chronicles* published: Neville's father-in-law, Henry Killigrew, is one of the editors.	Neville becomes M.P. for Sussex. Charles Neville, 6th Earl of Westmoreland, is one of the leaders of an invasion force at the time of the Spanish Armada.

Date	1589	1590	1591	1592	1593	1594
Shakspere, the actor from Stratford				Willelmus Shackspere in London: loans John Clayton £7 (see 1600).		Performs before the Queen at Greenwich on 28 December.
Shakespeare, the writer	Earliest date for *The Taming of the Shrew*. *The Troublesome Raigne of John King of England: co-written with George Peele.	*Henry VI: Part II (The First Part of the Contention)*. **Henry VI: Part III* performed.	**Henry VI: Part I*.	*Edward III*. *Two Gentlemen of Verona*. *Richard III*. *Henry VI part 1 performed. Nashe refers to 'brave Talbot' and the impact of the play in *Pierce Penniless*.	*Venus and Adonis* published (registered in April) by William Shakespeare: **FIRST USE OF THIS NAME**, dedicated to Southampton. Richard Stoney bought V&A and was the first to write the name 'Shakspaere' in his account book.	*The Rape of Lucrece* published as by William Shakespeare, also dedicated to Southampton. *Henry VI: Part II* registered. *Titus Andonicus* co-written with Peele published anonymously. *The Comedy of Errors* performed at Gray's Inn, 28 December.
Other works, possibly by the Bard	Thomas Nashe refers to *whole Hamlets, I should say handfuls of Tragicall speeches*.		*The Phaeton Sonnet.* **Troublesome Raigne of John* published anonymously.	*Arden of Faversham* published anonymously. *Thomas of Woodstock.*		*Taming of the Shrew* published anonymously. Henslowe lists a performance of *Hamlet* in his diary.
Events			In *The Troublesome Raigne* Falconbridge refers to Phaeton; Shakespeare refers to Phaeton in the 1590s.	Greene's attack on 'Shake-scene' (actually by Chettle?). Plague closes the theatres until 1594.	Marlowe killed. *Guy Earl of Warwick* by 'B. J.' lampoons 'Sparrow' from Stratford upon Avon. Peele praises Southampton as a star.	First mention by another author of Shake-speare, in *Willobye His Avisa* referring to *Lucrece*. The Lord Chamberlain's Men formed. Theatres reopen.
Neville's life and family	Neville becomes MP for Sussex.		Henry Killigrew, with Earl of Essex in France, meets Charles de Gontaut, Duc de Biron.	Neville obtained a five-year Royal Patent, a monopoly, to export cast iron guns.	Neville's father dies. Neville elected MP for New Windsor.	

Date	1595	1596	1597	1598	1599	1600
Shakspere, the actor from Stratford	First written record of 'Willm Shakspere' as an actor/manager, the only recorded payment to him as such.	Hamnet dies. Applies for coat of arms. W. Wayte accuses Shakspare of threatening him.	Buys New Place in Stratford for £60. Listed as tax defaulter in Bishopsgate, London.	Hoarded grain in a famine. Quiney's letter requesting a loan (never posted). Paid for load of stone.	Willelmum Shakespeare shareholder of the Globe Theatre. Shakspeare owes tax. John Shakspere's coat of arms granted.	William Shackspere goes to court for a debt of £7 (Clayton, 1592) and is referred to as a tax defaulter.
Shakespeare, the writer	*The True Tragedy of Richard Duke of York* (*Henry VI: Part III*) published anonymously. *Love's Labour's Lost* written 1594–5?	*The Raigne of King Edward III* published anonymously. *King John* *Merchant of Venice*	*Richard II, Richard III* and *Romeo and Juliet* published anonymously.	*Richard III* Q2 and *Richard II* published as by William Shake-speare; *Love's Labour's Lost* as by W. Shakespere: **THE FIRST PLAYS TO BE IDENTIFIED AS BY SHAKESPEARE.** *Henry IV: Part I* published anonymously.	*Much Ado About Nothing.* *As You Like It.* *Julius Caesar.* Thomas Platter records a performance of *Julius Caesar* in September.	*Merry Wives* written. *Merchant of Venice*, *Henry V, Henry IV* Part 2, *Much Ado About Nothing* and *A Midsummer Night's Dream* published. *Twelfth Night* has Count Orsino on stage.
Other works possibly by the Bard	*Locrine* published as 'by W. S.'	Thomas Lodge refers to 'y ghost which cried... Hamlet, revenge'.		*Mucedorus* published anonymously.		*Look About You* published anonymously.
Events	William Covell in an epistle in *Polimanteia* notes 'Lucrecia Sweet Shakespeare'.	The Northumberland Manuscript, owned by Neville, lists *Richard II* and *III*, quotes from *Lucrece, Love's Labour's Lost* and names William Shakespeare.		Barnfield praises Shakespeare's poetry in his *Poems in Diverse Humours*. Francis Meres lists Shakespeare's plays in *Palladis Tamia*.	Globe theatre opens. Weever's epigramme 22 addressed to 'Honey-Tongued Shakespeare'.	Neville's secretary Winwood tells him Orsino is coming to London in a letter dated 20 November.
Neville's life and family		Neville made Deputy Lieutenant, Berkshire.	Neville becomes MP for Liskeard.	Neville sells iron works; is knighted and chosen to be ambassador to France. Biron is ambassador to England.	Neville goes as ambassador to France; his baby son dies.	Neville returns to England in August.

Date	1601	1602	1603	1604	1605	1606
Shakspere, the actor from Stratford	His father dies. Thomas Whittington records in his will that "Wyllyam Shaxspere" owed him 40 shillings. Is listed as a tenant of the Globe.	Pays £320 for land and buys a cottage. The grant of a coat of arms to John Shakspere is challenged. His son is called 'Shakespear ye Player'.	Is named as an actor in James I's royal patent creating the King's Men; and in Jonson's play *Sejanus* cast list (but this is not published until 1616).	Rents lodgings with the Mountjoys in Silver Street. Is listed as a player in accounts for the coronation procession. Sues an apothecary and sells malt in Stratford.	Invests £440 in Stratford parish tithes. Augustine Phillips, actor, leaves 30s in gold in his will to his "fellow William Shakespeare".	
Shakespeare, the writer	*Hamlet.* *The Phoenix and the Turtle* published in *Loves Martyr* as by William Shake-speare.	*Troilus and Cressida.* *Othello.* *Merry Wives* registered 18th January. *Hamlet* registered 26 July.	*Measure for Measure.* *Troilus and Cressida* registered. *Hamlet* Q1 published. *Sir Thomas More*: Hand D.	*All's Well That Ends Well.* *Measure for Measure* performed at court 26 December. *Hamlet* Q2 published	*Timon of Athens.* *King Lear.*	*Macbeth.* *Antony and Cleopatra.* *King Lear* performed 26th December.
Other works possibly by the Bard					*A Yorkshire Tragedy.*	
Events	After the Earl of Essex's unsuccessful rebellion he is tried and executed. The Earl of Southampton is imprisoned.		Elizabeth I dies and James I comes to the throne. King's Men formed. Southampton dedicates a defence of Richard III to Neville: he refers to 'playes'.	Southampton, Neville and Lord Danvers arrested on rumours of a plot on 24th June but released next day.	Gunpowder plot.	
Neville's life and family	Neville arrested, tried and imprisoned in the Tower.	Edward Neville born: was Anne the mother of an illegitimate son? Did Neville have reason to be jealous?	Neville and Southampton released in April. Southampton stages *Love's Labour's Lost* for Queen Anne.	Neville elected M.P. and serves on committee concerned with illegitimate children.[2]	Neville awarded M.A at Oxford. James I and Southampton are present. *Tres Sibyllae* by M. Gwynne which refers to *Macbeth* performed.	Neville supports oath requiring Catholics to vow James is the lawful king; opposes James' wish for the Union of Scotland and England.

Date	1607	1608	1609	1610	1611	1612
Shakspere, the actor from Stratford	His brother, Edmund Shakespeare, 'a player' buried 31 December at St. Mary Overy, Southwark.	Mother dies; he owes £20 and is owed £6. Blackfriars theatre sharer. Godfather to a Stratford mercer's son.	Continues litigation for the debt of £6 against John Addenbroke.	Buys 20 acres of land near Stratford.	Acts to protect his real estate interests against default. Pays to improve Stratford roads.	Testifies in Belott vs Mountjoy and signs a deposition as 'William Shackp': his first signature.
Shakespeare, the writer	*Coriolanus*. *Pericles*.	*King Lear* published. *Pericles* and *Antony and Cleopatra* registered.	*Shake-speares Sonnets*, *Troilus and Cressida* and *Pericles* published. *Cymbeline*.	*A Winter's Tale*.	*The Tempest*.	*Cardenio/Double Falshood* and *Henry VIII* co-written with Fletcher.
Other works, possibly by the bard		*Yorkshire Tragedy* registered as by 'Wylliam Shakespere'; quarto states it was written by 'W. Shakspeare'.			Fletcher writes *The Tamer Tamed*: the only sequel to a Shakespeare play (*The Taming of The Shrew*).	'Cardenno' performed at court during Christmas.
Events	Susanna Shaxspere marries physician John Hall.		Second London Virginia Company (SLVC) given royal charter: Southampton and Neville are investors and directors.	Strachey letter (SLVC) was a source for *The Tempest*. Beaumont & Fletcher write *A King and No King* (see 1619).	Ben Jonson's epigram addressed to Neville. John Davies calls Shakespeare 'a companion for a king'.	Beaumont retired in 1612-13 to Kent.
Neville's life and family	In Parliament Neville, in a speech about the union of Scotland and England, refers to Richard III.	James I visits Neville.	'Henry Nevil poet' is encoded in the dedication to *Shake-speares Sonnets*.	Neville has access to the Strachey letter. Two of his daughters marry. Goes hunting with James I in Windsor forest.	Neville is a possible candidate to become Secretary of State.	In *Henry VIII* [3] there is a masque: Sir Edward Neville was disguised in the real event but he is not mentioned in the play.

Date	1613	1614	1615	1616	Seven year gap	1623
Shakspere, the actor from Stratford	Buys Blackfriars gatehouse and signs deed/mortgage.[4] Earl of Rutland pays Shakespeare for an impresa.	As a landowner seeks to enclose pastures in Welcombe.	John Combe, moneylender, leaves Shackspere £5. Legal cases about the gatehouse and theatres.	Daughter Judith married. William Shakspere signs his will three times [5] and dies, is buried on 25 April.		
Shakespeare, the writer	Two Noble Kinsmen based on Chaucer's Knight's Tale co-written with Fletcher.				1622 Walkley publishes Othello and states the author is dead.	First Folio printed: contained thirty-six plays, eighteen of which had never been published before.
Other works, possibly by the bard	Cardenio performed again on 8 June 1613 for Ambassador of Savoy.				1619 Two Noble Kinsmen performed at court.	
Events	29 June the Globe burned down during a performance of Henry VIII. Overbury imprisoned in the Tower and dies.		Edmund Howes lists 'M. Willi Shakespeare' as a poet in Stow's Annales.	Ben Jonson lists Will Shake-speare as an actor in Sejanus in 1598.	1619: A King and No King (Beaumont and Fletcher) printed with dedicatory epistle to Sir Henry Neville.	Ben Jonson, one of the compilers of the First Folio, is living at Gresham College, which was founded by Neville's great uncle.
Neville's life and family	Neville was related to Chaucer. He knew Overbury and in Two Noble Kinsmen reflects on his plight (see Chapter 11). Neville travels to Brussels.	Sir William Herbert supports Neville in Parliament (he is a cousin of Neville's chief backer in Privy Council, William Herbert, 3rd Earl of Pembroke).	Neville reported to have died on 10 July.	The Encomium on Richard III published by Thomas Thorp using Southampton's version but without his dedication to Neville. A copy of the Encomium on Richard III is amongst Neville's books in his library.		The First Folio is published with a dedication to William and Philip Herbert, 3rd and 4th Earls of Pembroke.

The Early Comedies and Tragedies 1589–1596

Home-keeping youth have ever homely wits.

The Two Gentlemen of Verona, 1.1.2

If William Shakspere was the true author of the canon, we might reasonably have expected the earliest works of a playwright from Stratford-upon-Avon to include some reference to the adventures of a young man arriving in London. They might contrast the city with life in a small country town. Yet Shakespeare never wrote such a play. His earliest comedies and tragedies were set in Italy: *The Taming of the Shrew* in Padua; *The Two Gentlemen of Verona* in Verona and Milan; *Titus Andronicus* in Rome; *Romeo and Juliet* in Verona and Mantua. His other early comedies were not set in England: *The Comedy of Errors* was set in Ephesus, at that time in the Ottoman Empire; *Love's Labour's Lost* occurs in France.

Neville travelled in Europe from 1578, reaching Italy in 1581 and returning to England in 1582. He spent time in France, the Holy Roman Empire (Germany, Bohemia, Prague and Vienna) and Poland, before arriving in Italy. 'Verona is the first Italian city a sensible traveller from England would reach, having first successfully crossed the Alps and come down through the Brenner Pass.'[1] Arthur Throckmorton travelled to Italy from Vienna in May 1581, arriving in Padua on 4 June. It is not clear what route he took. In his diary he recorded that 'Mr. Nevelle, Mr. Saville and Mr. George Carew' arrived in Padua on 7 August having come from Vienna. They then visited Venice. Throckmorton reported in his diary that on 10 September 1581, Savile and Neville left Padua and travelled in the direction of Vicenza (and so towards Verona).[2] In Neville's library there is a copy of Andrea Palladio's 1575 *I Commentarii di C. Giulio Cesare*. Palladio lived most of his life in Vicenza. His classical Teatro Olimpico was being constructed in Vicenza from 1580 to 1585. Palladio died in August 1580, just a year before Neville arrived.

Throckmorton's diary provides evidence that Neville visited Florence. Arthur had arrived in Florence in October and recorded that on 19 November 1581 'Mr. Savel came from Como' (north of Milan). We presume that Neville accompanied Savile. There are three plausible routes that Savile and Neville may have taken:
1. By land from Padua via Verona, Bergamo, Como, Milan, Genoa, then by sea to Pisa and overland to Florence;
2. by canal to Verona via Ostiglia, Cremona, Cassano, Milan, then by land to Como, returning to Milan and then on to Florence;[3]
3. by canal to Verona via Ostiglia, Mantua, then by land to Bergamo, Como, Milan and to Florence.[4]

Evidence of these possible routes can be traced through the cities mentioned in the early Shakespeare plays. Shakespeare referred to Padua in three plays: *The Taming of the Shrew, The Merchant of Venice* and *Much Ado About Nothing*, but by far the most references occur in the earliest play. Milan is also mentioned in three plays and scenes in *The Two Gentlemen of Verona* are set there.[5] Valentine 'embarked for' Milan and we can reasonably suppose the Savile party used the canals because they were the easiest way to travel.[6] Mantua is also referred to in three plays: *The Two Gentlemen of Verona, The Taming of the Shrew* and *Romeo and Juliet*. There is a consistent pattern of northern Italian cities, which could have been on the Savile party itinerary. Since the early twentieth century many scholars have agreed that not only 'must Shakespeare have visited Italy but he must have visited Milan, Verona, Venice, Padua and Mantua'.[7]

On 20 November, Throckmorton reported that 'Mr. Savel went to see Pratelina' (near Florence). In 1581 Francesco I de'Medici, Grand Duke of Tuscany, had just finished building his beautiful villa with its spectacular gardens in Pratelino. Just a year before, Michel de Montaigne, whose works influenced Shakespeare, had visited Pratelino.[8] During the period 1580–81 Montaigne travelled through Switzerland, Munich, the Brenner Pass, Verona, Vicenza, Venice, Florence and Rome, returning home via Pisa and Milan.[9] We do not know whether Montaigne met Savile and Neville although their paths may have crossed when Montaigne was travelling north from Rome to Milan and Neville was travelling south from Milan to Florence in October 1581. Montaigne's journal includes his descriptions of Pratelino, Florence and Milan but he does not mention meeting the Englishmen.[10] From Florence Savile also visited Rome. It was not until late 1582 that he arrived back in England.[11] In the absence of evidence to the contrary there is no reason to doubt that Neville stayed with his tutor for the rest of his journey.

The Italian *commedia dell'arte* has been identified as one of the theatre forms that inspired Shakespeare from his very earliest plays. Neville, having visited Italy, is likely to have seen the *commedia* in its native habitat. Neville may also have seen *commedia dell'arte* again in France, as Winwood wrote to him on 31 July 1600 that 'the King answered *he would not go to the Comedy* (for here are certain Italian Comedians where he passeth the Afternoons with much Contentment).'[12] (Italics and capitals in the original.)

Neville could read Italian. Shakespeare must have been able to read Italian because he translated whole lines from Italian sources.[13] In the Audley End House library there is a book about the Italian language, *De Commentarii della Lingua Italiana*, dated 1581 and published in Venice. Since Neville had visited Venice that very year he may well have bought it there. In letters of 1605 and 1608, Neville wrote in Italian.[14] Also in the Audley End House library are books published in Venice during the 1560s and 1570s as well as several other Italian books published in the 1550s when Neville's father and father-in-law were Marian exiles in Padua.

The Taming of the Shrew

'Shakespeare chose to change the Ferrarese setting of George Gascoigne's *Supposes* to "Fair Padua, nursery of arts" for his *Taming of the Shrew* and to have his Lucentio arrive there to "haply institute a course of learning and ingenious study" (1.1.8).[15] This shift of location is understandable when we know Neville had travelled to Padua for his own learning. 'In almost all the dramas set in Italy, learning and education are major themes.'[16] Since the purpose of Neville's travels was educational and he was travelling with his Oxford tutor, it makes sense for him to have used these themes. In the play there is a scene of a comic lute lesson. Throckmorton reported in his diary that he had lute lessons while in Padua. Neville himself had a lute and in 1603, when imprisoned in the Tower of London, he made a note for himself to 'send for my lute to Billingbeare'.[17] Of the sixteen references to the lute in Shakespeare's plays all but three are to be found in the early plays from the 1590s.

The only references to Bergamo and Pisa in the Shakespeare canon occur in *The Taming of the Shrew* where the latter is mentioned twelve times. Furthermore the Pedant in the play (who claims he has often been in Pisa) recalls a visit to Genoa:

Signior Baptista may remember me,
Near twenty years ago, in <u>Genoa</u>,
Where we were lodgers at the Pegasus. (4.4.4)

The Pedant tells us he has cheques ('bills for money by exchange' 4.2.89) from Florence. Throckmorton charted his own return journey through Florence, Pisa and Genoa.[18] The Pedant refers to an inn called 'the Pegasus' and we know from Throckmorton's record that he and the Savile party stayed at inns during their travels.[19]

The Taming of the Shrew dates from 1589. It opens with scenes which show a lord playing a trick on a drunkard by changing his identity, lifting him from the gutter and transporting him to a life of luxury. This lord enters with his huntsmen and hounds. He knows each dog and their qualities, naming them and caring about them. *The Two Gentlemen of Verona* also features dogs, including 'gentleman-like dogs, under the Duke's table' (4.4.17). In the 1550s Neville's father was Master of the Harriers, the king's pack of hunting dogs. Neville's father wrote to Sir Nicholas Throckmorton (Arthur's father) in 1561 about hunting the hare with hounds, using this as a metaphor about members of the council: 'I need not describe to you the nature of our fellows here. They can hold to the <u>hare</u> and <u>hunt</u> with the hounds' (our emphasis underlined).[20] Rosalind in *As You Like It* uses hunting as a metaphor: 'Her love is not the <u>hare</u> that I do <u>hunt</u>' (4.3.19). As we shall see below, this is not the only time Neville's father used a metaphor that is later used by Shakespeare.

Returning to *The Taming of the Shrew*, in the same speech the lord also talks of hawking. The play, like many of Shakespeare's works, contains much imagery from falconry. Petruchio describes the taming of Kate as if she was a falcon.

My falcon now is sharp and passing empty;
And till she stoop she must not be full-gorged,
For then she never looks upon her lure.
Another way I have to man my haggard,
To make her come and know her keeper's call,
That is, to watch her, as we watch these kites
That bate and beat and will not be obedient. (4.1.177)

Falconry was a sport of noblemen. Because his father was a falconer Neville would have learned about the sport as a boy. In 1610 Neville served on a parliamentary committee concerned with hunting and hawking. There is also evidence that Neville was a keen hunter, joining James I while he was hunting in the Windsor forest.

Of all the sports used by Shakespeare as imagery, Spurgeon identified bowls as his favourite, due to the sheer number of references.[21] We find one in this early play when Petruchio comments on Katharine's taming:

thus the bowl should run,
And not unluckily against the bias. (4.5.24)

It might be thought that bowls was a common game, so William from Stratford might play it, and these references to the game would be unexceptional. However Henry VIII, following the practice of Edward III and Richard II, made bowls illegal except to noblemen who paid a fee of £100 to play on their private greens. Neville would have been in a position to play bowls while William from Stratford would not. There is evidence that Neville's father played the game in a letter he wrote, dated 30 June 1570 (when Neville himself was a boy), in which he used bowls as a metaphor (just as Shakespeare was to do later). He wrote that he 'must needs utter unto my Lord his color [choler] as well tempered as may be by bools [bowls]'.[22] From this we can glimpse Neville growing up in a household where hunting with hounds and falcons and playing bowls led his father to use these sports as figures of speech.

Petruchio also refers to the raging depths of the sea, booming cannon and mathematics. Neville had sailed across the channel in 1578 and 1582 and, as a manufacturer of cannon, knew the roar they made. He studied mathematics at Oxford and owned at least three books on the subject. His 1538 celestial geometry of Ptolemy is in the library at Merton College; the 1558 *Sphaericorum* by Theodosius and Barlaam's *Monachi* are in the library at Audley End House. The last of these is dated 1600 and is a translation of a Greek manuscript found by Henry Savile during his European travels, during which Neville accompanied him (see Chapter 6). The first two were both annotated by Neville in Latin and Greek.

We wonder whether the scenes featuring the drunkard Sly, being led to believe he is a lord, may be the author showing us that William from Stratford (who shared the same initials as the actor who played Sly) was dreaming or deluded if he pretended he was the dramatist. The plot involves men exchanging identities: Lucentio and Tranio, as well as the Pedant pretending to be the latter's father. Petruchio complains, 'Why this is flat knavery to take upon you another man's name.' (5.1.31) Perhaps then the playwright was playing with his factotum who complained of his shrewish wife back in Stratford! However these references could just be coincidence because, if the first version of the play was written as early as 1589, William might still have been resident in Stratford, because there is no evidence that he was in London before 1592. If so then the idea of two men exchanging identity was clearly already in the playwright's mind even before William appeared on the scene. The use of disguise was popular as a theatrical device at the time. Neville's grandfather had been mistaken for Henry VIII on at least two occasions at a masque and at a tournament, and indeed he impersonated the king. This illustrates the way that the idea of hiding behind a false identity may already have been familiar to Neville.

When Neville's father died in 1593 an inventory of his goods listed many items including his horses, cattle and sheep, his kitchen and bedroom equipment. Amongst the latter we find 'a bedstead with a testerne and valance also curtaynes of Sarcenett, a featherbedd, a bolster, two pillow, a paire of blankets and a coverlet of Arris'.[23]

In *The Taming of the Shrew* Gremio, thinking he might die soon, makes such a list, including 'my arras counterpoints' and 'Valance of Venice gold in needlework' (2.1.344–7).[24] Petruchhio says, 'I'll fling the pillow, there the bolster, This way the coverlet' (4.1.188).

Shakespeare referred to 'sarcenet' in *Henry IV: Part II* and *Troilus and Cressida* (both written after 1593). He used the verb 'testerned' in *The Two Gentlemen of Verona* (1.1.138). In his list Gremio mentions 'tents and canopies', meaning bed hangings. 'Tents' were defined as 'testorne' in Baret's *Alvearie*, 1580, a word we find in Neville's inventory.[25] There are beds with 'curtains' in *Romeo and Juliet* (1.1.134) and *The Rape of Lucrece* (367). A 'feather-bed' is uniquely used as a metaphor by Launcelot in *The Merchant of Venice* (2.2.157). Shakespeare referred to a 'blanket' in four plays, the earliest being in *Hamlet* (2.2.505). Most of these words are not in *The Taming of a Shrew* which, being published in 1594, must have been composed earlier. Neville's father died in 1593. Neville would therefore have known of this inventory of his goods that year, even if he did not compose it himself. As we have seen, Gremio in the play makes the list of these items thinking he might die soon.

Ovid was Shakespeare's favourite poet. Among Neville's books there is a 1568 book of Ovid's *Ars Amatoria* and *Remedia Amoris*. Lucentio tells us in *The Taming of the Shrew* that he has read 'The Art of Love' (4.2.8). Bate confirmed that Ovid's *Ars Amatoria* had been a source for *The Taming of the Shrew*: 'Petruchio implicitly bases his taming on one precept within it: 'Vim licet appelles: grata est vis ista puellis' – 'may use what is termed force: girls like you to use it' (1 673)'.[26] In the copy of Ovid's *Ars Amatoria* in Neville's library this passage is highlighted. Indeed there is a small = mark against this very line:

Ovid's *Ars Amatoria* and *Remedia Amoris*. (Private collection)

In the play Ovid is contrasted with Aristotle.[27] There is a copy of Aristotle's *Ethics* in the Neville library, dated 1553. Neville's father went to Padua in 1553–4 so this volume is likely to have been purchased by him there. Padua was the centre of Aristotelianism at the time.[28]

The Two Gentlemen of Verona

In the annotated edition of Ovid's *Ars Amatoria* and *Remedia Amoris* in Neville's library someone has highlighted text about Orpheus, the archetypal poet and this passage is referenced in seven works by Shakespeare.

> Nec plectrum dextra,citharam tenuisse sinistra
>   Nesciat,arbitrio foemina docta meo.
> Saxa,ferasq; lyra monit Rhodopeius Orpheus,
>   Tartareosq; lacus,tergeminumq; canem.
> Saxa tuo cantu uindex iustissime matris
>   Fecerunt muros officiosa nouos.
> Quamuis mutus erat,uoci fauisse putatur
>   Piscis,Arioniæ fabula nota lyræ.

Ovid's *Ars Amatoria* and *Remedia Amoris*, 30 verso.

This passage translated reads:

No woman trained according to my will should fail to know,
How to hold her lyre in her left hand, a plectrum in her right.
Rhodopeian[29] Orpheus, with his lyre, moved <u>stones</u> and wild beasts,
And Tartarus's lake and Cerberus, the triple-headed dog.
At your[30] song, just avenger of your mother,
The <u>stones</u> obligingly made Thebes's new walls.
Though mute, a fish[31] is thought to have responded
To a human voice, as the story of Arion's lyre told.[32]

Shakespeare's first reference to Orpheus was in *The Two Gentlemen of Verona*:

For Orpheus' lute was strung with poets' sinews,
Whose golden touch could soften steel and <u>stones</u>,
Make tigers tame and huge leviathans
Forsake unsounded deeps to dance on sands. (3.2.77)

Here the Bard refers to Orpheus' musical instrument as a lute (as we have seen above, Neville wrote of his own lute: Shakespeare never used the word 'lyre': it was the Latin word 'lyra' that is used in Ovid's poem, see above), the playing of it by hand, stones, a fierce animal and fish, all in the same order as in the Ovid. In *The Merchant of Venice* (1596–8) we find: 'Orpheus drew trees, <u>stones</u> and floods' (5.1.80). In both of these Orpheus is moving stones: in the highlighted verse above the annotator has marked a passage which twice mentions 'saxa' (stones).

The Two Gentlemen of Verona is one of Shakespeare's earliest comedies, dated to 1590–3. It starts with two friends saying goodbye as one sets off on his travels 'to see the wonders of the world' (1.1.6). Similarly, Neville had had to say goodbye to family and friends as he set out on his European tour. In his *Shakespeare Guide to Italy* Roe provided convincing evidence that the details in the play about travels by boat were based on real canal and river transport. Furthermore he showed that many details could only be known to an author who has actually been there. He also showed that the playwright must have visited Italy after 1578 because he refers to events that took place there prior to that time.[33] Neville was in Italy in 1581.

This comedy is courtly, celebrates and reflects on love and male friendship and is concerned with the education of young nobles. Panthino recommends that Proteus be sent to the Emperor's court:

There shall he practice tilts and tournaments,
Hear sweet discourse, converse with noblemen,
And be in the eye of every exercise
Worthy his youth and nobleness of birth. (1.3.30)

This concern with the education of young noblemen recurs in several plays including *Love's Labour's Lost* and *Hamlet*. Neville travelled to Italy with his tutor and Robert Sidney (who remained lifelong friends) as part of his education. Neville also wrote about his desire to educate his children. In his 1603/4 draft letter to Robert Cecil he wrote, 'Either restrained or specially destinated, I would be glad of som small amenyties to my younger sonnes, whereby I might ~~hope~~ {be inabled} to give them good education at the least, ~~and~~ {that} being eased of that charge ~~might be able~~ to do the more for my daughters.'[34]

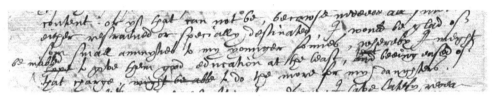

Neville's 1603/4 letter: Berkshire Record Office, Reading.

There is no evidence that William Shakspere from Stratford educated his children. His daughter Judith was unable to sign her name except by making a mark on a 1611 document.

Roe showed that Shakespeare had not made a mistake when he located both an emperor and a duke in Milan in the play: he had based his story of *The Two Gentlemen of Verona* on the brief visit of Emperor Charles V to Milan's Duke Francesco in 1533. Roe quoted Guicciardini's *History of Italy* about the Emperor's reason for leaving Milan to return to Spain. [35] A copy of Francesco Guicciardini's *Della Historia D'Italia* dated 1580 and published in Venice is to be found in Neville's library. As Neville was in Italy the very next year, 1581, he could well have bought the book in Venice. There are also copies of Guicciardini's *Discrittiones*, dated 1581 and his *Propositioni overo Considerationi*, 1583, amongst Neville's books.

Another source for *The Two Gentlemen of Verona* was Boccaccio's *Decameron*. This can also be found in Neville's library. The edition is in Italian and dated 1554. Neville's father was in Padua in 1554. Also amongst Neville's books that were sources for Shakespeare is a two-volume 1574 edition of the Spanish prose romance *Diana Enamorada* by Jorge de Montemayor that was printed in Venice. The book, a source for *The Two Gentlemen of Verona*, *A Midsummer Nights Dream* and *As You Like It*, was not published in English until 1598 after the first two of these plays had been written and so scholars have puzzled over how Shakespeare could have read this source.[36] It would not have been a problem for Neville as he could read and speak Spanish. He negotiated with Spanish diplomats in 1600 and used a Spanish phrase 'el nuevo regno di Granada'[37] in a letter of 13/11/1599.[38]. He was considered for the role of Ambassador to Spain in 1604.

A possible source for plot elements in *The Two Gentlemen of Verona* (Julia following Proteus disguised as a page and Valentine becoming leader of the robbers) was Sir Philip Sidney's *Arcadia*, which certainly influenced Shakespeare's later plays. It is possible that

Neville had early access to Sidney's epic romance. From his letters to his brother Robert in 1578 and 1580 it is clear that Sidney knew Neville because he referred to him in both letters by name. Robert and Neville were travelling through Europe together. In the 1580 letter Sidney mentioned his 'toyful book' (the Old *Arcadia*), which he said he would send to Robert by February 1581, so it is possible that Neville had access to an early manuscript copy of *Arcadia* from 1581.[39]

The Comedy of Errors

Another book in Neville's library is a collection of plays by Plautus in Latin, published in 1522. There is a marginal annotation at the start of *The Menaechmi*, which was the source play for *The Comedy of Errors*. Scholars had noted that this play was not available in translation in Shakespeare's time so he must have read it in the Latin. The faint annotation is against the text, 'Mercator quidem fuit Syracusis senex' (There was in fact an old merchant at Syracuse …). *The Comedy of Errors* opens with Egeon, whom Duke Solinus identifies as a 'Merchant of Syracuse' (1.1.3). Furthermore, rather than being identified as Egeon in stage directions in the First Folio, he is named as the 'Merchant of Syracuse' or 'Mer'.[40]

Plautus, 1522. (Private collection)

Because there must be some uncertainty whether this annotation is by Neville we have sought evidence to corroborate the hypothesis that it is by him, by comparing the style of his handwriting with that of the annotator. The capital 'A' of this annotation is the clearest letter here and we can compare it with several from Neville's manuscript copy of *Leicester's Commonwealth* (Worsley MSS 47: 1584–5) and compare these with other capital 'A's in the annotated volumes of Horace, Tacitus, Dionysius and Appian that are in Neville's library.

Plautus annotation detail.

Worsley MSS 47: 45V; 61V; 63V. Horace; Tacitus; Dionysius; Appian.

The annotation, which is faded, reads, 'Argument … favela': this may be translated as 'the argument of the story'. There is also a small mark on page 142, verso, and another on page 139, where the annotator has corrected the text, showing that he was a critical reader. Neville did this in other books. This volume also contains *Amphitryon*, the other source play for *The Comedy of Errors*. A translation of *The Menaechmi* by William Warner was not published until 1595, after the play had appeared on stage. It is not necessary to speculate that William Shakspere had access to Warner's unpublished manuscript when we know that Neville could read the original in Latin.

Scholars have noted links between Richard Edwardes' 1564 play *Damon and Pythias* and some of Shakespeare's plays. The older play is about the friendship between two men. Several of the Bard's plays explore male friendship, from *The Two Gentlemen of Verona* at the start of his career to *The Two Noble Kinsmen* at the end. *The Comedy of Errors* has further specific links with *Damon and Pythias*: in both plays a man is under threat of execution but is finally reprieved; men arrive by sea and explore an unknown city; two men are inextricably linked and exchange places; Syracuse is a location; a servant is torn between two masters; and both plays are tragicomedies. *The Comedy of Errors* ends with the words:

We came into the world like brother and brother
And now let's go hand in hand, not one before another.

In *Damon and Pythias*, written thirty years before, we find:

So we two linckt in frindshippe brother and brother,
Full well in the Courte may helpe one another. (1.1.71)

And:

Fear not that Jacke, for like brother and brother
They are knit in true Friendship the one with the other. (1.1.192)

While rhyming 'brother' and 'other' might be regarded as commonplace, the repetition of 'brother and brother' and the use of the words 'one … another' suggests Shakespeare might be recalling these lines. *Damon and Pythias* was performed at Merton College, Oxford in 1568.[41] Neville went to Merton in 1574. The play had been printed in 1571 so it is possible Neville came across the text of the play there. As the play was being quoted in Oxford eighty years later this is not fanciful.[42] Hamlet calls Horatio 'O Damon dear' (3.2.275) in what is believed to have been a reference to this play.[43] The close friendship of Sir Henry Neville and Henry Wriothesley, 3rd Earl of Southampton, was acknowledged by Henry Howard, Earl of Northampton, who, in a letter dated November 1613, wrote to Rochester describing Neville as Southampton's 'Dear Damon'.[44] Since the Greek legend tells of two friends, both of whom were imprisoned and under threat of execution, and were later pardoned, this reference in *Hamlet* resembles Neville and Southampton's situation in 1601–3. *The Comedy of Errors* long predates this but again we have evidence that Neville knew both the Latin and English source works.

Believed to have been written between 1589 and 1594, the first recorded performance of *The Comedy of Errors* was on the infamous 'Night of Errors' on 28 December 1594. On the front cover of the Northumberland Manuscript owned by Neville are listed 'Orations at Graies Inne revells … By Mr. ffrauncis Bacon'. These were additional speeches for the celebrations during which Shakespeare's play was premiered. Neville was related to Bacon, his stepmother being Bacon's stepsister.

Love's Labour's Lost

Set in France, the play shows intimate knowledge of the politics and culture of the French court and even of identifiable personalities. Neville had travelled through France in 1578 and 1582. The plot of *Love's Labour's Lost* seems to be based on the attempt in 1578 to achieve a reconciliation between Henry of Navarre and his wife, Margaret de Valois. Many details in the play suggest that the playwright must either have been present at the festivities or heard about them from someone who was there. For example, the presence of the Nine Worthies in the play may have been prompted by the tapestries that decorated the queen's apartments in Nérac which showed these figures. Costard refers to a 'painted cloth' showing the figure of Alexander. 'Numerous other details in *Love's Labour's Lost* betray Shakespeare's firsthand knowledge of personalities and circumstances at the French court.'[45] Francis Bacon was in France at this time attached to the English embassy to the French court.[46]

New evidence of Neville's authorship of the play can be found in the annotations of books that he owned. In the 1518 book of Ovid's *Ars Amatoria* and *Remedia Amoris* in Neville's library the annotator noted an 'Epitheton amoris' (an epithet of love) which refers to the text: 'Tenero amori: molli & lascivo' (Of tender love, soft and lustful).

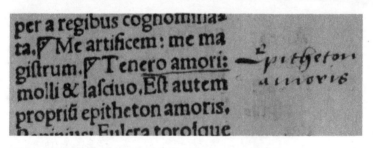

Ovid's *Ars Amatoria* and *Remedia Amoris*, 2.

The words 'epitheton' and 'epithet' occur in *Love's Labour's Lost* and 'epitheton' is associated with the word 'tender' in the same sentence (1.2.14). Furthermore Biron tells us that:

> Love's feeling is more <u>soft</u> and sensible
> Than are the <u>tender</u> horns of cockl'd snails;
> Love's tongue proves dainty <u>Bacchus</u> gross in taste:
> For valour, is not Love a <u>Hercules</u>,
> Still climbing trees in the Hesperides? (4.3.311)

The annotator also made marginal notes of <u>Bacchus</u> and <u>Hercules</u>. *Love's Labour's Lost* can be seen here to have Ovid's *Art of Love* and this book as a source. Ovid is mentioned by name in the play (4.2.123). The frequency with which the annotations in books from Neville's library are relevant to the Shakespeare canon goes far beyond coincidence. However, we cannot confidently attribute all these annotations to Neville because not only does the handwriting vary but the date of the volume (1568) means it could have been read and annotated by his father. Nevertheless we can be confident that another book, *Discources Politiques et Militaires*, dated 1587, was annotated by Neville. On page 151, there is an annotation in French: 'L'institution d(es) Academies':

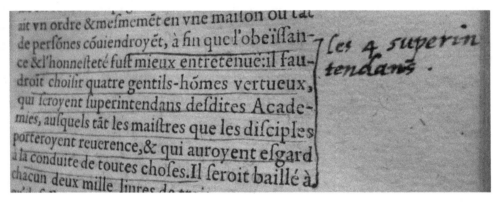

Discources Politiques et Militaires, 151. (Private collection)

Discources Politiques et Militaires, 153.

Love's Labour's Lost is set in France and begins with the King of Navarre setting up an academy with three courtiers. He says, 'Our court shall be a little academe' (1.1.14).[47] This French book is dedicated to Henry of Navarre. Another annotation, 'les 4 superintendans', is next to the text 'il faudroit choisit quartre gentils-homes vertueux, qui seroyent superintendans desdites Academies ...'

Ferdinand of Navarre and his three courtiers perhaps are these four superintendants. Only the fifth dialogue in the book (pages 129–158) is substantially annotated. It concerns the education of young men. On pages 151–2, Neville noted exercises of the body and of the mind, 'Les exercises du corps (et) de esprit', including dancing, the lives of the ancients, language and mathematics. In the play Longaville says of the academic life, 'The <u>mind</u> shall banquet, though the <u>body</u> pine' (1.1.25). In the play there are dances, an entertainment about the Nine Worthies (including Hercules) and much about language and numbers.

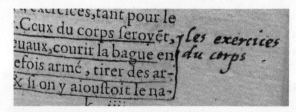 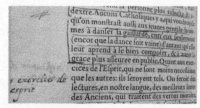

Discources Politiques et Militaires, 151-2.

This fifth dialogue is titled, 'De La Bonne Nouriture & institution qu'il est necessaire de donner aux ieunes gentilshommes Francais.'[48] The playwright seems to be making fun of such a regime. The play has been dated to 1594–5, just seven years after the publication of this book. While no source has ever been discovered for the plot, a number of works have been identified as influencing the play. Several of these books are in Neville's Audley End library. The word 'honorificabilitudinitatibus' occurs on page 662 of the *Adagia* of Erasmus, which is in Neville's library, dated 1558.[49] The word is used by Costard in the play (5.1.40). A version of this word, 'honorificabiletudine', appears on the Northumberland Manuscript, which has Neville's surname at the top and Shakespeare's at the bottom and dates from 1596–7, before *Love's Labour's Lost* was first published in 1598. The play dates from 1594–6 and the title page of the quarto states it was performed during 'this last Christmas', which would be 1597. This means that the writer of the Northumberland Manuscript (NHMS) must have had access to a manuscript of *Love's Labour's Lost* before it was ever performed. That the word is misquoted may be due to misremembering such a long word, an earlier version of the script, or indeed the poet noting the word for use: the NHMS covers the entire period during which the play would have been written. Thomas Nashe is believed to be playfully represented by Moth in *Love's Labour's Lost*, and his play *The Isle of Dogs* is listed on the NHMS.

Erasmus's *Colloquia* is also cited as a possible source for the play and an annotated copy, dated 1591, is also in Neville's library. *Love's Labour's Lost* is believed to have been written between 1594 and 1596.[50]

Another rare word in *Love's Labour's Lost* is 'thrasonical' (5.1.12) and this refers to the braggart Thraso in Terence's Latin play *Eunuchus*, a 1551 copy of which is in Neville's library. *Love's Labour's Lost* was also influenced by Castiglione's *Book of the Courtier*, an annotated copy of which, dated 1560, is in the library. The Latin poet Horace is seen as another possible influence and there are two small volumes of Horace's poetry with passages underlined showing they had been read. There is a major volume of the works of Appian on Roman history, dated 1551, and in the margin Neville noted 'veni, vidi, vici', which is quoted by Boyet in *Love's Labour's Lost* (4.1.68).[51]

Appian (Dionysius section), 135. (Private collection)

The Comedy of Errors and *Love's Labour's Lost* are linked by a notorious Spanish statesman, Antonio Perez, who was secretary to Philip II. In England after escaping from a murder trial in Spain, he was a guest of Francis Bacon on the 1594 Night of Errors at Gray's Inn when *The Comedy of Errors* was performed.[52] The Spanish braggart Don Adriano de Armado in *Love's Labour's Lost* is believed to be a parody of Antonio Perez. After his flight from Spain, Perez had offered his allegiance to Henry of Navarre, who sent him on a mission to Elizabeth I. Perez, as an imitator of Seneca and Tacitus and because he knew Anthony Bacon,

> was admitted to the group of Essex's learned secretaries. There was Henry Savile to welcome the man who prided himself on being a modern Tacitus, and there was Francis Bacon who shared with him an enthusiasm for the political aphorisms derived from Tacitus and from commentaries that followed in the wake of Lipsius' modern Tacitus edition. ... If Shakespeare should have needed an original document for his parody, he might have drawn on any of the Latin epistles Perez wrote to his English friends, among them the earl of Southampton.[53]

Copies of Lipsius' edition of Tacitus and of the *Relaciones de Antonio Perez*, dated 1598, are in Neville's library. It was in 1598 that Essex persuaded Neville to take the role of ambassador to France. Perez had returned to France but was writing letters to Godfrey Naunton, who passed them on to Essex. In these he ludicrously pretended to be in love with Godfrey's sister who lived in Windsor, near Neville's house in Billingbear (just as Armado falls inappropriately in love with Jaquenetta). Neville met Perez when he was ambassador and consulted him.[54] On 11 October 1599 he wrote to Robert Cecil, '*Antonio de Perez* I heare is restored to his Lands, and his Wife and Children all at Liberty.'[55] In the play Armado writes florid letters. Many letters written by Perez survive, including one to the Earl of Southampton giving him a copy of the *Relaciones*.[56] They had met on the Night of Errors. In a letter to Henry Savile, dated 5 August 1597, Henry Cuffe wrote that Perez was keen to communicate with Southampton and Essex and fearful that his letter 'not miscarry, for his jealousy is infinite.'[57] In *Love's Labour's Lost* Armado's letter to Jaquenetta does miscarry, comically ending up in the wrong hands (4.1.58). The play was first published in 1598. What we can witness here is that Perez, who ensured everyone had a copy of his book, was at the centre of Neville's social network of the Cecils, Essex, Southampton, Anthony and Francis Bacon, Robert Sidney.[58] There is no evidence that William Shakspere ever met Perez. Neville certainly knew him and his writings, and could have heard from Cuffe or Savile, or indeed from the man himself, about Perez's fear of his letters miscarrying.

Thus we can see that there are ten books in Neville's library which all contain material relevant to *Love's Labour's Lost*: the Ovid, Terence, Erasmus (x2), Castiglione, Horace (x2), Appian, the *Relaciones de Antonio Perez* and the *Political and Military Discources* and all these editions predate the play. Also amongst Neville's books is a small volume of poetry dated 1598, by Giovanni Della Casa, whose works have been thought to have influenced Shakespeare's sonnets and courtly plays either directly or indirectly.[59]

In *Love's Labour's Lost* Navarre is shown owing money lent to him for his wars and the princess/queen comes in an embassy to ask for it to be repaid. The negotiations are delayed while they wait for further documents. Neville was chosen as ambassador to France in 1598, just as the play was published, but must have known he was in line for the job before then. Neville's major task as ambassador in 1599 was to get Henry of Navarre to repay Queen Elizabeth money she had loaned him for his wars. Neville ensured he took with him all necessary documents proving the amounts of the loans. The play is also much concerned with sums and numbers and we have already noted that Neville was educated in mathematics at Oxford.

We also know that Neville met Charles de Gontaut, Duc de Biron, on whom Berowne is based. Neville would have met Biron when he came to England in 1598 as French ambassador because that same year Neville was chosen as English ambassador to France. Southampton borrowed money from Biron that year.[60] Neville mentioned Marshall Biron in a letter dated 24 April 1600. *Love's Labour's Lost* 'has serious political undertones, as it evokes the 1578 negotiations … between Henry IV of France (also King of Navarre) and his estranged wife Marguerite de Valois'.[61] In 1578, and again in 1582, Neville, travelling with his tutor Savile, passed through France.[62] Both *The Comedy of Errors* and *Love's Labour's Lost* contain references to Henry of Navarre's war in France. Neville's father-in-law, Henry Killigrew, fought in that war with Biron. There is an extant letter to Killigrew from Elizabeth I, dated 2 September 1591, warning him that he could not trust Navarre to pay his soldiers.[63]

Love's Labour's Lost may also contain covert criticism of Elizabeth I's long and ultimately sterile courtships, the play being literally about the lost/fruitless labours of love. Hunt suggested that the play both idealised the queen and hinted that death would interrupt her futile courtships, as it did when the Duc d'Alencon died in 1584 and Robert Dudley, Earl of Leicester, in 1588.[64] Many opposed her possible marriage with either d'Alencon or Leicester. Henry Neville had an interest in this controversy. He owned copies of Philip Sidney's letter to Elizabeth against the marriage to 'Monsieur' (d'Alencon) and the banned tract, *Leicester's Commonwealth* (both are to be found in the folder of the Northumberland Manuscript). That Neville should have a copy of Sidney's dangerous letter is explained by the close friendship between his father and Sidney's father. That Neville knew Sidney and his writing explains the influence that Philip Sidney had on Shakespeare, an influence that is evident in the sonnets, *Love's Labour's Lost*, *Romeo and Juliet*, *King Lear* and *Pericles*.

Titus Andronicus

Written about 1592–3, *Titus Andronicus* was published anonymously in 1594. This violent play deals with the politics of what might happen if the election of a ruler resulted in the wrong person becoming king. Bate wondered whether *Titus Andronicus* 'may be shot through with an unexpected vein of republicanism'.[65] Hadfield confirmed this and demonstrated the continuity between *The Rape of Lucrece* and *Titus Andronicus* in which he saw Shakespeare exploring republican politics.[66] The prefatory argument of *The Rape of Lucrece* ends with the words: 'the people were so moved, that with one consent and a general acclamation the Tarquins were all exiled, and the state government changed from kings to consuls.'

This last sentence hints at a political, even anti-monarchy, stance. We can clearly see the warning of the danger of civil war in the play and the tract. The authors of the banned 1584 *Leicester's Commonwealth* explicitly linked the Roman experience of civil war with the threat to the security and peace of the contemporary English state, as they wrote of the

> Romans who received notable damages and destruction also in the end by their divisions and factions among themselves, and specially from them of their own cities and countries who upon factions lived abroad with foreigners and thereby were always as firebrands to carry home the flame of war upon their country.'[67]

This passage effectively describes a theme in several of Shakespeare's plays: *Titus Andronicus, Coriolanus, Antony and Cleopatra* and *Julius Caesar.*

Titus Andronicus is a play created out of the playwright's imagination based on a thorough knowledge of Roman history and literature. Neville owned and annotated volumes of Roman history: the Dionysius of Halicarnassus *Roman Antiquities* (1546); Appian's *Civil Wars* (1551); and Tacitus's *Annales* (1574). He also gave a copy of Cassius Dio's *Roman History* to Merton College, Oxford.[68] There are clear links between *Titus Andronicus, The Rape of Lucrece* and Neville's annotations in the books he owned.[69] In *Titus Andronicus* Lavinia, struggling to reveal her rape, throws Ovid's *Metamorphoses* on the floor and then writes the word 'stuprum' (rape) in the sand (4.1.73). In Neville's volume of Ovid this word is underlined.

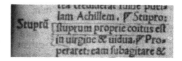

Stuprû:… Stupro: stuprum proprie coitus est in virgine & uidua.
Ovid's *Ars Amatoria* and *Remedia Amoris*, 14.

In the play Demetrius quotes two lines from Horace:

Integer vitae, sceleris purus
non eget Mauri iaculis, nec acru. (4.2.20)

This means 'The man of upright life and free from crime does not need the javelins or bows of the Moor.'[70] Neville annotated these lines in his volume of Horace.

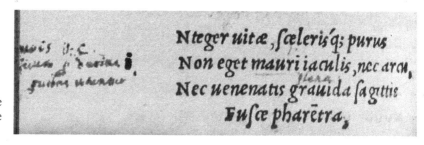

Horace Ode I, 22. (Private collection).

There are discernable links between *Leicester's Commonwealth* and *Titus Andronicus*. Neville owned manuscript copies of *Leicester's Commonwealth* and close examination of these shows that they were a source for Shakespeare.[71] The queen's proclamation against *Leicester's Commonwealth* labelled it a libel. *Leicester's Commonwealth* is in the form of a letter. When Titus sends letters complaining of his sufferings, Saturninus, the tyrannical ruler of Rome, complains that these are 'libelling against the senate and blazoning our injustice everywhere' (4.4.17). It has been suggested that Queen Tamora's lover, Aaron, the Moor, might represent Leicester (who was nicknamed 'the gypsy' because of his dark looks). In *Leicester's Commonwealth* the Gentleman speaks of how dangerous it was for courtiers who witness Leicester's 'errors or misdeeds ... for if it had been but only suspected that they had seen such a thing, it would have been as dangerous unto them as it was to <u>Acteon</u> to have seen <u>Diana</u> and her maidens naked; whose case is so common now in England as nothing more, and so do the examples of divers well declare, whose unfortunate knowledge of too many secrets brought them quickly to unfortunate ends.'[72]

In one speech Tamora says,

Had I the power that some say <u>Dian</u> had,
Thy temples should be planted presently
With horns, as was <u>Actaeon</u>'s; and the hounds
Should drive upon thy new-transformed limbs,
Unmannerly intruder as thou art! (2.2.61)

While this image might be considered a commonplace, there are a number of words used in both *Leicester's Commonwealth* and *Titus Andronicus* such as 'commonwealth', 'opportunity', 'tyrant', 'election', 'title', 'pretend' 'faction', 'dangerous', 'discontent', 'detested', 'ingratitude', 'conspirator', 'competitor', 'controlment', 'banquet' and 'trenches'. 'Stop the mouths' is found in *Leicester's Commonwealth* and 'stop their mouths' occurs twice in *Titus Andronicus* (5.2.161, 167) in the same scene as 'banquet' and 'trenches'. Shakespeare only used 'tattle' once: in *Titus Andronicus* (4.2.170); the word 'tattled' is used in *Leicester's Commonwealth*.[73] While this list is not exhaustive it is perhaps long enough to suggest that *Leicester's Commonwealth* was a possible source for *Titus Andronicus* and, of course, Neville had his own manuscript copy.

Titus Andronicus begins with an election of the Roman emperor: in the first scene the word '<u>election</u>' is used three times (1.1.16, 22, 185). The disaster is that Titus, a soldier rather than a politician, refuses the people's choice and suggests they '<u>elect</u>' Saturnine (1.1.232). The threat of civil war is never far away. In other words Shakespeare follows through the constitutional concerns in *Leicester's Commonwealth* but goes further, and begins to explore the possible consequences of electing a king. This is not of course an election in modern terms with universal suffrage. However, it does introduce the idea of choice rather than divine right or the hereditary principle. This interest in the election of those who have power in the realm is further evident in the annotated Hall's *Chronicle* where the annotator has highlighted one item (with #) in a list of charges against Richard II:

Hall's *Chronicle*, f.viii. (By permission of the owners of the annotated Hall's *Chronicle*)

19 Item at the sommons of the Parliament when knightes and burgesses should be <u>electe</u> that the <u>election</u> had bene full proceded, he put out diuers persons <u>elected</u>, & put in other in their places to serue his wyll and appetite.

Furthermore the annotator of Hall's *Chronicle* made a note, '5 article they complayne ageyinste Knightes of th(e) parliament electyd'.[74] The highlight # and this annotation both draw attention to the issue of elections being contested. Neville as a Member of Parliament would have been one of those who might have elected the next monarch in the event of a disputed succession after Elizabeth I's death. Casson dated the annotations in Hall to 1586–96, so within the period that *Titus Andronicus* was written.[75]

In *Titus Andronicus* there are the words, 'reuenge Vpon the Thracian Tyrant' (spelt thus in the first quarto: 1.1.140). In his copy of *Leicester's Commonwealth* Neville wrote in a unique annotation: 'A tiranous reuenge vpon a Tirante'.

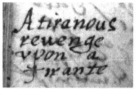

Worsley MSS47: 29V. (By permission of the Eighth Earl of Yarborough and Lincolnshire Archives)

In the 1609 edition of the sonnets, Shakespeare spelt the word 'tiranous' in sonnet 131. In the second quarto of *Romeo and Juliet* (which is believed to be based on the playwright's manuscript) 'tirannous' is spelt with an 'i' and double 'n' (1.1.168). Neville spells the word 'tirannous' in a letter dated 20 March 1600.[76]

Annotating his Worsley MSS 47 copy of *Leicester's Commonwealth* Neville often inserted a 'u' into words such as France, strange/stranger, change, danger, ancient, ancestors, Canterbury, tenant so we find: 'ffraunce', 'straunge/straungers', 'chaunge', 'indaungereth/daunger', 'aunciente', 'auncestors', 'Caunterb:', 'fflaunders', 'tenauntable', 'comaund' and 'mayntenaunce'. In the Hall's *Chronicle* annotations we find: 'fraunce', 'straungers', 'daungerose', 'commaundement', 'avaunced', 'raunso(ming)', 'deliveraunce', 'defiaunce', 'aunswer', 'sufferaunce', 'chaunce'. Neville used the following spellings in letters: 'straunge', 'commaundment' in a letter dated 15 May 1599; 'straungers' on 1 September 1599; 'daunger' on 7 August 1599.[77] In a letter to Sir T. Edmonde, 16 July 1613, Neville wrote the word 'commaund'.[78] In the first quarto of *Titus Andronicus* there are 'commaund', 'demaund' and 'raunsome'. In the Hand D section of *Sir Thomas More*, folio 9, there are 'comaund' and 'fraunc'.

When we compare the first quarto of *Titus Andronicus* with Neville's manuscript copy of *Leicester's Commonwealth* we find that both italicise names and Latin phrases. Both end with the word 'Finis'.

According to Henslowe's diary, the first recorded performances of '*Titus & Ondronicus*' were by Sussex's Men at the Rose Theatre on 23 and 28 January and 6 February 1594. Sussex's Men were established by Thomas Radcliffe, 3rd Earl of Sussex, and continued in existence under his successors. We know that Neville's father knew Thomas Radcliffe because the earl wrote to Sir Henry in the 1570s and the latter responded.[79] Thomas, as Lord Chamberlain, was in charge of the Revels Office, overseeing court entertainments from 1572 to 1583. During his tenure, in 1576, Sir Henry Neville supported Richard Farrant (who had been Master of the Children of St George's Chapel, Windsor) in acquiring rooms at Blackfriars for a theater rehearsal space.[80] Thomas Radcliffe married first Elizabeth, daughter of Sir Thomas Wriothesley, and second Frances Sidney, sister of Sir Henry Neville's good friend Henry Sidney. It was Thomas's brother's son Robert who was Earl of Sussex when the play was performed, having inherited the title the year before. Robert was sent on an embassy to Scotland the year after Neville had travelled there and was a supporter of Essex, being knighted by him at Cadiz. Neville lived in Sussex and became the Member of Parliament for Sussex in 1589. We can see then that the Earls of Sussex, whose company performed this early play, were in the Neville social network.

Romeo and Juliet

One printed *Leicester's Commonwealth* marginal note is: 'The happy cõiũnctiõ of the tvvoe houses.'

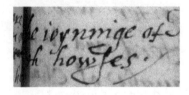

Worsley MSS 47, 41.

Neville rendered this as, 'The ioynnige of howses'. He had picked this wording up from an earlier printed annotation which he copied as 'The ioynnig of both howses'.[81] This refers to the marriage of Henry VII of Lancaster to Elizabeth of York, a marriage that sealed the end of the Wars of the Roses. Shakespeare looked back at that period in his history plays, fearing that a disputed succession to the throne, following Elizabeth I's death, would lead to civil war. *Romeo and Juliet* is a play which shows the disastrous consequences of division between 'houses' and the resultant 'civil brawls' (1.1.87). Three times Mercutio cries, 'A plague o' both your houses!' when he is fatally wounded in a brawl (3.1.92, 100, 108). In the annotated Hall's *Chronicle* Neville used the words 'males of bothe (t)he howses yorke and lan=(c)ast^re were destroyed' in a marginal note.[82]

We can now appreciate the political meaning of the play, which is not just about star-crossed lovers, but about the danger of civil war between two houses. The Bard was warning the country to stay united. We suggest that this was Neville's political motive behind his reading of *Leicester's Commonwealth* and his playwriting. *Romeo and Juliet* ends in reconciliation: after the tragedies of civil war citizens must live together again.

Of course the play is much more than a political allegory. It is a story of love, hate, youth, chance, time and fate. There are a number of sonnets in the play. Shakespeare was influenced by Philip Sidney's *Astrophil and Stella* sonnet sequence. As we have already seen Neville knew the Sidneys. However Philip Sidney was not the only sonneteer who influenced the Bard. For the only time in the canon, Shakespeare refers directly to greatest Italian writer of sonnets when Mercutio names Petrarch and his lady Laura (2.4.40). Amongst Neville's books at Audley End House library is a 1581 volume of Velutello's edition of *Il Petrarcha Con L'Espositione*. It was published in Venice. Many of Petrarch's sonnets in this volume have passages underlined. We recall that Neville was in Italy, indeed in Venice, in 1581. (See Chapter 12 for an illustrated example.)

Ovid's *Ars Amatoria* was a source for *Romeo and Juliet*. Juliet says, 'At lovers' perjuries/ They say, Jove laughs' (2.1.134). Bate showed that this derives from the line, 'Juppiter ex alto periuria ridet amantum'. The section within which this line occurs is highlighted by the annotator of the copy that is in Neville's library:

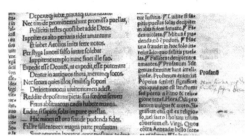

Ovid's *Ars Amatoria*.

The play is also substantially based on Arthur Brooke's narrative poem *The Tragical History of Romeus and Juliet*. This derives from French and Italian originals, one of which was a play by Luigi Groto called *Hadriana* which was written in 1578. Given that Neville was in Italy just three years later he could have seen a performance. It has one telling detail that Shakespeare used: a nightingale sings as the lovers part.[83]

One odd reference that condemns usury (lending at interest) distances Shakespeare the writer from Shakspere the Stratford moneylender. Friar Lawrence refers to usury in a metaphor as he confronts Romeo's suicidal ideas (3.3.122).

It has long been recognised that this play, whose tragic hero is a Montague, was a tribute to the Earl of Southampton, whose mother, Mary, was the daughter of Anthony Browne, 1st Viscount Montague. In 1575 George Gascoigne had composed a wedding masque which highlighted the connections between the earl's family and the Italian Montacutes who were rivals of the Capulets. The Montacutes are also mentioned in *Edward III* which was written between 1589 and 1594. A story in which Mercutio and Tybalt are both killed in brawling may have resonated with contemporary events. In 1594 the Earl of Southampton had concealed Charles[84] and Henry Danvers after the latter killed Henry Long in a brawl.[85] *Romeo and Juliet* was written between 1594–6. As we have seen, Neville had known the earl since he was a boy. No connection between William Shakspere and the earl has ever been discovered.

Conclusion

Shakespeare's earliest comedies and tragedies were set in Europe, especially Italy. Neville had travelled there and had personal knowledge of the places where the plays were set. The books he acquired while travelling were works that are widely believed to have influenced Shakespeare, and several prove Neville's interest in poetry. Neville's private library furnished him with the source material he needed to write the poetry and plays and these sources were annotated in a way that strongly implies they were used for that purpose. Neville's manuscripts, including his letters, show he used the same words, phrases and spelling that Shakespeare used, sometimes before they appeared in plays. Neville also had the political outlook and life experience that can be readily seen in the Bard's plots and imagery.

The Early History Plays
1589–1596

The reverence of mine age, and *Nevel's* name
Is of no little force if I command.
The First Part of the Contention, 1.1.161

The early history plays, the *Henry VI* trilogy, *Richard III*, *Edward III*, *Richard II* and *King John*, are a panoramic exploration of power politics: of what happens when the succession to the throne becomes problematic. Elizabeth I had decreed that discussion of the succession was treason. In telling the stories of previous monarchs Shakespeare was able to circumvent this ban by using history as metaphor for the current situation. It was a dangerous strategy as works regarded as seditious were banned and burned, and authors imprisoned and tortured. Thomas Nashe and Ben Jonson co-wrote a satirical play, *The Isle of Dogs*, in 1596–7. It was banned and destroyed. Jonson was arrested. Nashe escaped but his lodgings were raided and his writings seized. There is no evidence that William Shakspere from Stratford was ever arrested so it seems likely that it was known he was not the real author of the canon. Keeping his identity as a writer secret effectively protected the Bard. Neville listed *The Isle of Dogs* on the cover of the Northumberland Manuscript (NHMS), indeed he may have owned a manuscript copy of the play. The folder contained several works, including essays by Bacon and the banned *Leicester's Commonwealth*. It may have included manuscripts of *Rychard the second* and *Rychard the third* which are listed and their author identified as 'William Shakespeare'. The Bacon and *Leicester's Commonwealth* manuscripts remain in the folder but the plays have disappeared. Dated to 1596–7, the NHMS is the earliest document to name plays as having been written by Shakespeare, yet no play that identified him as the writer was published before 1598. *Richard III* and *Richard II* were first printed in 1597 without any author being named. The NHMS, which refers directly or indirectly to three plays (one word is quoted from *Love's Labour's Lost*, see Chapter 3) and *The Rape of Lucrece*, was written during the Bard's anonymous period.

Philip, Earl of Arundel's letter to Elizabeth is also listed on the front page of the NHMS. This was another incendiary document.[2] Philip spent the last years of his life in the Tower under sentence of death (1585–96), eventually dying of dysentery in the year before the NHMS received its last additions. *Leicester's Commonwealth* has been shown to be a source for Shakespeare's history plays.[3] These listed works show that Neville had access to dangerous, indeed banned, political material and he would certainly have needed anonymity to protect himself if he intended to use the material as a source for his own writings.

The Anonymous Period

During the years between 1589 and 1598 Shakespeare was writing plays but he was not identified as a playwright. The *Henry VI* trilogy was written between 1589 and 1591 yet there is no reference or record of Shakspere (the actor/manager in London) or Shakespeare (the writer) until 1592–3. The attack on 'Shake-scene' in the pamphlet *A Groatsworth of Wit* appeared in 1592. It is cryptic and may be directed at an actor or a writer or neither.[4] *Venus and Adonis* was registered on 18 April 1593, and this was the very first time the name Shakespeare was used to identify the poet.

We will now review evidence for Neville's authorship of the early history plays and present some of the textual and documentary evidence which supports this ascription.[5]

The Nevilles in the History Plays

Henry Neville was related to all the kings and many of their senior liegemen depicted in the history plays.[6] This makes it inevitable that some of his family members will feature in the historical account. What is unexpected is the frequency with which Neville's family members are featured in the plays, often with roles and characters altered at the expense of historical accuracy. The members of the Neville family that appear in the history plays often have their identity obscured by the use of their titles rather than their family name. This concealment is less evident in the earliest of plays to be written, *Henry VI: Part II*, in which the name 'Nevel/Nevil' occurs eight times in the first quarto edition of the play. Perhaps the author feared this was a little too obvious because some of these were cut in the First Folio version. As we examine the real identities of the people behind the titles we find that Shakespeare shows a Neville bias by inserting or foregrounding a member of the Neville family to bring them glory, or by removing Nevilles to avoid exposing them or damaging the family reputation. He also included many minor characters that have links to the Nevilles.[7] After highlighting the Neville name in *Henry VI: Part II*, the Bard became more circumspect but the bias remains evident.

Neville's handwritten copy of *Leicester's Commonwealth*, Worsley MSS 47, predates the writing of the history plays and has been dated to 1584–6.[8] Neville annotated and added to the text with information we later find in the plays. Sometimes Neville made changes to the text as he copied and these changes also point to his authorship as we show below.

We start with *King John*, the earliest reign of the Plantagenet kings that Shakespeare dramatised. There is evidence that the first version, *The Troublesome Raigne*, which was published in 1591, was co-written by Neville and George Peele.[9] The Bard revised this text to create the First Folio version of *King John* after Peele died in 1596.

King John

In *Leicester's Commonwealth* the story of *King John* is summarised as:

> Arthur ... was declared by King Richard his uncle ... lawful heir apparent to the crown
> of England ... albeit after King Richard's death his other uncle John most tyrannously
> took both his kingdom and his life.[10]

Shakespeare's play is about the dangers and damage done to the country when the wrong person inherits or usurps the crown, so it dramatises the forbidden topic of the succession, a core concern of *Leicester's Commonwealth*.

An example of the way Neville's annotated changes to *Leicester's Commonwealth* are related to the play is shown in five marginal annotations made where the word 'impediments' appears in the printed text. The word is used when examining the question of who might inherit the throne. Neville, when copying, substituted 'barrs' each time.[11] In *King John* Eleanor (the queen mother), fighting for John's right to succeed his brother, Richard I, reveals she has a will that expresses Richard's wishes for the succession. Eleanor says that the will 'barres the title of' Arthur (First Folio spelling with double 'r', 2.1.192).[12] Throughout the canon Shakespeare used 'bars' fifteen times, of which ten refer to restrictions (rather than physical iron bars). All these uses date from early works of the 1590s. It is only from the late 1590s that Shakespeare used the word 'impediments', and only in *Macbeth* does this word refer to the succession to the throne. Between these references to 'bars' to inheritance, Neville noted 'King John an vsurper'. The word 'usurper' occurs in the play when the King of France accuses John of usurping the throne (2.1.120).

The central character in *King John* is not the king but the invented figure of the Bastard Falconbridge and as shown below, this is an example of Shakespeare showing a concealed Neville bias. Falconbridge was possibly modelled on John's contemporary Hugh de Neville (d. 1234), chief forester under Richard I, John and Henry III, who, like Falconbridge in the play, extorted money from the Church to help the king's finances.[13] Ralph Neville (d. 1244), Bishop of Chichester, worked with Hugh de Neville: they were related. Ralph was illegitimate and served King John as chancellor.[14] The historical Bastard of Faulconbridge, Thomas Neville, lived much later (1429–71).[15] Neville was related to the Faulconbridges (his great-great-grandfather, Edward Neville, Lord Abergavenny, was brother of William Faulconbridge). Annotating his Tower notebook[16] in 1602 Neville wrote 'de fawconbridge' in the margin.[17]

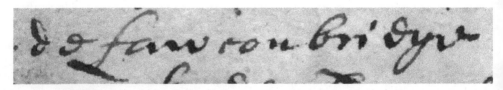

Worsley MSS 40.

In the play the fictitious character Falconbridge makes a famous speech on commodity (2.1.561–598). There is evidence that Neville was interested in commodities because, as the English ambassador to France, he wrote to the Secretary of State, Robert Cecil, concerned about 'commodity' trading in letters dated 21 June 1599, 24 September 1599[18] and 19 February 1601.[19] Neville took care to alert the government to the grievances of English merchants. He had inherited a fortune from his mother's uncle Gresham who was involved in trading of English–French commodities, including cannon, which feature so much in *King John*. Cannon appear anachronistically in both *King John* and *Edward III*. From 1583 to 1598 Neville owned an ordnance factory in Mayfield. In 1592, working in a syndicate with the Sackville family and two foreign partners, from Germany and Holland, Neville gained a royal patent or monopoly for the export of cast-iron guns. The Mayfield Furnace was one of the main gun production centres in Europe.[20]

The *King John* play text was first published in the First Folio in 1623 and so it may have been revised over many years. Indeed there is evidence that it was revised again after the Essex rebellion of 1601.[21] Neville made a note on King John in his Tower notebook of 1602, so proving his continuing interest in this reign.[22]

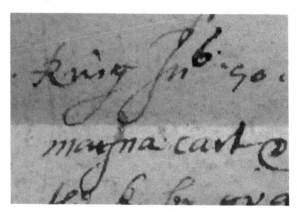

'Knig Jn's … magna cart', Worsley MSS 40.

Further evidence of revision is 'the absence of profanities in the text which suggests that it was revised at some point after the introduction in 1606 of the Act to Restrain the Abuses of Players. It also includes act divisions, which characterise plays prepared for performance at the indoor Blackfriars playhouse (used by Shakespeare's company from 1609).'[23]

Henry VI

Many members of the Neville family feature in the *Henry VI* trilogy. In his copy of *Leicester's Commonwealth* Neville made an annotation: 'The Nevills wth Hen: 6th and Edw: 4th.' The words 'the Nevils' occur three times in *Henry VI: Part II*, and the name is spelt with a double 'l' as 'Nevill' twice in the First Folio (in 2.2).

The text of *Leicester's Commonwealth* tells how the 'Nevilles took upon them to join with Richard of York to put down their most benign prince King Henry VI, and after again in the

Worsley MSS 47, 36.

other side to put down King Edward IV'.[24] This is what we see on stage in the trilogy. In his copy of *Leicester's Commonwealth*, Neville added details of the royal houses to a printed annotation (which only stated, 'How the kingdom was first broght to the house of Lancaster'), writing,

> Howe yᵉ knigdome was first brought into the howse of Lancaster
> Henr: 4.5 & 6 of <u>the howse of Lan</u>:
> Edw: 4th & Rich 3 of <u>the howse of Yorke</u>

(Our emphasis underlined.)

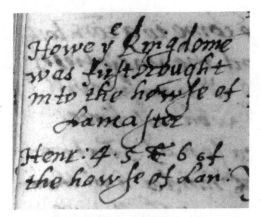
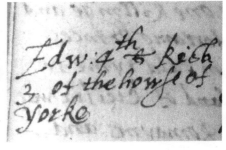

Worsley MSS47, 42V (italic).

The words 'house of Lancaster' occur thirteen times in the trilogy and *Richard III*. The words 'house of York' occur eleven times only in the trilogy. This is an example of Neville annotating material which, less than five years later, would appear on stage in the *Henry VI* trilogy. In Hall's *Chronicle* there is an annotation which uses the words 'heares males of <u>bothe (t)he howses yorke and lan=(c)astᵗ</u> were destroyed'.[25] This is a variation on Hall's actual text which reads, 'bothe the lines' (*Henry IV*, fxᵃ).

Hall's *Chronicle*, Henry IV, f.xᵃ (secretary script).

Neville used the words 'heires males' in a letter of 1603/4.[26]

Neville's draft letter.

The annotator of Hall's *Chronicle* spells '<u>howses</u>' with a 'w' three times. In the Hand D section of the manuscript of *Sir Thomas More* the spelling '<u>howses</u>' is used. Neville used this spelling again on his father's tomb[27] and in a letter dated 8 August 1599.[28]

We suggest that Neville wrote these plays as a way of warning the country to stay united. This would explain his close reading of *Leicester's Commonwealth*, his research in Hall's *Chronicle* and the notes he made in both these texts.[29] Neville's annotations and changes to the text of *Leicester's Commonwealth* reveal further manuscript evidence that he was preparing to write the history plays. When he chose a different word (as he did above with 'impediments' and 'bars') the change is in the direction of Shakespeare's vocabulary. Another example of this is where the printed words, 'all occasions of controversies' were varied by Neville to 'all occasōns of contrarietie' in his handwritten copy.

Worsley MSS 47, 50.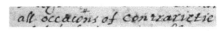

Shakespeare never used the word 'controversies' but did use 'contrarieties' in *Henry VI: Part I* (2.3.58) and 'contrariety' in *Coriolanus* (4.6.76). In place of the printed 'plots, packs and preparations to most <u>manifest</u> usurpation' Neville wrote, 'Plotts, <u>pranks</u> & pʳparacōns to most <u>manifest</u> vsurpacōn'.[30]

Worsley MSS 47, 58.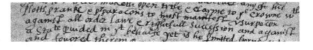

Shakespeare used 'packs' just once but used 'pranks' nine times.[31] In *Henry VI: Part I* Gloucester speaks of 'pranks' six lines before the word '<u>manifest</u>' (3.1.15) in the context of accusing Winchester of plotting murder and even treason.

In *Leicester's Commonwealth* the Lawyer asks rhetorically, 'Why should the rest be damnified thereby?' (Peck, 169/*112*). Neville copied this as 'whie should yᵉ rest be defamed'.

Worsley MSS 47, 52V.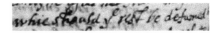

Shakespeare never used 'damnified' but did use 'defamed' in *Henry VI: Part II* (3.1.123). In *Leicester's Commonwealth* we read of the dangers of favourites and how in Henry VI's reign:

Queen Margaret's too much favor and credit … towards the Marquess of Suffolk that after was made Duke, by whose instinct and wicked counsel she made away first the noble Duke of Gloucester and afterward committed other things in great prejudice of the realm.[32]

This is enacted in Shakespeare's *Henry VI: Part II*. Neville varied the above text, changing 'committed other things in great prejudice' to 'she committed vnto him great matters preiuditiall to the Realme'.[33]

Worsley MSS 47, 62.

Shakespeare used 'prejudicial' in *Henry VI: Part III*: Richard Neville, Earl of Warwick, says:

Suppose, my lords, he did it unconstrain'd,
Think you 'twere prejudicial to his crown? (1.1.143)

Shakespeare suggested that Queen Margaret and Suffolk were lovers. There is little evidence of this in the historical sources. Holinshed does not even hint this, although Hall's *Chronicle* stated that the queen 'entirely loved the Duke'.[34] The authors of *Leicester's Commonwealth* state that Margaret loved Suffolk and that she favoured him for many years. *Leicester's Commonwealth* continues and tells of the death of Suffolk:

Worsley MSS 47, 63.

The text reads,

She was content first to commit him to prison and afterward to banish him the realm. But the providence of God would not permit him so to escape, for that he being encountered and taken upon the sea in his passage, he was beheaded in the ship and so received some part of condign punishment for his most wicked, loose, and licentious life.[35]

We see Suffolk meet his end on a ship in *Henry VI: Part II* (4.1). The words 'condign punishment' are used by Gloucester in a confrontation with Suffolk (3.1.130). One or two similarities in vocabulary might be considered coincidence but identical words used in the same context provide compelling evidence both that *Leicester's Commonwealth* was a source for Shakespeare and that Neville's copy, Worsley MS47, was the actual text used by the Bard.

Richard III

Leicester's Commonwealth also contains material about Richard III. Neville annotated this, calling Richard a usurper who killed his wife and the Princes in the Tower. In the printed text of *Leicester's Commonwealth* we read, 'Edward V and his brother, who after were both murdered in the Tower.'[36] However, in the copy he made, Neville named the brother as 'Rich: d: of york'.

MSS 47, 43V.

In *Richard III* the young Prince Edward greets his brother, naming him, 'Richard of York' (3.1.96). We later hear of their murder in the Tower.[37] In the play twenty characters appear or are mentioned who were related to Neville including Richard III himself and his queen, Anne.[38]

Neville continued his interest in Richard III, referring to him in a note in his Tower notebook of 1602–3. He mentioned Richard III in a speech he made to the House of Lords in 1607. At the time Neville had been chosen to represent the Commons in discussions about the Union of England and Scotland. He warned the Lords that if the Scots continued their special relationship with the French this could endanger the union: 'how dangerous this may be we may guess by the example of Richard III.'[39] Neville took a consistently negative view of Richard. In the copy of *Leicester's Commonwealth* which he made in 1585 he added a marginal notation, 'Rich: Duke of gloucester an vsurper'.

Shakespeare ends the play with Derby offering the crown to Richmond:

Lo, here, this long-<u>usurped</u> royalty
From the dead temples of this bloody wretch
Have I pluck'd off, to grace thy brows withal... (5.5.4)

Reinforcing his negative view in his final history play, *Henry VIII* (see Chapter 8), Shakespeare wrote of 'Th'usurper Richard' (1.2.197).

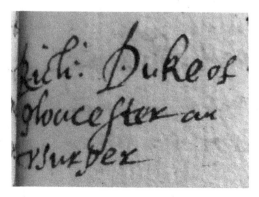

Worsley MSS 47, 57.

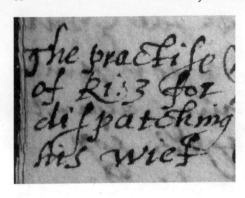

Worsley MSS 47, 34V.

Shakespeare gives prominent, positive roles to several women in *Richard III*. The Bard also seems to be endeavouring to protect the reputation of two women members of the Neville family. Despite the character assassination of Richard III in the play, his mother and wife, who were Cecily Neville and Anne Neville respectively, are not criticised and their behaviour is honourable.[40] When copying out *Leicester's Commonwealth* Neville, in a marginal note, wrote, 'The practise of Ri: 3 for dispatching his wief', namely Anne Neville.

In the play Hasting laments the 'momentary grace of mortal men', (3.4.96) in a speech that draws directly on Horace's *Odes* I.5, the Pyrrha poem.[41] Neville's copy of this poem in his little volume of the *Odes* is annotated, so showing that he had studied it.

The Encomium for Richard III

There is another manuscript pertaining to Richard III that points to Neville's authorship of the play *Richard III*. This was written by Henry Wriothesley, Earl of Southampton, in 1603 and dedicated to 'Sr Henry Nevill' while they were still both prisoners in the Tower.[42] This is to be found in the British Library.[43] The document is based on an *Encomium* in support of Richard III written by Sir William Cornwallis.

Shakespeare's play *Richard III* was written around 1592 but may not have been seen in London until the theatres re-opened after the plague in 1594. The *Encomium* could have been a response to the play: so dark a portrait of a king who had reigned just 100 years earlier was bound to provoke a reaction. We know that Southampton was keen on the theatre. In 1599 Rowland White wrote to Sir Robert Sydney, 'My Lord Southampton and Lord Rutland come not to the court ... they pass away the time in London merely in going to plaies every day.'[44] Southampton changed the text of Cornwallis's *Encomium* in two places with edits that indicate an interest in theatre. Halfway through (on folio 8) he altered the text from 'the partiall writings of an vndiscreete Cronicler a fauorer of the Lancastrian familye...' to 'the partiall writings of undiscreete Croniclers and <u>witty Play-makers</u>...' On the penultimate page (f. 16v) Southampton added: 'but that wee must still make him more Cruelle infamous <u>in pamphletts and playes</u>.'

Southampton may well have been referring to Shakespeare's plays *Henry VI: Part III* and *Richard III* in these additions. Southampton added more passages to Cornwallis's original, quite changing the nature of the document. Whereas Cornwallis had written a historical study and was attempting to redress the balance in Richard's favour, Southampton distorted this document for a political purpose: he was using the history as a metaphor for the present. Kincaid analysed these changes and concluded that the document had been sent to Neville to persuade him to join the Essex rebellion in 1600.[45] However, Casson discovered that Southampton's version of the *Encomium* was written on paper watermarked with the date 1603.[46] It now seems more likely that it was a belated self-justification in which Southampton offered arguments to support taking revolutionary action. He wrote that, 'new necessities require new remedies' and the ancient nobility should challenge 'new Statistes' (which Kincaid took to be a reference to the Cecils).[47] Shakespeare used the word just once when Hamlet refers to 'our statists' (5.2.33). This was written before Southampton used the word in his *Encomium*. Southampton was cautiously cryptic and ended his attempt to rehabilitate the last Plantagenet king, who had Neville blood in his veins, with the self-deprecating observation, 'I hold this but as a Paradox'.

This use of a historical context as a medium for the safe presentation of current issues can be seen throughout Shakespeare's history plays. The annotations in Neville's own manuscript copy of *Leicester's Commonwealth* show a parallel tendency to note historical events that had echoes of current relevance and connections to the Shakespeare plays.[48] Richard III is referred to several times in *Leicester's Commonwealth* and Henry Wriothesley's father, the 2nd Earl of Southampton, is also mentioned. Shakespeare certainly loved Wriothesley, the third earl, as is evident in his sonnets and the dedications of *Venus and Adonis* (1593) and *The Rape of Lucrece* (1594). Significantly, and perhaps in return, Southampton expressed his love to Neville: in the *Encomium* dedication he described the work as 'an ernest peny of my love'.

The *Encomium* was eventually printed in a collection of *Essays of Certain Paradoxes* in 1616, by Thomas Thorpe, who had published *Shake-speares Sonnets* in 1609. The date of publication of the *Encomium*, 1616, is one year after Neville died, two years after Cornwallis had died. It must have been popular because it was re-printed in 1617. A copy of the 1616 edition can be found in the Neville family library at Audley End House. The printed version is based on the Earl of Southampton's copy and includes virtually all of the additions he made to the text, including 'witty Play-makers' and 'but that we must still make him more cruelly infamous in Pamphlets and Playes'. However this printed version no longer has a dedication and was printed anonymously. 'The author hateth nothing more than coming in publick,' wrote Henry Olney in his dedication to Cornwallis's Essays. Cornwallis himself wrote in a letter to Sir John Hobart, who had commended the *Essays of Certain Paradoxes*, that 'in keeping them secret, he had shown some little discretion'.[49] He was not the only one who preferred to keep his writing secret. Given that Southampton's unique handwritten copy of the *Encomium* was given to Neville, it must have been this copy that became the source document for Thorpe's printing, although he did not include the dedication to Neville. This reminds us of Neville's express preference that Carleton's dedication to him of the 1603 *Heroici Characteres* be removed in a second printing.[50] The fact that the version printed by Thomas Thorpe is that given by Southampton to Neville is evidence of a connection between Neville and Thorpe, who had published *Shake-speares Sonnets*.

Why did Southampton choose to dedicate the *Encomium* to Henry Neville? Southampton and Neville were both in the Tower of London from 1601 to 1603, the scene of Richard III's crimes, so vividly portrayed in Shakespeare's play. Perhaps they discussed the historical events in which members of their families had taken part. Southampton's great-great-grandfather, John Writhe, as the Garter King of Arms, had officiated at the coronation of Richard III. It is possible that by composing his version of the *Encomium*, Southampton was attempting, albeit circuitously, to justify himself in Neville's eyes: if a bad king was not really so bad then maybe Southampton himself was not so bad for having betrayed Neville. It is possible that Neville was referring to Southampton's betrayal in Sonnet 34:

> For no man well of such a salve can speak
> That heals the wound and cures not the disgrace:
> Nor can thy shame give physic to my grief;
> Though thou repent, yet I have still the loss:
> The offender's sorrow lends but weak relief
> To him that bears the strong offence's cross.
> Ah! but those tears are pearl which thy love sheds,
> And they are rich and ransom all ill deeds.

The very next sonnet follows on with:

> No more be grieved at that which thou hast done:
> <u>Ros</u>es have thorns, and silver fountains mud;
> Clouds and eclipses stain both moon and sun,
> And loathsome canker lives in sweetest bud.

The choice of the rose imagery points to Southampton's name, Wriothesley, which was spelt 'W<u>ros</u>ely' in the baptismal register for his son in 1607.[51] Green has provided compelling evidence to support the view that the rose imagery in the sonnets refers to Wriotheseley.[52] The above sonnets of betrayal make sense when we see Shakespeare as Neville imprisoned in the Tower with Southampton (see Chapter 10). The poems show Neville working through his friend's betrayal and triumphing over the circumstances: however wounded, the friendship survived and we can see Southampton's work on Richard III as a peace offering.

Our final example of a connection between *Richard III* and Neville shows a close connection between the play, Neville's family and the company that performed the play. In December 1595 Sir Edward Hoby invited Sir Robert Cecil to supper and to see a play about King Richard. It is not clear whether this was *Richard II* or *Richard III*, but it was most likely the latter.[53] Hoby's mother, Elizabeth Russell, *née* Cooke, was a sister of Neville's mother-in-law, Katherine Killigrew, *née* Cooke. Sir Edward Hoby married Margaret, daughter of Henry Carey and sister of George Carey. Henry and George Carey were the patrons of the Lord Chamberlain's Men, who performed Shakespeare's plays.[54] Neville is believed to have owned the Northumberland Manuscript on which the earliest reference to the play occurs and which identified the playwright as William Shakespeare. From the fact that members of the Neville family appear on stage in the play, Southampton's *Encomium* on Richard III and the above report of a performance, we can see that Neville was a member of a social network of family connections within which this Shakespeare play appeared. Conversely no member of the Stratford Shakspere family is to be found in a similar position.

Edward III

Neville's family connections with Henry Carey offer an explanation of how Shakespeare might have gained access to a private library book which was a source for the play. Prior provided detailed evidence showing that *Edward III* was based on the annotated copy of Froissart's *Chronicle* belonging to Henry Carey, the Lord Chamberlain.[55] There is evidence that Neville's father knew Henry Carey because he wrote to Lord Burghley to be his friend in a contest with the Lord Chamberlain on 31 December 1590.[56]

Neville made his own notes on the reign of Edward III in *Leicester's Commonwealth* and in his Tower notebook. The play, written between 1589 and 1594, belongs to the anonymous period (being published in 1596 with no author on the title page) and was kept out of the First Folio. It would have been impossible to publish a play that ridiculed the Scots while James I was on the throne.

In Act 5 Scene 1 of *Edward III* Copland presents the captured Scottish King David to Edward. David had been defeated at the Battle of Neville's Cross in 1346.[57] Neville had visited Scotland in 1583, travelling through the disputed border region that we see in the play and so would have known the landscape where the Scottish invaders raided castles and threatened English inhabitants, such as the Countess of Salisbury, who appears in Act 1 Scene 2. He would also have had opportunities to observe the Scots and catch their ways of speaking as parodied in the play. His journey took him past the site of the Battle of Neville's Cross. We know this because Richard Eedes reported meeting Neville in Durham in his *Iter Boreale* and the battlefield was immediately to the west of the city.[58] Ralph Neville had set up the cross to commemorate the victory over the Scots.[59] In the play Henry Percy reports to the king in Calais after the Battle of Neville's Cross that, 'from her highness, and the lord vice-regent, I bring this happy tidings of success' (4.2.38–9). As Melchiori noted, the vice-regent was Ralph Neville.[60]

Before the play was generally accepted as having been written by Shakespeare, Professor Tillyard stated his opinion that the author was 'an intellectual, probably young, a University man, in the Southampton circle'.[61] This neatly describes Neville.

Richard II

Henry Neville was related to Richard II through John of Gaunt's descendants. *Richard II* opens with the king talking to Gaunt. The identification of Neville as the Bard explains why Shakespeare distorted both history and the character of Gaunt to make him such a positive figure, when in fact Gaunt was deeply unpopular during his lifetime.[62] In his copy of *Leicester's Commonwealth* Neville annotated the text: 'John of Gaunte The pedigree of ...'.

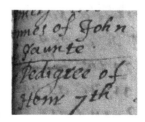

Worsley MSS 47, 43.

This is echoed in two Shakespeare plays: 'he from John of Gaunt doth bring his pedigree' in *Henry VI: Part I* (2.5.76) and 'John of Gaunt ... a pedigree' in *Henry VI Part III* (3.3.81–92). Furthermore, in the copy of Hall's *Chronicle* annotated by Neville, there is a marginal note 'John of Gaunt' against a passage referring to Gaunt's death, Bollingbroke's exile and the seizure of his lands by Richard, all of which is dramatised in the play.[63] Neville made notes on Richard II in his copy of *Leicester's Commonwealth* and his Tower notebook proving that he had continued his interest in this reign over twenty years.

The Northumberland Manuscript provides further documentary evidence of a link between Neville and the play because it is listed as *Rychard the second* on the front page. Just beneath *Rychard the second* someone had repeatedly written the name 'William Shakespeare' (correctly spelt). The NHMS has been dated to 1596–7. This is fifteen years before the first of the Stratford William's own signatures appeared, the earliest being 'Willm Shackp' on the Belott–Mountjoy deposition of 1612. *Richard II* was first printed in 1597 without any author being named. Thus Neville knew *Richard II* was by Shakespeare before anyone else. He also spelt the name correctly, which the Stratford Shakspere never did.

In July 1597 Sir Walter Raleigh wrote to Cecil telling him that the Earl of Essex had been 'wonderfully merry att the consait [conceit] of Richard the 2'.[64] It is not certain that this is a reference to Shakespeare's play but the date coincides with the time that the play would have been on stage. Neville was related to Cecil whose mother, Mildred Cooke, was a sister of Henry Killigrew's first wife, Katherine. Killigrew was Neville's father-in-law and he was one of the government editors of the 1587 edition of Holinshed, Shakespeare's main source for the history plays. Not only was Neville related to Cecil (they were cousins) but he was in correspondence with him and after the debacle of the Essex rebellion owed his life to Cecil's careful management of the situation. *Richard II* was especially famous because of the notorious performances just before the Essex rebellion in 1601. Some of the actors were called in for questioning and the man who had paid for the performance, Sir Gelly Meyrick, was executed. The fact that the actor William Shakspere was neither arrested, questioned nor punished on that occasion implies that it was known that he was not the author.

Conclusion

Many members of the Neville family appear on stage or are referred to in Shakespeare's early history plays, though they are often concealed by using their titles instead of their family names. His family had been powerful and influential in England since the Norman Conquest so any playwright might have been bound to introduce them into the plays. The Bard however displays a consistent pro-Neville bias. Some Nevilles appear on stage when other historical figures might have reflected the times more accurately. The author also manipulates historical truth by portraying ancestral family members in a positive light that they did not always deserve (see also Chapter 5). Neville had access to source materials on which the early history plays depend. In books and manuscripts he made notes that recur in the plays and, as we have shown, there are many examples of word choice, spelling and use that also appear in the early history plays. When taken together, this body of evidence makes a strong case that Henry Neville was an author of these plays.

Histories and Comedies
1595–1600

> Harry lives, that shall convert those tears
> By number into hours of happiness.
>
> *Henry IV: Part II,* 5.2.60

During this happy period of his life Shakespeare wrote six comedies and four history plays. This coincides with a period when we know that Neville was cheerful and that, at the end of this time, he was hit by tragedy. It was only then that Shakespeare wrote tragic, bitter plays. In this chapter we examine the happy period that sees all the fun of Falstaff make even the history plays verge on becoming comedies. Towards the end of this time a more sober mood emerges in the plays of 1600. We track this period through Neville's extant correspondence and are able to compare the vocabulary of these plays with his contemporary letters.

The plays of this period begin with *A Midsummer Night's Dream* and *The Merchant of Venice*, then the three Falstaff plays of *Henry IV* (both parts) and *The Merry Wives of Windsor*. We have devoted Chapter 6 to examining *The Merry Wives* as a special test case for the authorship so do not discuss it here. *Much Ado About Nothing* was followed by *Henry V, Julius Caesar, As You Like It* and *Twelfth Night*. For clarity's sake we deal first with the history plays and then turn to the comedies.

The Histories

Henry IV
In this two-part play, members of the Neville family and their relatives appear on stage. In *Part I* Ralph Neville (1354–1425) is identified only as the Earl of Westmoreland and the king calls him 'my cousin Westmoreland' (5.5.35). Ralph was grandfather of Edward IV, Richard III and father of Cecily Neville (wife of the Duke of York, mother of Edward IV and Richard III). The Earl of Westmoreland is a key figure in *Henry IV*. We know that Neville was proud of his descent from Westmoreland because he had this family connection carved onto his father's tomb at Waltham St Lawrence.[1] The annotator of Hall's *Chronicles*, whom we accept was Neville, made a note of 'the earle of Westmoreland'.[2] Neville also made a note of 'Ra. E. Westmerland' in his 1602 Tower notebook.

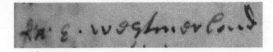

Worsley MSS 40. (By permission of the Eighth
Earl of Yarborough and Lincolnshire Archives)

In these plays Shakespeare continued to show a pro-Neville bias:[3] an example of this is
the unhistorical sleight of hand that removes responsibility for a treacherous trick from a
Neville, displacing it onto Prince John of Lancaster.[4] At the Battle of Gaultree it was Ralph
Neville who deceived Archbishop Scrope and the other rebel leaders into surrendering
and then arrested them. In the play Shakespeare gives this Machiavellian role to Prince
John who promises to redress the rebels' grievances and so persuades them to discharge
their army, enabling Neville to arrest them (*Henry IV: Part II*, 4.2.59). Stow and Holinshed
both stated that it was Westmoreland (Ralph Neville) who conducted this negotiation.
Their testimony is reinforced by the fact that Prince John was aged sixteen at the time and
so would have been an unlikely negotiator.[5]

A central plot theme of *Part I* is the rivalry between Hotspur and Prince Hal. The real
historical rivalry was between the Percys and the Nevilles.[6] Neville, annotating his copy of
Leicester's Commonwealth, made a note of the Percys during the reigns of Richard II and
Henry IV.

Worsley MSS 47, 35V.

The printed text reads:

> When the Percies took part with Henry of Bolingbroke against King Richard II, their
> lawful sovereign, it was not for lack of preferment, for they were exceedingly advanced
> by the said king ...

In the above illustrated text from *Leicester's Commonwealth*, Neville spelt Henry's surname
'Bullnigbrook'. In the first quarto of *Henry IV: Part I* the spelling is 'Bullingbrooke'.[7] Neville
used the spelling 'Bullnigbrook' (with his characteric 'ni'[8]) again as he annotated the text
naming Henry as 'the first sonne of John of Gaunte'.

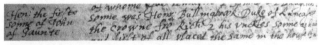

Worsley MSS 47, 42V.

Neville wrote 'sonne'. The First Folio uses the spelling 'sonne' 555 times, 'son' just sixty-
eight times.[9] Later Neville, using the spelling 'Bullingbrook', made a unique marginal
annotation of Henry as a usurper:[10]

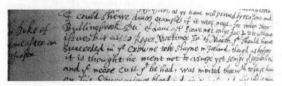

'Hen: Duke of Lancaster an vsurper,
Worsley MSS 47, 57.

The printed text states:

> I could show by divers examples if it were need. For when Henry Bolingbroke, Duke of
> Lancaster, saw not only Richard II to be without issue, but also Roger Mortimer, Earl of
> March, that should have succeeded in the crown to be slain in Ireland, though before (as
> is thought) he meant not to <u>usurp</u>, yet seeing the possibility and near cut that he had, was
> invited therewith to lay hands on his sovereign's blood and dignity, as he did.[11]

Roger Mortimer and his wife both appear on stage in *Henry IV: Part I*.

Neville's copy of *Leicester's Commonwealth* is not the only manuscript source for the
plays in which his use of language echoes Shakespeare. Mortimer is mentioned twice in
marginal notes on the annotated Hall's *Chronicle*.[12] On folio xxxiii[a] of the *Chronicle* Neville
made a note: 'Kinge henrye semithe to confess that he had the crowne wrongfullye and
died Ao dni 1413.'[13] In *Henry IV: Part II* Henry, on his deathbed, confesses to his son,
Prince Hal, that

> God knows, my son,
> By what by-paths and indirect crook'd ways
> I met this crown; and I myself know well
> How troublesome it sat upon my head. (4.5.183)

On folio xx[b] of the *Chronicle* there is an annotation which reads 'a prophecie of the
Mollwarpe, the dragon the lyon the wolf'.[14] In the play Hotspur pours scorn on Merlin's
prophesies 'of the moldwarp ... a dragon, ... a couching lion ...' (3.1.143).

One specific source for poetry in the play has been identified as Horace's *Ode* III.1 in
which there is a passage about sleep blessing the ploughman's but not the royal head.
This is echoed by Shakespeare when Henry IV complains he cannot sleep (*Henry IV:
Part II*, 3.1.917). In both Horace and Shakespeare the word 'sleep' is repeated twice in one
line. Neville annotated this page in his copy of Horace, proving he was familiar with the
passage. Two different inks suggest he revisited the page on more than one occasion.

Falstaff

The comic figure of Falstaff can be seen as an alter ego for the ambassador-to-be: like
Prince Hal, Neville was obliged to give up an enjoyable life for a more responsible role
in government.[15] Indeed the play has much to do with growing up, Prince Hal being an
irresponsible adolescent whom we see grow into a responsible adult. The father–son
themes are strong. It may be significant that Neville's father died in 1593.[16] The king's
deathbed scene in the play is particularly moving.[17]

One of Neville's annotations in Hall's *Chronicle* reads, 'Kinge henrye beinge but prince
strakes th(e) chief justice on the fa(ce) for <u>imp[ri]soninge</u> of a wanton <u>companion</u> of his'
(our emphasis underlined).[18] The only time Shakespeare used the word '<u>imprisoning</u>' was
in *Henry IV: Part I* (3.1.27) in which Hal describes Falstaff as his '<u>companion</u>' (2.4.442).
In *Part II* the Lord Chief Justice calls Falstaff the prince's '<u>companion</u>' (1.2.199) while
investigating this very incident. Falstaff, trying to avoid the attentions of the Justice, tells

his page to inform the judge that he is deaf (1.2.66). Neville was to try the same tactic in 1600 when, due to his frustrations with the role, he complained of deafness in an attempt to get out of his role of ambassador (his uncle had been notoriously deaf).

In Neville's annotated copy of Hall's *Chronicle* one marginal note reads, 'All flatterers & olde cõpanions banisshid x myle frõ court' (All flatterers and old companions banished ten mile from court).[19] When, in *Henry IV: Part II*, the new king Henry V banishes Falstaff, he uses the words:

> I banish thee, on pain of death,
> As I have done the rest of my misleaders,
> Not to come near our person by ten <u>mile</u>. (5.5.63)

The use of the singular 'mile' matches the annotation when the Bard could have written 'ten miles'.

Even minor characters can be seen to have Neville connections.[20] In *Henry IV: Part II* Prince John orders Sir John Blunt to guard Falstaff's captive, Coleville of the Dale, who is taken away for execution (*Henry IV: Part II*, 4.3.72). James suggested that Neville selected this minor character, Sir John Coleville, from Holinshed because he was suspicious of a man called John Colville who was an intelligence agent in France.[21] Colville had been previously employed by Walsingham as a spy.[22] 'By the time Neville used his services in Paris, Colville was already under suspicion of being a double agent … Sir Henry Neville wrote to Winwood: I distrust Colvel every day more and more; I will quit myself of him'.[23] This letter was dated 17 July 1600. In another letter dated 28 August 1600, Neville stated he would not pay Colville until he had performed some real service rather than just offering empty promises. *Henry IV: Part II* was registered on 23 August 1600, when Neville had arrived back in London. The first quarto was printed in 1600 and included the Coleville scene.

The *Henry IV* plays were written between 1597 and 1598 and we have letters from Neville dated 1599. Neville used a significant number of rare words in the letters that are also used in the plays. 'Confesseth' was used only once by Shakespeare, in *Henry IV: Part I*: Neville used it in his letter dated 8 August 1599.[24] 'Offensive' occurs only in *Henry IV: Part II* and *King Lear*: Neville used it in his letter dated 20 August 1599.[25]

'Peremptorily' is unique to *Henry IV: Part I*: Neville used it in his letter dated 26 September 1599.[26] 'Accommodated' occurs only in *Henry IV: Part II* and *Cymbeline*: Neville used it in his letter dated 11 October 1599.[27]

There is thus evidence for Neville's authorship in his manuscripts and letters. Not only do Shakespeare's distortions of historical incidents and inclusion of particular characters show a Neville bias, but also there are strong connections between them in the very language used.

Henry V

Written in 1599, *Henry V* includes scenes set in France (and in French) including the triumphal victory at Agincourt. The playwright introduces members of the Neville family who were not present at the battle, giving them an undeserved reflected glory.[28] Neville's time in France was not so successful but perhaps, setting out, he had high hopes. The play was registered on 14 August 1600, just after Neville had arrived back in London on 6 August.

Neville was a fluent French speaker and writer: letters by him in French dated 1599–1600, around the time that *Henry V* was written, are preserved in Winwood's *Memorials*.[29] To be able to write playfully in French suggests an easy familiarity with the language, which Neville certainly had. Rouen is mentioned twice in the play (3.5.54, 64). Neville traveled through Rouen on his way to Paris, mentioning this in a letter dated 6 June 1599.[30]

Henry V is unusual for including a direct reference to one of Neville's living contemporaries.[31] The Chorus of Act 5 refers to Robert Devereux, 2nd Earl of Essex, who was leader of the expeditionary force sent to conquer Ireland in 1599.

> How London doth pour out her citizens.
> The mayor and all his brethren in best sort,
> Like to the senators of th'antique Rome,
> With the plebeians swarming at their heels,
> Go forth and fetch their conqu'ring Caesar in:
> As, by a lower but by loving likelihood,
> Were now the general of our gracious empress,
> As in good time he may, from Ireland coming,
> Bringing rebellion broached on his sword,
> How many would the peaceful city quit
> To welcome him! (5.0.24)

The Chorus looks forward to a glorious homecoming, resembling a Roman Triumph, and we can therefore deduce that the play must have been written between Essex's departure for Ireland on 27 March and his unhappy return in September 1599. Neville was a supporter of Essex and enquired about his progress in his 1599–1600 letters to Cecil, reporting what he had heard from French and other sources. He had been reluctant to serve as ambassador to France but was persuaded to go by Essex. On 15 November 1600, with the political isolation of the Earl of Essex, Neville wrote to his secretary, Ralph Winwood in Paris, using a theatrical metaphor: 'The Earl of Essex is no <u>actor</u> in our Triumphs'.[32] There is much shared vocabulary in Neville's diplomatic correspondence dated 1599 and the play *Henry V*. We have identified the following examples.

'Commissioners' was used only once by Shakespeare in *Henry V*: Neville used it in his letter dated 13 July 1599 and again on 29 July 1600. 'Inconveniences' was used only in *Henry V*: Neville used it in his letter dated 1 August 1599.[33] 'Petit' was used only in *Henry V*: Neville used it in the same letter as 'inconveniences'. 'Acknowledgement' was used only in *Henry V*: Neville used it in his letter dated 7 August 1599.[34] 'Governors' was used only in *Henry V*: Neville used it in his letter dated 20 August 1599.[35] 'Passport' was used only in *Henry V* and *Pericles*: Neville used it in his letters dated 6 September 1599 and 27 February 1600.[36]

Many other passages in the play and letters can be seen to echo each other.[37] Two Neville manuscript sources can be seen to contain seeds of the play. These are *Leicester's*

Commonwealth and the annotated Hall's *Chronicle*. While Holinshed was the major source for the play, Hall's *Chronicle* was also used by the playwright. Advising the king, Ralph Neville, Earl of Westmoreland, says:

> But there's a saying very old and true,
> If <u>that</u> you <u>will</u> <u>France win</u>, then <u>with Scotland</u> first <u>begin</u>.

(First Folio italics, 1.2.166, our emphasis underlined.)

When annotating Hall's *Chronicle* Neville wrote in the margin of folio vii of the Henry V section:

> he <u>that</u> <u>wyll</u> <u>fraunce wynne</u>
> <u>with Scotland</u> he must <u>begynne</u>[38]

The quartos miss out the word 'that', which occurs in both the Hall's *Chronicle* annotation and the First Folio. The wording is almost identical and occurs in the same order.

The use of italics in the First Folio (as above) continues the use of italic script for just *France* and *Scotland* in the first (1600) and second (1602) quartos of the play. Neville used italics for names in both his copy of *Leicester's Commonwealth* and his letters.

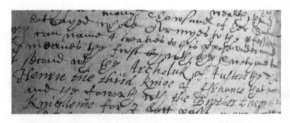

Worsley MSS 47, 9V. Italic script for names within a passage of secretary script including 'ffraunce'.

In both Hall's *Chronicle* and his copy of *Leicester's Commonwealth* France is spelt with 'au'.

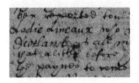

Worsley MSS 47, 13. Italic script for names within a passage of secretary script including '<u>Scotland</u>'.

Passages in French and Latin in *Henry V* are in italics in the First Folio and Neville used italic script for foreign languages in Worsley MSS 47 and his letters.

The annotated copy of Hall's *Chronicle* was discovered in 1940 by Alan Keen and the first thing he noticed was a passage which occurs in *Henry V*. He saw that the Latin words '<u>In terram salicam mulieres ne succedant</u>' had been underlined. In the play these very words are quoted by the Archbishop of Canterbury who helpfully translates them as, 'No woman shall succeed in Salike land' (1.2.39 First Folio spelling). The Hall's *Chronicle* annotator had written in the margin 'note the exposition'.[39] (Shakespeare used the word 'exposition' in five plays before and after *Henry V*.)

Hall's *Chronicle*, Henry V, f.iv[b].

The text referred to explains:

> which is to say, let not womē succede in the land *Salicque. This land Salicque the deceitful
> glosers name to be the realm of Fraunce. This lawe the logicall interpretours assigne
> to directe the croune and regalitie of the same region, as who would, say that to that
> preheminence no woman were liable to aspire, nor no heire female was worthy to inherite.

The asterisk refers to a printed marginal note '*The lands Salique'. Most scholars agree
that the Hall's *Chronicle* passage was the source used by Shakespeare for *Henry V*. Neville
annotating his copy of *Leicester's Commonwealth* also made an annotation which reads,
'The Lawe Salique in ffraunce'.

Worsley MSS 47, 39.

The phrase used in the main text of *Leicester's Commonwealth* is 'the Law Salick in
Fraunce' (original spelling). In *Henry V* the king says, 'the Law Salike, that they have in
France' (1.2.11, First Folio spelling).[40] The Archbishop of Canterbury also speaks of 'this
Salique Law' (1.2.91, First Folio spelling). Shakespeare spelt this as 'Salique' as does Neville
in his annotation in *Leicester's Commonwealth*. This identical spelling might seem like
coincidence at a time when spelling was not standardised. However it is precisely the shared
spelling of the river 'Elue' in the First Folio (as opposed to Elbe: 1.2.52) that proves beyond
reasonable doubt that Shakespeare's source was Hall's *Chronicle* rather than Holinshed:
this is because Hall made the 'Elue' spelling mistake whereas Holinshed corrected it. It
seems that *Leicester's Commonwealth* sparked Neville's interest in the 'Salique' law, which
he then researched in Hall and used in *Henry V*.

Another annotation in Hall's *Chronicle* reads, 'Hugh Capet an usurper of the crowne of
fraunce'.[41] The only time Shakespeare refers to Capet is in *Henry V*, fifteen lines after the mention
of 'that Law Salique' he wrote, 'Hugh Capet also, who usurped the crown' (1.2.69). The previous
line includes the words 'the crown of France'. A further annotation mentions 'blackeheathe'.
The only time Shakespeare referred to Blackheath was in *Henry V* (5.Chorus,16).

The annotated Hall's *Chronicle* has many more handwritten marginal annotations
relevant to the play and there is compelling evidence that these were written by Neville
(see Chapter 2).[42] Neville also made notes on Henry V in his 1602 Tower notebook.

Julius Caesar

During his Italian journey Henry Savile visited Rome and there is no reason to doubt that Neville accompanied his tutor to the city (see Chapter 3), in which case he would have seen the ruins of ancient Rome. As a young classics student he had several books on Roman history which he annotated. Amongst his surviving library books is a volume of the works of Tacitus edited by Justus Lipsius, dated 1574. Donaldson noted that

> Tacitus was read with great attention in Europe during the final years of the century, following the publication of the great edition of his work by the Belgian scholar Justus Lipsius. In England, the Earl of Essex and a group of Oxford scholars closely connected with his cause had shown particular interest in his work. They included Henry Cuffe, Regius Professor of Greek, soon to become Essex's secretary, and Henry Savile, Warden of Merton College, who in 1591 had published the first English translation of Tacitus (*Historiae*) ... and Richard Greneway, whose English translation of Tacitus' *Annales* and *Germanica* published in 1598, had been dedicated significantly to Essex.[43]

Neville showed his awareness of Lipsius' work with marginal annotations 'v. Lispiú': (e.g.: 216, 280, 301, 302, 376, 371). Richard Greneway's 1598 translation of the Tacitus *Annales* has been widely believed to be a source for Shakespeare's *Henry V* and *Julius Ceasar*. We can now see that Neville had access to this Latin text long before Greneway's version was published. Neville was in the Essex circle, close to Savile and met Cuffe in the lead up to the Essex rebellion.[44] Neville cited Tacitus when asked for his opinion by the Essex faction (see Chapter 7). At his execution Cuffe apologised to Neville for involving him in the rebellion and publicly exonerated him. Written in 1599 Shakespeare's *Julius Caesar* may have been a warning to the Essex faction about the dangers of honourable men staging a coup d'état.

The annotations made by Neville in Lipsius' 1574 edition of Tacitus show that he had an interest in the politics of ancient Rome at a time when this had contemporary relevance, as Shakespeare's plays and subsequent events show. Neville quoted Tacitus (*Annals* IV, 18) in a letter to Robert Cecil dated 24 September 1599 (the year that *Henry V* and *Julius Caesar* were written): 'Besydes your Honor remembreth the Saying of *Tacitus, beneficia læta sunt dum videntur exolvi posse; ubi multum antevenêre, pro gratia odium redditur.*'[45] This quotation tantalisingly suggests that Neville had his volume of Tacitus to hand and so, at the very time Shakespeare was writing the two plays that use this source, Neville had access to his own copy.

In Neville's Tacitus an annotation on page 253 reads, 'Theatralis dissensio' (= dissent in the theatre) against the text, 'Theatru(m) licentia proximo priore anno coepta' (= absence of restraint in the theatre began the year just before).

Tacitus, 253. (Private Collection)

From this it is clear that Neville, the annotator, was interested in theatre, and especially in the political aspect of theatre. He also wrote a note about the collapse of an Amphitheatre at Fidenae.

Tacitus, 361.

Amongst Neville's books is a volume of Appian's Roman history, dated 1551, in which he noted another theatre in Rome: the Theatre of Marcellus.

'Theatrum Marcelli', Appian (Dionysius section), 157.

These annotations prove Neville was interested in theatre. Another annotation, on page 328 of the Tacitus, reads, 'Theatrum Pompeii igne haustum' (Pompey's theatre was destroyed by fire). In another book Neville also noted 'Pompeij Theatrû(m)'.

'Pompeij Theatrû', Appian (Dionysius section), 68.

Shakespeare explicitly named Pompey's theatre in *Julius Caesar* (1.3.152). This volume of Appian/Dionysius is a major work on Roman history that contains many annotations about Brutus, Cassius, Antony and Caesar. In the play *Julius Caesar*, Brutus addresses the crowds at Caesar's funeral. 'Brutus' speech to the people on the Capitol' is a translation of

Neville's annotation, 'Bruti ad populû(m) in capitolio δημηγορια' (he started in Latin and switched to Greek):

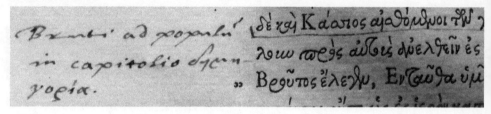

'Bruti ad populus in capitolio δημηγορια', Appian, 256. (Private collection)

In Shakespeare's *Julius Caesar* Brutus uses the words 'in the Capitol' as he is speaking to the people (3.2.38). Appian's *Civil Wars* is a recognised source for Shakespeare's *Julius Caesar*.

Brutus, the honourable man struggling to decide what political action to take against emerging tyranny, hears off-stage cheering and says to Cassius:

I do believe that these applauses are
For some new honours that are heap'd on Caesar. (1.2.132)

One annotation on page 225 of the Appian is, 'Honours decreed to G(aius) Julius Caesar.'

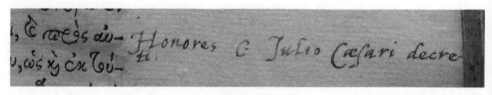

'Honores C. Julio Caesari decreti', Appian (Dionysius section), 225.

On page 250 there is an annotation stating that Antony fled to his house after the assassination.

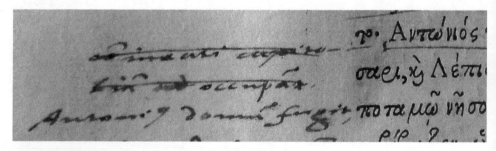

'Antonius domû(m) fugit', Appian, 250.

In North's *Plutarch*, the major source of the play, it states Antony 'cast a slaves gowne upon him, and hid him selfe', and with Lepidus, 'fled into other mens houses, and forsook their own'.[46] Neither of these details are in the play which more directly follows the annotation in Appian:

Cassius: Where is Antony?
Trebonius: Fled to his house amazed. (3.1.96)

The Appian contains some annotations referring the reader back to the Tacitus with page numbers. The handwriting of the annotations also looks similar, as if Neville returned to the Appian when he was reading the Tacitus. If both these books were sources for *Julius Caesar* this is evidence that Neville annotated them in tandem and that the notes relate to the plays.

The central scene in the play is Caesar's funeral at which the competing oratory of Brutus and Antony show the fickle nature of the mob. Antony speaks over Caesar's coffin (3.2.107). Another annotation in the volume of Appian states: 'Caesar's tomb and Antony's words of epitaph.'

'Caesaris sepulcra, et Antonii λογος επιταφιος', Appian, 259.

On page 170 of the Dionysius section of the Appian volume an annotation reads, 'the words of Mark Antony's epitaph for Julius Ceasar' in Greek and Latin:

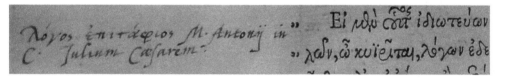

λογος επιταφιος M. Antonii in G. Julium Caesarem': Appian (Dionysius section), 170.

In the play Antony makes great play with Caesar's will in order to rouse the mob against his assassins and another annotation on the same page states, 'When Caesar's will was read the people were excited again by Antony's speech'.

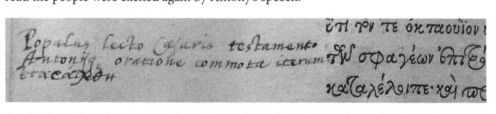

Populus lecto Caesaris testamento Antonii orattione commota iterum ἐταραχθη, Appian (Dionysius section), 170.

Antony tells the crowds:

You all did see that on the Lupercal
I thrice presented him a kingly crown,
Which he did thrice refuse ... (3.2.)

Another Neville annotation translated reads, 'Caesar returns a crown put on him by Antony in the Capitol at the Lupercal.'

'Caesar Lupercalibus diadema capiti ab Antonio impositû(m). in Capitoliû(m) remittit': Appian (Dionysius section), 161.

Neville's annotations in the volume of Appian also tell of Portia, Brutus's wife who features in *Julius Caesar*. In the play she describes herself as, 'A woman that Lord Brutus took to wife … Cato's daughter.' (2.1.292). One annotation translated reads, 'About Portia, M. Brutus' wife, Cato's daughter.'

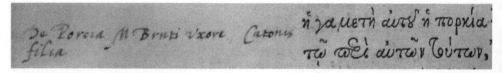

'De Porcia M. Bruti uxore Catonis filia': Appian (Dionysius section), 162.

Portia's death is reported in the play. Brutus says, 'she fell distract, and her attendants absent, swallowed fire' (4.3.153). Later he kills himself (5.5.51). Another annotation states, 'Brutus lays hands on himself. Portia, his wife eats a hot coal.'

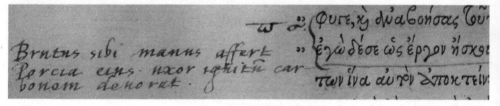

'Brutus sibi manus affert Porcia eius uxor ignitû carbonem devorat': Appian (Dionysius section), 238.

Julius Caesar culminates in the Battle at Philippi. On page 234 of Neville's Appian there is an annotation which when translated reads, 'The War at Philippi waged by Octavius and Antony against Brutus and Cassius':

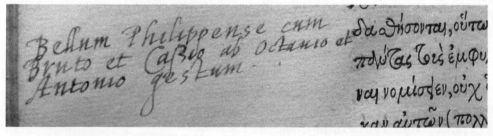

'Bellum Philippense cum Bruto et Cassio ab Octavio et Antonio gestum': Appian (Dionysius section), 234.

One annotation in Neville's volume of Tacitus refers to Quintus Antistius Labeo, a jurist, who died by suicide after the battle of Philippi and Brutus' suicide. The first annotation is 'Labeo Antistius' on page 330 where a whole passage about Labeo is underlined.[47] As noted, Tacitus is a recognised source for Shakespeare's *Julius Caesar*, and indeed Labeo features in the play when Brutus orders, 'Labeo and Flavius, set our battles on.' (5.3.108) A second annotation on page 388 concerns another man called Pomponius Labeo: 'Poponii Labeonis Mors'. He also committed suicide.

There is an obvious difference between the handwriting of some of Neville's annotations. This suggests that they were made at different times and that some may date back to Neville's youth, perhaps to 1577, when he was a student at Merton College, Oxford. If this is the case, Neville's knowledge of Roman history would long predate any decision to write the Roman plays.

The Comedies

A Midsummer Night's Dream
Written between 1595 and 1596, the play was influenced by Chaucer's 'The Knight's Tale' (as would be Shakespeare and Fletcher's last play *The Two Noble Kinsmen*, see Chapter 11). Neville was related to Chaucer.[48]

At the start of the play Theseus laments how

This old moon wanes! She lingers my desires,
Like to a step-dame or dowager
Long withering out a young man's revenue. (1.1.4)

This has a parallel in Neville's experience: after his father's death in 1593 Neville became embroiled in a legal dispute with his stepmother (see Chapter 6).

The play must date from after September 1594 because the Bard seems to have been aware of a comic incident in Scotland when, at Prince Henry's baptism feast, a lion was withdrawn for fear of frightening the guests.[49] This incident is reflected in *A Midsummer Night's Dream* when the lion reassures the audience that he is not really a lion, but actually Snug the joiner (5.1.218). Neville, who had traveled to Scotland and whose father-in-law had been on diplomatic missions to James VI, was likely to have heard of the lion being withdrawn for Prince Henry's baptism feast.

The Merchant of Venice
The Merchant of Venice was written between 1596 and 1598. Neville had spent time in Venice in 1581 and so Roe's discoveries of specific details of the city that only a visitor could have known make sense when we posit Neville as the author. When examining the sources for *The Merchant of Venice* we find compelling evidence of the necessity for its author to have had knowledge of foreign languages. We have already seen that Neville owned the volume 1574 edition of the *Diana Enamorada*, which was printed in Venice. The book was a source for *A Midsummer Nights Dream* and *As You Like It*. It is generally

accepted that Shakespeare relied on *Il Percorone* in the original Italian as source material when writing *The Merchant of Venice. Il Percerone* was published in Milan in 1554. Neville's father went to Padua in 1553 so this book could have been purchased by him there, though no copy survives in the Neville library today.

The Merchant of Venice was certainly written before the end of 1598. Writing letters the following year Neville used rare vocabulary that occurs in the play. 'Discontinued' occurs only in *The Merchant of Venice*: Neville used it in his letter dated 26 May 1599.[50] 'Vendible' only occurs in *The Merchant of Venice* and *All's Well That Ends Well*: Neville used it in his letter dated 18 July 1599.[51] 'Questionless' only occurs in *The Merchant of Venice* and *Pericles*: Neville used it in his letter dated 20 March 1600.[52]

Of all Shakespeare's plays perhaps it is *The Merchant of Venice* that can best represent Shakespeare's encyclopedic knowledge of the law, which has been acknowledged by many lawyers. Neville became a Justice of the Peace at the age of twenty-one and was involved in legal cases and lawmaking as a Member of Parliament throughout his life. Amongst his papers stored at the Berkshire Records Office are legal documents with his notes in the margin. These date from the 1590s onwards. In *King John* Shakespeare used the word 'interrogatories' (3.1.147) and he used the singular 'inter'gatory' in *The Merchant of Venice* (5.1.300). This is a legal term for questions answerable under oath.[53] He also used a shortened form ('inter'gatories') in *All's Well That Ends Well* (4.3.184) and in *Cymbeline* (5.4.393). At the Berkshire Records Office there are legal documents belonging to Neville, headed 'Interrogatories'.[54]

The play is a condemnation of usury and so one would not expect its contents to have been endorsed by William Shakspere from Stratford. One of the few facts we know about him is that he was a usurer, charging interest on loans, as was his father (see also Chapter 9).

Much Ado About Nothing

Thomas Hoby published a translation of Castiglione's *Courtier* in 1561. The book was a source for *Much Ado About Nothing*. There is a 1560 edition of the original Castiglione in Italian in the Neville family library at Audley End. Passages are underlined, showing it had been read, though it has not been otherwise annotated. Neville was related to Hoby through his mother-in-law: Hoby married her sister, Elizabeth Cooke. Hoby had spent time in Padua with Neville's father and father-in-law. In the play Benedick is a young lord from Padua and Claudio a young lord from Florence. Neville visited both cities during his travels in Italy. There is a 1555 edition of Boccaccio's *Decameron* in Neville's library signed by Thomas Hoby.

There is also a 1580 edition of *Orlando Furioso* by Ariosto printed in Venice in Neville's library. This was another acknowledged source for *Much Ado About Nothing*. As Neville was in Venice in 1581 it seems reasonable to presume the book was bought there by him and brought back to England. It has many passages underlined, showing that it was read throughout. Cairncross concluded that the evidence showed that Shakespeare read *Orlando Furioso* in the Italian and there is evidence that Neville did so.[55] The play starts in Messina in Sicily. Amongst Neville's books is a volume of *Del L'Historia di Sicilia* by Tomaso Fazello, published in Venice in 1574.

In a letter dated 8 September 1599 Neville used the word 'seavennight' which only occurs in *Much Ado About Nothing* and *The Winter's Tale*.[56] *Much Ado* was written at about the same time as this letter. The spelling in the first quarto (1600) is 'seuennight' (2.1.337).[57] Neither in Neville's letter nor in the quarto does the word have the hyphen commonly used in modern editions.

As You Like It

Set in France (in the forest of Ardennes), the play was written in 1599–1600, during the time that Neville was in France. Writing letters at the same time as the play was written, Neville was using words that occur in the play, such as the following examples. 'Insomuch' only occurs in *As You Like It*: Neville used this word in his letter dated 27 June 1599.[58] 'Employed' only occurs in *As You Like It*: Neville used this word in his letter dated 16 September 1599.[59] 'Propositions' only occurs in *As You Like It*: Neville used this word in his letter dated 22 October 1599.[60] 'Diminish' only occurs in *As You Like It* and *The Tempest*: Neville used this word in his letter dated 28 December 1599.[61]

Other connections between *As You Like It* and Neville's life and family include a letter that 'Neville wrote to Cecil in December 1599, in which he registered his wish that, rather than continue the arduous work of ambassador, he wished to "be a hermit in Ashridge[62] or the forest and do penance for the faults committed here", which very much echoes the character of the exiled Jacques' in the play.[63] Furthermore Thomas Morley wrote a musical setting of the song 'It was a Lover and his Lass' in *As You Like It*. Morley married a maidservant of Neville's stepmother. He studied with William Byrd. *My Ladye Nevells Booke* of music by Byrd survives to this day in the British Library.[64] The book proves that the Neville family had an interest in music and a connection with the song that features in *As You Like It*.

Twelfth Night

The play was performed at court during the Christmas period of 1600 (perhaps on Twelfth Night, 6 January 1601), during the visit of Count Orsino, who is mentioned in Neville's correspondence with Winwood. The play opens with Duke Orsino who is named as 'Count Orsino' three times in the play.[65] Written in 1600, it offers us a special opportunity to see Neville's authorship in the writing and circumstances of the play. It is a comedy that has gathering shadows and a poignant lyricism that is not without bitterness. This echoes Neville's humour, which, like that of Jacques in *As You Like It*, was going sour. Neville was possibly disillusioned by his experiences in France and had less optimism and more cynicism.

James and Rubinstein showed that *Twelfth Night* provides evidence of Neville's authorship and that there is material in his letters relevant to the play.[66] Ralph Winwood informed Neville that Don Virginio Orsino was coming to London in a letter dated 20 November 1600. In another letter of 4 December 1600, Winwood, informing Neville that he had given Orsino a letter of introduction to him, asked Neville to present Orsino to the queen. Later in a letter dated 29 January 1601 Neville wrote to Winwood that 'Don Virginio Orsino hath been here and very graciously and honourably entertained by her Majesty; he is gone hence to the Archduke'.[67]

Winwood also wrote about a Don Antonio whom he describes as the 'natural brother' of the new French queen in a letter dated 29 October 1600.[68] Neville was also especially interested in a mysterious Sebastian and on 15 November 1600 he wrote that this man had 'been so long a prisoner at Venice, is now believed to be the true Sebastian, by many secret tokens upon his Body; confirmed out of Portugal by those which knew him both Child and Man'.[69] John Chamberlain, in two letters of 8 November 1598 and 17 January 1599, explained the identity of this man: 'The newes now comes very hot that Sebastian the king of Portingale that was said to be slaine in the battell in Barbarie is at Venice' and 'sayes he was not slaine ... but taken prisoner, and concealed himself till he might conveniently get away'.[70] King Dom Sebastian had reportedly been killed at the Battle of al-Qaṣr al-Kabīr in 1578. Winwood wrote to Neville in a letter dated 2 January 1601 that Sebastian had been released, deported from Venice and might be sent to England. Their correspondence about Sebastian continued into February. Thus Neville was concerned with an Orsino, Antonio and Sebastian just before Shakespeare's *Twelfth Night* was first performed.[71]

Of 1,273 words to be found in Neville's letter of 29 July 1600, 372 words (29 per cent) occur in *Twelfth Night*. The letter pre-dates *Twelfth Night*, although it may have been written when Neville was beginning work on the play. In this letter Neville used the word 'implacable' (which Shakespeare only ever used once and that was in this play) in the context of the threat posed to Elizabeth I by too close a relationship between the French king and the Pope:

> what cause of jealousy it giveth to the Queen, to see him combine himself so much more strictly with the Pope, then any of his Predecessors have done, <u>considering</u> how <u>implacable</u> an Enemy he is unto her.

In *Twelfth Night* the word occurs in a comic context of the threat posed by Sir Andrew Aguecheek to Viola (disguised as Cesario). Sir Toby Belch warns,

> He is knight, dubbed with unhatched rapier and on carpet <u>consideration</u>; but he is a devil in private brawl: souls and bodies hath he divorced three; and his incensement at this moment is so <u>implacable</u>, that satisfaction can be none but by pangs of death and sepulchre. (3.4.237)

In the letter there is the word 'considering' and in the play 'consideration' close by. See the Addendum at the end of this chapter for the list of individual words, pairs of words, phrases and near misses to be found in the play and in the letter.

Another Neville letter dated 19 February 1601, includes the word 'notoriously', which Shakespeare used twice, only in *Twelfth Night*. This letter, written as Neville hastened back to France following the Essex Rebellion, was composed after the first performances of *Twelfth Night*.[72] Neville was arrested in Dover after his involvement in the aborted uprising was revealed. In the play Malvolio complains, 'There never was a man so notoriously abused.' Malvolio is unjustly locked up in a dark room. Just after writing this letter Neville found himself likewise imprisoned and a darkness entered Shakespeare's plays.

So the happiest period of young Neville's career came to an end. This period was happy for Shakespeare too, although gathering shadows threatened the fun. Falstaff dies and Brutus fails, despite his honourable intentions. Neville now faced the greatest challenge of his life: surviving a coup d'état and a state prison. But before we enter this dark period we will look carefully at *The Merry Wives of Windsor* as a special test case for the Authorship Question.

Addendum

In Neville's letter of 29 July 1600 the following words occur that are to be found in *Twelfth Night* (capitals and italics in the original edition of the letters: Sawyer, 1725, Vol. 1).

Single Words

Our, Business, End, twice, already, yesterday, Ship, Truth, action, among, continue, Days, Queen, whither, induced, Town, case, refuse, chuse, cases, Countrey, courtesy, Presence, point, all, way, neither, think, yield, while, besides, first, directly, own, part, meet, now, send, unless, before, Notwithstanding, willing, conceived, otherwise, partly, reason, grown, time, place, next, Meeting, upon, Sides, withal, Breach, sooner, *War*, Opinion, new, well, turn, small, Assurance, finds, least, certain, Enemies, finds, Friends, take, occasion, conceived, cut, off, Trade, very, either, three, Months, therein, directly, Honour, Policy, Copy, Letter, lately, sent, meantime, best, solicit, Order, write, stay, Pleasure, further, known, therefore, instant, fair, manner, good, present, either, follow, Court, advise, about, matter, yourself, down, cause, need, promise, satisfy, pains, little, halting, Fellow, deal, Mind, constant, Nature, always, found, ready, find, bethink, means, build, Argument, King, thing, Alliance, jealousy, *himself*, implacable, observe, return, after, Speech, News, nothing, last, Count, from, before, Action, Strength, lately, slew, sent, Charges, else, Sir, dead, receive, letters, Friend.

Pairs of Words

here is, went away, my part, there be, it shall, which time, if the, will be, to enter, into the, some of, any other, sending into, of these, so that, to come, in question, like of, she is, she shall, Continuance of, I suppose, these two, *being in*, Point of, of Honor, hath been, all this, having been, *and then*, And for, I see, they will, therefore I, we are, to have, therefore I, to give, of late, the other, should be, for all, *you find*, you may, tell him, and Safety, to touch, late Arrest, the wrong, between the, let fall, the better, desire to, the first, make some, till the, may be, know what, hath made, seems to, for our, with him, Name is, have seen, come with, I wish, you should, with some, would I, *out of*, to embrace, with all, she may, of state, her will, As if, chance to, fall into, hard a, *see him*, to hold, much more, than any, have done, an Enemy, *unto he*, leave to, with her, from me, a Month, hear of, favour to, of mine.

Phrases of Three or Four Words

fit for the, with the same, the Opinion of, of your self, be drawn in, I pray you, in all these, you shall hear more, I pray you.

Near Misses

There are some significant near misses, for example: 'memorials' in *Twelfth Night* (the only instance in Shakespeare) instead of 'memorial' in Neville's letter; 'restraint' in the play instead of 'restraints' in the letter; 'commission' in the play instead of 'commissioners' in the letter: the only time Shakespeare used 'commissioners' was in *Henry V*.

In Neville's letter we find 'for my own part, I see no other way': in *Twelfth Night* we have 'my part' and 'no way'; in the letter, 'that partly', in the play, 'that I partly'; in the letter, 'so would I not' in the play, 'Would I or not'. Furthermore, in the letter there is 'you may ease yourself', in the play: 'you can separate yourself'; 'you do usurp yourself'; 'you must confine yourself'; 'you yourself were saved'.

In the letter there is, 'you may very seriously urge': this is echoed in the play by, 'You may have very fit occasion for't'. In the letter we find, 'the setting down'; in the play 'down' is used seven times, three of which are with the word 'set' (all in the second half of the play): 'set 'em down'; 'sets down'; 'I will set down'.

In the letter we find 'three or four Months', in play 'three months' is mentioned twice; in the letter there is 'ready to embrace', in the play 'apt to embrace'; in the letter, 'small assurance', in the play, 'modest assurance'. Looking at one sentence in the letter there is a close correspondence with words in the play:

> In both which cases, her Majesty sending into their Countrey, is of courtesy to have the *Preseance*, and so that point not to come in question at all. If she like of neither of these, she is to propose any other way that she shall think fit for the Continuance of the Treaty.

The words 'point' and 'presence' occur within ten lines in the play, indeed the word 'presence' occurs in a letter read out by Malvolio. Earlier in the play Viola says, 'You call in question the continuance of his love.'

Other rare words are used by Neville in this letter before Shakespeare used them: 'distasted' occurs in the letter and appears uniquely in *Troilus and Cressida* which dates from 1602. 'Remonstrance' is in the letter and Shakespeare used it just once in *Measure for Measure*, 1604. Likewise 'dependance' is only found in *Measure for Measure*. 'Pretending' is to be found in *Measure for Measure* and *Cymbeline*.

6

The Merry Wives of Windsor
A Test Case

Falstaff: Let the court of France show me such another.
The Merry Wives of Windsor, 3.3.48

When testing the hypothesis that Henry Neville was the author of the works of Shakespeare, *The Merry Wives of Windsor* is a very important play. The play is a unique work by Shakespeare. It is the only play that is set in an English town chosen by its author and not dictated by historical events or literary sources. It is also the only play whose characters mainly consist of ordinary English people rather than royalty and aristocrats. We now compare the evidence of the authorship for William Shakspere of Stratford-upon-Avon with that for Henry Neville of Billingbear near Windsor. In considering the authorship question there are several different but associated questions to address: how much did its author know of Windsor, especially as a locale for ordinary people apart from royalty; why should he have set a play there; and when and why was it written?

Windsor

That its author was thoroughly familiar with Windsor and its vicinity has been confirmed by scholars and researchers. As William Green put it in his *Shakespeare's Merry Wives of Windsor*:

Antiquarians have shown that Shakespeare depicts Windsor as it was in the 1590s. A Garter Inn had been located in High Street opposite the castle during the sixteenth and seventeenth centuries. The two points at which Caius and Evans await each other for their duel – Frogmore and the Fields – lay, as in the play, at opposite sides of the town (although the exact area of the Fields is somewhat in doubt). The route by which the servants carry Falstaff in the buck-basket from town through Datchet Mead to the Thames actually existed in Elizabethan Windsor. Even the topography of the park setting of the final scene accords with the Little Park as it was in Shakespeare's day. The castle ditch from which Page, Shallow and Slender are to watch the fairy lights; the pit from which the fairies are to rush upon Falstaff; and Herne's Oak all had actual counterparts to one another on the park grounds.[1]

According to Olwen Hedley, in her *Windsor Castle,* the play is:

> a comedy rich in local associations. Shakespeare was a member of the Royal Household and clearly knew Windsor well. He used familiar names for his principal characters. Those of Ford and Page are found in the sixteenth-century registers of Windsor Parish Church, and Master Fenton, who successfully courted 'sweet Anne Page', bore a name well known at Datchet. The action of the play is set in places near the Castle. Frogmore and Datchet Mead would have been known to everyone, from Sovereign to scullion; and when Simple looked 'pittie-ward' for Dr. Caius, the audience would have been at no loss. He was referring to the Field through which Queen Mary I's water pipes were laid. It was the known as Pitt's Field ... Shakespeare knew it as a pasture and recreation ground ... The Garter Inn, which stood almost at the corner of High Street and Peascod Street, facing Castle Hill, was another landmark as familiar to Queen Elizabeth as to Shakespeare ...[2]

Before proceeding, several points might be made about the claims in the quotation above. First, Shakspere was of course not 'a member of the Royal Household'. He was a member of a company of actors who performed chiefly at the Theatre and the Curtain in Shoreditch, and then, from 1599, at the Globe theatre on Bankside. He was also an increasingly prosperous property owner in Stratford. While from time to time the company performed before the Royal Court in London, although not at Windsor, Shakspere could in no sense accurately be described as a 'member of the Royal Court' until May 1603, when King James became his company's patron and it changed its name to The King's Men. *The Merry Wives* was certainly written before then: it was registered in the Stationers' Register in January 1602 and a quarto version of the play was published in the same year. Secondly, as we shall see, Queen Elizabeth did not habitually spend time in Windsor.

Time and again the playwright demonstrates obvious eyewitness acquaintance with the town of Windsor and its environs. As well as showing an intimate knowledge of Windsor, the play also displays further evidence of a direct knowledge of other areas in Berkshire when it refers to such places as 'Readins [Reading], Maidenhead, Colebrook [Colnbrook]' (4.5.74). At the time these were small towns or villages which were off the beaten track and not located near each other. Another important feature of the play is its author's knowledge of Herne the Hunter. Shakespeare was apparently the first to tell this story in print. Although it is often referred to as a traditional 'local legend', there are no written references to Herne the Hunter prior to the publication of *The Merry Wives.* Olwen Hedley stated that 'according to tradition handed down through generations of dwellers in Windsor Forest, Herne was wounded by a stag which he finally killed'.[3] Hedley noted that 'a manuscript of King Henry VIII's reign in the British Museum reveals that there was a Richard Horne [*sic*] who had confessed to poaching in His Majesty's forests'. However he was not specifically associated with Windsor. This manuscript only exists in an unpublished form and it was not recorded in any published source previous to the play.[4] In the first quarto edition of the play the spelling of Herne as 'Horne' occurs twice so there is a possibility that this story may be the source for Herne (the spelling in the First Folio), but then Neville as a royal forester and Justice of the Peace would be more likely to have access to such a legal manuscript than Shakspere from Stratford. *The Merry Wives* is quite specific about the legend, giving it a precise origin. Mistress Page tells us that

There is an old tale goes that Herne the Hunter,
Sometime a keeper here in Windsor forest,
Doth, all the winter-time, at still midnight,
Walk round about an oak, with great ragg'd horns;
And there he blasts the trees, and takes the cattle,
And makes milch-kine yield blood and shakes a chain
In a most hideous and dreadful manner. (4.4.25)

Neville and his father were keepers of the royal forest at Windsor and owners of milch-kine so would have known any such local story.[5]

The Case for William Shakspere as Author of *The Merry Wives of Windsor*

We now turn to the central issue: just how William Shakspere could have acquired such detailed local knowledge of a place where there is no evidence that he ever set foot. Perhaps he visited Windsor as a tourist or traveller? It is doubtful if there were tourists in the modern sense in Elizabethan times. Windsor is located about 25 miles (40 kilometres) from central London, inconveniently far to travel on a day trip on horseback, coach or via the river. After the local religious shrines of the murdered King Henry VI and an alleged fragment of the true cross held at Windsor were declared to be superstition by the Reformed Church, Windsor went into decline for many decades. 'The town began to stagnate about ten years after the Reformation [*c.* 1550] … Most accounts of Windsor in the 16th and 17th centuries talk of its poverty, badly made streets, and poor housing.'[6] Windsor is situated on the wrong side of the Thames for Shakspere to have passed through it going to or from Stratford-upon-Avon.

The most likely explanation for Shakspere's knowledge of the minutiae of Windsor and its environs is that he and his acting company performed there before the royal court, perhaps staying at the Garter Inn named in the play. By this plausible scenario, Shakspere (as was his wont, according to Stratfordian historians) gossiped in the local inn with the citizenry, picking up and storing facts about the town by clever conversations and by osmosis, in the same way he allegedly learned, by casual conversation with experts and eyewitnesses, about the geography of Italy, astronomy, medicine, and a dozen other subjects used in the plays. Quite possibly so, except for one inconvenient fact: from 1593 until August 1601, and with the exception of a few days in 1597 when she attended the Garter Knights' installation at which her cousin Lord Hunsdon was officially made a Knight of the Garter, Queen Elizabeth did not visit Windsor, apparently because 'the howse [Windsor Castle] be colde'.[7] Shakspere and his acting company thus never performed before the queen and her court at Windsor during this period, the only possible exception being at the Garter Installation of April 1597 when, according to Leslie Hotson (echoed by many subsequent writers), the play was premiered.

If there is no evidence that William Shakspere ever set foot in Windsor, let alone became familiar with the minor details of ordinary life there, how could he have included them in a play, and why would he? The answer to these questions is, plainly, that he couldn't and he wouldn't. Shakspere might well have written a similar play about Stratford-upon-Avon but not Windsor, of which he had no knowledge.[8]

The Case for Henry Neville as the Author

Contrast this with the life and career of Sir Henry Neville and, as always, the mystery vanishes. For much of his life, Neville lived at Billingbear Park, his country house, which was situated about 12 miles from Windsor. During the period from 1584 to 1589, and again in 1597, he was the Member of Parliament for New Windsor and, from 1604 until his death, Member of Parliament for Berkshire.[9] He was a Justice of the Peace for Berkshire from 1583; High Sheriff of Berkshire from 1594 to 1595; a Burgess of New Windsor in 1584; Bailiff of Crown Lands in Newbury; High Steward of Wokingham and Steward of the Royal Manors of Donnington and Sonning, all towns in Berkshire. In all probability, there was literally no one in the Elizabethan Establishment who was more familiar, by personal experience, with Windsor and its environs than Neville. The town of Windsor is mentioned twenty-two times in five plays. As Jiménez put it, 'Maybe "Shakespeare" was a Berkshire boy.'[10]

Billingbear Park, Neville's country house, was in the north-western portion of Binfield parish and Neville left money for the poor of Binfield in his will. Binfield, Berkshire, was at the very centre of Windsor Forest, which, as old maps make clear, was far more extensive then than today. The old inn that exists today at the spot marking the forest's centre, the Stag and Hounds, was then used as the royal hunting lodge and 'may originally have been the headquarters of the Royal Gamekeepers.'[11] The play contains references to the forest and Falstaff states, 'I am here a Windsor stag, and the fattest, I think, i'the forest … Am I a woodman, ha? Speak I like Herne the hunter?' (5.5.12, 27). Neville was a keen hunter. He went hunting in the Windsor forest with James I and served on a parliamentary committee on hawking and hunting. On 6 September 1612 Neville wrote a letter from Windsor stating that 'this tumultuary and uncertain attendance upon the King's sports affords me little time to write.'[12] Long before this in 1582, 1593 and 1603 documents at the Berkshire Record Office, Reading, show that Neville and his father were providing timber for Windsor Castle and concerned with a lease under the Dean and Canons of St George's Chapel, Windsor.[13]

At the start of the play Shallow tells Slender that he is 'Robert Shallow esquire' (1.1.3) and Slender elaborately labels him as a gentleman and 'Armigero' which Melchiori translates as 'esquire', while pointing out that Slender is incorrectly using an Italian rather than Latin form of the word. On the first page of a book dated 1538, about the Celestial Geometry of Ptolemy in Merton College library, Oxford, is a note, 'Ex do:[no] Henricj Nevilli armigeri de Pillingbear.'[14] On the first page of his volume of Cassius Dio's *Roman History* also at Merton we also find the word 'armigeri'.[15] This Latin word means 'entitled to bear heraldic arms', i.e. a gentleman or esquire. However 'armigeri' is deleted and 'Militis' inserted.

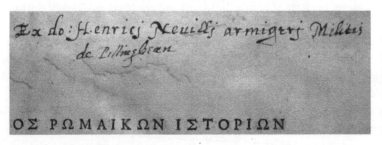

'From a gift of Henry Neville, gentleman, knight of Pillingbear'. (By permission of the Warden and Fellows of Merton College Oxford)

This deletion is presumably because Neville's status had been raised from an esquire to a knight, so the gift must have been made about 1598 or the note altered at or after that time. Neville knew both Latin and Italian so the sophisticated linguistic joke of Slender using the wrong word fits Neville but certainly not William from Stratford, who never signed himself 'armigeri', esquire or knight. In a Latin Bible at Audley End House Library, Neville also described himself as 'Militis': a knight or soldier. Neville was knighted before going to France as ambassador. He was responsible (like Falstaff in *Henry IV: Part II*) for mustering men. In 1596 he was Deputy Lieutenant for the county of Berkshire. In 1597 he was on parliamentary committees dealing with the 'Reformation of sundry abuses committed by soldiers' and the cost of 'having to maintain sundry sort of armour and weapons'.[16]

The Merry Wives of Windsor starts with Falstaff being accused by Shallow: 'Knight, you have beaten my men, killed my deer and broke open my lodge … The Council shall know this.' In response to Shallow's demand, 'This shall be answered', Falstaff replies, 'I will answer it straight: I have done all this' (1.1.104–110). After his father's death in 1593, Neville became embroiled in a legal property dispute with his stepmother, Elizabeth, *née* Bacon. She instituted a suit in the court of Chancery, accusing him of breaking into her manors, that he had 'chased and hunted' on her property and forced her tenants to acknowledge him as the owner.[17] Neville had seized all the documents so she could not go to the local courts and was obliged to apply direct to the chancellor. Neville answered the case by asserting his inheritance from his father. He also showed that he knew the law, by stating that the case was one of common law and had no place in Chancery. This is echoed in *The Merry Wives* when Evans states, 'It is not meet the Council hear a riot', referring to Shallow's demand that the (Privy) Council hear the case (1.1.32).

The only time Shakespeare used the word 'bucking' (meaning washing) was when Falstaff hides in the laundry basket (3.3.121). In the inventory of Sir Henry Neville's goods on his death in 1593 'two bucking tubbes' are listed.[18] Neville, as his son, would have overseen the preparation of this list.

Ford, speaking to Falstaff, suggests he use his art of wooing (2.2.224), which is possibly a reference to Ovid's *Ars Amatoria*. Neville had a copy of Ovid's *Ars Amatoria* in his library (see Chapter 3).

The Date and Occasion of the Play's Composition

For many years, virtually all scholars accepted the theory put by Leslie Hotson in 1931 that *The Merry Wives* was written as a royal entertainment for the feast held to accompany the Installation of Garter Knights at Windsor on 23 April 1597, when (among others) George Carey, 2nd Baron Hunsdon, who was also the Lord Chamberlain and the patron of Shakespeare's acting company, was officially admitted to the Order.[19] Given the play's many references both to Windsor and to the Order of the Garter, and Shakespeare's direct connection to Hunsdon in the latter's role as the company's patron, this theory seemed eminently plausible. In subsequent discussions of the play, Hotson's view was constantly reiterated, and so was generally accepted, as Elizabeth Schafer put it, 'because it had been repeated so many times'.[20] This theory was also given credence because of the well-known statements of John Dennis in 1702, and of Nicholas Rowe in 1709, that Queen Elizabeth directly commanded Shakespeare to write the play in order (in Rowe's famous words) 'to show [Falstaff] in love.'

In fact, the dating of the première of *The Merry Wives* to the Garter Installation in April 1597 is highly implausible and has recently been discarded by scholars. There is, first of all, not a shred of direct evidence that the play was performed at that Garter Installation (or at any other time in Windsor). There were eyewitnesses who gave written accounts of the ceremony, but none mentioned the play. Given its ribald, slapstick, facetious nature, a performance of *The Merry Wives* to accompany such a solemn, magnificent occasion as a Garter Installation might well have been scandalously inappropriate, and might have resulted in severe penalties being applied to Shakspere and his company. Apart from the statements written by Davies and Rowe over a century later, there is no evidence of any kind that the queen directed Shakespeare to write the play, let alone (as Davies claimed in 1702), in two weeks' time. This story appears to be no more than a romantic fiction created by subsequent generations.

Apart from these considerations, there is an even more important reason why the play must have been written sometime after 1597, namely, as Schafer and Melchiori have pointed out, that many of the characters in *The Merry Wives* associated with Falstaff must have already appeared in Shakespeare's plays to be familiar to the audience, especially both parts of *Henry IV* (usually dated to 1597–8) and possibly *Henry V* (generally dated to 1598–99).[21] April 1597 is thus simply too early to have been the première date of the play. (It is an interesting commentary on Shakespearean scholarship that no one spotted this obvious fact until Schafer's 1991 discussion in *Notes & Queries,* published sixty years after Hotson's book.) Moreover, *The Merry Wives* was not mentioned in Meres's famous 1598 list of Shakespeare's plays. The quarto edition of the play was entered into the Stationers' Register in 1602, making 1599 to 1601 the most likely period in which the work was premièred. Melchiori also noted that *The Merry Wives,* as it now exists, apparently contains a much briefer and more courtly masque-like component, far more appropriate for performance at a Garter Installation, which, in Melchiori's view, suggests that this section may have been performed at the 1597 installation, and the rest of the play written later.[22] Most recent scholars now agree that the play, certainly in its quarto form, was written after April 1597, between 1599 and 1600.

If the full play was actually written by Neville around 1599, it is easy to arrive at a likely set of circumstances which prompted him to write it. The play was his nostalgic, affectionate, humorous depiction of his home town and its environs written when he was ambassador to France, possibly in response to a request from the Lord Chamberlain's Men for another play about the enormously popular Falstaff. Shakespeare killed off Falstaff. His death is foretold at the end of *Henry IV: Part II* and mentioned in *Henry V.* These plays were written when Neville was taking up his post as ambassador, and if Falstaff was a sort of alter ego for Neville, he was perhaps proving his new seriousness of purpose to himself and to those in the know. However, he may have felt nostalgic for his old haunts because Shakespeare depicted Falstaff as a knight in retirement in Windsor and as a living contemporary rather than a historical figure. We know that Neville wanted to return home especially once he had become disillusioned with the role of ambassador. He had not wanted to take the role in the first place and so to suggest he was homesick is reasonable. In Paris, Neville may have been without many of the source books he had used, especially those concerning English history, and had to rely on his own imagination (as in *The Merry Wives*) or on works readily available in France, such as biographies of Julius Caesar. Most scholars now date Shakespeare's play to 1599 and, as we saw in Chapter 5, Neville may have taken his edition of Tacitus with him.

This apparent sequence of events seems far more plausible than that William Shakspere, in all likelihood a total stranger to Windsor and its neighbourhood, had anything to do with writing the play. Furthermore there are numerous references to France in the play which indicate that the writer was interested in the country. As with *Henry V*, written in the same year, Shakespeare not only wrote a French character into the play (Dr Caius) but also included lines in French. Falstaff declares, 'Let the court of France show me such another!' (3.3.48). Neville at the time was indeed at the French court! Falstaff, being impecunious, proclaims that he will 'learn the humour of this age: French thrift …' (1.3.80). While in France, Neville had found that the French government was unwilling to pay its debt to Elizabeth I, so this joke, previously unexplained, makes sense when we posit Neville as the author.

Evidence for this dating occurs in Neville's letters of the period. In his letters of 1599 Neville used a number of words that Shakespeare only used once, in *The Merry Wives of Windsor*. These hapax legomena are: 27 June 1599: 'decipher';[23] 1 August 1599: 'Canaries';[24] 11 October 1599: 'fidelity' (used again by Neville in a letter dated 20 March 1600).[25]

Furthermore in his letters Neville used vocabulary that also occurs in *The Merry Wives of Windsor* and other Shakespeare plays. For example on 15 May 1599 Neville wrote the compound word 'well-nigh', which Shakespeare only used in *The Merry Wives of Windsor* and *Much Ado About Nothing* (dated 1598–99).[26] In this letter he also used the word 'intention', which only occurs in *The Merry Wives of Windsor* and *The Winter's Tale*. Thus we can see that between May and October 1599 Neville was using rare words that occur in the play.

Two Poems of 1599–1600

In 1600 Neville wrote a little poem that relates to the themes of *The Merry Wives of Windsor*. Inside the cover of a book he once owned there is a poem written by Neville in his own hand on a piece of parchment:

> The man is blest that lives in rest
> and soe kan kepe him still
> But he is curst that was the first
> that gave his wife her will
> By me Henrie Neuill
> which is a verie true sentence

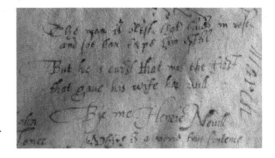

Rodolpho Gualtero Tigurino's 1554 *Argumenta*.
(Private collection)

This poem shows that Neville:

1. Could write a poem;
2. could rhyme;
3. had a sense of rhythm: the lines are regular iambs alternating four and three stresses;
4. had a sense of humour;
5. used Shakespeare's characteristic antithesis (blest/curst). The words 'curst' and 'bless'd/blessed' occur in *The Taming of the Shrew*, a play whose central theme is the relationship between a man and his wife and the struggle for control between them; Shakespeare had used the words 'cursed-blessed fortune' in *The Rape of Lucrece* (stanza 124) in 1594 and used the word 'blest' fifty-one times. Neville's little poem echoes Boyet in *Love's Labour's Lost* who says:

> Do not <u>curst</u> wives hold that self-sovereignty
> Only for praise sake, when they strive to be
> Lords o'er their lords? (4.1.36)

In *The Merry Wives of Windsor* the words 'cursed' and 'blest' both occur in the final scene, the first word being especially concerned with marriage.

6. The theme of women and their assertiveness and the impact of this on their husbands interested Shakespeare as a source of fun and comment. This is especially true in *The Merry Wives of Windsor*. Neville had witnessed such an assertive woman in his stepmother: his father wrote about her that 'Betty doth wear the breeches', suggesting it was his third wife who was in fact in charge.[27]
7. Neville used alliteration: 'can', 'keep', 'curst'. In *The Merry Wives of Windsor* Falstaff also uses the words 'can' and 'keep' in the same order: 'it is as much as I <u>can</u> do to <u>keep</u> the terms of my honour precise' (2.2.21). The words 'can keep' occur together in *Twelfth Night* and *Hamlet*, both written 1600–1. Hamlet twice uses three similarly alliterated words saying, 'the players cannot keep counsel' (3.2.137) and 'I can keep your counsel' (4.2.10).
8. Is there a pun on the final word 'will'? Shakespeare puns on 'will' in a sexual sense. This is especially evident in sonnets 135 and 136. Pistol uses the same pun in *The Merry Wives of Windsor* (1.3.46).[28] In these sonnets and perhaps in Neville's little poem, which concludes with a statement of authorship, there may also be a pun on William (= I am Will)! The way the poem is written makes the juxtaposition of 'will' and the 'vill' of 'Nevill' just below very obvious. When we turn to sonnets 135 and 136 we see Shakespeare rhyming 'will' and 'still', as in Neville's poem; indeed Shakespeare often rhymes these words, including in *Venus and Adonis*:

> He kisses her; and she, by her good <u>will</u>,
> <u>Will</u> never rise, so he <u>will</u> kiss her <u>still</u>. (Stanza 78)

Both sonnets contain the name Nevill: sonnet 135, twice, has 'One will' which spells out 'O nevvill'. The last line of sonnet 136 spells out 'Henry Nevvill': And <u>then</u> thou louest me for <u>my name</u> is <u>Will</u>.[29]

9. There is also a half-hidden Biblical reference to Adam (the first man) and Eve: 'he is curst that was <u>the first</u> that gave his wife her will'. Shakespeare refers to Adam and Eve

in a number of plays. In *Henry IV: Part I*, written 1596–7, Falstaff compares himself to Adam: 'Dost thou hear, Hal? thou knowest in the state of innocency Adam fell; and what should poor Jack Falstaff do in the days of villany?' (3.3.165). Benedick in *Much Ado About Nothing* says of Beatrice:

> I would not marry her, though she were endowed with all that <u>Adam</u> had left him before he transgressed: she would have made Hercules have turned spit, yea, and have cleft his club to make the fire too. Come, talk not of her: you shall find her the infernal Ate in good apparel. I would to God some scholar would conjure her; for certainly, while she is here, <u>a man may live as quiet</u> in hell as in a sanctuary; and people sin upon purpose, because they would go thither; so, indeed, all disquiet, horror and perturbation follows her. (2.1.234)

Benedick's 'a man may live as quiet' compares with the opening line of Neville's poem, 'The man is blest that lives in rest'. *Much Ado About Nothing* was written in 1598–9 and published in 1600: the little poem therefore is exactly contemporary and includes similar sentiments as to whether a man can live a quiet life ('live in rest' in the poem) with a strong-minded woman. The date of 20 March 1599 is to be found on the back cover of Tigurino's *Argumenta*, where Neville's handwriting is also preserved:

Henrie
Neuill
with my
Hand
at Paris the twintth
of march 1599 william
garrard y..
his adge 24
years

Rodolpho Gualtero Tigurino's 1554 *Argumenta*.

As the year ended on 24 March in the old calendar, this date was actually 1600. Neville had arrived in Paris in May 1599. Neville names William Garrard and states his age as twenty-four. This is likely to be the son of William Garrard who contributed funds to the building of Sir Thomas Gresham's Royal Exchange.[30] Gresham was Neville's maternal uncle and he had inherited his fortune. It seems young William had accompanied Neville on his ambassadorship or met him in Paris. This little poem looks like a spontaneous bit of fun and Neville felt safe to put his name on it because he was in Paris. The same day the poem was written, 20 March 1600, Neville wrote a long diplomatic letter to Cecil.[31] This proves that Neville had the capacity both to act as a diplomat and to write comic poetry. This is confirmed by a Latin poem written that very year (see below).

Just a month later Neville wrote in a diplomatic letter dated 27 April 1600 about meeting the 'Ambassador of Wirttenberg'.[32] Here is a further example of how a mystery in the text of *The Merry Wives of Windsor* can be solved when we put Neville as author into the picture. In the play there is a half-hidden joke about horse-stealing Germans in Act 4, Scene 3 and Act 4, Scene 5. This may refer to Frederick I, Duke of Württemburg, who had visited Windsor in 1592 and was elected to the Order of the Garter in 1597. His surname, Mompelgard, is punned upon as 'Cozen-Garmombles' in the 1602 quarto (4.5.73). We can therefore see that Neville was in an excellent position to make covert references to European political figures in a play about a foolish knight in pursuit of the women of Windsor. Frederick was eventually installed in the Order of the Garter at Stuttgart on 6 November 1603. This was after Neville had been released from the Tower. There is, however, another possible interpretation of the horse-stealing incident which implicates a Monsieur de Chastes who, in 1596, stole horses in his rush to tell the French king he had been elected to the Order of the Garter.[33] In either case, Neville, as ambassador to France, was well placed to know these stories.

Another Poem of 1599–1600

In 1600 a book was published in Paris by John Chamber. It was a Latin translation of the Greek writings of Barlaam, a mathematician (*c.* 1290–1348). The original manuscript had been found by Savile and Neville during their European travels and given to Chamber to work on. At the start of the volume this is acknowledged in a Latin poem by Chamber, praising Neville (what follows is our translation):[34]

> TO THE MOST DISTINGUISHED MAN, THE LORD HENRY NEVILLE,
> AMBASSADOR OF THE MOST SERENE QUEEN ELIZABETH
> TO THE KING OF FRANCE.

> You may count your family and ancestors in long succession, so that kings' high courts grant you access. Yet nothing in such great good fortune is so greatly deserving as the honourable quality of your character and the glory of your genius.

> It is with these qualities that you manage all your royal duties and conduct such high negotiations; and in the same spirit, leaving the earth behind, you joyfully enter the realm of the stars.

> Joyfully you go to the stars, where your many faceted qualities make you immortal and admit you amongst the gods before your time.

> Too little is your excellence seen by the common people of the Earth, were it not for the kindly company of the Muses who sing through you, granting you various arts: the refined Muse of Comedy[35] giving you the eloquence[36] to pour forth <u>what you Will</u>.[37]

> Euclid teaches you, revealing origins and first principles, and the ancient Egyptian, Pelusiachan[38] Ptolemy, leads you to the stars. Not content with this you make it your practice to raise the ghost and stir up the buried ashes of Barlaam the Monk!

> I do not now remind you how often you have asked me, please, submit his writings to the printing press.

> So, look, see! For you at last, the Monk's writings now in print, giving voice again to the teacher's learned words.

For had not Savile been earlier in his praise, Barlaam would now be indebted to you for his ransom from oblivion.

And now through your promptings and equally your requests, the man's Muse survives who otherwise was about to be lost.

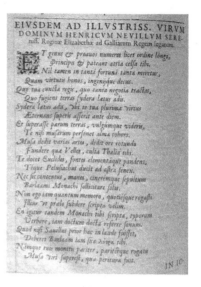

John Chamber's poem addressed to Neville, 1600. (Private collection)

For some reason Chamber has used a capital V on 'Velles': perhaps he is making this word, meaning 'You Will' into a name? *What You Will* is the subtitle of *Twelfth Night*, written the same year that Chamber's poem was published. We are not suggesting Chamber knew the play, which had not been written in 1599 when he must have composed the poem. He is however perhaps punning on the name Will, safely transposed into Latin. There may also be a pun on the Neville family motto 'Ne Vile Velis': Wish nothing vile. Velles is close to Velis. We suggest that Chamber is pointing to Neville's authorship because of the reference to Thalia, the comic Muse, in the poem: by 1599 Shakespeare-Neville had written eight comedies. When, in 1603, George Carleton published *Heroici Charactères,* written in Latin verse, he dedicated it 'Ad Illustrissimum Equitem, Henricum Nevillum', ('To the Most Distinguished Knight, Henry Neville') and referred in his opening poem to Tragedy.[39] By 1603 Shakespeare had written five tragedies. Carleton knew John Chamber. In the 1600 Barlaam volume Carleton had contributed a dedication poem on the page facing Chamber's poem to Neville. In his 1603 *Heroici Charactères* poem, like Chamber, Carleton referred to the Muses. He also exhorted Neville to 'grasp firmly the rewards of your achievements, you who will have the Muses to bear witness to you, and your unspotted excellence to guide you'.[40] These two Latin poems both praise Neville, refering to the Muses and to the theatre of comedy and tragedy.

Unsurprisingly there is a copy of Chamber's volume of Barlaam's mathematical treatise in Neville's library. On the first page an extra piece of paper has been glued with a dedicatory message: 'En tibi, grande decus, rerum columénque mearum, Mentis & oficij pignora plena pij'. This translated states: 'Here, for you, mighty pride and pillar of my estate, is a full pledge of my intent and sacred duty'.[41]

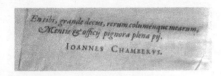

John Chamber's dedicatory note to Neville, 1600.

Neville would have recognised the quotation from Horace, Odes Book 2, Ode 17, lines 3–4 ('grande decus, rerum columénque mearum'). Horace was addressing Maecenas, who was patron to both Horace and Virgil. There is an annotated volume of Horace's poetry in Neville's library (see Chapter 7).

Luces, Lucy, the Fishmongers and Gardiner

Another significant matter that bears directly on the authorship question is the apparent reference to Sir Thomas Lucy (1532–1600) near the beginning of the play.

> Slender: All his successors – gone before him – hath done't; and all his ancestors – that come after him – may. They may give the dozen white luces in their coat.
> Shallow: It is an old coat.
> Evans: The dozen white louses do become an old coat well. It agrees well passant. It is a familiar beast to man, and signifies love.
> Shallow: The luce is the fresh fish – the salt fish is an old coat. (1.1.11–20)

'Luce' (a pike, the freshwater fish) is apparently pronounced something like 'lucy', or (on some readings) like 'louses'. Three (*not* twelve) silver luces (heraldic depictions of the pike fish) are found on the coat of arms of the Lucy family of Charlecote, near Stratford-upon-Avon. A romantic story of Shakspere poaching deer on Lucy land was thought to be the original incident behind Shallow's accusations against Falstaff: 'knight, you have beaten my men, killed my deer and broken open my lodge' (1.1.103). Although the two passages are often linked by Stratfordian biographers, they have no obvious connection and are not adjacent to each other in the play. The latter lines have no mention of 'luces'. We have already shown the connection between Henry Neville and the deer killing incident. These two extracts, generally taken together, have, countless times, been associated with the well-known claim about the youthful William Shakspere. First written down by Revd Richard Davies sometime between 1688 (at the earliest) and his death in 1708, we are told that young Shakspere stole venison and rabbits from Sir Thomas Lucy (and others) who 'had him oft whipt [*sic*] and sometimes imprisoned'. Shakspere apparently got his revenge in the 'allusion to his name' which 'bore three louses [*sic*] rampant for his arms' in *The Merry Wives of Windsor*. This claim was repeated and expanded in 1709 by Nicholas Rowe, Shakspere's first biographer, who stated that Shakspere 'more than once' stole deer from 'a Park that belong'd to Sir Thomas Lucy of Charlecote', for which he was prosecuted by Lucy. In revenge, Shakspere 'made a Ballad upon him' which was so bitter that it resulted in a further prosecution, driving Shakspere to leave Stratford for London and eventual immortal fame as a writer. This must have occurred when Shakspere was around nineteen or twenty years old, in 1583 or 1584, but was not recorded in print in any source for a minimum of 104 years and possibly not for 125 years.[42] Despite its total lack of contemporary documentation, this story has generally been accepted as authentic by the majority of Shakespeare's biographers, who need a good reason why the young Bard should have left Stratford, possibly in a great hurry, and migrated to the capital.

In considering the Sir Thomas Lucy story, it is important to keep in mind that there are two separate questions to consider: do the lines in *The Merry Wives* cited above actually relate to Sir Thomas Lucy, and did Shakspere actually poach Lucy's deer, resulting in his fleeing to London? (Since we take the view that Shakspere did not write the works attributed to him, these points are simply academic, but are well worth considering carefully because of what such a review of the evidence reveals.) Lucy was Member of Parliament for Warwickshire from 1559 until 1586, and so has an entry in *The History of Parliament: The House of Commons*, the multi-volume biographical dictionary of all persons who have served as Members of Parliament, beginning in the Middle Ages. It is researched and written by academic historians, who have little time for unsubstantiated and apocryphal tales first written down more than a century after they allegedly occurred, and has this to say in the concluding portion of its entry on Lucy:

> Lucy acquired a dubious posthumous notoriety as the villain in the story of Shakespeare's deer stealing. The authenticity of this episode, first popularised by Aubrey nearly a century after Shakespeare's death, has long been a subject of controversy. The description of Shallow's arms in Act I, Scene I of *The Merry Wives of Windsor* has been adduced as supporting evidence of Shakespeare's animosity to the Lucy family, although the quotation could equally refer to the arms of the Fishmongers' Company, and a recent author has claimed that Shallow was a caricature of William Gardiner. As this scene is missing from the defective quarto [of 1602], it is not impossible that if the remark refers to a Lucy at all, it might be an allusion to the suit about poaching brought by this Member's grandson. Even if early, the statement 'come from Gloucestershire' applies more readily to this Member's son, who in his father's lifetime lived on his first wife's Gloucester estates.[43]

The reference here to 'the suit brought by this Member's grandson' refers to a Star Chamber prosecution brought by another Sir Thomas Lucy, the better-known man's grandson, on 27 June 1610, against three deer poachers in Warwickshire, William Wall, Rowland Harnage, and Edward Bennett.[44] While there is no written evidence of any kind that the elder Sir Thomas Lucy brought a lawsuit for poaching against William Shakspere, or that Shakspere was ever 'whipt and sometimes imprisoned', something for which written evidence could have survived the centuries in legal records, in contrast there is written evidence that Lucy's grandson did launch a prosecution for poaching. This Sir Thomas Lucy (1585–1640) bore an identical name and title as his grandfather, was also a long-serving Member of Parliament for Warwickshire, and brought this prosecution in 1610, when Shakspere was still alive (and probably living mainly in Stratford-upon-Avon) and less than thirty years after Shakspere's alleged run-in with his grandfather. Given the complete absence of written evidence about the earlier alleged prosecution, it seems plausible that local gossip had somehow attached it to Shakespeare and the earlier Lucy, possibly because the lines in the play had already become well known and required an explanation of some kind.

More basically, there is also the question of whether *The Merry Wives* actually refers to Sir Thomas Lucy at all. As the *History of Parliament* entry notes, this could well be a reference to the Worshipful Company of Fishmongers. This is a City of London livery company founded in 1272, whose coat of arms has on it, among other things, three fish. An apparently pointless reference to fish is just the kind of irrational, punning, stream-of-consciousness humour that its author presented throughout *The Merry Wives*, somewhat like a twentieth-century Marx Brothers film or a play by Samuel Beckett. There is, moreover, a distant connection between Neville and this livery company. Since 1555 the Fishmongers' Company has acted as the Trustee of Gresham's School in Holt, Norfolk, which was founded by Neville's relative Sir Thomas Gresham.

The other possibility suggested above is that the reference is not to Sir Thomas Lucy, but to William Gardiner, whose coat of arms also had three fish on it. The case for Gardiner was first put by Leslie Hotson in 1931 in his book *Shakespeare versus Shallow*. Hotson found a document in the rolls of the Queen's Bench in London from November 1596, in which one William Wayte 'craved sureties of peace' against 'William Shakspere, Francis Langley, and two women.'[45] Three weeks later, Langley in response was 'crav[ing] sureties of peace against William Gardener [sic] and William Wayte'. Langley (1550–1601) was the builder of the Swan Theatre on Bankside, and these procedures appear to have been some kind of feud over property rights. Hotson also found that Gardiner was a remarkably unpleasant and dangerous character, universally despised, whose career he described as 'a tissue of greed, fraud, cruelty, and perjury', and speculated that these lawsuits led to Shakespeare ridiculing him in *The Merry Wives*.[46] Hotson, however, was unaware that William Gardiner (1531–97), as remarkable as this may seem, was also a Member of Parliament, sitting for Lostwithiel in Cornwall from 1589 to 1593, and for Helston in Cornwall from 1593 until his death in October 1597.[47] Again, most remarkably, one of the patrons for both seats was none other than Sir Henry Killigrew, Neville's father-in-law.[48] Moreover – the coincidences multiply – Neville himself was from 1597 until 1601 Member of Parliament for Liskeard, Cornwall, a nearby seat in the remote county, although apparently he obtained this seat through the influence of the Trelawny family, the local magnates.[49] Neville was the Member of Parliament for Mid-Sussex from 1589 to 1597, while Gardiner served as High Sheriff for Surrey and Sussex from 1594 to 1595. Neville must therefore almost certainly have known Gardiner and encountered him in various guises many times. If Gardiner was the intended target of the 'luces' references in *The Merry Wives*, this may have been meant either sarcastically or even affectionately: it is difficult to tell.

If the pun on 'luces' was a contemporary satiric reference it is sufficiently cryptic to ensure that only those whom it was intended to hit would recognise it. So successful was this disguising that we cannot now say for sure what it refers to. One thing is clear from this exploration of the Luce/Lucy material: it cannot be said for certain to refer to an apocryphal story about young William Shakspere's poaching in the woods around Stratford. Armstrong dismissed the story, stating, 'Shakespeare's deer-stealing is a manifest fiction – Sir Thomas Lucy had no deer park at Charlecote when Shakespeare was a boy.'[50]

Conclusion

Whereas there is no evidence for William Shakspere being the author of *The Merry Wives of Windsor*, there is much circumstantial evidence for Henry Neville's authorship, not least his home being near Windsor and his authorship of a comic poem, dated 1599, about assertive wives.

Neville in the Tower
1601–1603

Forfeit to a confined doom.

Sonnet 107

Hamlet, The Phoenix and the Turtle, Othello and *Troilus and Cressida*

In the middle of 1600, Neville was at last given permission to return to England from France, where he had served as ambassador since May 1599. Neville arrived in Dover on 2 August and, as previously noted, was in London on 6 August. On 4 August 1600 there appeared in the Stationers' Register a listing of four plays 'to be staid': *As You Like It, Henry V, Much Ado About Nothing* and Ben Jonson's *Every Man in His Humour.* Why this listing appeared, on whose instructions, and for what purpose has been much debated. The normal interpretation is that these were registered either by the Lord Chamberlain's Men or by Shakespeare himself to forestall piracy. One possibility is that once Neville knew he would soon be returning to England, he sent word to the Lord Chamberlain's Men, or through other channels, to register these plays, which he had brought with him or previously sent across. Another possibility, given his role later in the First Folio, is that Ben Jonson acted in some capacity on Neville's behalf. We do not know. The timing may be simply coincidence or, we suggest, further circumstantial evidence for Neville's authorship of these plays.

The Essex Rebellion

Neville was now at the peak of his reputation as a successful, well-connected, rising and trusted court insider and appointee, destined in all likelihood for high office and for a possible restoration of the Neville family to its leading historical role in the governance of England. Within months, however, all of these high hopes and expectations had crumbled to dust. Neville had become a convicted traitor, confined to the Tower of London. Struggling to pay an enormous fine and stripped of his knighthood, he was lucky to have his head still attached to his shoulders and had no prospects of holding further government office of any kind.

Sir Henry Neville Was Shakespeare

This traumatic catastrophe occurred because Neville became involved in the Essex rebellion. Robert Devereux, 2nd Earl of Essex (1565–1601), was a charismatic nobleman, a favourite of Queen Elizabeth, and a general with a widely admired military reputation which may or may not have been deserved. His maternal great-grandmother was Anne Boleyn's sister, so he was a relative of the queen. His enemies (and others) believed that he himself had designs on becoming king. This possibility may seem far-fetched to us, but at the time few would have forgotten that Henry Tudor, Earl of Richmond, with only a remote claim to the English throne, had successfully seized power and become Henry VII a century earlier. The strength of this view was fanned by the fact that Queen Elizabeth had no clear-cut heir and it was not by any means clear that James VI of Scotland would in fact succeed her as James I of England. Open discussion of the succession to the throne was illegal. Essex was a cultured man, a patron of the arts and of poets, a poet himself, and a royal favourite.[1] His father had died young, probably of dysentery, in 1576 (though many believed he had been poisoned). In 1599 Essex was sent to Ireland as Lord Lieutenant, but failed in his mission to suppress the rising led by Hugh O'Neill, Earl of Tyrone. Essex then had a spectacular falling out with the queen, and lost his monopoly of sweet wines, a lucrative sinecure and his main source of income. He was now poor and rather desperate, but still generally regarded as a charismatic figure who would become extremely powerful when the old queen died, either in his own right or as a dominant figure if James VI of Scotland (with whom he was probably in secret negotiations) came to the throne. Essex was, in particular, disliked and feared by the Cecils: William Cecil, Lord Burghley (1520–98), Lord High Treasurer, and his son Robert Cecil (1563–1612), Secretary of State, the chief ministers of England, who had given the country stable government for decades.

Essex had gathered around him a diverse group of his supporters from varying points of the Elizabethan political compass: disaffected noblemen; intellectuals, especially those associated with Henry Savile, Neville's Oxford tutor; strong Protestants who feared a Catholic succession upon the queen's death; Catholics who thought that Essex might end their persecution; some City merchants; advocates of a strong military and foreign policy; and virtually everyone disaffected by the Cecil family's political domination. These groups had little in common apart from their status as outsiders or their unsatisfied ambitions. Early in February 1601 Essex and his supporters met (Neville was not present at this meeting) and decided to launch an insurrection in the City of London ostensibly designed to secure a Protestant successor to Queen Elizabeth. This poorly conceived revolt quickly petered out. Essex and his key supporters were arrested. On 19 February 1601 Essex and Southampton were tried for treason by a jury of peers in the House of Lords. Edward de Vere, 17th Earl of Oxford, was the jury foreman and Francis Bacon was a prosecuting barrister. Found guilty, Essex was beheaded on 25 February 1601. His supporters, Sir Christopher Blount, Sir Gelly Meyrick, Sir Charles Danvers and Henry Cuffe, were also executed. The life of the Earl of Southampton, one of Essex's most prominent supporters, was spared, but he was stripped of his titles (for the next two years he was known as plain 'Mr Henry Wriothesley') and sent to the Tower of London for an indefinite period. Essex and the rebellion he fomented polarised late Elizabethan politics, deeply dividing both the Elizabethan elite and the common people. It is also evidence that much of late Elizabethan England had turned against the old queen by the closing years of her long reign, her goddess-like reputation as 'Gloriana' being sorely tested. In particular, many in the elite wanted a definite assurance of a Protestant successor, which Elizabeth had pointedly declined to provide until she was literally on her deathbed, when at last she signalled that James was to succeed her.

There were several reasons why Neville would have been drawn to Essex. There are also good reasons why he would wish to keep his distance from this charismatic nobleman and his movement. It seems likely that Neville was attracted to the personality of Essex in the 1590s. Neville had a long association with pro-Essex intellectuals like Sir Henry Savile and Henry Cuffe (Essex's secretary). However there were many reasons why he would not wish to join the Essex faction. His status as a relatively young, admired, rising Member of Parliament and diplomat, plainly marked out for higher things, would be in grave danger if the rebellion failed. Neville's ambivalence is evident in his Delphic response to Southampton's invitation to join the planned invasion of the court to confront the queen with Essex's demands. Neville cited Tacitus, 'non laudantur nisi peracta', namely that 'the effort would be judged by its success'.[2] Neville owed much to the pro-Cecil faction, especially to his father-in-law Sir Henry Killigrew, and he was also a cousin of Robert Cecil.

When Neville arrived back in London on 6 August 1600, he found a note from Henry Cuffe (*c.* 1562–1601), waiting for him, requesting a meeting. Cuffe, a contemporary of Neville, was an old friend whose career had in some respects run parallel to Neville's own.[3] Cuffe had entered Trinity College, Oxford in 1578, where he was noted for his great ability in Greek. He then progressed to Merton College, becoming, like Neville, a protegé of Henry Savile. He was made a Fellow of Merton College in 1586, and, from 1590 until 1597, was Regius Professor of Greek at Oxford. He was also a friend of Southampton. Through Savile, he became close to the Earl of Essex and, from 1595, was his principal secretary and arguably his most important adviser, a hardliner who wanted Essex to seize power.[4] He accompanied Essex on his military expeditions to Cadiz and Ireland and, in 1600, produced the manuscript of his only book, *The Differences of the Ages of Man's Life.* In 1592 he participated in a debate that was presided over by Savile and attended by the queen herself at Merton College on the incendiary topic of 'the usefulness of civil dissent to the state'.[5]

After receiving Cuffe's note, Neville prevaricated, visiting his estate at Billingbear and spending time in London. Finally in late October 1600 Neville held a meeting with Essex at his house in London. Neville left by the back gate and kept the meeting a secret.[6] He subsequently had several meetings with Cuffe.[7] On 2 February 1601 he attended a formal meeting with Essex's key associates at Drury House in London. At these meetings, it was hinted to him that, should Essex come to power, Neville would be made Secretary of State in place of Robert Cecil.[8] Neville again met with Cuffe a day or two later, on 3 or 4 February 1601. On 7 February 1601, five days after Neville's meeting with the Essex conspirators, the famous performance of *Richard II* took place at the Globe Theatre. Its performance at this time has long been regarded as inexplicable: who had come up with this idea? *Richard II* concerns the justifiable deposition of an English king. If Neville was indeed its author, it is possible that it was he who suggested performing one of his own plays as a way of rousing sympathy for Essex and his cause.[9] If he were not its author, this sequence of events remains baffling. The Essex circle had no obvious links with the Lord Chamberlain's Men, and it is unlikely that the idea of performing a play written in 1595, which the actors said was 'so old and so long out of use', would have occurred to anyone associated with Essex besides its author.

Essex's rebellion took place in London on 8 February 1601. It was a complete failure, leading to the arrest of Essex, Southampton, and their key supporters including Cuffe. Following his trial on 19 February 1601 Essex, backed by Southampton, made a frank confession, naming those who had assisted the conspirators, including Sir Henry Neville, 'whom no man did suspect.'[10] Shortly after the rebellion, Neville hastened to return to his role as ambassador to France. He had reached Dover when the warrant for his arrest for treason reached the authorities there. Neville 'leaped to his horse and, abandoning his wife, his children, and his servants, rode off to court with … two men in pursuit.'[11] In London, Neville was placed under arrest at the Lord Admiral's House in Chelsea, where he wrote accounts of his actions for the authorities which comprehensively minimised the already minor role he had played in the rebellion. His father-in-law, Sir Henry Killigrew, an influential court figure was so enraged that 'he would not permit' Lady Neville (his daughter) 'in his house' until ordered to do so by the Privy Council.[12] In May 1601 Neville was sent to the Tower of London where he was ordered to stay until he had paid an enormous fine of £10,000, the equivalent of perhaps £10 million today. He had been extremely lucky to escape with his life. By negotiating with Cecil, his kinsman by marriage, Neville managed to reduce the original fine by half, to be paid in annual instalments of £1,000. Neville was thus doomed to remain in the Tower for five years. He had already spent £3,000 of his own money to finance his role as ambassador to France. The role was largely unfunded and, although in letters Neville asked for adequate expenses to be reimbursed, it seems he was disappointed by Cecil's replies. The queen was notoriously parsimonious. His financial situation was greatly reduced and he spent much of the rest of his life attempting to recoup his losses. Neville was also stripped of his knighthood, his ambassadorship, and, of course, any prospect of further appointment to high office. The only person with whom he could immediately share his burden was his fellow prisoner the Earl of Southampton, who had initially been sentenced to death but had had his sentence commuted to life imprisonment in the Tower. After they were released, they became political associates.

Another man drawn into the rebellion, Thomas Smyth (later Sir Thomas, *c.* 1558–1625), at the time Sheriff of London, and later head of the Second London Virginia Company and the grandfather of Neville's eldest son's wife, was also sent to the Tower for assisting Essex, but was soon released.

Shakespeare's Tragic Period

We now turn to examine the Shakespeare works written during this time, and consider the evidence for Neville's authorship.

Essex's rebellion had a profoundly traumatic effect upon Neville, marking a dividing line in his career, indeed in his life. He was never the same man again. The smile was erased from his face, certainly for years to come. It is, however, an ill wind which blows no one any good, for what was a catastrophic misfortune for Henry Neville proved to be a profoundly beneficent occurrence for humanity and for Western culture. The period of the Essex rebellion transformed William Shakespeare from an outstanding late Elizabethan playwright and poet into the greatest writer in the English language, an author whose peers in history include only Homer, Virgil, Dante and Goethe, if indeed he does not stand supreme. For it was only then, in 1601, that Shakespeare began to write his great tragedies, starting with *Hamlet* and *Othello,* and continuing with *Macbeth* and *King Lear.* That 1601 marked a dramatic transformation in Shakespeare's writings has been agreed by virtually all commentators since it was first proposed by Edward Dowden in 1875 in his *Shakspere [sic]: A Critical Study of His Mind and Art,* which is a work of the greatest importance when attempting to understand Shakespeare's career in a realistic way.[13] Dowden's chapter on 1601 is entitled 'The Revolution in Shakespeare's Soul: The Growing Melancholy of the Following Period - Pessimism, Misanthropy'.[14] '[T]he time is now approaching,' Dowden wrote of the great break of 1601, 'when mirth, and even the joy of life, are extinguished in his soul. We can only divine what gnawing sorrows and disappointments have beset him; we observe its changing expressions, without knowing its causes'.[15] With Neville identified as the Bard we can do better than that, and provide actual reasons.

Shakspere's Contented Life in Stratford

Before examining the works produced when Neville was imprisoned, it is worth considering the known life of William Shakspere as it relates to the great change in the Bard's output which began in 1601. What happened to the Stratford man in 1601 that would cause 'the revolution in Shakespeare's soul'? Orthodox commentators have proposed two possible causes: the death of Shakspere's son Hamnet in August 1596, and the death of his father John in September 1601. Both suggestions are implausible: there was a five-year gap between the death of Hamnet Shakspere and the Bard's *Hamlet,* almost certainly the first play written (or substantially revised) after the revolution in Shakespeare's soul. As was pointed out many years ago, during this five-year interval Shakespeare wrote the Falstaff plays, as well, in all likelihood, as *Twelfth Night,* with Sir Toby Belch. This hardly sounds like deep grief for his son. As to the death of Shakspere's father, in 1601 William Shakspere was thirty-seven, an established man of property and (ostensibly) a well-known author. There is no reason to suppose that he was close to his father. He did not follow in his father's occupation, apparently left Stratford for London at a young age, and, most notably, did not erect a monument to his father in Stratford Church (or anywhere else), although he could certainly have afforded to pay for a memorial to a man who had been Stratford's bailiff and a local JP, an altogether worthy recipient of a stone tablet of remembrance (unless of course the monument in Holy Trinity Church was originally in memory of John Shakspere, see Chapter 1). As will be shown, Neville's Tower plays (and some of his later works) are, under the surface, obsessively concerned with the figure of the Earl of Essex. But William Shakspere had nothing whatever to do with the Earl of Essex. The Lord Chamberlain's Men has been seen by some historians as the pro-Essex acting company (in contrast to its rival, the Lord Admiral's Men, regarded as the pro-Cecil, pro-Establishment, company) and it was asked to perform *Richard II* by the Essex faction.[16] We know of no direct links between either Shakspere himself, or his acting company, and Essex. Actors were regarded as little better than vagabonds and few actors would have risked their lives by taking visible sides in a controversial political dispute involving the monarchy, the court, and the succession, in which heads literally rolled. It is often suggested that Shakspere was close to Southampton. The story, first published in Nicholas Rowe's 1709 biography of Shakespeare and 'handed down by Sir William D'Avenant,' is that Southampton 'at one time gave him [Shakespeare] a thousand pounds, to enable him to go through with a purchase which he heard he had a mind to.' Apart from bring *a priori* unbelievable, £1,000 then being roughly equivalent to £1 million today, it would actually have been impossible, because Southampton was deeply in debt and could not have given anyone even a fraction of that sum.[17] There was, in other words, no known reason why William Shakspere should have altered the nature of his work so profoundly in 1601, and no reason why he should have been obsessed by Essex.[18]

Neville Writing in the Tower

Neville was sent to the Tower of London in May 1601, remaining there for just under two years. With ample time to fill, he wrote three of his most notable works. The first question one might ask is whether he was allowed to write plays, or do anything else, in the Tower. Neither Neville nor Southampton were in close confinement and they could do virtually anything they wanted, except leave. Both wrote letters while in the Tower, and were apparently treated as gentlemen by the Tower authorities. Neville's notebook full of historical research dated 1602 is extant as well as a long document about Richard III written by Southampton and presented to Neville in 1603.

Shortly after this time Sir Walter Raleigh was also a prisoner in the Tower for many years. There he was so prolific that the section of his entry in the standard *Oxford Dictionary of National Biography* dealing with this period is headed, 'The Tower Scholar, 1603–1618'.[19] In the Tower, Raleigh wrote *The History of the World,* from the creation of the world to 146 BC, totalling 1 million words.[20] He also wrote overtly political works, such as *A Dialogue Between a Counsellor of State and a Justice of the Peace.* Writing plays and poems with no apparent direct political content or commentary on English politics would certainly have been permitted. Another earlier example of a poet in the Tower is Charles, Duke of Orleans, who, after Agincourt (1415), was a prisoner for twenty-four years. He wrote many poems during his confinement.[21] The duke appears on stage in *Henry V.*

Hamlet

The first play that Neville worked on in the Tower was almost certainly *Hamlet.* There are two key questions which might be asked concerning this work: when was it written and what is it really about? New research on the first two quartos of *Hamlet* (dated 1603 and 1604–5) has opened up the first question in a startling way. By comparing these texts and researching all references to a *Hamlet* from 1589, when Nashe referred to 'whole Hamlets I should say handfuls of Tragicall speeches',[22] Jolly offered the possibility that the play was first conceived in the 1580s.[23] Henslowe listed a performance of *Hamlet* in 1594 in his diary.[24] Jolly showed how the first quarto, which may represent the early version, was closer to the French source text, Belleforest's *Les Histoires Tragiques.* The latter was printed first in Lyon and then

Paris, in 1576 and 1582 respectively. Neville passed through Paris on European travels in 1578 and 1582. He could read French so may have bought the book there.

Whether Shakespeare wrote an early version which he then revised, scholars agree on the dating of the final version of *Hamlet* to 1600–1601. Revising an old play would perhaps have afforded Neville protection from being accused of referring to contemporary events. In re-working the play Neville used the title, characters and the plot of the old play to disguise what he had in mind. Evidence for a 1601 dating of the revised version of the second quarto and First Folio was offered nearly a century ago in a now little-remembered book by Lilian Winstanley, *Hamlet and the Scottish Succession*.[25] Winstanley pointed out, citing Edmund Malone in the late eighteenth century, that the famous lines by Horatio at the end of the play, 'Now cracks a noble heart. Goodnight, sweet Prince, And flights of angels sing thee to thy rest,'[26] are clearly based on part of the speech given by Essex in his defence at his trial on 19 February 1601: 'And when my soul and body shall part, send thy blessed angels to be near unto me which may convey it to the joys of heaven.'[27] Essex was executed six days later, on 25 February 1601. The first quarto of *Hamlet* does not contain these words based on Essex's statement.[28] The words 'the late innovation' (2.2.331), which are believed to refer to the Essex rebellion, are not in the first quarto but do occur in the second quarto of 1604. The play therefore must have been revised after Essex's death, in all likelihood around the second, or possibly the third, quarter of 1601. Other evidence also points to mid-1601 as the time it was written.[29]

A myth about Shakespeare's *Hamlet* is that its title and principal character derive from the name of William Shakspere's deceased son Hamnet (1585–96), who had died five years earlier. This is simply a coincidence, perhaps remarkable, but just a coincidence. The boy was named after his godfather Hamnet Sadler, a baker in Stratford-upon-Avon. As all authorities agree, the name Hamlet derives from Amleth,[30] the name of the prince in Belleforest's 1576 *Les Histoires Tragiques* which is the acknowledged source for the play.[31] The early version of *Hamlet* had been performed onstage in London from at least in 1589, when Hamnet Shakspere was only four years old.

The second key question is what *Hamlet* is centrally about. Of course, like most of Shakespeare's works it has multiple meanings, and has been interpreted in many different ways. However, we suggest that the play revised in 1601 is centrally about Essex and his failed rebellion, with the character Hamlet being, in large measure, Essex. However Hamlet is also based on Neville himself, his hesitancy in joining the rebellion and the near-fatal consequences of his decision.[32] Neville disguised his intention by grafting multiple identities onto the one character, hiding autobiography in multifaceted fiction. As to Essex, the parallels with the character of Hamlet are abundant. By nature, Essex was a student and soldier far more than a courtier. Francis Bacon advised him to appear 'bookish and contemplative'. In his *Apology* addressed to Anthony Bacon, Essex wrote: 'For my infection in nature, it was indifferent to books and arms and was more inflamed with the love of knowledge than with the love of fame ... Witness your rarely qualified brother ... my bookishness from my very childhood.'[33] Edward Abbott stated that 'physically and mentally Essex was as unstable as Hamlet' and that 'during the last years of his life, continually suffer[ed] from melancholy'.[34] Winstanley enlarged on this description: 'Essex, in fact, in the last years of his life, was, as Mr. Abbott so justly points out, startlingly like Hamlet: he was irresolute almost to the point of insanity, he was surrounded by cunning enemies who plotted against his life, he had a premonition of disaster.'[35] Like Essex, Hamlet 'treat[ed] the players with the utmost courtesy, was on terms of familiarity with them, [and] interested in their art'.[36]

'The Mousetrap' ('The Murder of Gonzago'), the play within a play 'to catch the conscience of a king', recalls the performance of *Richard II* just before Essex's rebellion. Polonius, as many commentators have suggested, is clearly based on Lord Burghley. The character may also blend aspects of his son Robert Cecil (who asked Neville when he was in France to spy on his son's potential French teacher/companion) and of Neville's father-in-law Sir Henry Killigrew, who was of a similar character.[37] Even the gravedigger's scene seems to have a parallel with Essex. In a letter written to the queen on 20 May 1600, Essex said that he felt 'as if I were thrown into a corner like a dead carcass. I am gnawed upon and torn by the basest and vilest creatures upon earth. The tavern-haunter speaks of me where he lists. Already they print me and make me speak to the world, and shortly they will print me in what forms they list upon the stage.'[38] As Winstanley observes, 'Now surely we have here remarkable parallels to the grave-digging scene: Yorick's skull is thrown into a corner, it is "gnawed upon" by the vilest of creatures; the clown is a tavern-haunter, for he sends his boy for a "stoup of liquor", even over his work, thus bringing the dead insulted bodies in close connection with the tavern.'[39] (How would William Shakspere have had access to a letter from the Earl of Essex to Queen Elizabeth?) In this scheme Fortinbras, the Prince of Norway, who has Hamlet's 'dying voice' to succeed to the throne, is James VI of Scotland, who actually succeeded as James I. Essex had supported James's claim to the throne. There are many other similar parallels between Hamlet and Essex, and between Hamlet and Neville.

Given that *Hamlet* was written or revised just after the failure of a major insurrection in London by a charismatic nobleman, we propose that the play contains Neville's reflections on Essex, as well as his contemplation of the dangerous situation he was now in ('Denmark's a prison', 2.2.242).[40] Spurgeon, in her study of Shakespeare's imagery, described the playwright's state of mind as revealed in the imagery he used at this time. She suggested he experienced 'some deep perturbation, shock and revulsion of nature, emotional, moral and spiritual … the springs of life – love, laughter, joy, hope, belief in others gradually infected by the disease of the spirit which is … killing him … In *Hamlet* we find in the sickness images a feeling of horror, disgust and even helplessness … a general sense of inward and unseen corruption, of the man helplessly succumbing to a deadly and foul disease.'[41] Letters from Neville and his wife when he was in the Tower reveal he was ill. Spurgeon showed there were more images of illness in *Hamlet* than any other play.[42] Furthermore she showed how from this time onwards images of the plague take on a more sombre tone, being 'used in such a way that the gravity and horror of the disease are emphasised'.[43] This makes complete sense when we know Neville was trapped in a state prison, unable to escape from the plague (as he did after his release, leaving one house and moving to another in the country, according to his letter dated 16 February 1604).[44]

The names of Rosenkrantz and Guildenstern were among the ancestors of Tycho Brahe, the astronomer. Brahe sent an engraving of himself, which included the names and arms of these two families on its border, to Henry Savile's brother Thomas, with the request to distribute it to his friends in England. Neville could thus have seen a copy. He may also have met Brahe on his European travels during which he and Savile did meet several prominent astronomers. These included Tadeáš Hájek who was in frequent scientific correspondence with Brahe and played an important role in persuading Rudolph II to invite Brahe to Prague.[45] Hájek sent Savile and Neville to Wrocław, Poland, where they met Paul Wittich, an astronomer who had, until a couple of months before, been a colleague and confidant of Tycho Brahe.[46] Furthermore Brahe's island observatory was just a short distance from Elsinor. We do not know whether Neville visited Brahe. William Shakspere never left England and would not have received a copy of Brahe's engraving.

Shakespeare changed the name of the usurping king in *Hamlet* from Fengon, in his source, Belleforest's *Les Histoires Tragiques*, to Claudius. Shakespeare's reading of Tacitus informed *Hamlet*. 'Tacitus was particularly merciless in his judgement of Claudius' rule. Claudius was ugly, uxorious, cruel, and addicted to drink and gaming. He was also the second husband of Julia Agrippina, with whom he was in an incestuous marriage. She was his brother Germanicus' daughter. The parallels of incest and corruption between Tacitus' account of Claudius and Shakespeare's Claudius are unmistakable.'[47] Before speaking to his mother, Hamlet says to himself, 'Let not ever the soul of Nero enter into this firm bosom' (3.3.363–4). 'According to Tacitus' account, to which Shakespeare is clearly referring, Nero had his mother Agrippina stabbed to death'.[48] Neville sketched a family tree on the end pages of the Tacitus in his library which included Claudius and Nero (see Chapter 5).

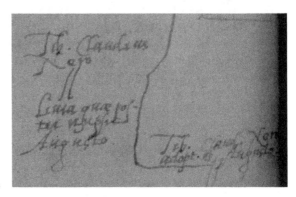

Tacitus, end page.

In his copy of Appian's volume on Roman History Neville made many annotations about Claudius, including one about him being poisoned by his wife Agrippina.

'Claudius ab Agrippina veneno interficitur': Appian (Dionysius section), 473.

Neville may have made these annotations in the late 1570s when he was a student at Oxford and they show that he knew this material long before the play was written.

Neville's letters and documents of the period 1599–1601 contain much rare vocabulary used by the Bard in *Hamlet*, including many instances of hendiadys (when two words are paired, as in 'slings and arrows'). His trial deposition written in March 1601 contains 1,379 words of which 426 occur in *Hamlet*: 30.9 per cent, nearly one-third of the statement, sharing vocabulary with the play. It contains sixteen hendiadys, twelve of which contain words used in the play.[49]

On 9 May 1600, when he was ambassador to France, Neville wrote in a letter about Denmark, where Shakespeare set *Hamlet* (the only time he ever named that country):

> The Ambassador of Wirttenberg told me lately, that he had received Advertisement from a Friend of his in Hambourg, that the King of Denmark makes very great Preparation by Sea.[50]

The word 'preparation' is also used by an ambassador in *Hamlet*, about war (Fortinbras's intended invasion of Poland, 2.2.63). In the first scene Horatio and Marcellus discuss Denmark's 'preparations' for a war, including ships and cannon, against Norway (1.1.108). In 1574 and 1578 Sir Thomas Gresham received licences to export cannons to Denmark. One of his ships, containing cannon, sank in the Thames and was rediscovered in 2003.[51] Neville inherited Gresham's iron foundry and exported cannons during the 1590s. Cannon are mentioned four times in *Hamlet* and in *King John*, the only other play in which cannon are referred to so frequently.

James noticed that Neville used the word 'clemency' in a letter of July 1601 to Cecil, in which he hoped the queen would not ruin him.[52] 'Clemency' is unique to *Hamlet* (3.2.140).

Jost offered evidence that Shakespeare intended Horatio in *Hamlet* to evoke the Latin poet Horace. Horatio replies to Barnardo's enquiry, 'Is Horatio there?' with, 'A piece of him' (1.1.22).[53] In Horace's Ode 3.30 the words 'pars mei' can be translated as 'a part of me'. This page of Neville's small volume of Horace is annotated, proving it had been studied. Neville referred to Horace in a letter written in 1604.[54]

Of course Hamlet is much more than a reaction to the debacle of the Essex rebellion. It is a meditation on human frailty and culpability, on folly and mortality. This greater meditation, however, makes sense when we know its author had experienced the greatest challenge, indeed tragedy, of his life and was now working through his own self-judgement for errors, delays and folly as he waited in prison facing financial and political ruin, illness and death. Hamlet himself reflects on the fact that one fault can ruin a man's reputation (1.4.20–38). Much more has been and will be written about *Hamlet* and Neville.[55] For further reflections on Neville's psychology at this time see Chapter 12.

The Phoenix and the Turtle

Another work which Shakespeare almost certainly wrote in 1601 was *The Phoenix and the Turtle*, a strange allegorical poem, often classified as a metaphysical work, first published in that year.[56] In 1601 Richard Field, who had produced Shakespeare's two long poems in 1593–4, printed a collection called *Loves Martyr: Or Rosalins Complaint*, for Edward Blount. It contained fourteen poems, two of which were by Ben Jonson, and one each by John Marston, George Chapman and Shakespeare. The other poems in the collection were anonymous. Shakespeare's poem, although almost always known as *The Phoenix and the Turtle*, is untitled, and begins, 'Let the bird of loudest lay …' (The turtle in the poem is a turtle dove, not the reptile.) The poem, which is sixty-seven lines long, celebrates an ideal marriage which, nevertheless, is apparently unconsummated and produces no children. The whole purpose of the poem is to mourn what might have been, but regrettably did not occur. The work concludes:

To this urn let those repair
That are either true or fair;
For these dead birds sigh a prayer.

Many explanations of what this mysterious poem might mean have been offered. Once modern criticism began, it did not take commentators long to offer the most obvious explanation of the poem's meaning, one which is virtually forced upon us by its date of 1601, namely that it is about Elizabeth and Essex. The queen was regularly known as the 'Phoenix', one of her portraits being 'the Phoenix portrait' (now in the National Portrait Gallery, London). This identification of the Phoenix and Elizabeth is confirmed by the lines:

Hearts remote, yet not asunder
Distance, and no space was seen
'Twixt <u>this turtle and his queen</u>:
But in them it were a wonder.

This Elizabeth–Essex interpretation was first offered by A. B. Grosart in the earliest modern edition of *Loves Martyr* in 1878.[57] Many critics have accepted this interpretation, for instance Richard McCoy, in an essay published in 1997.[58] The poem is certainly not a mournful dirge about, literally, the failure of the queen and Essex to marry and produce children. Elizabeth was sixty-eight in 1601; Essex had, in 1590, married Frances Walsingham, the daughter of Sir Francis Walsingham and the widow of Sir Philip Sidney, and had three surviving children. Indeed, Shakespeare probably wrote the poem apparently regretting a childless marriage in order to disguise the fact that he was writing about Elizabeth and Essex. For similar reasons, both the Phoenix and the Turtle die in the poem, while Elizabeth was still alive, however much the imprisoned Neville might have wished for her death. For Neville, perhaps, the queen, as the lode star of his world, had died when she unjustly imprisoned him and refused all appeals of clemency. What the poet laments in the poem is the death of hope, the end of the Elizabeth–Essex era and the regret that this great queen and her favourite could only be united in death. In the alchemy of poetry he eulogises these archetypal figures into a jewel of grief for lost love and faith. The poem praises loyalty and we can infer from his story that Neville remained loyal to both Elizabeth and Essex despite paying a high price for his dichotomous position. From the dualism inherent in the poem a synthesis emerges, antithesis resolving into unity: 'How true a twain seemeth this concordant one!' As Roe put it, 'duality, the necessary medium for expressing hopes of recovery and redemption, persists as part of the design, even as the earlier antithetical clamour gives way to a mood of sadness and surrender.'[59] Neville's letters at the time of his imprisonment express both sadness and surrender: he had to surrender to survive and had much to grieve, including his concern for his wife who was close to a mental breakdown. The line of 'Hearts remote, yet not asunder' might also speak of Neville's own marriage which survived the disaster.

Other interpretations of *The Phoenix and the Turtle* have been offered. The best-known is that the Turtle is Sir John Salusbury and the Phoenix is his wife Ursula Halsall, the illegitimate daughter of the Earl of Derby.[60] The poems in *Loves Martyr* were collected and edited by Robert Chester, who dedicated the book to Sir John Salusbury and apparently worked for him as a chaplain and secretary. However, as both Sir John and his wife were alive in 1601 and had many children, this suggestion seems far-fetched. Similarly, it has been suggested that the poem was actually written in 1587 to celebrate Salusbury's forthcoming marriage to Ursula, a suggestion that is even more implausible, since the poem states that both spouses have died, childless, which would not be your usual marriage ode! Salusbury (1565–1612) was a local landowner in Denbighshire. In 1601 he became known as an anti-Essex partisan, and was knighted in that year, apparently for his loyalty during the rebellion.[61]

About Robert Chester, who edited the volume, virtually nothing is known.[62] The only man of that name who attended a university matriculated at Clare College, Cambridge in 1569. *Alumni Cantabrigiensis,* the biographical dictionary of everyone who ever attended the university, states only this fact about him and provides no further information. If this was the same man, he was presumably about fifty in 1601. Elsewhere, Chester apparently compared himself adversely as a poet to those he encountered in London.[63] Thus he, and possibly Salusbury, may have been familiar with the London literary scene. However, there are no known links between either man and Neville, Shakespeare, the Lord Chamberlain's Men, or any of the other contributors to *Loves Martyr,* with the possible exception of Ben Jonson, who apparently knew the family.[64] A link must, necessarily, have existed. It seems likely that Neville would wish to contribute his controversial poem to a work dedicated to a high-profile anti-Essex activist in order to disguise its true message. Perhaps an intermediary, such as Jonson or Chester, asked Neville to contribute, which he did. Beyond this little is clear apart from the date of the poem.

The Phoenix and the Turtle is by far the most cryptic poem Shakespeare wrote. There was no reason for William from Stratford to write such a mysterious piece in 1601. There was every reason for Neville to encode his lament for the end of the Essex era in Neoplatonic obscurity. Posit him as the author and its meaning emerges more clearly than ever before. The Neoplatonism that has been noted as the cultural background to the work, with its possible sources in Lactantius, Petrarch, Chaucer and Philip Sidney, is illuminated when we know that Neville had researched the early Church fathers, such as Lactantius, with Savile; had two copies of Petrarch amongst his library books (the editions being dated 1550 and 1581); was related to Chaucer and a friend of Sidney.[65] Neville had also noted the image of a Phoenix in two of his books. In his copy of Ovid's *Ars Amatoria* and *Remedia Amoris*, page 9, a marginal annotation on the mythical bird was underlined, as shown in Chapter 3. We illustrate the example of a phoenix annotation that occurs in his copy of Tacitus in Chapter 8.

Othello

Othello is traditionally dated to 1602–3. In the third Arden edition[66] of the play Honigmann noted that the work must have been written between 1601 and 1604, and, after a long discussion of its date, concluded that the play 'would have been performed not later than March 1603, a *terminus ante quem* that again points to 1602 as the probable year of the play's first performance'.[67] In 1905, A. C. Bradley, the eminent Shakespearean critic, concluded that 'there is practically no doubt that *Othello* was the tragedy written next after *Hamlet* ... [This] is confirmed by similarities of style, diction, and versification.'[68] Assuming that the play was written in or about 1602, the key question, again, is what is *Othello* about? The resemblances between *Hamlet* and *Othello*, plays superficially so different, were also noted more than a century ago by Bradley. This view, that the two plays have an underlying nature in common, is also sustained by what we know of who wrote the plays and why. Like *Hamlet*, *Othello* is also about Essex's rebellion. Like Prince Hamlet, General Othello is also a synthesis of Essex and Neville himself. Of course, Othello's target is not a usurping king but his faithful, innocent wife. Neville's mishandling of the Essex debacle caused great distress to his wife Anne. Othello is not driven to tragic action by a ghost seeking posthumous justice but by a malevolent and evil assistant, Iago. Who, in this schema, is Iago? We suggest Iago was based on the character of an actual man, Henry Cuffe, Essex's secretary and Neville's friend from Oxford, who tempted him into joining the rebellion, with catastrophic consequences. According to Cuffe's entry in the *Oxford Dictionary of National Biography*, '[a]t his own trial, and in the official propaganda which described the insurrection, Cuffe was cast as an Iago-like figure in Essex's fall, "the very seducer of the earl" (*State Trials*).'[69] In Neville's submission to the enquiry into the rebellion, dated 2 March 1601, he described how Cuffe had left a message for him awaiting his return from France, telling him that 'I had had evil offices done me, as my Lord of Essex was informed by his friends in Court,' and that some great blame was like to be cast upon me for the breach at Bulloigne ...'[70] Here Cuffe was sowing seeds of fear and distrust, just as Iago does. Neville, in the interim, found out this was not true: he went to court and 'found no such matter'. At the end of the play, Iago dies under torture. Cuffe was hanged, drawn and quartered. Although the description of Cuffe as an 'Iago-like figure' in the *Oxford Dictionary of National Biography* is meant as a simile, it may be literally true. According to Honigmann, both Othello and Iago 'are in some ways opposites or complementaries, yet Elizabethans would have thought them curiously alike ... Both are outsiders, Othello as a Moor, Iago as a malcontent with a grudge against privilege; both stand apart from their fellow men.'[71] Essex and Cuffe were in a similar position. It has also been argued by recent critics that there is a homosexual motivation underlying Iago's relationship with Othello.[72] According to the *ODNB* entry on Cuffe, '[He] never married and apparently had no interest in women. In *The Differences of the Ages of Man's Life* he mentions women only in connection with ... their physical inferiority to men.'[73] All of this would have been known to Neville, who knew both and who was lured to destruction by Cuffe. If William Shakspere wrote *Othello* and if the two main male characters were based on Essex/Neville and Cuffe, how could the Stratford man have known any of this? There is no reason to suppose that he ever met Essex or Cuffe, let alone was familiar enough with them to base a play around their intimate characters and events in English high politics.[74]

Another striking mystery, but similar to those recurring throughout the Shakespeare canon, is that *Othello* is largely based on an Italian work, Giraldi Cinthio's *Hecatommithi*, a collection of short stories of which one, 'A Moorish Captain', was used for much of the plot of the play. Cinthio's work was written in 1565, but had not been translated into English when *Othello* was written. The Italian work had been translated into French in 1584. However there is no evidence that William Shakspere knew French or Italian, and the play is apparently closer to the Italian original than to the French translation. How, then, did William Shakspere read it, and why would he use a story in an Italian collection of short stories, one which has a striking parallel to the situation of Essex/Neville and Cuffe? Cinthio's work consists of no less than 110 short stories, strongly suggesting that the author of *Othello* must have read most of them, in order to identify one suitable for the plot of this particular play. Stratfordians, needless to say, can offer no explanation. Honigmann, like all mainstream commentators at a complete loss for an explanation, suggested that 'Shakespeare could have read … a lost English translation [of either the Italian original or the French translation] … [A] lost English translation, one that perhaps made use of both the Italian and the French texts, cannot be ruled out'.[75] Nor can it be ruled in: this is obviously not evidence, but an attempt, like so many others, to offer an explanation for the extraordinary erudition of William Shakspere in the complete absence of evidence, in order to save the Stratfordian paradigm. Lost translations are both handy and fulfilling, since, most conveniently, by definition they do not exist and their existence cannot be confirmed or disconfirmed. In complete contrast, Neville certainly knew both Italian and French, as well as other ancient and modern languages, and owned a large library of books.

The most obvious single feature of *Othello* is, of course, that its central character is a Moor, almost always played onstage by a black actor. Yet some critics, like E. C. Bentley, have questioned whether Othello's race is actually central to the play. Othello is, after all, a high-ranking and senior Venetian general, married to the daughter of an equally high-ranking Venetian senator, a member of that country's ruling elite. While not explicitly discussed, it is inconceivable that Othello could be anything other than an orthodox Catholic Christian; he is certainly not a Muslim, as were, presumably, most Moors. In other words, in everything but his skin colour, Othello was a member of the Venetian establishment, given high and responsible office, apparently well regarded and, like Essex, an impressive military leader: Shakespeare gives both Essex (in the Prologue to Act 5 in *Henry V*) and Othello the rank of general. Othello is neither a member of a persecuted and despised minority, nor seen as an enemy of the normal order of things distinguished by his otherness. To be sure, Shakespeare did write plays with these themes, most obviously *The Merchant of Venice*, and, also, in a sense, the triumphalist History plays which emphasise England's inherent superiority to the rest of the world. Shakespeare was also well aware of the fact that black men were often hated, feared and despised, as is shown in the following passage:

> Mislike me not for my complexion,
> The shadowed livery of the burnish'd sun,
> To whom I am a neighbour, and near bred.
> Bring me the fairest creature northward born,
> Where Phoebus' fire scarce thaws the icicles,
> And let us make incision for your love,
> To prove whose blood is reddest, his or mine.

Readers may be forgiven for thinking that these lines come straight from Othello's lips, but they do not: they are spoken by the Prince of Morocco in *The Merchant of Venice* (2.1.1–7), when seeking Portia's hand. Othello arguably has nothing to say about his persecution as a black man. Iago and others in the play do disparage Othello for being black but this is not central to the plot. Why, then, did the author of *Othello* choose to dramatise a story whose main character was a Moor? We suggest that his blackness is a metaphor.[76] Shakespeare used this for two reasons: first, to disguise that he is writing in large measure about Essex; and, second, to signal his own otherness as an imprisoned traitor, a man with a blackened reputation, and to camouflage this. In many other respects, Essex is a close parallel to Othello. Essex was sent to Ireland as general-in-chief, just as Othello was sent to Cyprus. Both had 'done the state some service' (5.2.337). Both were led to perdition by an evil counsellor.

Other aspects of Neville's experience can be seen to inform this play. Neville had been to Venice but not to Cyprus and the vividness of location detail is greater for Venice than Cyprus. Twice, for example, 'the Sagittary' is referred to: Roe following the work of previous scholars, was able to track this street name to an actual place, the Frezzeria (an Italian word meaning the street of the arrow makers, whereas the Sagittary is the same but from a Latin root).[77] Shakespeare did not add to the sketchy information given by Cinthio about Cyprus. However the Bard was well aware of the military threat posed by the Turks. In many of his letters to Cecil in the summer of 1599, Neville reported news he had heard of 'the Turk', of wars, truces, peace treaties, revolts.[78] Neville arrived back from France in August 1600, the very same month as the Moorish ambassador of the King of Barbary, Abd el-Ouahed ben Messaoud, arrived in London.[79] Neville mentioned this in his letter written from London on 28 August 1600. 'Here is an Ambassage[80] lately arrived from the King of *Barbarie*, what he brings I know not yet, but will advertise by my next. My Lord of *Essex* was yesterday by order from her Majestie, *set at full Liberty* only *his repair to Court forbidden*' (italics in the original).[81] Here we have documentary proof that Neville knew about the ambassador and we see him immediately referring to Essex, so our suggestion that he might later use a Moor as a metaphor for Essex is supported by this immediate association. A magnificent portrait of Abd el-Ouahed ben Messaoud graces many editions of *Othello* and he is seen as a possible inspiration for the play's protagonist.[82] The Moorish ambassador was looked after by Sir Lewes Lewkenor. Another source for *Othello* is Lewes Lewkenor's book *The Commonwealth and Government of Venice*, published in 1599. As James pointed out, Lewkenor was a friend of Philip Sidney, a Member of Parliament, who had interests in metals and became master of ceremonies for James I.[83] All of which would bring him within Neville's circle of acquaintances. Lewkenor was looking after the French ambassador in 1600 when Neville, as English ambassador to France, had meetings with him.[84] Neville's daughter Mary married Edward Lewkenor, Member of Parliament, in 1610. His entry in the History of Parliament states that it was probably through this marriage that Edward gained a Cornish seat in the House of Commons through the influence that Neville and the Cornish Killigrews could exert on his behalf.[85] From 1610 Neville continued his contact with Venice through Dudley Carleton who became ambassador to Venice.[86]

Neville himself may have been drawn to examine jealousy and the fear of marital infidelity by his own position as a husband separated from his wife by imprisonment. Anne gave birth to a son, Edward, in 1602 and this child was conceived when Neville was incarcerated in the Tower. Neville's grandfather, also called Edward, was executed in the Tower of London, so perhaps this name was chosen because Neville was reminded of his grandfather in the Tower. Whether this boy was the result of a conjugal visit or an extramarital affair we may never know. Shakespeare wrote two plays about a husband's jealousy: *Othello* and *The Winter's Tale*. In both the jealousy is intense but unfounded: Neville could well have felt insecure in his marriage when he was forced to spend two years apart from his wife. Edward later became a fellow at King's College, Cambridge, dying in 1632.[87] On several pages of the annotated Hall's *Chronicle* there are squiggles and blots on the opposite page.[88] They are all in the same area, about three inches up from the bottom of the page, as if the writer could not reach higher.

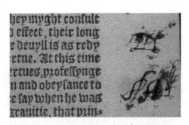 

Hall's *Chronicle*: squiggles and blots.

On one page this writer copies one of the annotations: the word 'execution' (correctly spelt in secretary script). The copyist wrote 'exesucion', sloping upward to the right. This is clearly not by the original annotator: the handwriting and ink are different. Underneath is the name 'Edward' in a large childish hand.

   Hall's *Chronicle*, Henry IV, fxiv[a].

As the annotated Hall volume must have stayed in the family during this time we can here see the young son scribbling in the margin, and proudly leaving us his name. These blotted marks must have been made between 1607 and 1612 by a boy young enough to innocently but brazenly vandalise his father's book, yet old enough to read and write.[89]

Neville used some rare vocabulary in his letters of 1599–1604 which Shakespeare only used once, in *Othello*: 'Depute' in a letter dated 18 July 1599;[90] 'Solicitation' in letters dated 1 August 1599 and 29 June 1600;[91] 'Affinity' in a letter dated 4 January 1600.[92] Neville spelt this 'affinitie' which is the spelling in the First Folio; 'Favourably' in the draft letter 1603–4.[93]

Perhaps most remarkable of all is the word 'muttering'. This occurs in Neville's letter of 1 November 1604, written from 'my bed at the Star-Chamber' in London where he was in 'much paine of the gout'.[94] The first recorded performance of *Othello* was on the same day as the letter was written, 1 November 1604, in the Banqueting House in Whitehall (according to the Revels Office account).[95] The Star Chamber was nearby in the Palace of Westminster. The word 'muttering' occurs only in the first Quarto of 1622 in Desdemona's speech which begins, 'Why then tomorrow night' (3.3.60). The word became 'mammering' in the First Folio.[96] The word 'mutter' also occurs in *Othello*, when Iago tells of Cassio talking in his sleep (3.3.419). Earlier the same year, 'When Parliament came together on March 19th, 1604, Neville's name was "muttered" … for speaker of the house.'[97] The use of this word in the Journals of the House of Commons means it would have been current for a Member of Parliament.

Troilus and Cressida

The third Tower play was *Troilus and Cressida*, which is normally dated to 1602. It was recorded in the Stationers' Register on 7 February 1603, 'as yt is acted by my lord Chamberlens Men'. At that time Neville was still incarcerated. In many respects, the play is far more blatantly about Essex than its two predecessors because, even in his lifetime, the earl was compared with Achilles. In 1598 'George Chapman claimed in the dedicatory epistle to his translation of Homer's *Iliad* that the character of Achilles "did but prefigure the Earl of Essex".'[98] The play is notable for its cynicism and bitter tone, and may present Neville's view of Essex and the rebellion changing from respect to a more ambiguous response. One major oddity of the play is that it was published in 1609 in two separate and differing editions. While the 'first state' quarto of 1609 notes that it was written by William Shakespeare 'as it was acted by the Kings Majesties servants at the Globe,' the second edition omits any reference to the Globe but contains a long preliminary epistle, beginning with, 'A neuer writer, to an euer reader. Newes.' The epistle later states that, 'Eternall reader, you have here a new play, never stal'd with the Stage, never clapper-clawd with the palmes of the vulger,' and concludes, 'Since by the grand possessors wills I beleeue you should have prayd for them rather than be prayd. And so I leave all such to bee prayd for (for the states of their wits healths) that will not praise it. Vale.' The epistle is unsigned, and we do not know who wrote it, or why the play was published in two different formats in 1609. Quite possibly, Neville thought that it was now safe to publish a work which would be seen to be about Essex (whereas it was not so obvious that *Hamlet* or *Othello* were concerned with the earl and his rebellion). He may have felt more positive by 1609, which may explain his publishing *Shake-speares Sonnets* that year. That *Troilus* came via 'the grand possessors' wills' implies that Neville, by then both an influential Member of Parliament and a knight, and perhaps Southampton, his former fellow prisoner and close friend, may have been directly involved in its publication.

Palmer, in his introductory essay to the play, wrote about Time, Treason and Prophecy.[99] He showed how Time betrays us and how all other treasons derive from its passage. He further showed how betrayal and treason are central themes. For Neville, a man betrayed by friends and a prisoner accused of treason and serving time, these obsessions make sense. For a prisoner, survival and perseverance are essential skills. Ulysses advises that 'perseverance, dear my lord, keeps honour bright' (3.3.150). Palmer virtually describes the ruined Neville's situation. 'Personal reputation can never remain what it was, since Time either disregards what has been, or else destroys it … Honour, as Sidney maintained in the *Arcadia*, must be constantly renewed. This was the way to oppose Time, and frustrate him;

but it does so knowing that the very condition of continuing is to leave behind the "husks and formless ruin of oblivion" (4.5.165). Essentially this way is hinted at in Agamemnon's opening words to the Greek council: it is in some degree a way of settling for second-best, since no action proceeds as you expected, and you must bear your time of trial in patience, while at the same time persevering.[100] This neatly describes Neville's experience.

In her analysis of Shakespeare's imagery Spurgeon discovered that the Bard was concerned with poor quality food in *Troilus and Cressida*. Her list of images including crusty bread, 'cheese … mouse eaten and dry, an addled egg, … a fusty nut, a hard sailor's biscuit, fair fruit rotting untasted in an unwholesome dish, and greasy remnants of food … hunger, appetite, ravenous eating, fasting … drinking up the lees and dregs of wine', all of which may suggest a prison diet.[101]

Neville used 'distasted' and 'dependance', which only occur in *Troilus and Cressida*, in his letter of 29 July 1600.[102] In his letter dated 2 November 1600 Neville used the word 'negotiations' which is also unique to *Troilus and Cressida*, and here again Neville anticipated Shakespeare. At about the time he wrote *Troilus and Cressida*, Neville wrote the phrase 'to persist in', which is also unique to the play, in his letter of 31 July 1602.[103] In the same letter Neville wrote the following words: 'Reversion' occurs in *Troilus and Cressida* and two other earlier plays; 'Imposed' is in *Troilus and Cressida* and *Measure for Measure* and two earlier plays. 'Presuming' is only used in two plays: *Richard II* and *Troilus and Cressida*; 'Soiled' is unique to *King Lear*; 'soil'd' is used in three plays: *Richard II*, *Hamlet* and *Troilus and Cressida*.

Neville used the word 'imbecility' in his defence statement of March 1601 and again in his draft letter of 1603–4, when he also used the words 'fee-farm': both are unique to *Troilus and Cressida*. Thus Neville used the word 'imbecility' both before and after it was written into the play. Neville also used another word that occurs only in *Troilus and Cressida* in his deposition in 1601: 'proposition'. Because the trial statement and 1603–4 draft letter are both concerned with the aftermath of the Essex rebellion, the use of this rare vocabulary in the play further links Neville, Essex and Shakespeare's bitter satire on Achilles.

In the play Hector refers to Aristotle's *Ethics*:

> … young men, whom <u>Aristotle</u> thought
> Unfit to hear moral philosophy …
> The reasons you allege do more conduce
> To the hot passion of distemper'd blood
> Than to make up a free determination
> 'Twixt right and wrong, for pleasure and revenge
> Have ears more deaf than adders to the voice
> Of any true decision. (2.2.440)

This matches Aristotle's argument that 'political science is not a proper study for the young' man who is 'swayed by his feelings … Acts which are the effects of passion are surely the very last that can be called acts of deliberate choice … When Pleasure is at the bar, the jury is not impartial. So it will be best for us if we feel towards her as the Trojan elders felt towards Helen … If we are for packing her off, as they were with Helen, we shall be the less likely to go wrong.'[104] Here Aristotle is using the very topic Hector is discussing in the play as an analogy. Palmer offered compelling proof that Shakespeare had read the *Ethics* carefully and had used Aristotle's arguments throughout the play. Amongst Neville's books at Audley End House there is a volume of Aristotle's *Ethics* dated 1553. In 1604 Neville purchased copies of Aristotle's *Politics* and *Rhetoric*.[105]

Conclusion

The three plays and one short metaphysical poem that Neville wrote in the Tower form a coherent unit. They are all about Essex, his rebellion and Neville's peripheral and catastrophic participation. He was working through the grief, betrayal, bitterness, anger and disappointment of the Essex debacle. After Neville was freed from prison in 1603, this obsession, at least in its acute form, ceased, as evidenced by the first play he wrote after his release, *Measure for Measure*. Neville apparently retained a keen interest in Essex, arguably using him as a role model in such later plays as *Antony and Cleopatra* and *Coriolanus*, but not in the highly focused manner of his Tower plays (see Chapter 8). Essex and the rebellion had had such a catastrophic impact on his life that Neville had real reasons for writing his Tower plays. With Neville identified as the author, intractable puzzles are resolved and the reasons for the tone and content of the plays become apparent. In contrast, what possible motive would William Shakspere have had for being obsessed with Essex, or for losing that focus after 1603? Apart from the performances of *Richard II* just prior to the rebellion, Shakspere had no known connection with Essex, and, as a mere actor, would certainly have steered clear of any dangerous involvement in high politics. He would also have wished to preserve his growing wealth as a man of property in Stratford. If William Shakspere wanted to prove to the authorities that he was innocent of any controversial political involvement, he would surely have written more Falstaff plays, or more triumphalist histories like *Henry V*, or some kind of soothing, lightweight comedies, not *Hamlet*, *Othello* or *Troilus and Cressida*.

Release from the Tower, Tragedies and Problems 1603–1609

Pray thee take this mercy to provide
For better times to come.

Measure for Measure, 5.1.482

Queen Elizabeth I died in March 1603. Shakespeare responded to this event with a deafening silence. Unlike many other well-known poets, the Bard did not write a memorial ode or tribute to the queen. Shakespeare's lack of public grief was criticised at the time by Henry Chettle:

Nor doth the silver tongued Melicert
Drop from his honeyed muse one sable tear
To mourn her death that graced his desert
And to his lays opened her Royal ear.
Shepherd, remember our Elizabeth,
And sing her Rape, done by that Tarquin, Death.[1]

We presume Chettle is pointing to Shakespeare because of the reference to *The Rape of Lucrece*. Why use the pseudonym 'Melicert', unless the real identity of the poet was to be kept hidden? Daugherty pointed out that in Greene's *Menaphon* 'Melicertus' was the name assumed by a man in disguise, whose real name was Maximus.[2] Chettle then is pointing to a figure hidden behind a pseudonym.

William Shakspere, the Stratford man, had absolutely no reason not to commemorate the memory of the queen. During her reign he apparently rose from unknown provincial to leading playwright and a successful man of property. As Chettle hints, the queen was known to be fond of Shakespeare's works. There was no discernible reason for William Shakspere not to have written a commemorative work to mark the queen's death. In complete contrast, Neville had been imprisoned by her in the Tower and had every reason to maintain a discreet silence at her death. His real feelings were more frankly expressed in sonnet 107, which has been seen by commentators as a reference to the queen's death and was written immediately afterwards. Its author was 'forfeit to a confined doom' and cautiously celebrated that

the mortal moon hath her eclipse endured,
And the sad augurs mock their own presage;
Incertainties now crown themselves assured,
And peace proclaims olives of endless age.

If Neville had honestly and straightforwardly expressed his feelings about the queen's death, it would hardly have been 'to drop from his honeyed muse one sable tear'. While Neville's silence is entirely understandable, the silence of William Shakspere is inexplicable (unless of course he was not a poet and so could not write an ode).

When King James came to the throne Neville's situation changed. One of his first acts, on 10 April 1603, was to release both Southampton and Neville from imprisonment in the Tower, restoring both to their previous honours. A glimpse of things to come for Neville however may be seen in the royal warrant which granted their freedom. It contains twenty-nine lines of fulsome praise for Southampton, following with four lines at the end, a virtual afterthought, also releasing Neville:

We have also written to our aforesaid Lieutenant [of the Tower] for the present delivery of Sir Henry Neville knight whom we are pleased you of your counsell shall bring with you, when you shall wayte upon us.[3]

Now popular heroes and martyrs for their roles in the Essex rebellion, Southampton and Neville were widely expected to be favoured with high appointments in the new reign. The Venetian ambassador reported that James had 'destined great rewards to the Earl of Southampton and Sir Henry Neville'.[4] Southampton was indeed made a Knight of the Garter in July 1603 and restored to all of his former privileges. The king also gave him the positions of Captain of the Isle of Wight and Carisbrooke Castle, granted him three manors, awarded him the lucrative monopoly (previously held by Essex) of the farming of customs on sweet wines, and also made him one of two Lord Lieutenants of Hampshire.[5] In contrast, Neville received nothing, certainly no high office or lucrative sinecure. For obscure reasons, the new king appeared to have taken a rapid dislike to him. James's mistrust also appears to have extended, at least temporarily after his initial burst of generosity, to Southampton as well as to other surviving Essex rebels. In 1604, Southampton's allies in the House of Commons, among them Neville, Sir Herbert Croft and Sir Maurice Berkeley, argued against James's plans for a permanent tax to support the Crown and opposed the king's proposal for a formal union with Scotland (which was not enacted until 1707). Then in June 1604 James had Southampton, Neville and others arrested because of suspicions of a pro-Catholic and anti-Scottish conspiracy.[6] Although they were only in custody briefly, Neville's arrest diminished his reputation in the eyes of the king. From this time he increasingly became a champion of the House of Commons when it competed with the prerogatives of the Crown, a position which became more marked in the later phases of his parliamentary career.

The most important outcome of this sequence of events was that the widely held expectation that Neville would be greatly favoured by the new king was never realised. Neville never recovered from the financial losses he had experienced as ambassador to

France and as a prisoner in the Tower. He did, however, become a leading figure in the House of Commons, serving on many committees and emerging as something of a popular hero, even a kind of moderate proto-Roundhead radical, in the context of the early part of James's reign. Perhaps because of the lack of royal favour and the consequent financial return from such, he also became involved in money-making schemes, especially, from 1607 until his death, as a member of the council of the Second London Virginia Company. One important effect of these changes on Shakespeare's plays was that, from about 1603, the Bard usually wrote only one play a year, gradually tapering off to co-author his later plays with John Fletcher. In the 1590s, Shakespeare had generally written two plays per year. Although there were good reasons why Neville would write at half the frequency of the earlier phase of his career, it is difficult to see why William Shakspere, the Stratford man, would produce at a slower rate than previously. He was certainly still a sharer in the King's Men (as the Lord Chamberlain's Men were officially known from 19 May 1603) and appears, from what limited evidence exists, to have acted less frequently, and so had rather more time on his hands. Certainly his apparent reputation as a playwright had not diminished, while the works he was supposed to have written in this period, including *King Lear, Macbeth* and *Antony and Cleopatra*, show no evidence of diminished ability, rather the reverse.

After he was released from the Tower, Neville had an enormous number of things to do. Since 1599 he had not spent more than a minimal amount of time at his country house, Billingbear, or with his family and his many children. He had to be re-elected to Parliament, which he accomplished at the 1604 election, the first of the new reign and the first held after his release. He was elected Member of Parliament for Berkshire as a 'knight of the shire' (as county members were known), a prestigious position, although unremunerated (MPs who were not government ministers were unpaid until 1908). He had all manner of fences to mend and friendships to renew, and had, above all, to repair his diminished fortunes as best he could. So Neville had less time for writing plays during the year or so after his release from prison than at any time in his career. The gap between the last play he wrote in the Tower, *Troilus and Cressida,* and the first one he wrote after his release, *Measure for Measure*, is apparently the longest in the Shakespearean canon, just as one might expect if Neville were the author. This gap may well have been abetted by the plague, which limited theatrical performances of plays in London between 16 March 1603 and 9 April 1604.[7] On 16 February 1604 Neville wrote to Winwood that he had had to leave his house to escape the plague.[8] *Measure for Measure* was on stage in December 1604, long after the theatres re-opened. If William Shakspere from Stratford were the author of the canon, he would have had much more time to write plays while the theatres were closed, not less.

Measure for Measure

Bawcutt, editor of the Oxford edition of the play, suggested that *Measure for Measure* 'must necessarily have been written in the second half of 1604'.[9] The play contains scenes in prison where one character narrowly escapes being executed. Neville had avoided this fate after being implicated in the Essex rebellion and only just emerged from two years in prison.

Troilus and Cressida and *Measure for Measure* are the so-called 'problem plays', which cannot be classified as comedies or tragedies, and are difficult and complex.[10] These are darkly cynical plays that question the motives of those in power and are perhaps what one would expect Neville to produce as he recovered from his time in the Tower. Ostensibly, *Measure for Measure* is about the law and fornication, and is sometimes seen as an attack on English Puritanism.[11] This may be superficially accurate, but it is far more likely that, given when and under what circumstances it was written, Neville had something broader and rather different in mind, namely the act of sitting in judgment about any fault, including alleged treason. As John Masefield wrote of the play, 'Wisdom begins in justice. But how can man be just without the understanding of God? Who is so faultless that he can sit in judgment on another? Who so wise that he can see into the heart, weigh the act with the temptation, and strike the balance?'[12] From this perspective we can see that Neville was writing about his own moral predicament during the Essex rebellion, and not about sexual sin, which is used in the play as a smokescreen metaphor for Neville's real dilemma. Disguise is, in fact, central to the play. 'Shakespeare's use of disguise is the most interesting single feature of *Measure for Measure*. The play is built around this device.'[13] Neville's ability to disguise his real intention in writing the play is one reason why it is often seen by commentators as 'strange … a play of undeniable but somehow evasive peculiarities'.[14] The work seems to be the product of some personal upheaval and crisis in the life of the author, and one which accords, as is so often the case, with nothing in the known life of William Shakspere. In 1604, life appears to have been completely normal for the Stratford man, who was lodging at the time with Christopher Mountjoy at Silver Street, Cripplegate, according to the testimony he gave in 1612 in the Bellott–Mountjoy lawsuit. In July 1605, Shakspere paid £440 to buy the interest in a lease of tithes in Stratford and surrounding parishes.[15] While there was no obvious reason for Shakspere to have been concerned with the profound issues raised in *Measure for Measure*, there was every reason for Neville to be concerned with the moral considerations raised in the play, given that he acted in the Essex rebellion with cautious, honourable discretion, but was branded and punished as a traitor motivated by opportunism and disloyalty and then again arrested on false accusations that same year. The play also contains what are apparently references to Neville's life just before 1604. As noted above, Neville returned home from his time as ambassador to France and was fined £5,000 for his role in the Essex rebellion, and probably paid £3,000 by the time he was released. He was in danger of being executed, and was apparently suffering at this time from gout and lameness. On 1 November 1604 Neville opened his letter to Winwood with the words, 'Though in much paine of the Gout …'.[16] In a letter written just one month later, on 8 December 1604, Neville used the word 'mitigation'. Consider these lines from the play:

Lucio:	Behold, behold where Madam <u>Mitigation</u> comes!
	I have purchased as many diseases under her roof as come to –
Second Gentleman:	To what, I pray?
Lucio:	Judge.
Second Gentleman:	To <u>three thousand</u> dolours a year.
First Gentleman:	Ay, and more.

Lucio:	A <u>French</u> crown more.
First Gentleman:	Thou art always figuring diseases in me; but thou art full of error; I am sound.
Lucio:	Nay, not, as one would say, healthy: but so sound as things that are hollow; thy bones are hollow; impiety has made a feast of thee.
First Gentleman:	How now, <u>which of your hips has the most profound sciatica</u>?
Mistress Overdone:	Well, well! There's one yonder arrested and carried to <u>prison</u>, was worth <u>five thousand</u> of you all.
Second Gentleman:	Who's that, I prithee?
Mistress Overdone:	Marry sir, that's Claudio; Signior Claudio.
First Gentleman:	Claudio to prison? 'Tis not so.
Mistress Overdone:	Nay, but I know 'tis so. I saw him arrested, saw him carried away: and which is more, within these three days <u>his head to be chopped off</u>! (1.2.41–63)

Neville, writing from Paris in a letter to Robert Cecil dated 19 November 1599, told him about a money transfer. He wrote that the banker wanted 'two-pence upon every *French Crowne* … he is to pay <u>fyve thousand</u> Pound Sterling in this sort, viz. <u>three thowsand</u> Pound within twenty Days after Sight of his Bill, and the two thowsand Pound within fyftie Dayes'[17] (Neville's italics and spelling, our emphasis underlined). The First Folio was the first printing of *Measure for Measure* and in this passage the spelling of 'Crowne' includes the final 'e'. We can conclude that this passage of *Measure for Measure* is richly redolent of Neville's experiences.

The Politics of *Measure for Measure* and Henry Neville

Lever suggested that *Measure for Measure* contains echoes of the effect of a treaty with Spain that was negotiated and ratified between May and August 1604, the period when the play was probably written.[18] Neville had been involved in negotiations with Spain in 1600. In August 1604 he wrote in a letter about 'The Spanish Ambassadors', and said that 'we are now full of Jollity, giving Entertainment' so there is evidence that he was aware of and possibly involved in these negotiations.[19] In another letter dated 8 December 1604 he was concerned with a report of 'our Merchants are ill used in Spaine'. In this period Neville was being considered for the role of ambassador to Spain. John Chamberlain wrote in a letter dated 18 December 1604, ten days after Neville's letter, that 'here is speech that … Sir *Henry Neville*' was a possible ambassador 'for *Spaine*'.[20]

It has been suggested that the duke in *Measure for Measure* is modelled on James I. Neville's 1604 letter shows that he was in direct touch with the king over negotiations about the Union of England and Scotland. He opened the letter with:

We have at length concluded the Conference about the Union, to his Majestie's very good Satisfaction, as he witnessed by the Speech he made unto us, when we presented him the Instrument under our Seales.

Neville's letter is much concerned with law, justice and judges. *Measure for Measure* is concerned with the balance of law, justice and mercy. The duke grants clemency to Angelo at the end rather than rigorously applying the law. James I wanted to be known for balancing justice and mercy. Neville had indeed benefited from James I's clemency just the year before. However, James could also be severe: 'Most commentators believe that the exchange between Mistress Overdone and Pompey (Act 1, Scene 2) refers to the proclamation by the king on 16 September 1604 calling for the demolition of houses in suburban London.'[21] Neville had visited Vienna in 1581 and through his tutor, Henry Savile, had contact with eminent humanists and Calvinists in the city, thus gaining insights into beliefs that underlie the plot of the play. The play explores public and private morality, especially concerns about sex outside marriage leading to illegitimate children. We know these were matters that concerned Neville because from 1604 to 1606 he served on a parliamentary committee considering the plight of illegitimate children.[22]

There is a striking overlap in Neville's vocabulary as found in letters written between 1602 and 1604 and the occurrence of rare and unique words in *Measure for Measure*. He also used words to be found in *All's Well That Ends Well*, dated by Bate and Rasmussen to 1603–6, and by Wells and Taylor to 1604–5.[23] Bate and Rasmussen noted *All's Well That End Well*'s 'similarity to *Measure for Measure*'.[24]

The Vocabulary of *Measure for Measure* in Three Neville letters, 1602–4

1. Neville's Letter of 31 July 1602

This letter, written when he was still in prison, must have been written before *Measure for Measure*. It is in the collection of manuscripts of the Marquis of Salisbury at Hatfield House.[25] In this letter, we can see how much of Neville's vocabulary is used by Shakespeare in *Measure for Measure*, here highlighted in bold, with pairs of words/phrases underlined.

> And **therefore howsoever** my **evill** destyny **hath**[26] **made me** hitherto uncapable of **the good** you **intended** mee, **and so** peradventure may do **hereafter**, **yet I** vow (and **that from my soule**) to **hold** a **perpetual** remembrance of your **honourable dealing** w^th **mee**, and to **dedicate whatsoever remains in mee** unto **your service** before **all the world**, my soveraigne **only** excepted.

Of the fifty-seven words in just this one sentence, thirty-eight (66.6 per cent) are to be found in the play. We also note that the words not to be found in *Measure for Measure*, such as 'destiny', 'hitherto', 'uncapable', 'remembrance' and 'sovereign', all occur in *Othello*, which was written at about the time of this letter. Of the 536 words in the letter as a whole, 182 (33.9 per cent) occur in *Measure for Measure*, including thirty-eight pairs of words and four three-word phrases and one four-word phrase (see Addendum at the end of this chapter). The pair of words 'no more' occurs thirteen times in the play. In this letter Neville begged for a pardon to be granted to him.[27] As we shall see below the word 'pardon' is especially significant in the Hand D section of *Sir Thomas More* and occurs more often in *Measure for Measure* (twenty-five times) than in any other play in the canon.

2. Neville's Letter of 1603–4

This is an undated draft found in a collection of Neville papers at the Berkshire Record Office. Neville was released from the Tower on 10 April 1603 so the letter, which refers to him meeting the addressee at Greenwich, must be some time after that.[28] Neville refers to the addressee forgiving him his previous offences: 'You had fully <u>remmitted</u> all former displeasure.' Although Shakespeare never used the word 'remitted' he did use the word 'remit' in three plays.[29] In *Measure for Measure* the duke forgives Lucio:

> Thy slanders I forgive; and therewithal
> <u>Remit</u> thy other forfeits. (5.1.517)

Furthermore Shakespeare used the word '<u>remit</u>' again in the play when Angelo says:

> It were as good
> To pardon him that hath from nature stolen
> A man already made, as to <u>remit</u>
> Their saucy sweetness that do coin heaven's image
> In stamps that are forbid: 'tis all as easy
> Falsely to take away a life true made
> As to put metal in <u>restrained</u> means
> To make a false one. (2.4.42)

In his letter Neville also wrote '<u>restrained</u>' and in the same sentence used the word '<u>immoderate</u>', a word which Shakespeare only ever used once, in *Measure for Measure*. Claudio uses the words 'immoderate' and 'restraint' in the same sentence:

> From too much liberty, my Lucio, <u>liberty</u>:
> As surfeit is the father of much fast,
> So every scope by the <u>immoderate</u> use
> Turns to <u>restraint</u>. (1.2.117)

Having checked the LION[30] database, it is evident that between 1600 and 1624 only Shakespeare and Neville used the words <u>remit/remitted</u> with <u>restraint/restrained</u> and <u>immoderate</u> in one document. Neville had also used the word <u>liberty</u> in his letter of 31 July 1602. Angelo's speech above, about coining and unjustly spoiling a person's image, fits Neville's situation when his reputation was damaged by his indictment following the Essex rebellion. Indeed Neville wrote about 'the hazard of my poore reputacion' in this letter. The words 'hazard', 'my poor' (three times) and 'reputation' all occur in *Measure for Measure*, the latter when Angelo suggests Mariana's reputation had been damaged. Over eighty other words and phrases occur in both this letter and *Measure for Measure*.[31]

3. Neville's Letter of 8 December 1604

Of 1,004 words to be found in this letter, 256 (25.5 per cent) occur in *Measure for Measure*. The earliest recorded performance of *Measure for Measure* took place on 26 December 1604, just eighteen days after this letter. The letter also contains vocabulary used in *All's Well That Ends Well*. 'In rare vocabulary, *All's Well* is linked most closely' to *Measure for Measure*.[32] Various tests suggest *All's Well That Ends Well* was written after *Measure for Measure*. In this letter there are the following words found in both plays: 'reputation', 'restraint', 'intents' and 'purposes'. In *Measure for Measure*: 'sufficiency', 'mitigation' and 'proof'; in *All's Well That Ends Well*: 'privelidge', 'exempted' and 'debate'. 'Exempted' is unique to this play.

All's Well That Ends Well

Most commentators now date *All's Well* to the 1600s, although the precise time when it was written is much disputed. Stanley Wells and Gary Taylor suggested 1604–5.[33] Alexander Leggatt, in his introduction to the New Cambridge edition of the play, noted the difficulties in arriving at a clear date, but concluded that 'if we place it in 1603, we may not be far wrong'.[34] Leggatt also saw in 'the convoluted prose of its first few speeches a manner … that can be seen in *Measure for Measure* and *Troilus and Cressida*', and which continues in *Cymbeline* and other late plays.[35] G. K. Hunter, in his introduction to the third Arden edition of the work, claimed that '*Measure for Measure* and *All's Well* are obvious twins', and that 'a tentative dating of *All's Well* [to] 1603–4 is therefore the outcome of this inquiry'.[36] A date just after Neville's release from prison seems most likely: indeed the very title *All's Well That Ends Well* fits his likely relief and happiness at his release. Given its mood, it might have been written just before *Measure for Measure*, around the same time as Sonnet 107, before Neville was overtaken by a mood of pessimism and distress (a normal post-traumatic reaction after what had been the worst experience of his life). *All's Well* was apparently not performed in its author's lifetime, or for many years thereafter: its first known performance onstage did not occur until 1741.[37] Its setting in France, where Neville had recently been ambassador, and with a cast of characters including the King of France (whom Neville had met in his ambassadorial duties) and French noblemen and women, may well also be relevant to when it was written. Shakespeare's play is based on a section of Boccaccio's *Decameron*. A 1555 copy of the *Decameron* is to be found in the Neville family library at Audley End. The author of *All's Well* appears to have read both the Italian original and a French translation by Antoine Le Maçon. According to G. K. Hunter, 'the atmosphere of the play is decidedly French; the names Parolles, Lavatch, and Lafew seem to indicate a mind at work strongly imbued with the consciousness of French meanings.'[38] Neville was fluent in both Italian and French, and had conversed in French on a daily basis when he was ambassador a few years earlier.

In the play there are scenes in Florence, and, as Roe discovered, these contain details which show the playwright had visited the city.[39] In August 1581 Arthur Throckmorton joined Neville and Savile and 'the whole group moved on to Ferrara, Florence and Bologna in September'.[40] Neville's visit to Florence is evidenced by two books in his library: a 1581 volume of the *Historie di Matteo Villani*, published in Florence and a 1580 edition of the *Historia Fiorentina*, di M. Piero Buoninsegni, published in Florence. Given the dates of these volumes it seems likely that Neville bought them while in the city.

In 1598, John Chamberlain reported in a letter that Neville had been chosen as ambassador to France, stating, 'We hear the French king is sicke of a carbuncle or carnositie in his yard [sic] which is thought wilbe [sic] a very difficult cure'. *All's Well* begins with the French king being cured of a fistula. The recent English ambassador to France might well have known of this and used it in a play, but how and why would William Shakspere? In a letter written in France on 24 April 1600, Neville used the word 'emblem', which is found only once in the Shakespeare canon, in *All's Well*.[41] Neville's letter of 1 November 1604 also includes 'descents' which is also unique to *All's Well*.[42] Neville wrote 'three or four descents' in his letter and there are 'four or five descents' in the play. While some may regard all this as coincidence, it does accord with Neville's authorship of *All's Well* at that time, just after his release from the Tower. Indeed it would seem that at this point Neville felt that all was well that had ended well. He was soon to be disillusioned.

Sir Thomas More and Hand D

Before discussing the other plays that Neville wrote in this period, we turn to the Hand D section in a manuscript copy of a play entitled *Sir Thomas More*, a stage account of More's life. In 1871 it was suggested by Richard Simpson that the manuscript[43] of this play, which was written by six different authors, each writing (by hand) a section of the play, included one section, known as Hand D, that was actually in the handwriting of William Shakespeare.[44] This suggestion was generally greeted with enthusiasm. The world wanted an example of an actual manuscript of a work by Shakespeare. Simpson's suggestion was made at a time when the Baconian challenge to the Stratford man as the real author had gathered many followers. Support for the claim that Hand D was actually an example of Shakspere's own handwriting came in 1916 from Sir E. Maude Thompson, a leading palaeographer, who compared it with the six known signatures of William Shakspere (one of which, from 1612 and the Bellott–Mountjoy lawsuit, had been discovered only in 1910) and concluded that the *More* fragment was indeed probably by the Stratford man, but that the case for his penmanship must rest on 'the convergence of a number of independent lines of argument – palaeographic, orthographic, linguistic, stylistic, psychological – and not on any one alone'.[45] Seven years later, Thompson contributed to a volume of essays edited by A. W. Pollard, *Shakespeare's Hand in the Play of Sir Thomas More*, whose authors came to the same conclusion.[46] In recent years, interest in *More* has revived and grown, for much the same reasons as in the nineteenth century: it would be wondrous to have an actual example of the manuscript of a Shakespeare play. At the same time the proposition that someone other than the Stratford man actually wrote the works has also become much more popular. In addition, there has been a growing interest in the Shakespeare Apocrypha, works attributed by some to the Bard but not normally included in the canon, as well as in Shakespeare as a collaborator with other playwrights.[47] This renewed interest has resulted in recent scholarly works on *Sir Thomas More*, and, in 2011, in the publication of the play in the standard third Arden edition of all of Shakespeare's works.[48] It is commonly, but by no means universally, accepted that Hand D was indeed actually written by William Shakspere. The portion attributed to him was almost certainly written around 1603, although part of the full manuscript was probably written around

1593 and then revised ten years later. It is now generally believed that the portions of the manuscript dating from around 1593 were written by Anthony Munday and Henry Chettle, while the revisions from 1603 were written by Thomas Heywood, Thomas Dekker and William Shakespeare.

There are, however, several salient reasons for questioning the proposition that Hand D was penned by William Shakspere. The only examples of the handwriting we have of the Stratford man are six signatures on legal documents, plus the words 'by me' with his last signature on his will. None of these were written prior to 1612, probably nine years after the date of Hand D. Moreover, a person's signature may well differ from their normal handwriting. Professor David Crystal warned against taking Shakspere's signatures as evidence of his normal handwriting: 'Signatures are automatic, formulaic things, meant to be recognised but hardly read. They tend to look nothing like a person's other handwriting.'[49] Perhaps more importantly, none of the other presumed authors of the *More* play were associated with the Lord Chamberlain's/King's Men, Shakespeare's acting company (it became the King's Men in May 1603): all the others apparently wrote for the Lord Admiral's Men, the rival acting company. If the Bard wrote even a play fragment for another acting company, that at least requires a good explanation. Shakspere was a sharer in the King's Men, his acting company, which means he received part of the profits from their performances, but had no known connection with a rival company and presumably did not receive any of its profits, while any plays he wrote for them were, by definition, put on in competition with those of his own acting company. Moreover, it is often argued that Shakspere was the in-house playwright of his acting company, contracted to write plays, which makes any suggestion of writing for a rival company even more unlikely. Some scholars, most notably Carol Chillington, believe that Hand D was actually that of John Webster, who is known to have collaborated with other playwrights at that time.[50]

Assuming that the extract from *Sir Thomas More* known as Hand D was written by the same man who wrote the plays and poems attributed to Shakespeare, there are many significant reasons for believing that this extract was actually written by Sir Henry Neville:

1. The handwriting used in Hand D and Neville's own handwritten documents share specific characteristics which have previously been identified as Shakespearean.
2. Neville's letters and memoranda written around this time (1603) contain many rare words and phrases that are also found in the Hand D section. This is especially remarkable given that Hand D is only three pages long.
3. The watermark on the paper on which Hand D was written is similar to that on paper used by Neville to write a letter in 1603–4.
4. Deletions in Neville's draft letter of 1603–4 and those in Hand D are made in an identical way.

We will now offer detailed evidence to support these points. For comparison we are using Neville's 1585 copy of *Leicester's Commonwealth* (Worsley MSS 47 at the Lincoln Archives), the Northumberland Manuscript 1596–7 (Alnwick Castle[51]), his letter of 1601 (British Library[52]), his 1602 letter (Hatfield House[53]) and a draft of a letter 1603–4 (in the Berkshire Record Office, Reading[54]).

The Handwriting of Hand D: Shakspere and Neville

As we noted above a number of scholars have examined Hand D and suggested it is by Shakspere, as evidenced by the six extant signatures. These signatures date from 1612 to 1615 and are the only authenticated examples of Shakspere's handwriting. With only these six signatures to go on, scholars have identified two key similarities between Hand D and the Shakspere signatures, when compared with samples of 250 contemporary hands. These are summarised as follows:

1. A Form of Joined 'ha', Featuring a Spurred 'ȧ' (the Spur Is a Curled Extension)
The spurred 'ȧ' occurs in only one of the Shakspere signatures:

 William Shȧksper, 1612, the Blackfriars Gatehouse deed.

We can compare this spurred 'ȧ' to those in Hand D:

  'a' and 'as' with spurred 'ȧ's in *Sir Thomas More*, Hand D, folio 9. (© The British Library Board)

Note that the spur here comes much further over than that of the signature. The writer of Hand D, in penning the word 'mȧiestrate' ('magistrate') used both a spurred 'ȧ' and a normal '*a*':

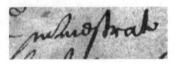 'mȧiestrate' in *Sir Thomas More*, Hand D, secretary script.

In his letter of 1601 Henry Neville used spurred 'ȧ's:

Five spurred 'ȧ's: Neville's letter of 1601, italic.
'ȧnd ordniȧry ȧbuses mȧy' and 'ȧm'.
Cotton Manuscripts, Caligula EX folio 21V. (© The British Library Board)

Note the spurred 'ȧ' in 'ordniȧry' and 'ȧm' have the same backwards hook as in the *Sir Thomas More* 'mȧiestrate'. When we turn to Neville's handwritten copy of *Leicester's Commonwealth* (c. 1585) we find he did use a curled spur when writing the word 'ȧny':

    'ȧny': Worsley 47, 1, NHMS, Neville letter 1601, Hand D.

Note that, unlike the Shakspere signature, the loop of the spurred 'a̡'s come all the way back over and this is evident in 'a̡m', above, and the word 'ha̡ppen' in Neville's 1601 letter.

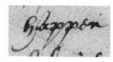

Neville's letter of 1601: italic.

We can compare these with Hand D:

'wha̡t' and 'tha̡t' in *Sir Thomas More*: Hand D, secretary script.

Dawson[55] suggested that the bulbous link of the 'h' and the 'a̡' were uncommon and matched that of the Blackfriars signature but we can see that Neville also links his 'h' and 'a' with a bulbous shape:

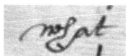

Neville's letter 1601; Neville's letter 1602.

Indeed Neville's writing here is more like Hand D, despite being in italic instead of secretary script, than is the Shakspere signature. Neville wrote in secretary script, italic and court hand and so was able to use different styles of handwriting. Hand D is in secretary script. Neville combined elements of both secretary script and italic in some of his handwritten documents and in his copy of *Leicester's Commonwealth* he switched from one to the other.

2. A Form of 'W' (Or 'M') with a Long Initial Upstroke

The second distinguishing feature is a form of 'W' with an initial upstroke which is also found on the letter 'm' of 'me': this <u>only</u> occurs in the final signature on Shakspere's will:

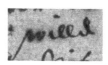

'By me William Shakspear'.

We can see these in Hand D:

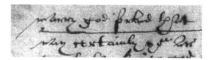

Sir Thomas More, Hand D: 'willd', 'we ma̡y'.

Sir Thomas More: Hand D, 'ma̡rry god forbid tha̡t na̡y certainly yo[u] a̡r'.

In *Sir Thomas More* 'w', 'm' and 'n' have long upstrokes. There are also upstrokes on other letters such as 'u' of 'unto' and 'i' of 'incident'. There are upstrokes on the letters 'i', 'm', 'n', 'u', 'w' in Henry Neville's 1601 letter:

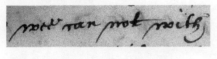

'wee can not with' in Neville's letter of 1601.

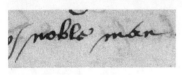

'noble man' in Neville's letter of 1601.

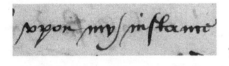

'upon my instance' in Neville's letter of 1601.

As the young Neville learned to write he would have been influenced by his father's writing. A letter from Sir Henry Neville in the Berkshire Record Office, dated to the 1570s, shows he used spurred 'a's and long descenders on the letters 'i', 'm', 'n', 'u' and 'w'.[56]

Other Similarities Between Hand D and Neville's Writings

We can also compare the word 'noble' which is found in Hand D and Neville documents:

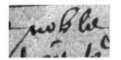

Above left: 'noble' (with long descender on initial 'n') *Sir Thomas More*: Hand D.

Above middle and right: Neville letters: 1601 (with long descender), 1602, 1603–4.

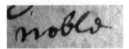 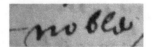

Worsley MSS 47, 12V, NHMS folio 16.

In several of these there are gaps between the letters as in Hand D and the form of the final 'le' is similar.

Capital C

The writer of Hand D used capital 'C' instead of the lower case. Melchiori noticed the occurrence of a capital 'C' instead of the lower case in the quarto of *Edward III*: 'This may reflect the author's habit, noted in the three pages of Hand D ... of nearly always capitalising initial "C" not only in nouns and adjectives but also in verbal forms, a feature absent from the rest of that manuscript or in fact from any other manuscript of the time.'[57] In Neville's 1601 letter the words 'Company', 'Counsaile', 'Conference', 'Contribucions' and 'Clothiers' on the recto and 'Coullour', 'Commodities', 'Content' and 'Complement' on the verso page are capitalised. None of these are at the start of a sentence.

'Company' and 'Counsaile', 'Conference' on the recto of Neville's letter 1601.

'Coullour', 'Commodities', 'Complement': on the verso of Neville's letter 1601.

We can compare these with examples in Hand D:

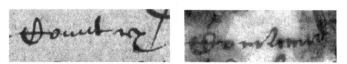

'Country' and 'Comaund' in *Sir Thomas More*: Hand D.

'Comforts' and 'Charterd' in *Sir Thomas More*: Hand D.

What these show is that Neville closed his capital 'C' whereas in three of the above examples, Hand D left the top left corner open, perhaps due to writing at speed. Neville's letter is a formal, neat italic letter to Robert Cecil. However in Neville's copy of *Leicester's Commonwealth*, Worsley MS 47, there are many open capital 'C's:

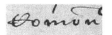 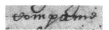

Worsley MSS 47, 'Comon' on the title page, 'Companie' 2, 'Catholique': 3V.

The last word, 'Catholique', enables us to compare the shape of the 'h' as it loops back up to connect with the next letter in Hand D's 'Charterd' above. There are no capital 'C's in the Shakspere signatures for comparison.

Capital 'S'

Crystal suggested that the capital 'S' at the beginning of line 49 of Hand D 'bears a striking resemblance to the "S" in the signatures', especially in the 1612 Blackfriars deed.[58] We can compare these with Neville's capital 'S'.

Hand D folio 8 and 9   Shaksper *1612*   Neville 1601,   1602   NHMSf24.

Abbreviation of 'pro/par'

In the Hand D section there are words beginning with 'pro' and 'par' with only the initial 'p': 'psnyp' (parsnip), 'ptly' (partly), 'pcure' (procure), 'pdon' (pardon), 'pclamation' (proclamation), 'pvnice' (province) and 'pceed' (proceed). These can be seen to mirror examples to be found in Neville's copy of *Leicester's Commonwealth*.

 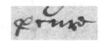

Above left: 'pcure' (procure): *Sir Thomas More*: Hand D.

Above right: 'pcure' (procure): Worsley MSS 47, 8V.

Above left: 'pdon' (pardon): *Sir Thomas More*: Hand D.

Above right: pdon' (pardon): Worsley MSS 47, 12V.

It could be objected that this 'pro/par' abbreviation might be made by any writer. Checking the entire text of *Sir Thomas More*, which is in several hands, we find that neither the principal writer, Anthony Munday, used this abbreviation and nor did Chettle, Heywood or Dekker. Just one example occurs: Hand C, a copyist, wrote 'pdon' (pardon). Hand C may have been copying text written by the Bard and accurately copied Neville's abbreviation of 'pdon'. This then provides possible evidence that Shakespeare wrote more of *Sir Thomas More* (as some editors have wondered) than just folios 8 and 9. Indeed as the scene is one in which a man is disguised and standing in for someone else (More's servant disguised as More to test Erasmus), the situation reminds us of Neville and William from Stratford.[59] (Can Erasmus tell the real man from the stand-in?) There are also examples of the 'pro/par' abbreviation in the Northumberland Manuscript: 'pvidence' (providence) in folio 16 and 28; 'pfit' (profit) in folio 27; and 'ptie' (party) in folio 28. There are many examples of this abbreviation in the annotated Hall.[60]

Superscript Letters

Hand D abbreviates 'Majesty' to 'matie'. Neville used this abbreviation with superscript letters writing 'Matie' for 'Majesty' in his 1601 letter as well as his 1602 and 1603–4 letters.

'her Matie': Neville letter 1601.

In Hand D there are small superscript letters for 'yo^u' for 'you' and 'yor' for 'your'. Neville used these superscripts in his copy of *Leicester's Commonwealth* (Worsley MSS 47):

Above left and middle: Worsley 47, 19: yo^u 23: yor.

Above right: 'yo^u' to yor' *Sir Thomas* More: Hand D.

The similarities are clear: the 'y' loops back to join the next letter in the words 'you' and 'your'. Note also the 'v' shape of the upper part of the 'y'.

Spelling and Handwriting

In some instances the spellings used by Hand D and Neville are the same, such as 'hart' (for heart), 'bin' (for been), 'yt' (for it). Weis pointed out that 'y' was frequently used by Hand D instead of 'i'.[61] Neville used 'yf' and 'yt' instead of 'if' and 'it' in his letters. In his 1602 letter he wrote 'destyny'; in his 1603–4 letter he wrote 'imbecillyty',[62] 'pryvytie'[63] and 'disabylyty'.[64] These repeated 'y's matches the following words in Hand D: 'auchtoryty', 'inhumanyty' and 'quallyfy'.

The writer of Hand D spells the word 'addition' with a 'c': 'adicion'. Neville used the letter 'c' instead of 't' in many words, such as 'interpretacion', 'intencion', 'reputacion', 'approbacion' in his 1603–4 draft letter and 'obligacion', 'mediacion' and 'preservacion' in his 1602 letter.

Hand D spelt the word 'rebell' with a double 'll' four times, once in the plural. Neville used this spelling of 'Rebells' in diplomatic letters dated 8 August 1599, 9 September 1600 and 28 December 1600.[65] In a marginal annotation on a letter from Robert Cecil dated 12 May 1600, Neville noted 'Irish Rebells'.[66] In the First Folio, the word 'rebell' is spelt with a double 'll' in *Henry VI: Part III* (1.1.50).[67]

In the Hand D section the writer used 'au' in the following words: 'Comaund', 'ffraunce' and 'straungers'. Neville wrote 'commaundment' in his letter of 15 May 1599.[68] In a letter to Sir T. Edmonde, 16 July 1613, Neville wrote 'commaund'.[69] In the first quarto of *Titus Andronicus* (1594) there are 'commaund', 'demaund' and 'raunsome'. This 'au' spelling may be due to the French influence on English and, of course, Neville was fluent in French. Neville spelt France with a double 'ff' and 'au' in his copy of *Leicester's Commonwealth* and we can compare this with the same word in Hand D:

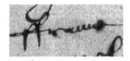 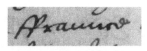

Sir Thomas More: Hand D, Worsley 47, 8V.

Neville used the following spellings in letters: 'straunge' in the letter dated 15 May 1599; 'straungers' in one dated 1 September 1599. We can compare the handwriting of these words in Hand D and Neville's copy of *Leicester's Commonwealth*:

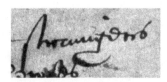 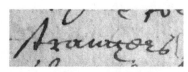

Sir Thomas More: Hand D, Worsley MSS 47, 8.

Here we can see the long 's' attached to the 't'; the backward sweep of the 'g'; the 'e' turned over to the left; the rising tail of the 's' at the end of 'straungers'.

Neville had a habit of writing 'ni' instead of 'in': such as 'knig' (king), 'aganist' (against), 'hmi' (him). This habit is to be found in Hand D, for example 'knig', 'aganist' and 'hmi'.[70] There are similarities between the way Neville writes the word 'king' and as it appears in Hand D.

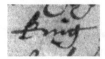 

Sir Thomas More: Hand D.   Neville 1601, Worsley MS 47, 7.

In two of the Hand D 'king's the spelling is 'knig', as it is in Neville's 1601 letter and Worsley MS 47. The curl of the 'g' to the right is a feature of Hand D but not all 'g's go to the right, as is evident with the first 'knig' above. Neville does occasionally use these rightward curling 'g's, as is evident in his copy of *Leicester's Commonwealth* (Worsley MS 47) above and in his 1601 letter:

'judgement' and 'congratulate' in Neville's 1601 letter.

We have already seen see the rightward curling 'g' in 'strangers' in Neville's copy of *Leicester's Commonwealth* and Hand D above. Not all Hand D's 'g's curl to the right. We can compare Neville's 'god' with that in Hand D:

Sir Thomas More: Hand D, Neville 1602.

The Watermarks in Hand D and Neville's 1603–4 Draft Letter

While not exactly identical, these watermarks are very similar, being placed in the same positions in relation to the chain lines, with the pot handle just over the left-hand line. A similar watermark is found on folios 6 and 16 in *Sir Thomas More*.[71] Jowett pointed out that 'the watermark on fol. 9 is unique for having a crescented orb at the top instead of the three-petalled flower of the others.'[72] It is not unique. The watermark on Neville's letter has the crescented orb. That Neville used the same type of paper may simply be coincidence: namely that the paper was available. However no document written by Shakspere exists to show William from Stratford had access to such paper.

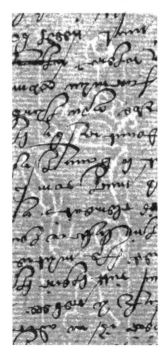 

Sir Thomas More Hand D, folio 9, Neville's 1603-4 letter.

The Form of Deletions

In both Hand D and Neville's draft letter of 1603–4 passages are deleted and corrections inserted in the space between the lines of writing. Insertions are also deleted in both.

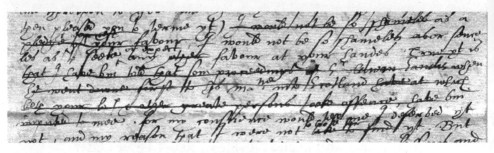

Neville's letter of 1603–4. (By permission of the Berkshire Record Office, Reading)

Sir Thomas More: Hand D.

It is evident on close examination that in both documents the deleting lines start rising and then dip like a wave, perhaps as the hand moved across the paper.

We will now examine the vocabulary of the three of Neville's letters between 1601 and 1604, comparing it with the Hand D section of *Sir Thomas More*.

The Vocabulary of Hand D and Neville's Letters

In the Hand D section of *Sir Thomas More* and Neville's letters of 1601, 1602, and 1603–4, there are numerous shared words that recur, such as 'noble', 'hart' (heart), 'pardon', 'nature', 'power', 'mediation' and 'the state'. There are also some near misses between Hand D and Neville's letters:

Hand D: lawe	Neville's 1601: lawes
Hand D: offend; th'offendor	Neville 1603–4: offence, offensive
Hand D: thoughts	Neville: 1601 and 1603–4: thought
Hand D: charge	Neville 1603–4: charged
Hand D: comforts	Neville 1603–4: comfortable, comfort
Hand D: pleasd	Neville 1601: please; in 1602, 1603–4 pleased

Hand D: growne   Neville 1603–4: growen.
Hand D: reasons   Neville 1601 and 1603–4: reason.
Hand D: have till now   Neville 1602: now till I have

In the Hand D section of *Sir Thomas More*, we also find:

you shall p(er)ceaue howe horrible a shape
your ynnovation beres, first tis a sinn
which oft thappostle did forwarne vs of vrging obedienc to aucthory[ty]
and twere no error yf I told you all you wer in armes gainst g[od]

Shakespeare used the word 'innovation', meaning civil disorder in *Henry IV: Part I*, *Hamlet* and *Othello*, all of which pre-date Hand D. On 27 April 1600, Neville wrote a letter in which he used the word 'innovation', just three days after he had used the word 'inhibition' in another letter.[73] In *Hamlet*, Rosencrantz says, 'I think their inhibition comes by the means of the late innovation' (2.2.328). Shakespeare here was referring to the Essex rebellion. Neville's letter predates *Hamlet*. Neville had bitter experience of the cost of such civil disorder and had the motivation to write a passage for *Sir Thomas More* where the hero argues against such an innovation. It is also relevant that the Neville family had personal connections with Sir Thomas More.[74]

Taken together, these facts present a strong case that Hand D was written by Neville. There remains the unanswered question, why was Neville writing for the Lord Admiral's Men, not for the King's Men? This cannot be answered definitively, and some scholars actually believe that the 1603 revision of *More* was written for the Lord Chamberlain's/ King's Men, despite its origins in a rival company. When Neville was arrested for his part in the Essex rebellion, he was initially confined at the Lord Admiral's House in Chelsea, where he drafted an account of his role in the rebellion. It is possible that he received a sympathetic reception there from Lord Nottingham, the Lord Admiral, who had shared the command of the Cadiz raid of 1596 with Essex. Perhaps in revising the play Neville was helping the Lord Admiral's men in return for the Lord Admiral's hospitality. Another possible explanation of Hand D is simply that, in 1603, Neville needed a great deal of time to normalise his affairs and to resume his previous life, and so was only in a position to write the fragment of a play, not an entire drama. As we noted earlier, the gap between his emergence from the Tower and the apparent première of *Measure for Measure*, his next play, in December 1604, was the longest in the canon. The evidence we have presented here for Neville's authorship of Hand D far outweighs that for William Shakspere, for whom there are only six signatures to compare and some of these may in fact be by legal clerks.

King Lear

King Lear was probably the third of the four great tragedies to be written. It was penned about the same time as *Macbeth*, but which of the two came first is unclear. The earliest performance of *King Lear* was before the king at Whitehall on 26 December 1606, but the play was not recorded in the Stationers' Register until nearly a year later, on 26 November

1607. The first quarto edition of the play was published in 1608. The question of its date is further confused by two other factors. An anonymous play, *King Leir* [*sic*], was recorded in the Stationers' Register in May 1594 and again, curiously, in May 1605. This play was also printed in 1605. *Leir* was performed in 1594 by two acting companies, 'the Queenes men and my lord of Sussex together' at Philip Henslowe's Rose Theatre, not by the Lord Chamberlain's Men (which was established in 1594). That play (unlike Shakespeare's) ends happily and does not contain the Gloucester subplot. If Neville relied on *Leir* for inspiration for his version, he may have written his play after *Leir* was published in 1605. The second anomaly is that the version of the play published in the First Folio in 1623 omits about 300 lines of text found in the quarto version, and also includes about 100 lines not found in the earlier version. Whether these revisions came from Shakespeare or were theatrical changes, possibly made by the actors, or by someone else, is unclear.

The basic plot of *King Lear* derives from Holinshed's *Chronicles*, as well as from works by Edmund Spenser, Sir Philip Sidney and others, which its author must therefore have known and read. However, it almost certainly drew upon two other important contemporary sources. The first was the case of Cordell Annesley in 1603–4. As R. A. Foakes put it in his introduction to the third Arden edition of *King Lear*, 'In 1603–4 the eldest daughter of Brian Annesley, an ageing wealthy gentleman pensioner of Queen Elizabeth, tried to have her father declared a lunatic so that she and her husband could control his affairs. His second daughter seems to have played no part in the matter, but the youngest, Cordell, appealed successfully to Sir Robert Cecil, and when Annesley died in 1604 he left most of his property to her'.[75] Annesley (who was apparently known more often as Ansley or Anslowe) had sat briefly as a Member of Parliament for Peterborough from 1571 to 1572, and so has an entry in the *History of Parliament* series which is of interest:

Ansley's father was an officer of the royal cellars under Henry VIII and he himself was one of the band of gentlemen pensioners to her Majesty the space of thirty years. He received a monopoly to import steel, another to export coney skins, and the wardenship of the Fleet prison [from *c.* 1574 to *c.* 1588]. The last he farmed for £100. In Mr. Anslowe's time, it was later reported, were insurrections, slaughters of servants, and irons and stocks inflicted. As far as we know, Ansley was as unconnected with Peterborough as he was with the county - unless he inherited his father's office of woodward [*sic*] of Braden near Towcester - and it was unusual for the borough to be represented by strangers at the time. Presumably his return was due to Cecil [*sic*] influence, after Henry Cheke had chosen to sit for Bedford. Towards the end of his life Ansley fell into 'such imperfection and distemperature [*sic*] of mind and of memory' that was thought 'altogether unfit to govern himself.' He was cared for by his younger surviving daughter, Cordell, who claimed that her sister Grace's husband Wildgoose [Sir John Wildgoose] wished to have Ansley 'begged [*sic*] for a lunatic, whose many years service to her late Majesty deserved a better agnomination [*sic*].' Ansley resolved the situation by dying, 7 July 1604, leaving Cordell executrix, who proved the will the same day. Wildgoose unsuccessfully challenged the will, and Cordell erected a monument in Lee Church, where Ansley was buried on 13 July 1604 'at her own proper cost and charges in further testimony of her dutiful love… against the ungrateful nature of oblivious time.'[76]

One of Annesley's executors was Sir William Harvey (*c.* 1565–1642), who in 1598 had married Mary (d. 1607), the widowed mother of Lord Southampton. In 1608 he married Cordell Annesley.[77] In 1604 Harvey was Member of Parliament for Petersfield, and would certainly have known Neville either through his connection with Southampton or because they were both Members of Parliament. In April 1604 Harvey was 'among those appointed to consider the bill for the restitution of his stepson, the 3rd Earl of Southampton (2 April) who rewarded him with a life grant of Soberton [near Southampton in Hampshire]'.[78] Neville would plainly have had an interest in this bill, as he would certainly have hoped for similar generosity towards himself following his support for Essex. In contrast to these links, how could this family dispute between two daughters, one named Cordell (later spelled Cordelia), of a wealthy, elderly, mentally ill man, possibly be known to William Shakspere, and why would he have used this situation in a play? There were no newspapers then, and the proceedings in this case were heard in the Court of Wards. Neville had specific links with Harvey and Southampton. We have already traced some of these in Chapter 2.[79] The point cannot be made too often that William Shakspere, the Stratford man, had no known connections of any kind with Southampton. Southampton's surviving papers have been combed for evidence of any association with Shakspere, but none has been found.

The second contemporary case from which *King Lear* may in part derive was that heard in the Star Chamber between June 1604 and June 1605 in which Sir Robert Dudley, the illegitimate son of Robert Dudley, 1st Earl of Leicester, attempted to establish his legitimacy and his claim to Leicester's property. Sir Robert lost his case. This occurred in part due to direct intervention by King James and as a result, Sir Robert's cousin, Robert Sidney, was declared Leicester's rightful heir.[80] This lawsuit divided the English Establishment, with Robert Cecil opposing these claims.[81] Judgment was delivered against Dudley in May 1605.[82] Factors which might have motivated Neville to use this dispute in *King Lear* include his own possible illegitimacy and the fact that, like Neville, Dudley 'had been waiting for [Queen] Elizabeth to die, as he was well aware that she would not have allowed him to raise the issue', Leicester having been her favourite.[83] There were also other personal and political factors affecting Neville. Robert Sidney (1563–1626), born at around the same time as Neville, had been at Christ Church, Oxford when Neville was at Merton, and had served as a Member of Parliament in the 1580s and 1590s at the same time as Neville.[84] They had travelled together on the Continent. During the 1590s, Sidney had been an ally and supporter of Essex, but later turned against him.

It has sometimes been claimed that Sidney clung to Essex's party while it was to his advantage, but, at the critical moment in 1601, abandoned the Earl to his fate. This suggestion is unwarranted. At least two years earlier their friendship was becoming cooler and, in fact, it was Essex who began the process … His appearance for the government at the time of the Essex rebellion in 1601, to try to persuade Essex to surrender since his cause was lost, was not a treacherous act.[85]

In 1601, no longer a Member of Parliament, Robert Sidney intervened in a contested election for the seat of Kent by supporting the candidacy of one Sir Henry Neville. This was not our man, but his identically named cousin (*c.* 1575–1641), who was also an Essex supporter. Sidney supported him against the candidate favoured by Francis Fane, Lord

Cobham, whose mother was a claimant to the Barony of Bergavenny against the claims of the cousin's father.[86] In the end, both Neville and Fane were elected for the two-member seat. In 1603, Sidney was created Baron Sidney. In 1605 he was made Viscount Lisle of Penshurst and, in 1618, Earl of Leicester. He also received other rewards from the new king, including 'numerous lucrative grants, and a place in the queen's household'.[87] Neville, who had received no rewards from the new king, might well have been vexed by Sidney and his case. For obvious reasons, the Dudley lawsuit is thought to have influenced the Gloucester subplot about bastardy in *King Lear,* which is not found in the earlier *King Leir* play. A further connection with Sidney is the fact that the Gloucester subplot is drawn from Philip Sidney's *Arcadia.*[88] At the time that *King Lear* was written, Neville was serving on a parliamentary committee concerned with illegitimate children. During the time of the lawsuit, which was heard in the Star Chamber, Neville wrote a letter on 1 November 1604, from 'my bed at the Star-Chamber'.[89] Robert Sidney was later to be a supporter of Neville in his bid to become Secretary of State.

The timing of these two lawsuits, especially the conclusion of the Dudley affair (May 1605) appears to offer the earliest date at which Shakespeare's play could have been written.[90] It thus seems likely that *King Lear* was written in late 1605 or in early 1606. As Foakes notes, there is no evidence that William Shakspere from Stratford knew of either of these affairs.[91] It is possible that he might have known of the Dudley lawsuit because, in contrast to the Annesley/Ansley litigation, it was apparently a top talking point, but why would he have added it as a subplot to *King Lear*? Yet again, we are comparing a possible author who had an immediate and obvious reason for taking note of an actual event with a supposed writer who had no known interest in this matter.

In Neville's letter of 4 June 1606 he used the word '<u>affectionate</u>', which is unique to *King Lear.* The letter was written about the same time as the play. Neville ended this 1606 letter with 'my affectionate commendations and best wishes unto yourself and Mrs. Winwood'. He used the word again at the end of another letter dated 21 June 1608.[93] In *King Lear* the word occurs at the end of a letter as the writer signs off: 'Your – wife, so I would say – <u>Affectionate</u> servant, Goneril'. In his letter of 21 June 1608, Neville used the phrase '<u>to deal plainly</u>' which is unique to *King Lear*. While Shakespeare used the words 'deal' and 'plainly' separately many times this was the only time he used the phrase. The first quarto of *King Lear* was published in 1608, the very year of this letter.

In *King Lear* Edmund, pouring scorn on his father's superstitious astrological prognostications, refers to 'spherical predominance' (1.2.120). Astronomy was called 'Spherics' by the Pythagorians. Neville's book on spherical geometry by Theodosius of Tripoli is still in his library and the front page is signed by him. It is annotated in Latin and Greek, showing Neville had studied it closely.

In the play Edgar describes the cliffs at Dover: the writer had clearly seen the dizzying height of the cliffs and observed men gathering samphire (4.6.15). Neville had travelled through Dover at least twice.[94] He wrote a letter from there as he waited for a favourable wind in 1599 and he stayed at Dover Castle on his return from France in 1600. Neville was arrested in Dover in 1601, so we can be sure he had vivid memories of the town. By contrast, there is no evidence that William Shakspere travelled anywhere except London and Stratford.

Macbeth

Macbeth was probably the fourth of the great tragedies to be written, although once again it is not possible to date it precisely. Its earliest recorded performance was in April 1611, witnessed by Simon Forman, but it was presumably put on many times before this. Wells and Taylor date the play to 1606, immediately after *King Lear*.[95] Virtually all commentators give 1606 as its date, noting the many apparent contemporary references in the play, especially to the Gunpowder Plot of 1605. Wells and Taylor summarise the mainstream view:

> The choice of a Scottish and demonic subject, and the prophetic references to James, make clear that the play was written after James I's succession. James was touching for 'the King's evil' as early as November 1604. The reference to equivocation coupled with treason … very probably alludes to the trial of the Gunpowder Plot conspirators (January–March 1606). The reference to 'The Tiger' (1.3.6–24/84–102) may allude to the terrible voyage experienced by a ship of that name which arrived back at Milford Haven on 27th June 1606 and at Portsmouth Road on 9th July, after an absence which lasted almost exactly 'Wearie Sen'nights, nine times nine' … [There is] a circumstantial case for the play's performance before James I on 7th August 1606, during a visit of King Christian of Denmark.[96]

These scholars also note apparent allusions to *Macbeth* in two plays composed in 1607.[97]

There is no reason to question any of this, nor their view that *Macbeth* was composed after *Lear* and *Timon* but before *Antony and Cleopatra*.[98] A date of composition in late 1606 or even early 1607 thus seems most likely. Perhaps the most striking of many features of *Macbeth* is that it is more focused than the plays which immediately preceded it, and lacks the ambiguous moral world view of the plays written slightly earlier. Indeed, *Macbeth* appears in many respects to parallel *Hamlet* (and also *Othello*) and it offers a kind of distorted mirror image of the first of the great tragedies. In *Hamlet* and *Macbeth* one sees the play's protagonist urged by supernatural beings to do something necessary (for him) but illegal and we see the same hesitation. There is also a comic parallel in the Gravedigger and the Porter. Of course there are differences: Hamlet's revenge is arguably justified, while the murder of Duncan by Macbeth is urged on a combination of prophecy by the witches, ambition and an evil counsellor, Lady Macbeth. The play was written when a Scottish king was on the English throne, and this fact is presumably relevant to the play's setting in Scotland.

Neville had several important links with Scotland. He had traveled there in 1583, in the company of the Earl of Essex and Sir Francis Walsingham, as a member of an ambassadorial visit to what was then a foreign country. Of course, visiting a place is not a *sine qua non* for writing a play set there, but it is worth reiterating that the plays show a detailed knowledge of such places as Italy, Scotland and the environs of Windsor, which Neville is certainly known to have visited, while there is no evidence that William Shakspere from Stratford ever did.

Through his ancestors, the Barons Bergavenny, Neville was descended from the eighth king of Dalriada in Scotland 'in the shape of the line of Anglo-Scottish thanes and mormaers who held sway on the English–Scottish borders long before the original

Nevilles even arrived in England [from Normandy]'.[99] Neville was actually descended from King Duncan and from a close relative of Macbeth.

James I was in Oxford in 1605 when Neville was awarded an MA degree. On that occasion Matthew Gwinne (or Gwyne, 1558–1627) presented a pageant in Latin, *Tres Sibyllae*, which referred to the prophecy that Banquo's descendants would inherit an endless empire, 'the concept whereof the King did much applaude'.[100] As the work was not published until 1607, after *Macbeth*, but seems plainly to have influenced it, Iain Wright, the author of Gwinne's entry in the *Oxford Dictionary of National Biography*, suggests that it 'seems plausible to argue that Shakespeare may have been present at the performance'.[101] There is, needless to say, no evidence that William Shakspere from Stratford was present at the performance, but Neville was certainly in Oxford at the time. Moreover, from 1601 until 1607 Gwinne was a professor at Gresham College in London, founded by Neville's famous relative, where the Neville family had continuing rights of administration. Neville could have known Gwinne personally because they had been at Oxford University at the same time.[102]

Macbeth appears to be welcoming the Scottish king to the English throne, but with more than a hint of ambivalence. This double-edged viewpoint almost certainly mirrored Neville's opinion of the new king in 1606 and 1607: still hopeful of office and reward; glad that a Protestant monarch was on the throne; grateful to have been released from the Tower and restored to his knighthood; but increasingly disappointed and frustrated by the king's vexatious refusal to grant him high office. More and more, Neville looked to his growing role in the House of Commons as a conduit for his evolving political views and ambitions.

In the play King Duncan is assassinated. King James was fearful of assassination. Indeed he had been held prisoner more than once and in the Gowrie Conspiracy of 1600 had been assaulted. Neville knew of this and referred to it in his letters, indeed he knew John Ruthven, 3rd Earl of Gowrie, having met him in Paris earlier that year. In his report to Cecil, Neville described Gowrie as a strong Protestant and Anglophile, 'a nobleman of whom, for his good judgement, zeal and ability, <u>exceeding good use could be made on his return</u>' (our emphasis underlined).[103] Mystery surrounds the deaths of John and Alexander Ruthven on 5 August 1600. It is possible that they were involved in a plot against James VI on behalf of several hidden figures including Cecil. John travelled from Paris to London where he was well received and liked. Shortly after he returned to Scotland he and his brother were killed in a fracas involving James. At the subsequent treason trial their bodies were propped up so they could be found guilty and their lands sequestered.

In December 1604, the King's Men (Shakespeare's company of actors) gave two performances of a play, *The Tragedy of Gowrie*. It was banned and no copies survive. On 18 December 1604, John Chamberlain wrote to Neville's secretary and replacement as ambassador to France, Ralph Winwood, about the play speculating that, 'whether the matter or manner be not well handled, or that it be thought unfit that Princes should be played on the Stage in their Life-time, I hear that some great Councillors are much displeased with it and so 'tis thought shall be forbidden'.[104] No evidence survives of this play's plot or author. However *Macbeth* is thought to be an oblique response to the Gowrie incident. A number of incidents in *Macbeth* can be seen to replay those that occurred on Tuesday 5 August 1600: a Tuesday is mentioned in the play as being ominous (2.4.11); a porter played a significant role in both; according to Holinshed, Shakespeare's main historical source, Dunsinane was in the Gowrie lands.

James's attempted extirpation of the entire Gowrie family is curiously reminiscent of Macbeth's wholesale slaughter of Macduff's family in Act 4 of the play ... James ordered the arrest of the boys William and Patrick Ruthven who escaped from the king's clutches by fleeing to England and France just as Duncan's sons, Malcolm and Donaldbain, flee to England and Ireland following their father's murder. These similarities between James and the tyrant Macbeth would not have been lost on those members of the original audience of the play familiar with the circumstances of the Gowrie Conspiracy.[105]

Shakespeare also inserted a Scottish noble into the Macbeth story who is not in Holinshed's account: Lennox. Ludovick Stuart, 2nd Earl of Lennox, was James's companion during the Gowrie incident and was a principal witness to the events.[106] None of his potential assassins survived their plot against him and it was suspected that James had perhaps arranged the whole affair to eliminate a family who had previously threatened him and to whom he owed a great deal of money. Neville wrote to Winwood from London, in a letter dated 28 August 1600, 'The Erle of *Gowry* and *a Brother of his*, have been lately slaine in *Scotland, in the Erle's own House, and in the King's Presence.* They were charged *to have conspired the King's Death at that tyme*, but God would not suffer them, they had prepared for it, to *execute their Desseign, allthough they attempted it*; and so they fell into the Pitt themselves had digged. This is the Relation sent hither to of it, *which notwithstanding is diversely ansured according to Men's divers Affections*.'[107] (Italics in original.)

Neville here is recording doubts about the truth of the official account. In November he had found out more details which he put into two letters, the first being dated 2 November 1600: 'Some other Ministers are put from their Charges, and banished *Edinbourg* Town and the Court, *with an express Prohibition not to come into* England. Their Crime is, *that they refused to declare the Conspiracy* and Attempt of *Gowry* and his Brother against the King *in such sort as they were required*.'[108] In other words men were being pressured to support the official account and refusing to do so. Two weeks later Neville wrote, using code numbers[109] perhaps because the information was sensitive, 'Out of (205) *Scotland* we hear, there is no good Agreement, but rather an open Difference between (165 Counsail) *the King of* Scots and his wife; and many are of Opinion, that the Discovery of some *Affection between her and the Earle of* Gowry's *Brother, (who was killed with him) was the truest Cause and Motife of all that Tragedy*.'[110] Neville here used the same word that appears in the title of the lost play: *The Tragedy of Gowry*. If Neville wrote this play it might explain James I's antipathy to him.

Clark showed how one possible source for *Macbeth* was a unique Scottish royal historical manuscript, William Stewart's *Buik of the Chroniclis of Scotland*.[111] It was not printed until 1858. We suggest that the diplomat Henry Neville, who visited Scotland, met James I on several occasions and who was known for his 'book-learning', was more likely to have had access to this rare document than William Shakspere from Stratford. Clark made a case for William having visited Scotland and been allowed access to the book but there is no evidence in support of his speculation.

In the copy of Ovid's *Ars Amatoria* to be found amongst Neville's books an annotator has drawn a hand pointing to a passage about 'Tigris ... Hircani'. In other books and documents Neville drew these little hands to highlight text.[112]

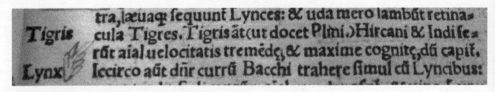

Ovid's *Ars Amatoria* and *Remedia Amoris*, 12.

Shakespeare referred to the 'th'Hircan tiger' in *Macbeth* (3.4.102). The original spelling in the First Folio is 'Hircan' with an 'i', though later editors change this to 'Hyrcan' with a 'y'. According to LION, between 1584 and 1611 no other writer referred to a Hircan tiger. In 1612, Hervey Peacham in *Minerva Britanna* wrote, 'No Hircan tyger' but this was well after *Macbeth*.[113] The text in the *Ovid* reads, 'Tigris āt (ut docet Plini) Hircani'. The editor of the Oxford *Macbeth* offered a footnote suggesting that 'Pliny, *Natural History*, viii, 18, uses Hyrcanian sea for the Caspian ... his book was widely read in grammar schools, and translated by Philemon Holland in 1601'.[114] The Ovid text mentions 'Plini', showing that Neville had access to information on the tiger and a reference to Pliny as a source long before Holland's translation. Hamlet refers to 'th'ircanian beast' (2.2.441; this spelling is in the second, third further and fifth quartos: 1604–37). This spelling suggests an elision between the 'h' of 'the' and 'Hircanian' spelt with an 'i'. Only in the First Folio does this become 'th'Hyrcanian beast' with a 'y'.[115] In the First Folio version of *Henry VI: Part III*, the Duke of York (who married Cecily Neville) refers to the 'tigers of Hyrcania' (1.4.155).

Macbeth, the darkest of all the plays, is a meditation on how men can be seduced by ambition into evil actions and pay a terrible price. Neville was still ambitious and, as his parliamentary career shows, he manoeuvred to succeed Robert Cecil. He knew the dangers inherent in political ambition and that frustrations might well lead to failure. He was in a position to observe the king and the ambitious men about him with their court factions. The next play takes these meditations to their disillusioned culmination.

Timon of Athens

One of Shakespeare's least known plays, *Timon of Athens* was almost certainly written about this time. 'Taking into consideration all the available evidence ... we lean to a date of 1607, though it is possible that the play was written a little earlier,' two recent editors have concluded.[116] Wells and Taylor put its date at around 1605, 'just after *All's Well* and before *Macbeth*'.[117] H. J. Oliver, the editor of the second Arden edition of the play, suggests 1607–8, around the same time as *Coriolanus* and *Antony and Cleopatra*, while Sir E. K. Chambers concluded that 1608 was the probable date.[118] It seems that the play was certainly written between 1605 and mid-1608, with 1607–8 as its probable date. There are several important anomalies about the play which should be noted. Most commentators believe that it remained unfinished, and that Thomas Middleton probably wrote some of it, supplementing the portions written by Shakespeare. Middleton had been a student at Queen's College, Oxford between 1598 and 1601.[119] Neville kept in touch with Oxford as is evident by the award of his MA in 1605 and his continuing friendship with Henry

Savile. It is also widely believed that the play, which was unpublished in any format until its appearance in the First Folio in 1623, was only published there because its editors had some difficulty in securing permission to use *Troilus and Cressida,* and included *Timon* only to fill the gap.[120] When permission to include *Troilus* was secured, *Timon* was still printed despite its unfinished condition.

The play is also anomalous in other ways. Since some readers will not have read it, it might be useful briefly to summarise its plot. Timon, a wealthy Athenian, is overly generous with his money. When he needs financial help he discovers that his fair-weather friends have deserted him. He becomes a misanthrope and goes to the woods as a hermit, living on roots. There he discovers a trove of gold, which he offers to Alcibiades, a rebel besieging Athens, who is accompanied by two prostitutes spreading venereal disease. The play ends with Timon having just one friend left, a loyal servant. He dies in the wilderness. His epitaph is:

Here lies a wretched corse, of wretched soul bereft:
Seek not my name: a plague consume you wicked caitiffs left!
Here lie I, Timon, who, alive, all living men did hate.
Pass by and curse thy fill, and pass and stay not thy gait. (5.4.69)

'Seek not my name' is a *cri de coeur* echoed in sonnets 71 and 72. Neville's name does not appear on the tomb where he is buried. This epitaph, indeed the whole play, is not necessarily one of Shakespeare's more inspired, or inspiring, works, and many commentators have wondered just what it is really about and why Shakespeare wrote it when he did. It is, in fact, one of the few plays Shakespeare wrote about money and the effects of wealth and poverty. In his post-1601 phase, Shakespeare wrote about revenge, ambition, jealousy, military greatness, and so on, but not centrally about money, and seldom in so wholly negative a way, even in his great tragedies. It is also a play in which the protagonist finds himself absolutely alone, or nearly alone. Something appears to have been definitely amiss with its author at this time, a condition acknowledged even by those critics who seldom draw inferences about the author's life from his writings. Most notably, the great Shakespearean scholar Sir E. K. Chambers believed 'that Shakespeare's failure to finish the work resulted from a mental breakdown' and also that '*Timon* was the last of the tragedies, abandoned before a revived and spiritually whole Shakespeare began composing the romances'.[121] Wells and Taylor note that Chambers' 'biographical speculations represent a wholly uncharacteristic lapse' from the latter's normal, renowned refusal to speculate about Shakespeare's life without direct evidence.[122] However, with Neville in the picture it becomes evident that Chambers may have been more perceptive than Wells and Taylor credit. By 1606, Neville was a disappointed man. He had lost a vast sum of money as ambassador to France and as a prisoner in the Tower. Although it was rumoured in late 1604 that he would be appointed ambassador to Spain, he never received any offices or appointments of any kind from the new king. He was in financial difficulty for which Sir Robert Cecil could offer no help.[123] It is possible, indeed likely, that Neville turned a psychological corner of some kind in 1607, when he was appointed to the council (i.e., becoming a director) of the Second London Virginia Company, and to a number of local offices in Berkshire, but his mood at the time that *Timon* was written was far from buoyant, and he was almost certainly obsessed by his money woes and personal disappointments, exactly the mood one might expect of the author of *Timon of Athens*. By 1606–8, Neville had been out of prison for three or four years, but had not made good his losses and many of his hopes had been disappointed.

In complete contrast to Neville, this was, so far as we know, a time of growing prosperity for William Shakspere of Stratford. In July 1605 (as noted above) he bought the interest of a lease of tithes in Stratford and surrounding parishes for £440, a very substantial sum of money at the time, especially for a provincial townsman not in the aristocracy and not a successful merchant. In August 1606 his daughter Susanna married Dr John Hall, a prominent physician; the following year Susanna produced a daughter, Elizabeth. In August 1608 Shakspere became the owner of a one-seventh share in the indoors Blackfriars Theatre.[124] Thus the only actual evidence we have about the life of William Shakspere at this time is of his growing prosperity as a man of property, and, in all likelihood, personal happiness.

One theory about *Timon of Athens* is that the play embodied 'the Southampton judgment on the crying injustice of the Essex affair, particularly the part played by Francis Bacon'.[125] As H. J. Oliver describes this theory, *Timon* is 'a play about a lavish nobleman (Timon = Essex) who was let down by those he befriended (particularly Ventidius = Bacon) and finally rebelled against the sovereign state (the rebellion being 'transferred' from Timon to Alcibiades for safety)'.[126] Oliver labels this theory 'implausible,' but it is difficult to believe that the Bard had failed to see a parallel with the Essex rebellion, given how obsessed the author had been with those events.[127] If this theory is rejected as implausible, that is perhaps due to the play's ambiguity and its concern with other matters, especially money. At the time *Timon* was written, its author appeared to be turning his back on the centrality of Essex, at least for the time being, viewing these events in a much more ambiguous light. Meanwhile Neville kept some contact with Essex's son, the young Robert Devereux, 3rd Earl of Essex, and was later to be involved in his divorce (see Chapter 11). Another possible interpretation also connects the play with Neville's concerns at the time. Jowett suggested that

> King James's Timonesque generosity in gift-giving had been especially evident in the celebration of the marriage of the Earl of Essex to Lady Frances Howard … James's reliance for financial relief on the Members of Parliament, an equivalent of the play's senators, was a matter of public comment in the months that followed. In early 1606 Parliament voted to grant funds to the King and then debated whether to increase its subsidy. It is at this time, according to the *Oxford English Dictionary*, that the noun *supply* began to be used in this context, and the sense is used in *Timon of Athens* at 3.27.[128]

Indeed, the word 'supply' is used six times in *Timon of Athens* (twice as many times as in any other Shakespeare play), including Timon's 'supply of money' (2.2.196). Neville was one of those Members of Parliament who had debated the question of the king's supply.

In Neville's letter of 8 December 1604, he used three words that only occur in *Timon of Athens*: 'imported', 'bankrupts' and 'ardent'. As *Timon of Athens* has been dated to 1605–8 we can see that Neville used these three rare words before the play was written. Like Timon, Neville was financially ruined: in his draft letter of 1603–4 he begged Cecil for financial relief which never came. This letter has over thirty words to be found in the play including the words 'my occasions' which Shakespeare only used in *Timon of Athens*.[129]

Antony and Cleopatra

Antony and Cleopatra has been dated to 1606 by Wells and Taylor, who place it after *Lear*.[130] Bate and Rasmussen claimed it was written and 'performed at Court Christmas 1606 or Christmas 1607'.[131] Two recent editors have concurred. John Wilders in the third Arden edition (1995) concluded that the evidence 'strongly suggests that it was finished by the Christmas of 1606–7'.[132] Michael Neill, in the Oxford edition of the play, stated that the evidence 'suggest[s] a probable date of late 1606 or early 1607 for the first performance of *Anthony* [*sic*] *and Cleopatra* – that is to say, just a little later than *Macbeth* (*c.* 1606) and about a year after *King Lear* (*c.* 1605)'.[133] There is virtual unanimity about both the play's date and its chronological order in the Shakespeare canon. It was apparently recorded in the Stationers' Register on 20 May 1608, although no author was given for 'A booke called Anthony and Cleopatra', and the play was not published until the First Folio of 1623. Despite the obvious appeal of its subject matter, there is no record of an actual performance of the play during the seventeenth century.[134]

Antony and Cleopatra may be seen as one among a group of plays written within a few years (1601–1609), and including *Troilus and Cressida* and *Coriolanus*, which were based on classical sources and have at least two characteristics in common: obsession with Essex and Elizabeth and a growing concern with the nature of proper governance and how this had been and was being abused. Of course, these themes figure in other works by Shakespeare, but the similarities among these particular plays are clear. That *Antony and Cleopatra* has parallels with the story of Essex and Elizabeth, however much its plot differs from actual events, has been noted by many critics. Geoffrey Bullough, for instance, in his *Narrative and Dramatic Sources of Shakespeare*, argued, in Neill's words, that 'in this story of a great soldier betrayed to his death by a queen, there were uncomfortable parallels with the story of Queen Elizabeth and her disgraced favourite, Essex, executed in 1601'.[135] Although Neill added that 'the parallel may seem strained to us', in fact it is blatantly obvious.[136] As Neill noted, the poet and playwright Fulke Greville (1554–1628) wrote a play about Antony and Cleopatra, and then destroyed it in 1601 because of its highly visible, and dangerous, parallels with Essex and Elizabeth.[137] Helen Morris, in her 'Queen Elizabeth "Shadowed" in Cleopatra' article, highlighted not merely the many parallels between Cleopatra, as depicted in the North translation of Plutarch's *Lives*, the main source used by Shakespeare in writing the play, but also many aspects of the life and character of the queen and incidents in her life not found there.[138] Dr Morris noted that several descriptions of the appearance, mood and activities of Queen Elizabeth were set down in the *Memoirs* of Sir James Melville, emissary of Mary, Queen of Scots to Elizabeth in 1564, which were not published until 1683.[139] Neville had numerous well-defined links with the leading figures in England who were engaged in negotiating with Scotland, most notably his father-in-law Sir Henry Killigrew, who was English ambassador to Scotland from 1572 to 1575, and might well have been friendly with Melville.[140] Neville had visited Scotland as a young man and had met Queen Elizabeth who had appointed him ambassador to France. Recent commentators on the play have also highlighted the anomaly of a female ruler at that time, and how Shakespeare handled this situation in his works. There is evidence of Neville recalling Elizabeth I in his portrayal of Cleopatra in a letter to Winwood from London dated 2 November 1600, in which Neville observed the queen's tendency 'to desire things till they are <u>offered</u>, and then to neglect them'.[141] This reminds us of *Antony and Cleopatra*, where Menas, conversing with Pompey, has this aside: 'Who seeks, and will not take when once 'tis <u>offer'd</u>,/Shall never find it more' (2.7.82).

Neville had known the story of Antony and Cleopatra since he was a student of classical history and literature at Oxford. Among his books were volumes of Ovid, Tacitus and Appian. The 1574 volume of Tacitus's *Annales* combines with the Ovid to furnish source material for Shakespeare's *Antony and Cleopatra*. On the last page of the Tacitus, Neville drew a family tree starting with Julius Caesar:

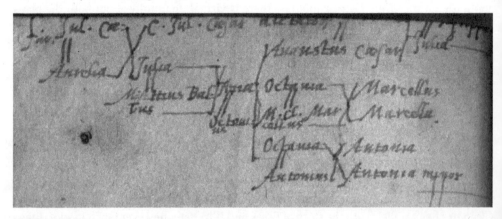

Tacitus, end page.

This genealogical list includes Augustus, Octavia, Antonius, Marcellus and (lower down on the same page) Agrippa, all of whom appear in *Anthony and Cleopatra*.[142] Anthony is called 'Antonius' four times in the play and this is the spelling used by Neville here and in annotations in his copy of Appian (see below). Another annotation on page 89 reads, 'Dolabella interfectus'. Dolabella is in *Antony and Cleopatra*.

An important image for Shakespeare was the Phoenix. It recurs throughout the canon, especially in the final plays. It has meaning and relevance to Neville's authorship.[143] The annotator of the Tacitus wrote, 'De Phœni(x)', in the margin:

inlustri tamen fortuna egere.   Paullo Fabio, L. Vitellio p. v. c.
Coss. post longum sæculorū ambitū auis Phœnix in Aegy- DCCXXCVII.
ptum venit, præbuitq₃ materiem doctißimis indigenarum, & De Phœni
Græcorum, multa super eo miraculo differendi. de quibus ce -

Tacitus: De Phœni(x), 387.

The text refers to the 'Phœnix Aegyptum', the Egyptian Phoenix, and so is an appropriate image for a play set in Egypt. The Phoenix is recalled when Agrippa exclaims, 'O Antony, O thou Arabian bird!' (3.2.12).

Cleopatra describes Antony as a perspective painting:

> Though he be painted one way like a <u>Gorgon</u>,
> The other way's a Mars. (2.5.117)

Bate suggested Ovid's *Ars Amatoria* was a source for *Antony and Cleopatra* and that a passage from it was a source for this image.[144]

> Pertinet ad faciem rabidos compescere mores:
> Candida pax homines, trux decet ira feras.
> Ora tument ira: nigrescunt sanguine venae:
> Lumina <u>Gorgoneo</u> saevius igne micant. (III. 501–4)

This very passage is underlined by the annotator of the copy of Ovid's *Ars Amatoria* in Neville's library:

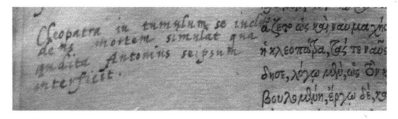

Ovid's *Ars Amatoria* and *Remedia Amoris*, 33.

Bate explained that Shakespeare was using the Gorgon/Mars images to alert the audience to Antony's questionable ability to manage his anger and his fitness to rule. We can therefore see a psycho-political aspect to this imagery, and indeed Tacitus' *Annales* is concerned throughout with Roman Emperors' fitness to rule. Shakespeare examines this question, and we know that Neville was also concerned with these issues, from his copy of *Leicester's Commonwealth* (1584–5), to his dialogues with James I and Parliament in the 1600s as he strove for a solution to the relationship between the monarch and Parliament. Neville was now an influential Member of Parliament and questions of governance, good and bad, loomed larger in his concerns and in his writings.

In the Dionysius section of the 1551 volume of Appian's *Roman History* in Neville's library there are numerous annotations concerning Antony and Cleopatra. One annotation tells how 'Cleopatra feigns death by shutting herself up in her tomb and when he hears this Antony kills himself.'

Cleopatra in tumulum se includens mortem simulet qua audita Antonius seipsum interficit, Appian (Dionysius section), 304.

Mors Antonii in sinu Cleopatrae, Appian (Dionysius section), 305.

We see this in Shakespeare's play when Mardian tells Antony that Cleopatra is dead. Another annotation on the next page reads: 'The death of Antonius in Cleopatra's net.' ('Sinus' may also be translated as 'hiding place'.)

In the play we see Cleopatra pull Antony up to her (perhaps in a net) for their final kiss. Another annotation states, 'Cleopatra, having feared lest she should be led in triumph by Caesar at Rome, committed suicide.'

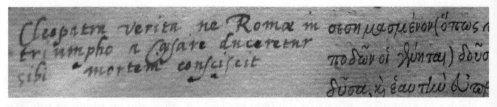

Cleopatra verita ne Roma in triumpho a Caesare duceretur sibi mortem consciscit, Appian (Dionysius section), 306.

In the play Cleopatra says:

> Do Caesar what he can. Know Sir that I
> Will not wait pinioned at your master's court …
> Shall they hoist me up
> And show me to the shouting varletry
> Of censuring Rome? (5.2.52)

Although these annotations may long predate the writing of the play, they show Neville was familiar with this story and it is possible he would choose to dramatise episodes he had previously highlighted.

Horace's *Odes* I.37 is also considered to have been a source for the play. Horace was Cleopatra's contemporary and his description of her death ennobles her. Gillespie suggested that Shakespeare could have derived his conception of the dying Cleopatra from Horace and that Horace's *Odes* were possibly a source for the play's style as a whole.[145] Neville heavily annotated his copy of *Odes* I.37. Though mostly too faint to be sure what these notes say they are nevertheless proof that Neville knew this passage.

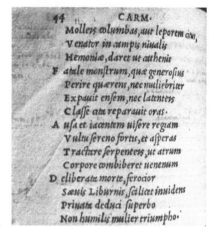

Horace *Odes* I.37.

One faint annotation, 'Alexandria', can just be made out above the words 'uisere regiam': Alexandria is referred to five times in *Antony and Cleopatra*. The last of these references is when Antony is speaking to Cleopatra (4.8.30). Alexandria is mentioned in no other Shakespeare play.

In his letters from 1599 to 1605 Neville used words that only occur in *Antony and Cleopatra* or other later plays: 'forborne': in a letter dated 6 June 1599;[146] 'favouring': 20 August 1599;[147] 'president': 6 September 1599;[148] 'acknowledged': 16 September 1599 (also found in *King Lear* and *The Winter's Tale*); 149 'diminution': 24 September 1599 (also found in *Cymbeline*);[150] 'dismission': 22 October 1599 (also found in *Cymbeline*);[151] 'slackness': 1 November 1599 (also found in *The Winter's Tale*);[152] 'mariners': 20 December 1599 (also found in *The Tempest*);[153] 'maritime': 3 January 1600;[154] 'engender': 12 March 1600;[155] 'persisted': 9 May 1600;[156] 'entangled': 21 June 1605, this last being written just the year before the play was composed. The words in the letter are: 'entangled in some other business. But I am out of my proper orb when I enter into state matters.'[157] All these words occur separately in *Antony and Cleopatra*. The two words 'state matters' occur together only in *Othello* which was written by 1604. We acknowledge that these words might have been widely used at the time but their occurrence in his letters is proof that they were already in Neville's vocabulary when the play was written.

Coriolanus

Bate and Rasmussen tentatively dated *Coriolanus* to 1608; they noted that the 'theatres were closed because of the plague for the majority of the time in these years [1607–8], so the play may belong to the open period of April–July 1608'.[158] The play is more confidently dated to 1608 by Wells and Taylor, who claim that 'stylistic tests uniformly place the play after *The History of King Lear*, *Macbeth*, and *Antony and Cleopatra*'.[159] All commentators highlight the reference to 'coale of fire upon the Ice' (1.1.171) as referring to the great frost of December 1607 to January 1608, and also to the apparent references to the Midlands food riots of 1607–8. The First Folio (1623) edition of the play contains regular act divisions which the King's Men began to use when they acquired the indoor Blackfriars Theatre in

August 1608.[160] However, there is no reference to a performance of the play before it was published for the first time in the First Folio.[161] The play is largely based on Plutarch, and on other works including Camden's *Remaines* of 1605. Camden knew Neville and was present when he confessed his role in the Essex rebellion.[162]

Coriolanus has seemed to many to be a commentary on contemporary English politics. The evidence for this is striking, and is fully consistent with Neville's career at that time, but clearly not with the career of William Shakspere. The most frequently noted aspect of English politics seemingly dramatised in the play is that the Coriolanus character appears to be similar to the actual character and life of the Earl of Essex.[163] Indeed, these are so similar to the actual biography of Essex, but different from the life of Coriolanus as depicted by Plutarch, that it is difficult to believe that the play's author did not have Essex in mind.[164] For Neville, this would suggest that he was returning to his former obsession with Essex in a more focused way than in the plays that he had written shortly after his release from the Tower.[165] As always, it is very difficult, perhaps impossible, to see why William Shakspere should still be obsessed with Essex, or use an Essex-like character as the protagonist of a play written seven years after the earl's execution, when the dust had settled on him and his rebellion.

Coriolanus has also been seen as a commentary on parliamentary elections and, in particular, on the franchise, with its author opposing challenges to the system that prevailed in English parliamentary elections of the time.[166] It appears that the play's author was arguing for the greater supremacy of Parliament, and especially of the elected House of Commons, as the people's tribune. He seemingly hoped that the leadership of the nation, increasingly found in the lower House of Parliament, would result in the traditional leaders of the nation, those most likely to be elected to the Commons, gaining the upper hand over both royal and executive privilege, but without engaging in demagoguery aimed at gaining the support of the masses outside of the elite and gentry: a balance had to be struck. To a remarkable extent, this mirrored Neville's increasingly important position in the House of Commons at the time, which was as a proto-radical, yet moderate, critic of the arbitrary power of both the king and Robert Cecil (who was by then Lord Salisbury). It is also worth noting that in May 1608 Cecil assumed complete control of English public affairs, becoming Lord Treasurer as well as Secretary of State.[167] It is difficult to believe that the author did not have this in mind when he wrote the play.

Neville still hoped for high office for himself, but had been denied by the king since his accession. In 1611, rumours circulated that Neville would succeed Cecil as Secretary of State, but the king declined to appoint him. Had he done so, Neville would have achieved the restoration of the Neville family to its old pre-eminence. Neville and his associates also had a programme aimed at the diminution of royal monopolies, the establishment of free trade, and of Protestant hegemony, which foreshadowed that of the Puritans a generation later. In 1612, Neville offered to act as 'undertaker', an organiser of parliamentary business for the king in the House of Commons, provided that James refrained from making inflammatory remarks, sought parliamentary approval for funding, and instituted discreet consultations between the Crown and a committee of Parliament.[168] Neville was supported in the Lords by his close ally Lord Salisbury and by William Herbert, 3rd Earl of Pembroke.

Nevertheless, it is important to keep in mind that Neville was not Cromwell and remained a moderate reformer, more in favour of reforming a pre-existing order than of a revolution. Despite that, he and his allies have been seen by some scholars of the early twentieth century as foreshadowing not only the Commonwealth but also the American Constitution. For E. P. Kuhl, 'Shakespeare [in his later works] expresses his age, in fact distills the spirit of the time of the Virginia Colonization: its ideals of representative government, religious toleration, prospect of trade [*sic*]'.[169] This viewpoint had also been expressed earlier by Charles Mills Gayley, in his *Shakespeare and the Founders of Liberty in America* (1917), who also saw many parallels between the works of William Shakespeare and the ideas of Richard Hooker (*c*. 1554–1600), the champion of a balanced constitution, whose writings apparently influenced the famous speech on degree by Ulysses in *Troilus and Cressida*.

Even if the linkages between Shakespeare and later theorists of good government are exaggerated, it seems clear that *Coriolanus* is heavily political in nature and well-informed about the monarchical and parliamentary politics of the day. Neville was a Member of Parliament for virtually the whole of his adult life, with the exception of the period following his imprisonment in 1601.

In complete contrast, William Shakspere had no direct experience of English politics at either the national or local level. Although his father had served as Burgess of Stratford-upon-Avon and as a local Justice of the Peace, William was never appointed or elected to either office (or any other) after retiring to his home town (or at any other time), although he had become one of Stratford's richest men and had been officially recognised as a gentleman with a coat of arms. Possibly, if he had lived longer, he would have held a local office of some kind, but at the time of his death he had no political experience as an office holder at any level. There is, in fact, no evidence that Shakspere took any interest in holding a political or even parochial office, which is perhaps the reason why he never held any, and there is no evidence that he took any interest in national politics.

Stratfordian commentators have, however, had to account for the fact that *Coriolanus*, and other plays of that time, were clearly very political in nature. Some have postulated a connection between the Stratford man and wider political events. For instance, Richard Wilson, the author of *Will Power: Essays on Shakespearean Authority*, quoted by Lee Bliss, saw 'the play's handling of its political struggle as solidly grounded in Shakespeare's Stratford viewpoint on the troubled 1601 election of Sir Fulke Greville as Member of Parliament for Warwickshire'.[170] There is, of course, no evidence of any kind that William Shakspere held any view whatever on the 1601 Warwickshire election, or used it in *Coriolanus*, written seven years later. *The History of Parliament*, with its account of the history of every parliamentary electorate of that period, has this to say about the Warwickshire election:

> In 1601 there was an attempt by the Warwickshire gentry, led by Sir Thomas Lucy, to break
> Fulke Greville's monopoly of the senior county seat, but Greville was in favour at court,
> and the Privy Council put such pressure on the sheriff that Greville was again elected.[171]

Lucy was supported by the Stratford aldermen, including Richard Quiney (d. 1602), whose son Thomas (1589–*c*. 1655) married Shakspere's daughter Judith in 1616 (fifteen years later).[172] According to Wilson's scenario, William Shakspere apparently sided with Sir Thomas Lucy (1552–1605). He was the son of the identically named Sir Thomas Lucy (1532–1600) who, according to the famous alleged account, caused the young poacher William Shakspere to flee to London. Surely this would have been an unlikely preference for the Bard (and one for which, needless to say, there is no actual evidence). In addition, Greville failed to secure election to Parliament after 1601 because 'his fall from favour after Elizabeth's death removed any hope effect of a sixth victory'.[173] The next parliamentary election, that of 1604, the last before the writing of *Coriolanus,* was uncontested, although one of the successful candidates was Sir Edward Greville (1566–1634), apparently a cousin of Sir Fulke. Sir Edward had been a wealthy supporter of Essex as well as an unpopular encloser of lands in Warwickshire. Essex knighted him at Cadiz in 1597.[174] There was nothing to link this parliamentary election with William Shakspere, although there is much to link it with Neville.

Perhaps the current events most frequently cited as evidence that *Coriolanus* reflected the affairs of England of its time are the apparent references to the food riots of 1607–8, known as the 'Midlands Revolt'.[175] According to Bliss, these were 'agrarian protests against the enclosure of formerly open-field farming units into commercially profitable large tracts of hedged-off sheep pastures [which] meant fewer jobs for agricultural labourers'.[176] *Coriolanus* is apparently on the side of the labourers. Most of the 1607 rioting was in Northamptonshire, although the Stratford-upon-Avon area was affected. These riots must have been of national, rather than purely local, importance, or they would not have been dramatised in a London stage play. Indeed they were, as Bliss puts it, of concern to the audiences at the Globe and Blackfriars theatres at that time. 'All would have seen the effects on the poor in the streets, and, for those not themselves suffering, in the increased amount they were taxed for the relief of the poor; all would have experienced the high price of bread in 1607–8 and of fuel from 1606 to 1608'.[177] The author of *Coriolanus* need not have been directly connected with the Midlands food riots, but merely with their national effects, experienced in London by everyone.

If William Shakspere was the author of *Coriolanus,* it is especially curious that he himself was a grain hoarder. The play opens with the famished citizens of Rome rioting for grain: one of them accuses the governing class of hoarding grain and supporting usurers (1.1.79). An official return of those holding stock of corn or malt contrary to law in a time of dearth of 4 February 1598 noted that 'Wm. Shackespere' of 'Stratforde' held 'x [ten] quarters of grain'.[178] He was also affected by the enclosure of the Welcombe open fields, a mile from Stratford, of which, in 1605, he had purchased the corn and hay tithes. In 1614, two local investors proposed to enclose these fields, compensating William Shakspere and his cousin, Thomas Greene, another tithe holder. The two promoters were then joined by William Combe (William Shakspere left £5 in his will of 1613 to Combe's nephew and the legacy of 'my sword' to his great-nephew). 'We cannot be certain what Shakespeare thought about the scheme, though it may be that he was not unfavourable,' F. E. Halliday has suggested.[179] Park Honan, in his mainstream scholarly biography of William of Stratford, stated that 'the Welcombe affair … illustrates Shakespeare's wish to seem impartial without being disloyal to his friends, and to protect the value of his assets'.[180] There is no evidence that he took the welfare of agricultural labourers into account in determining his attitude. As with what happened at other points in his career, William Shakspere's personal life appears to have been grossly inconsistent with the views apparently expressed by the author of the Shakespeare plays.

The young scholar Henry Neville, annotating his Greek copy of Dionysius of Halicarnassus's *Roman Antiquities*, noted on page 45 that the writer had missed out Ancus Martius and Tarquinius Collatinus:

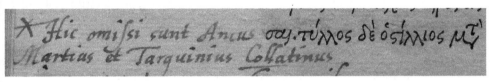

Hic omisi sunt Ancus Martius et Tarquinius Collatinus, Dionysius of Halicarnassus *Roman Antiquities*, 45. (Private Collection)

The name Ancus Martius is to be found in *Coriolanus* (2.3.235) and Dionysius of Halicarnassus is an acknowledged source for the play.[181] Collatinus is named in the argument of *The Rape of Lucrece*, being Lucretia's husband (his full name being Lucius Tarquinius Collatinus).

In his letters of 1599–1608 Neville used words that are unique to *Coriolanus* or shared with other plays written after the letter: 'inclinable': in a letter dated 26 May 1599;[182] 'conveying': 1 August 1599 and 25 January 1600;[183] 'particularly': 20 August 1599 (also found in *Timon of Athens*);[184] 'recommend': 24 September 1599;[185] 'disadvantage': 24 September 1599;[186] 'temporized': 2 April 1600;[187] 'priority': 1 November 1604 (also found in *Troilus and Cressida*);[188] 'pretext': 21 June 1608.[189] *Coriolanus* has been dated to 1608–9. Neville had also used this word in letters dated 27 June 1599 and 20 August 1599.[190]

Conclusion

The plays written between 1603 and 1609 cannot simply be regarded as allegorical essays on political dilemmas: they are great literature exploring the problematic, indeed often tragic, human condition. Nevertheless their political context illuminates their meaning. When we posit Neville as the author many aspects of the plays light up with contemporary significance and match his life experience, studies and letters.

Addendum

Single Words in Neville's Letter of 31 July 1602 Found in *Measure for Measure*

Right, Honourable, favour, goodness, towards, hath, many, waies, shewed, whether, greater, kindness, therefore, howsoever, evill, intended, peradventure, hereafter, vow, hold, perpetual, honourable, dealing, dedicate, whatsoever, remains, before, only, profess, noble, kindness, wrought, because, nature, which, respect, much, any, further, sute, fortune, god, witness, affection, strength, desire, pleased, pray, incline, thinkes, better, service, sort, away, possible, liberty, men, serve, stand, possess, already, freends, value, marks, ready, pay, composition, security, both, part, tooke, fine, made, satisfy, sure, kinde, pardon, neither, recompence, receave, mony, bad, fortune, brought, pitty, shall, neede, prayers, rest, evermore.

Pairs of Words

Hath made, made me, the good, and so, yet I, that from my soule, wth mee, in mee, your service, my mind, my hart, the rather, I know, lay hold, the greater, way of, I trust, your Ho^r, to continue, my life, might be, even for, no other, meanes to, I might, my bloud, The state, upon my, according to, put in, a yeare, the first, a good, my wife, would have, Therefore I, no more.

Phrases or Three or More Words

all the world, to the contrary, I speak not, in this place, occasion to use.

Near Misses

Letter: 'she hath occasion to use men';
Play: 'if you have occasion to use me' (4.2.55)

Letter: 'in her eye';
Play: 'in his eye' (5.1.493).

Letter: '2000 marks and I am ready to pay';
Play: 'five marks ready money' (4.3.7)

Letter: 1000;
Play: thousand (x3)

Letter: '1000 marks a yeare';
Play: three thousand dolours a year (1.2.46);
Play: four score pound a year (2.1.122).

Single Words in Neville's Letter of 8 December 1604 Found in *Measure for Measure*

Length, Satisfaction, under, Seales, agreed, shortly, Laws, likewise, Justice, hereafter, free, Trade, without, paying, except, Sheep, sufficient, given, said, Parts, lawfull, subjects, paying, Custom, used, appears, Men, English, pay, therefore, whatsoever, less, here, French, River, either, natural, Place, common, Subject, free, one, Company, Sort, *bear*, already, Judges, either, born, since, Death, Intents, Purposes, before, Voice, Office, Crown, three, thought, good, till, perfect, things, Article, touched, both, particular, Side, Form, forced, taken, send, short, kind, Oath, purpose, sufficiency, answered, part, far, permit, others, Lord, Reputation, somewhat, about, Value, Ambassador, hope, some, mitigation, Rigour, reported, besides, nothing, expected, partly, become, poor, able, upon, Days, play'd, brought, back, rather, sell, Credit, reason, long, Restraint, themselves, making, care, ever, better, now, ours, cheap, little, fruit, Peace, regard, Affairs, Affection, carried, strongly, some, even, greatest, short, Proof, understand, Service, Charge, complaine, cold, Answers, receive, sometimes, proceeded, worthy, wishes, remain, evermore, assured, Friend.

Pairs of Words

We have, he made, when we, which we, shall be, That there, between the, about the, very good, the Speech, according to, for all, so as, to transport, any of, for all, to bring, the other, where they, because it, than we, much more, such as, it appears, but so, of our, to carry, as those, the same, this time, be done, most in, The last, to seek, very well, the End, the Matter, have been, of late, a great, to buy, many of, do make, of any, of State, will be, under the, I find, your knowledge, this time.

Phrases or Three or More Words

out of the, as great as, all the rest.

Near Misses

'Discourse' in *Measure for Measure* instead of 'discourses' in the letter. 'Privileges' in *Measure for Measure* instead of 'privelidge' in the letter. 'Furnished' in *Measure for Measure* instead of 'furnish' in the letter. 'Proofs' in *Measure for Measure* instead of 'proof' in the letter. 'Transport' in *Measure for Measure* instead of 'transportation' in the letter. 'Lawful trade' occurs in *Measure for Measure* while 'lawful' occurs three times and 'trade' five times in the letter. This is the only time Shakespeare used these words together. 'Witness' in both *Measure for Measure* and *All's Well That Ends Well* instead of 'witnessed' in the letter. 'Minister' in both plays instead of 'ministered' in the letter. 'Commodity' in both plays instead of 'commodities' in the letter.

The Romances
1607–1611

Whom best I love I cross; to make my gift,
The more delay'd, delighted.

Cymbeline, 5.3.195

Some falls are means the happier to rise.

Cymbeline, 4.2.403

Pericles, Cymbeline and The Winter's Tale

These three plays all show the disasters of a hero who is hurt and hurts others, is shamed and falls from grace, but who is eventually redeemed and reunited with his family. They match Neville's experience of his fall, imprisonment and release to be reunited with his family. They trace a psycho-spiritual process that mirrors Neville's experience.

Pericles

Written between 1607 and 1608 and printed in 1609, this play shares a source story with *The Comedy of Errors* and *Twelfth Night*: that of Apollonius of Tyre as originally told by John Gower in his *Confessio Amantis* (which he completed in 1390). This story resonated for the Bard throughout his career, impelling him, like an *idée fixe*, to create plays based on a figure from the earliest period of the Christian era: Apollonius of Tyana. When Neville travelled with Henry Savile from 1578 to 1582 they were researching the early church fathers, especially St John Chrysostom. Apollonius of Tyana lived at the same time as Christ, with whom he has been compared. In the play Pericles refers to his own suffering as 'crosses' (see also the above quotation from *Cymbeline*). Apollonius of Tyana spent his life travelling through Asia, specifically to Antioch and Ephesus. Like Pericles in the play, he observed a period of silence (reportedly five years). There is, however, no direct evidence that Shakespeare knew of this early figure behind the legendary story of Apollonius of Tyre as told by Gower and translated by Laurence Twine in *The Pattern of Painful Adventures*, the latter being reprinted in 1607 and perhaps therefore re-stimulating

Shakespeare's interest in this tale. These two were the Bard's main sources, with some material possibly drawn from Sidney's *Arcadia*. Neville knew Sidney and it has been suggested that the name Pericles was taken from the *Arcadia*'s Pyrocles.[1] The latter is a companion of Musidorus. Casson has shown that the early play *Mucedorus* was based on the *Arcadia* and was Neville's first play.[2] Orthodox scholarship has now begun to accept that *Mucedorus* shows signs of Shakespeare's authorship, at least in part.

We can therefore see that, while there is no evidence that Shakspere from Stratford knew anything about Pericles or Apollonius, two separate pieces of evidence point towards Neville. Furthermore there are more specific textual links in the plot, ideas and words of the play that have connections with Neville's life and letters at this time. We will now examine some elements common to the three plays that have the Apollonius story underlying their plots.

The Comedy of Errors starts with the threat of an innocent man's execution. *Pericles* likewise begins with the heads of the executed princes who could not solve the riddle posed by Antiochus. Pericles himself is threatened with execution if he fails, or assassination if he succeeds, in resolving the riddle: here we see the connection between the two plays made evident in the first scene. Both *The Comedy of Errors* and *Pericles* end happily in Ephesus in a religious context (an abbey or temple) but they begin with the threat of execution which had hung over Neville's own life and haunted his family history, especially the execution of his grandfather Edward.

Long before *Pericles* was written Neville had studied Greek at Oxford and annotated his copy of the Appian, a volume of Roman History in Greek, with a large family tree of Antiochus, including Antiochus the Great (Magnus) and Antiochus Asiaticus, King (Rex) of Syria.

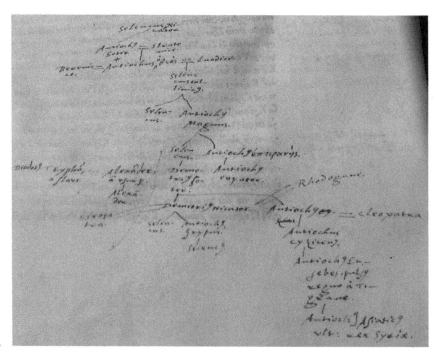

Appian, 91.

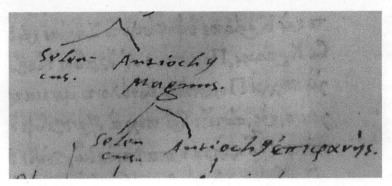

Appian, 91, detail.

Antiochus, named 'great' by Pericles, is the king of Syrian Antioch. His incestuous relationship with his daughter is the basis of the riddle in the first scene. In a footnote on Antiochus the Great in his edition of *Pericles*, Warren explained that he ruled the Asian empire inherited by his forefathers from Alexander the Great and that in the play he is conflated with his son, Antiochus IV Epiphanes, in the account of his death.[3] Neville, in his family tree, shows Antiochus Epiphanes, writing the latter in Greek as ἐπιφανής, under his father Antiochus Magnus.

Another source for *Pericles* was Plutarch's *Lives*. The names of several characters in the play – Cleon, Aeschines, Philemon, Simonides and Lysimachus – occur in Plutarch, 'all but the last two within the Life of Pericles'.[4] We know that Neville had read Plutarch because, in a paper presented to James I and Parliament, he wrote of Antigonus, whose history Plutarch tells.[5] The latter name also occurs in *The Winter's Tale* (see below).

Having escaped from Antioch, Pericles survives a shipwreck and joins knights who joust for the hand of Thaisa, daughter of the king of Pentapolis, Simonides. Each knight presents a shield which has a symbolic picture (a device) and a motto (a word). The princess introduces the first as:

A Knight of *Sparta*, (my renowned father);
And the <u>deuice</u> he beares vpon his Shield
Is a blacke Ethyope reaching at the Sunne
The <u>word</u>: *Lux tua vita mihi*. (First quarto spelling and italics, 2.2.18)

Neville, writing in a letter to Robert Cecil dated 24 April 1600, described an emblem set up to represent the state of France at Henry IV's court (italics in the original, our emphasis underlined):

The <u>Devise</u> is this, a Globe supported by fower Pillers, every Piller representing a principall Personage, as the one the *Chancellour*, with this <u>Word</u> *Inutilis aequitas* …

Neville described the other figures, each of which has a Latin motto which he labelled as a 'Word'. It is also noticeable that both the quarto and Neville's letter put the Latin text of the 'Word' in italics. Neville also used italics for Latin quotations in his copy of *Leicester's Commonwealth*.

Tompkins suggested that the name Pericles and the story of Apollonius were chosen because both were exemplars of patience.[6] In the play the king must go through the suffering, submit and accept. Looking at Marina he says, 'thou dost look like Patience gazing on kings' graves and smiling extremity out of act' (5.1.128). The word 'patience' is used 184 times across the canon and eight times in *Pericles*. Only *Othello*, which was written when Neville was incarcerated and needed to be patient, uses the word more often (namely fourteen times). 'Patience' is used eight times in *As You Like It*, which was written at a time when Neville was frustrated in France. The image of patience in *Pericles* recalls one in *Twelfth Night* (which was written in the autumn of 1600 after Neville had returned from France). Viola says:

She sat like patience on a monument,
Smiling at grief. (2.4.115)

The word 'patience' is also used eight times in *Cymbeline* (which followed *Pericles*). In a letter dated 21 June 1608, Neville declared, 'Patience is a great Virtue and hath great efficacy. I confess I want it often times both for myself and my Friends.'[7] *Pericles* was registered on 20 May 1608, just a month before this letter. The play was probably being performed at the time of Neville's letter, which provides evidence that he was in London at the time.

Pericles ends in a joyous reunion at the temple of Diana in Ephesus: she was the twin sister of Apollo, the god of poetry. *The Comedy of Errors* also ends in a happy reunion in Ephesus. We can identify the abbess in *The Comedy of Errors* with Neville's mother, because she says it is 'thirty-three years' since she was pregnant with the twins (5.1.400). The play was premiered in 1594 and thirty-three years before that would be 1561. Elizabeth could have been pregnant that year with Henry, who, we believe, was born in the summer of 1562.[8] Whether he was a twin, we do not know. He did have an elder sister, Elizabeth, who was born in 1561. Neville's mother died on 7 November 1573 when he was between ten and eleven years old: a terrible loss for such a young boy.[9] Shakespeare shows great knowledge of grief and loss. Linking grief and mothers, the Bard wrote scenes of mothers saying goodbye to sons, scenes where mothers die, are missing, turned into statues and grieving the loss of loved ones. In *The Comedy of Errors*, the mother is lost until the very end. In *Pericles* the mother apparently dies in the storm. But a child may have a fantasy of eventual reunion with the lost mother: the aching hope of being re-united once more.

The lost mother may be idealised into a sainted figure such as the nun in a temple/abbey at Ephesus in both of these plays. Ephesus was the centre of the Mother Goddess cult, Artemis/Diana, and it was also where the Virgin Mary was believed to have settled and died. All these figures were idealised virgin goddesses. Posthumus in *Cymbeline* says that his 'mother seem'd the Dian of that time' (2.4.158). Diana was the Roman name of the Greek goddess Artemis who had a spear, and some have seen a connection between the name Shakespeare and Artemis. Artemis/Diana was also goddess of forests and so would perhaps have appealed to Neville who was a forester.

Pericles' wife, Thaisa, apparently dies in childbirth aboard the ship in a storm. Neville had the experience of travelling by ship with his pregnant wife when they went to France in 1599: the baby boy died, if not on ship, then soon afterwards. Like Pericles, Neville could exclaim:

O you gods!
Why do you make us love your goodly gifts,
And snatch them straight away? (3.1.22)

George Wilkins: the Co-Author

George Wilkins is believed to have co-authored *Pericles*. He wrote several works between 1606 and 1608 and then fell silent. His experiences as a brothel keeper might have equipped him to write the scenes in the brothel in *Pericles*. Three years after *Pericles* appeared on stage, Wilkins and William Shakspere were both witnesses at the 1612 Belott–Mountjoy legal case about a marriage settlement dating back to 1604. Shakspere was a witness to the agreement between the bride's father, Mountjoy, and the groom. The young couple then went to live with Wilkins, so there can be little doubt that William Shakspere and George Wilkins knew each other.[10] Wilkins had by then ceased writing and his career deteriorated into a series of criminal cases in which he was accused of violent assaults on women, keeping a disorderly brothel and theft.[11] In Wilkins' play *The Miseries of Enforced Marriage*, written in 1606–7, one character is called Faulconbridge, a Neville family name. This play is related to *The Yorkshire Tragedy* which, as Casson showed, has hidden Neville connections.[12]

Cymbeline

Cymbeline dates from 1610. The first record of a public performance was in 1611. In June 1610 James I's son Henry was invested as Prince of Wales and during the investiture Sir James Hay was made a Knight of the Bath.[13] One of Hay's ancestors had defeated the Danes with his two sons at the Battle of Luncarty, just as Belarius defeats the Romans with his two adopted sons in the play. The setting of Milford Haven may be intended to celebrate the Prince of Wales' newly adopted country and recall Henry VII's arrival there to found the Tudor dynasty (just as James I was the founder of the Stuart dynasty: his ancestors included Henry VII). Neville did have an interest in Wales, as is evident in his letter dated 21 June 1605, when he wrote, 'Concerning *the Disorder in* Wales, whereof I made mention in my last, it seems the Lords have taken some Apprehension of it, and have sent down my Lord of *Worcester*, who is potent in those Parts, *to settle and quiet all Things there*' (Italics in the original; our emphasis in underlined).[14] The words 'Wales', 'whereof', 'apprehension', 'potent', 'parts' and 'quiet' all occur in *Cymbeline*. 'Settle' is only found in *Antony and Cleopatra* and *The Winter's Tale*, plays that preceded and followed *Cymbeline*. The words 'sent down' only occur together in two late plays, *Cymbeline* and *Henry VIII*.[15] Yet again, in using this vocabulary, Neville anticipated the Bard. In the same letter of 21 June 1605 Neville felt, 'I am out of my proper Orb when I enter into State Matters; I will therefore leave these Considerations to those to whom they appertain, and think of my husbandry in the Country ...' These sentiments are echoed in *Cymbeline* by Belarius. The play has much to say about the dangers of the royal court and Belarius praises life in the country compared to the city and the court:

Did you but know the city's usuries
And felt them knowingly; the art o' the court
As hard to leave as keep; whose top to climb
Is certain falling, or so slippery that
The fear's as bad as falling; the toil o' the war,
A pain that only seems to seek out danger
I' the name of fame and honour; which dies i' the search,
And hath as oft a slanderous epitaph
As record of fair act; nay, many times,
Doth ill deserve by doing well; what's worse,
Must court'sy at the censure ... (3.3.45)

William Shakspere was a usurer, charging interest on loans, as was his father who was fined for this practice when his son was six years old.[16] It would have been odd for him to have given a sympathetic character a line complaining against 'the city's usuries'. By contrast, Neville had reason to complain about the frustrations of city and court. Neville was able to advise his friend Ralph Winwood, who continued his ambassadorial duties, warning him of the frustrations of life at court in a letter dated 11 March 1606: 'For the Place here, it is that which they are all extreamly weary of that are in it; the Attendance is more exacted than ever, and the Profit less then ever.'[17] In *Cymbeline* the queen offers to promote Pisanio:

I'll move the king
To any shape of thy preferment such
As thou'lt desire; and then myself, I chiefly,
That set thee on to this desert, am bound
To load thy <u>merit</u> richly. (1.5.70)

Neville's letter to Winwood continued (italics in the original, our emphasis underlined):

And for *<u>Merit</u>, <u>be you assured</u> it will wear as fast as a <u>Tear</u> will <u>dry</u>*, neither is it found so ready a Way to <u>Honor</u> and *<u>Profit</u>*, as some other which I know you have some skill of. In Sume, perhaps you have not *all Contentment there*, but believe it you will have none here.

Both the queen and Pisanio use the words 'be assured' (1.1.71; 1.3.24; 1.5.81), the third instance being just seven lines after the word 'merit' quoted above. The letter was written in 1606, the date of *Antony and Cleopatra*, where we find the words:

In thee't had been good service. Thou must know,
'Tis not my <u>profit</u> that does lead mine <u>honour</u>;
Mine <u>honour</u>, it. (*Antony and Cleopatra*, 2.7.71)

Neville's image of the tear drying recalls *The Rape of Lucrece* where we find 'Many a <u>dry</u> drop seem'd a weeping <u>tear</u>' (1375). This is relevant to *Cymbeline* because the play recalls that poem in incident and language when Giacomo invades Innogen's bedroom.[18] While Neville would not be writing *Cymbeline* for another three years we can see the germ of the play's themes and vocabulary evident in this letter.

Neville suffered from rumours and accusations from nameless rivals who sought to ruin his reputation and disempower him at James I's court. He was briefly arrested on an unfounded accusation in 1604 and, although released, the damage was done; James I never fully trusted him again and thwarted his political ambitions. Belarius complains of just such injustice:

> My fault being nothing, as I have told you oft,
> But that two villains, whose false oaths prevailed
> Before my perfect honour, swore to Cymbeline
> I was confederate with the Romans ... (3.3.65)

Pisanio also complains of the 'viperous slander' suffered by Innogen (3.4.39) who, reading Posthumus's letter commanding Pisanio to murder her, speaks of her pain: 'Those that are betrayed do feel the treason sharply' (3.4.85). Neville experienced the pain of being accused of treason and served on a parliamentary committee to clarify the laws of treason in 1604.

The play is set against an international political backdrop, moving between Britain and Italy. Lucius, the Roman ambassador, is treated with the respect such a diplomat deserves. His demand for the payment of £3,000 of unpaid tribute recalls Neville's diplomatic task of requesting that the French king repay Elizabeth I's loan (2.3.55; 3.1.9).

Britain was the name proposed for the newly united kingdoms of England and Scotland. Neville was involved in the negotiations between king and parliament 'about the Union' from 1604.[19] Britain is specifically named in *Cymbeline* twenty-three times (*Love's Labour's Lost* and *Henry VIII* mention Britain, but then only once). Warren considered the possible contemporary political references in the play, noting the play ends with peace between two nations: 'James I, who liked to be known as <u>Jacobus Pacificus</u>, prided himself especially on his achievements as a peacemaker who had brought about the union of the British Isles.'[20] The play ends with Cymbeline declaring, 'My peace we will begin' (5.4.460). In a letter dated 4 June 1606, Neville wrote to Winwood about a possible war with Spain over '*much Injustice and Oppression done there to our Nation, besides some particular Contumely to the King personally*, the like Complaint was made before to the Lords. I hear it hath *moved much*, and this I will assure you, *that the Kingdom generally wishes this Peace broken, but* <u>Jacobus Pacificus</u> *I believe will scarce incline to that Side*.'[21] (Italics in the original, our emphasis underlined.) This proves that Neville was both aware of, and involved in, the international politics of war and peace. Neville's previous international experience is further evidenced in the play when the banished Posthumus travels to Italy and he remembers when he was 'a young traveller' (1.4.41), as Neville would have done. A Frenchman in the play remembers meeting Posthumus in Orleans (1.4.32) and, in a letter to Winwood dated 5 March 1601, Neville referred to 'mine host of Orleans'.[22] France is mentioned four times in the play, although no scene takes place there: experiences in France are recalled, which makes sense when we posit Neville as the author.

Feeling the full weight of his guilt, Posthumus decides to seek death in battle and when captured submits to the hangman. Neville, when imprisoned, had written of his own willingness to risk death in battle in order to recover Elizabeth I's favour. Whether his words were hyperbole or evidence of his desperation, in a letter dated 31 July 1602, he offered: 'yf I were at liberty, I might shed so much of my bloud in som place where she hath occasion to use men as might serve for a laver for the crime which hath made me so ugly in her eye.'[23]

In earlier letters Neville used rare words that occur in *Cymbeline*, showing again that Neville already had this vocabulary years before the Bard used it : 21 June 1599: 'shunned' is only found in *Othello* and *Cymbeline*;[24] 20 August 1599 and 16 September 1599: 'pretending' is only in *Measure for Measure* and *Cymbeline*;[25] 6 September 1599: 'procuring' is unique to *Cymbeline*;[26] 24 September 1599: 'diminution' is only in *Antony and Cleopatra* and *Cymbeline*;[27] 22 October 1599: 'dismission' is only in *Antony and Cleopatra* and *Cymbeline*;[28] 26 January 1600: 'consign' is only in *Henry V* (written 1599) and *Cymbeline*;[29] 2 April 1600: 'abatement' is only in *King Lear* and *Cymbeline*;[30] 18 July 1600: 'venison' occurs in *Merry Wives of Windsor* (which we have suggested dates from 1599–1600, see Chapter 6), *As You Like It* (also 1599–1600) and *Cymbeline*.[31] Neville, as a keeper of the Windsor forest and a keen hunter, knew about venison. In his letter of 28 December 1600: 'resume' is to be found in *King Lear*, *Coriolanus* and *Cymbeline*.[32]

Cymbeline's queen is a wicked stepmother. Neville had experience of a stepmother and their relationship deteriorated to such an extent that she took him to court (see Chapter 6). If, as a boy, he had idealised his dead mother, then he might well have demonised his stepmother. Elizabeth Neville (who married three times but had no children) was certainly a powerful woman, as her tomb in St Mary's Church, Henley-on-Thames, attests, where her effigy lies, still formidable.[33]

Several academics have independently suggested that the appearance of Jupiter in the play with four circling ghosts is a reference to Galileo's discovery of the moons of Jupiter. He published his book *Siderus Nuncius* in March 1610. *Cymbeline* was probably completed by the autumn of 1610, giving time for the Bard to have heard of Galileo's discovery, which had spread through Europe like wildfire. Sir Henry Wotton[34] was in Venice when the book came out and sent a copy to James I.[35] Neville knew his astronomy: he had books on astronomy and was praised by John Chamber as an astronomer (see Chapter 6). Henry Savile, Neville's Oxford tutor and lifelong friend, also had a copy of Galileo's book *Siderus Nuncius*, which is now in the Savile collection in the Bodleian Library, Oxford. Since Neville remained in touch with Savile all his life, there can be little doubt that he would have known what was being discovered across Europe. Neville would also have known Sir William Lower, astronomer and fellow Member of Parliament, who had a copy of *Siderus Nuncius* and who praised Galileo, contrasting the importance of his discoveries with those of 'the Dutchmen that were eaten by bears on Novaya Zemla'.[36] In Shakespeare's next play, a man is eaten by a bear (see below).

Cymbeline, though based on Holinshed, has several other possible sources in ancient Greek literature, some of which had not been translated at the time the play was written. Chariton of Aphrodosia's *Chaereas and Callirhoe* (in which the heroine, like Innogen, is left for dead and revives) was not translated until the eighteenth century.[37] Another source for

Innogen's false death was Heliodorus' *Aethiopica*, which the Bard certainly knew because he referred to it in *Twelfth Night*.[38] The *Aethiopica* appeared in translation in 1569 but Neville would have been able to read the original in Greek and he had a French translation in his library, *Histoire Aethiopique d'Helidorus*, dated 1596. It had already influenced Philip Sidney's *Arcadia* and Neville knew the Sidneys. 'It seems likely that Heliodorus is the source of the structural elements and some of the plot materials which make *Cymbeline* a modern example of Greek romance.'[39] Neville's copy of Heliodorus is annotated throughout with underlined words, some of which occur in the late plays. On page 149 'cataracts' is only found in *King Lear*; page 475 we find 'opulemment': the word 'opulent' occurs in *King Lear* and *Antony and Cleopatra*; page 365 'parangon' is underlined: the word 'paragon' is in *Cymbeline* and in seven other plays; page 521 provides 'tromperie': 'tromperie' occurs in *The Winter's Tale* and 'trumpery' in *The Tempest*. That the spelling of 'tromperie' is the same in the annotated Heliodorus and in the First Folio version of *The Winter's Tale* may be evidence that Neville had recently read the book and noticed the word.

The source for the subplot of Iachimo's wager, and his hiding in a chest to gain entrance to Innogen's bedroom, was Boccaccio's *Decameron*, a copy of which is to be found amongst Neville's books in the library at Audley End House. It is in Italian and there was no translation earlier than 1620.[40] Neville could, of course, read Italian.

Another source for the play was *The Rare Triumphs of Love and Fortune*, 'a romantic drama that was apparently performed before Queen Elizabeth at Windsor Castle on 30th December 1582'.[41] Neville had arrived back in England from his European travels earlier that year and so could have attended this performance because his father lived so close to Windsor and, as the royal forester, might be expected to attend upon the queen on such an occasion. By contrast, in 1582 Shakspere was in Stratford, wooing and wedding Anne Hathaway.

Innogen names one of her maids Dorothy. This name only occurs in *Cymbeline*. Neville had two daughters called Dorothy (or Dorothea), one born in 1593, who died in infancy, and another born in 1605.[42] Neville specifically mentioned Dorothy in a document about his estate in July 1612.[43] The father–daughter theme in all the romance plays is very strong, perhaps because two more daughters were born to Neville in 1610: Anne and Elizabeth. The play ends in a reunited family, reconciliation between enemies, peace, harmony and contentment. These themes continue in the next play.

The Winter's Tale

In this play, dating from 1610–11, we see again the importance of the father–daughter relationship which is especially significant in all the Romance plays: *Pericles, Cymbeline, The Winter's Tale* and *The Tempest*. Neville celebrated the marriages of two daughters at the time the play was written: Mary, who married Edward Lewknor, and Frances, who married Richard Worsley, in May 1610. Neville took great care to ensure Frances' rights by signing a substantial marriage settlement. This legal document is still extant and provides evidence of his concern for and involvement in her financial wellbeing.[44] Shakspere's daughter Susanna married John Hall on 5 June 1607. His other daughter, Judith, did not marry Thomas Quiney until 1616, so neither of these marriages matches the chronology of the Bard's celebration of a daughter's wooing and wedding in *The Winter's Tale*.

The play was also politically topical. James I asserted the divine right of kings and preferred to inculcate fear in his people rather than love. In 1610, he told Parliament that 'kings are justly called gods, for that they exercise a manner or resemblance of divine power upon earth.' He went on to insist that 'Parliament not presume to call the royal prerogative in question.' Nor should the Commons presume to advise him 'how to govern, for that was his craft, and to meddle with that would be to lessen him.' John Chamberlain observed that this 'bred generally much discomfort to see our monarchical power and royal prerogative strained so high and made so transcendent every way'. Leontes' insistence in Act 2, Scene 3 that he is not accountable to his advisers, and his lords' and Paulina's equally tenacious questions and protestations, are informed by a debate that persisted throughout James's reign.

Leontes is, in the dramatic contest, ultimately the loser. Parliament similarly declined to ratify the Great Contract.[45] Neville was involved in the negotiations over the Great Contract, which was an attempt to provide the monarch with an assured annual income. He certainly knew James I's writings on kingship because, in a speech delivered on 16 July 1610, Neville proposed that all Members of the Commons be permitted to attend the committee appointed to discuss one of the king's papers. Neville's concern for the royal finances may explain why he was the first Member, after the privy councillors and law officers, to be appointed to the committee established on 15 March to consider the assignment of debts to the king. Robert Cecil, by that time Earl of Salisbury, regarded him as one of the leading figures in the Commons, and on the evening of 10 July, Salisbury summoned Neville and seven other Members to a secret gathering in Hyde Park. The state of the royal finances was not Neville's sole preoccupation in 1610 for he was also chosen to consider measures on bastardy. Leontes suggests Perdita is a bastard six times in just one scene (2.3).[46]

Like *Cymbeline*, *The Winter's Tale* contrasts life at court with life in the country. The dangers at court are those of tyranny and betrayal whereas those in the country are of wild nature (the storm and the bear) and the petty crime of the confidence trickster Autolycus, who makes an ironically smooth transition to courtier! Neville experienced these two worlds and wrote about them in his letters. The theme of the loyal courtier, who is unjustly accused, is continued from *Cymbeline* when Camillo is accused by Leontes. Camillo is forced to be dishonest, even betray Leontes and Florizel, in order to be true to himself and ultimately loyal to them. Neville had experience of navigating the treacherous shifting loyalties at court. In Chapter 11, we will see that another character, also called Camillo, who is a worried father in *Double Falshood*, can be considered as an alter ego of Neville.

Exit Pursued by a Bear

The incident when Antigonus is devoured by a bear on the coast of Bohemia is not in Greene's *Pandosto*, the main source for the story. It is Shakespeare's invention. Three elements of this have been shown to have Neville connections: Bohemia, the bear and the name Antigonus.

Ben Jonson famously criticised Shakespeare for having suggested that Bohemia had a coast. For a long time it was presumed Jonson's contempt was justified but he was wrong because, in *Pandosto*, Greene had explicitly stated that Bohemia had a coast.[47] In the sixteenth century Bohemia did indeed have an Adriatic coastline and Neville would have known this because he had travelled through Bohemia in 1579–80 when he visited Prague.[48]

One of Neville's annotations in his copy of *Leicester's Commonwealth* is the word 'Beares' written in italic, against a passage in secretary script.

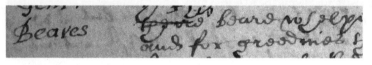

Worsley MSS 47, 6V.

This is spelt the same way as the word 'Beare' (also with a capital '*B*' italicised) is spelt in the first quarto text (1594) of *The First Part of the Contention* (later printed in the First Folio as *Henry VI: Part II*). The bear was a symbol of Richard Neville, Earl of Warwick, as we see in *Henry VI: Part II*:

Old Neuels crest,
The Rampant *Beare* chaind to the ragged staffe, (5.1.202)

Casson has shown that *Mucedorus*, in which there is a stage direction: 'Enter ... pursued with a bear' was Neville's first comedy.[49] He showed the links between *Mucedorus* and *Leicester's Commonwealth* as the hero rescues Amadine (Elizabeth I) from a dangerous bear (Leicester).[50] He dated the first version of *Mucedorus* to 1584–5, the same time that Neville made his annotations in *Leicester's Commonwealth*. This is significant because *Mucedorus* is a possible source for the bear incident in *The Winter's Tale*. *Mucedorus* was the most popular play of its time and was reprinted in 1610. Bate and Rasmussen speculated that the additional passages inserted into the text of this edition might be by the Bard, who was writing *The Winter's Tale* at the time.[51]

Greene did not name the character of the shipman who cast the baby Perdita adrift in a boat. It was Shakespeare who gave this role to Antigonus. James pointed out that Neville referred to a King Antigonus in a treatise presented in Parliament on 14 May 1614.[52] Neville only reluctantly admitted that he had written this paper, once again showing that he was a man who preferred to keep his authorship secret. By using the name Antigonus he was referring to 'one of the immediate and mightiest successors of Alexander' as an example of a proud father (of Demetrius) and a metaphor for the ideal relationship between James I and his people/Parliament. Although this paper was written after the play, it nevertheless shows Neville using the name as a metaphor of the right relationship between monarch and people. In the play Antigonus shows a duty and compassion greater than King Leontes whose loyal servant he is. 'Alexander, Demetrius and Antigonus were successive kings of Macedonia who lived just about sixty years after Pericles. One of the main sources of knowledge concerning them in Neville's time was Plutarch's *Lives*. This work has always been considered a major source for Shakespeare's Roman plays ...'[53]

The Statue That Comes to Life

Another of Shakespeare's inventions in retelling the story of *The Winter's Tale* is the statue that comes to life when Hermione, who has been hidden by Paulina awaiting the fulfilment of the oracle, is presented to a repentant Leontes. The sculptor is named as Giulio Romano (5.2.95). Romano (*c*. 1499–1546) left works in Rome and Mantua and was involved in creating theatrical spectacles in Mantua. Shakespeare was criticised for suggesting Romano was a sculptor when he was mainly known as a painter. However, his friend Vasari stated he was a notable sculptor in plasterwork. Romano was also described as a sculptor on his tomb.[54] Neville may have seen his works in Italy or indeed in Britain. After their joint period in the Tower of London, Neville and Henry Wriothesley, Earl of Southampton, were regarded as friends and political associates. Southampton was born at Cowdray House and spent much of his youth there.[55] A 1717 catalogue of works of art at the house listed two copies of paintings by Julio Romano, both entitled 'Marriage of Cupid and Psyche'.[56] Also listed were paintings of Richard Neville, Earl of Salisbury (who appears on stage in *Henry VI: Part I*), and numerous other Nevilles. Sadly these paintings were destroyed in a fire in 1793. Here again we find evidence linking Southampton, Shakespeare and members of the Neville family. Cowdray House is on the way to the Isle of Wight from Neville's home in Billingbear and it is known that Neville visited his daughter Frances, who married Richard Worsley, on the island in about 1610 (the year *The Winter's Tale* was written). Southampton had been appointed captain of the island in July 1603. According to a letter from John Chamberlain, Neville visited his daughters again on the Isle of Wight in 1612.[57]

The Vocabulary in Neville's Letters

In letters written by Neville before the play we once again find words that the Bard later used in the play: 18 July 1599: 'anchor hold' is unique to *The Winter's Tale*;[58] 8 August 1599: 'magnificence' is unique to *The Winter's Tale*;[59] 6 September 1599: 'continuing' is unique to *The Winter's Tale*;[60] 24 September 1599: 'requisite' is unique to *The Winter's Tale*;[61] 26 February 1600: 'importunate' occurs only in *Hamlet*, *Othello*, *The Winter's Tale* and *Timon of Athens*;[62] 27 April 1600: 'scandalous' occurs only in *Measure for Measure* and *The Winter's Tale*;[63] 14 May 1600: 'vouchsafed' occurs only in *Twelfth Night*, *The Winter's Tale* and *Antony and Cleopatra*.[64] The last three examples of shared vocabulary show that up to ten years before the play was written Neville was using these words, again anticipating Shakespeare.

Among Neville's library books there is a 1602 copy of Battista Guarini's *Il Fido Pastor*, a 'tragicommedia pastorale'. This is known to have influenced John Fletcher's *The Faithful Shepherdess* (1608–9) and *A King and No King* (1611, see Chapter 11)[65] and may also have influenced *The Winter's Tale* with its pastoral scenes of shepherds, its surprising denouement and its use of metatheatre.[66]

Towards Completion

The final period of great artists (Leonardo, Rembrandt, Beethoven) is often a time when they achieve a summation or transcendence beyond earlier works. The romances start this final period with plays that evoke just such transcendental joy and wonder after disaster and suffering. They are characterised by patience, hard-won forgiveness, release from shame and reunion with family members. Some of what was lost may be irredeemable but the central figure is transformed by grace and, while there is grief for the past, there is also joy. These themes are continued in Shakespeare's last plays, with wonder, forgiveness, compassion overcoming evil and the new life of the next generation is assured. Power is only sought in order to reconcile old enemies. These themes resonate with Neville's life experience and his behaviour as reported by John Chamberlain, in a letter dated 3 November 1612 in which he told Sir Ralph Winwood that Neville 'takes great pains to reconcile and set all in tune'.[67] As he realises the error of his ways in *The Winter's Tale*, Leontes promises to reconcile himself to Polixenes (3.2.153). The latter acknowledges Leontes as the 'reconciled king' (4.2.23). At the end of *Cymbeline* the soothsayer, significantly called Philharmonus, interpreting the vision of Jupiter proclaims, 'the powers above do tune the harmony of this peace' (5.4.467). In reflecting on Neville's character, Chamberlain unwittingly matched the mood and even the words of these last plays.

The father–daughter and reconciliation themes continue in *The Tempest*, which we examine in the next chapter.

The Sonnets and *The Tempest*
1609–1611

When in disgrace with Fortune and men's eyes …

Sonnet 29

Shake-speares Sonnets was entered for publication on the Stationers' Register on 20 May 1609. Ever since Shakespeare became the English National Poet, indeed the central figure in English literature, this little volume of poetry has been the subject of endless speculation over both its mysterious dedication and the meaning of the 154 sonnets themselves. There are many questions: when were they written; why were they published in 1609; to whom were they addressed; whether and in what sense are they autobiographical; and were they published with the author's knowledge and approval? Most critics have given up attempting to provide definitive answers for any of these questions: to them, the meaning of the sonnets and the circumstances of their publication are simply unknowable. However, if one accepts Henry Neville as their author, one can provide cogent answers to all of these questions, and in a way which is simply impossible if William Shakspere were the author.

We suggest that the publication of *Shake-speares Sonnets* was timed to coincide with the granting of the Charter of the Second London Virginia Company on 23 May 1609, and as celebratory verse to mark the marriage of Neville's eldest son on 2 May 1609. Evidence for the first of these propositions can be seen in the dedication itself.

The Dedication to *Shake-speares Sonnets*

T. T. is believed to stand for Thomas Thorpe (*c.* 1571–*c.* 1625), although his full name does not appear anywhere in the book. On the frontispiece it is only signified by the initials T. T., which is strange because other names involved in the publication were spelt out in full (Shake-speare, G. Eld, William Aspley and John Wright).[1] The wording of the dedication concludes with the words, 'wisheth the well-wishing adventurer in setting forth'. But who is the 'adventurer'? The wording is apparently deliberately ambiguous (as one might expect of Shakespeare, but not of Thorpe). We do not think the term 'adventurer' refers to the risk involved in publishing the sonnets. Rather we suggest that it refers to subscribers to the Second London Virginia Company, who were providing 'venture capital' to the

TO.THE.ONLIE.BEGETTER.OF.
THESE.INSVING.SONNETS.
M.W.H. ALL.HAPPINESSE.
AND.THAT.ETERNITIE.
PROMISED.
BY.
OVR.EVER-LIVING.POET.
WISHETH.
THE.WELL-WISHING.
ADVENTVRER.IN.
SETTING.
FORTH.

T. T.   The dedication to *Shake-speares Sonnets*.

Company. While the term 'venture capital' was coined in more modern times (and so may appear to be anachronistic in this context) the word 'venture' was used for trading risks in the seventeenth century, as the naming of one of the Company's ships as the *Sea-Venture* shows. Shakespeare wrote of how 'merchants venture trade abroad' in *Henry V* (1.2.192).

Neville and Henry Wriothesley, Earl of Southampton, were subscribers and we suggest that 'Mr. W. H.' was intended to be understood as Henry Wriothesley, disguised by his initials being reversed. The lists of its 659 shareholders is readily available online and in print. They paid a minimum of £12 to become subscribers in the Company. William Shakspere from Stratford, who as a property owner and businessman had ample means and opportunity to become an adventurer, did not do so. Similarly, Thomas Thorpe's name is absent from the list although he seemingly referred to them in the above dedication he allegedly signed. We suggest that this dedication was written by Neville himself, signing himself as 'T.T', and that it was dedicated to his friend Henry Wriothesley. Many of the sonnets were addressed to Southampton, recognised by the Bard as the 'onlie begetter' of these verses. Some of the sonnets were written while Neville was in the Tower, bewailing his imprisonment but also forgiving Southampton for providing confirmatory evidence that he had been involved in the Essex rebellion (see below).

The first question to address in more detail is why *Shake-speares Sonnets* was published when it was, on 20 May 1609. Why then and not five years earlier or five years later? Why not posthumously, given the controversial nature of many of the verses? If the volume was unauthorised and pirated by Thomas Thorpe it might have been published when it was by random circumstance. We suggest the publication was authorised, the date chosen by the Bard, and that this coincided with the launch of the Second London Virginia Company, a suitably important occasion to be celebrated. We suggest that the publication occurred when, for the first time in years, Neville felt optimistic and upbeat about the future. His mood was to change over the following two years after a shipwreck off Bermuda and the failure of the Virginia Company to make a profit, events that led directly to the writing of *The Tempest*, which was apparently first performed in November 1611.

Few critics who have written on the sonnets are aware of a publication which appeared shortly beforehand and on which the dedication may be based. This was *A Good Speed to Virginia*, written by one Robert Gray, whose introduction, signed by him, was dated 28 April 1609, and reads as follows (our emphasis underlined):

To the Right Honorable earles, barons, and lords, and to the Right Worshipfull knights, merchants, and gentlemen, adventurers for the plantation of Virginea, all happie and prosperous success, which may either augment your glorie, or increase your wealth, or purchase your <u>eternitie</u>.

The beginning of Gray's pamphlet reads:

Time the devourer[2] of his own brood consume both man and his memorie. It is not brasse nor marble that can perpetuate the immortalitie of name upon the earth. Many in the world have erected faire and goodly monuments, whose memorie together with their monuments is long since defaced. The name, memorie and actions of those men doe only live in the records of <u>eternitie</u> ...

The conclusion of Gray's pamphlet reads:

From mine house at the Northend of Sithes lane London, April 28. *Anno* 1609. Your Honours and Worships in all affectionate <u>well wishing</u>, R. G.

There is a clear resemblance between the beginning and end of Gray's pamphlet and the *Shake-speares Sonnets* dedication. Gray's pamphlet itself is a highly erudite and learned exposition of the reasons why English settlement in Virginia would be beneficial both to England and the local natives, especially, as the pamphlet argues, in elevating the Indians 'from brutishness, to civilitie, to religion, to Christianitie, to the saving of their souls'.[3] This latter sentiment reminds us of Prospero's attempt to civilise Caliban.

Quite who Robert Gray was is uncertain. The most likely candidate is a man named Robert Graye [*sic*] who entered St John's College, Cambridge and received a BA from Cambridge University in 1592/3. The university's alumni register, *Alumni Cantabrigiensis*, notes that a man of this name was Rector of St Benet Sherehog in the City of London from 1606 to 1612. Nothing more is known of him, but the estate of a Robert Gray of Bread Street, City of London, was probated in June 1612, which is consistent with these other dates. The learned author of *A Good Speed to Virginia* is very likely to have attended Oxford or Cambridge, and they have no other man of this name on record for the appropriate period, so we conclude he was the author. St Benet Sherehog was a church, situated at the heart of the City of London, near Cheapside and Old Jewry, in what was formerly the wool-dealing district of the City. Originally built in the twelfth century, it burned down in the Great Fire of 1666 and was never rebuilt.[4] Its clergyman would thus have preached to a congregation largely consisting of City merchants, where many of the 659 'adventurers' of the Second London Virginia Company would have worshipped, most of whom were resident in London and the proprietors of businesses there. An especially erudite work such as *A Good Speed* might have attracted the attention of someone like Henry Neville, himself a learned man as well as a senior 'adventurer' in the Company.

In complete contrast Thomas Thorpe, supposedly the author of the mysterious dedication to the sonnets, was the son of an innkeeper, lacked a university education, and was possibly a secret Catholic. Although his entry in the *Oxford Dictionary of National Biography* states that he had 'a long-standing interest in exploration' (he had published two pamphlets on the East India Company in 1603; Neville was an investor in the East India

Company), he was not a subscriber to the Second London Virginia Company.[5] Thorpe apparently never maintained a printers or a bookshop, but acted as a commissioner of printers and arranged for booksellers to sell the books others printed. *Shake-speares Sonnets* was printed by George Eld for T.T., 'to be solde by William Apsley'.[6] Some copies were printed as being sold by 'John Wright, dwelling at Christ Churchgate'.[7] Thorpe was, in other words, a man who could arrange to produce works at short notice. It is also relevant to note that the dedication apparently signed by Thorpe is unlike any of his other printed dedications, which were, as Dr. John Rollett has shown, far more elaborate and flowery both in their wording and appearance.[8] So why would Thorpe pattern his dedication in the way he did, seemingly referring to the launch of the Second London Virginia Company? There is nothing in the sonnets which bears in any way on the Company. It might be suggested that Thorpe was drawing a comparison between the launch of the Company and the launch (publication) of *Shake-speares Sonnets*, but this seems improbable. The launch of the Company was a huge public event whereas *Shake-speares Sonnets* was a tiny volume and its sale price was only five pence.[9] It is difficult to estimate the number of copies actually printed in 1609, but 200 is a reasonable guess. Just thirteen copies survive today and only one person, Edward Alleyn, is known to have listed the purchase of 'a book Shaksper sonnetts 5*d*' in his accounts in June 1609.[10]

We question the near-universal assumption that Thorpe was the author of the dedication and this has a bearing on the issue of who ordered the publication of this complete collection of Shakespeare's sonnets. Some sonnets were mentioned by Francis Meres in 1598 in his list of works by Shakespeare, and so must have been written at least eleven years earlier. Thorpe might have obtained some of these early sonnets from sources, such as the 'private friends' amongst whom, according to Meres, sonnets had been circulated, but surely he could only have obtained *all* of them from one of two sources: the author himself, who presumably retained all of the sonnets he had written, or from the person to whom they were addressed and dedicated, assuming that *all* of them were addressed to the same person, and that he had retained all of them. The latter possibility seems remote, because the sonnets do not appear to have been addressed to just one person, and even if there were a sole addressee, there is no reason why he might have presented them to Thorpe for publication at that time. This puzzle is resolved by accepting that the volume was collected together by its author and presented to Thorpe for publication.

Many have wondered who 'Mr. W. H.', the sonnet's 'onlie begetter', was. Some have seriously argued that these initials might stand for 'William Himself', or that the 'H' was a misprint for 'S'. But these suggestions seem too far-fetched to be credible. The answer might be better informed by combining the question of identity with the issue of why there would be any deliberate concealment of that identity.[11] We propose that 'Mr. W. H.' was Henry Wriothesley, 3rd Earl of Southampton. The identification as 'Mr. W. H.' was apparently intended as an ironic remembrance of the time, between 1601 and 1603, when he and Neville were confined to the Tower and stripped of their titles, with Southampton being known officially as 'Mr. Henry Wriothesley'. He signed one document written at that time as 'Hen W.' (see Chapter 4). 'Mr. W. H.' is simply his initials with the letters reversed. Many scholars now agree that Henry Wriothesley was the dedicatee, his initials having been reversed to avoid any embarrassment by indicating him too obviously. Confirmation of this came in 1999 when Rollett published his discovery that the names Henry and Wriothesley were encoded in the dedication to the sonnets. Brenda James discovered that the name Henry Neville was also hidden in the dedication and since then other researchers in America and Australia have confirmed this.[12] The linking then of Neville, Southampton and the Virginia Company with the *Shake-speares Sonnets* publication makes sense. It also means it is unlikely that Thorpe was the author of the dedication, which seems to have been written by someone with a close and immediate interest in the Company who addresses that dedication to someone who would have understood the coded wording. We therefore conclude that Neville was the author of the dedication and of course the sonnets themselves. Evidence for this can be found in Neville's letters and other surviving manuscript documents.

The dedication wishes Mr. W. H. 'all happinesse'. Neville signed off his letter of 11 March 1606 with, 'I will end somewhat abruptly and wish <u>all happiness</u> unto you and yours'[13] (our emphasis in underlined). It is widely accepted that some of the sonnets were written to Southampton because the use of rose imagery and the word 'hue', spelt 'hew' in sonnets 20, 67, 82, 98, 104 in the 1609 edition, points to him. They do so because his surname was Wriothseley, pronounced <u>Rose</u>ly, and his initials could be written <u>He</u>(nry) <u>W</u>. as they were when Southampton dedicated his *Encomium* of Richard III to Neville in 1603, signing himself as 'Hen W'. This suggestion is reinforced by the fact that the word 'hew' is repeated twice in one line in Sonnet 20, and in the 1609 printing the second time it is not only capitalised as if it was a name, but also in italics: 'A man in hew all *Hews* in his controwling'. Neville wrote names in italics in his copy of *Leicester's Commonwealth*. Sonnet 20 may refer to an extant miniature painting of Wriothesley, aged twenty, by Nicholas Hilliard, that is now held in the Fitzwilliam Museum, Cambridge.[14]

Henry Wriothesley, 3rd Earl of Southampton, by Nicholas Hilliard. (© The Fitzwilliam Museum, Cambridge (Accession number: 3856))

The number '20' can be seen in the top right-hand corner of the picture (after 'Etatis Suæ': 'his age'.) Sonnet 20 opens:

A woman's face with Nature's own hand painted
Hast thou, the master-mistress of my passion;

The poet also noticed Wriothesley's bright eye, as we can still see in the portrait. This would date the sonnet to 1594 when Wriothesley was twenty. This was the same year that *The Rape of Lucrece*, which was dedicated to him, was published.

The mysteries of the dedication and the sonnets, which have puzzled commentators for generations, vanish if one posits Neville as their author. It is not clear why Neville would have titled the work '*Shake-speares Sonnets*', rather than 'Sonnets by William Shakespeare'. He may have been hinting that the name was a pseudonym and emphasising that these intimate works were not by William Shakspere who, at that time, appears to have been living mainly, or perhaps entirely, in Stratford-upon-Avon. The latter had no apparent interest in the London literary world, and may well never have heard of the tiny book of verses, printed in a limited run, which bore a version of his name on the title page.

Neville's Son Henry's Marriage to Elizabeth Smythe

Neville's official parliamentary biography reveals that 'by the beginning of 1609 Neville was in financial difficulty, occasioned perhaps by the recent marriages of two of his daughters. He beseeched Salisbury, to whom he had recently become reconciled, for a lease of some Crown land or the grant of annuities for his younger sons to compensate him for the £4,000 he had spent in royal service. However, the Crown was also impoverished, and consequently Neville was forced to sell timber from his estate to remain solvent. The subsequent marriage of his eldest son also brought him a dowry of £3,200.'[15]

So alongside the launch of the Second London Virginia Company there was another major reason why *Shake-speares Sonnets* was published at this time. On 2 May 1609 Neville's eldest son, also called Henry,[16] married Elizabeth Smythe[17] at St Margaret's Lothbury in London. Their wedding occurred just over two weeks before both the publication (on 20 May 1609) of *Shake-speares Sonnets* and the official launch of the Virginia Company (on 23 May 1609). Elizabeth Smythe was the daughter of the recently deceased Sir John Smythe (1557–1608) who had been a wealthy Member of Parliament for the previous twenty-four years. Elizabeth was thus an heiress and the marriage brought a dowry of about £3 million in today's money. This must have been extraordinarily welcome to the groom's financially struggling father, who had feared just the previous year that he would 'sink beneath the burden of his debts'[18] and was now keen to set up his eldest son in appropriate style.[19] The bride's deceased father had been the elder brother of Sir Thomas Smythe (1558–1625), who was also a Member of Parliament (from 1597 until 1624). Sir Thomas had been, like Neville, a member of Essex's circle and was briefly imprisoned in 1601. He was also one of the greatest tycoons in early Jacobean London. Most significantly, it was Thomas Smythe who had obtained the Charter of the Second London Virginia Company and who acted as its treasurer from 1609 until 1619. He was also a governor of the Muscovy Company, the East India Company, the Levant Company and the North West Passage Company, and held many other offices.[20] During 1604 and 1605 he had been ambassador to Muscovy. In 1605 he referred to *Hamlet* in his *Voyage and Entertainment in Russia*, comparing the government of Boris Godunov to 'the *Poeticall Furie in a Stage-action*, complete yet with horrid and wofull Tragedies: a first, but no second to any *Hamlet*; and that now Revenge, just Revenge was coming with his Sworde drawne …' (italics in the original text). Sir Thomas Smythe and Neville had much in common: they were both ambassadors and supporters of Essex, had both been imprisoned in the Tower after the Essex rebellion, were Members of Parliament and subscribers to the Second London Virginia Company. Neville named Smythe in three letters between 1604 and 1608,[21] telling Winwood, in a letter dated 11 March 1606, 'I chanced to meet Sir *Thomas Smith* in *Westminster-Hall* in good leisure and fell into some Speech with him.'[22] Sir Thomas's wife, Sarah, daughter of William Blount, is widely believed to be the unnamed 'Noble Lady' to whom William Strachey addressed his letter about the Bermuda shipwreck that is normally accepted to have been one of the main sources for *The Tempest* (see below).

Evidence that the recent marriage of his eldest son was a factor in the timing of the publication of the sonnets can be found in the first seventeen poems, which we suggest were written by Neville to his eldest son urging him to marry. The publication was, in effect, a wedding celebration, and so it is no coincidence that they were printed first in the collection. These sonnets are addressed by their author to a young man with whom the author is intimately acquainted, urging him to wed and produce an heir. Leslie Hotson summarised the puzzle that their pre-eminence has previously presented (our emphasis underlined):

> [P]erhaps no feature of the whole series [of *Shake-speares Sonnets*] has been more puzzling than its opening: the first seventeen poems urge, persuade, beg, and warn the Friend to marry and beget a child. *Why?* There is nothing like it in all poetry. Ordinary common sense dismisses the Just So Story which informs the credulous reader that 'Shakespeare was hired by a worried mother to write a lot of poems to make her son marry.' Only complete bafflement would force even a theorist quite unacquainted with the Elizabethans to suggest such an absurdity. The truth is that no *explanation* has ever been offered. As the late C. S. Lewis acutely remarked of this 'incessant demand' to marry, 'It is indeed hard to think of any real situation in which it would be natural. What man in the whole world, except a father, or potential father-in-law, cares whether another man gets married?'[23]

It is sometimes suggested that Shakespeare was hired to write these sonnets to convince Southampton to marry Lady Elizabeth Vere, the granddaughter of Lord Burghley and the daughter of the 17th Earl of Oxford. Southampton refused this marriage and was compelled to pay a fine of £5,000 as a result. Southampton's refusal to marry Lady Elizabeth Vere came no later than July 1590.[24] If Southampton was the dedicatee of *Shake-speares Sonnets*, as is widely believed (and is argued here), the last sonnets the Bard was likely to include in the book, let alone place first in the collection, would be those written nearly twenty years earlier, urging an unwanted marriage on him when in 1598 he had happily married another woman, Elizabeth Vernon.

There are other hints of Neville's authorship in the early sonnets. The author of Sonnet 2 may be implying that he was around forty years old; Neville was in his mid-forties in 1608. The author, in Sonnet 10, asks the subject to 'make thee another self for love of me' so using the term 'thee', reserved at the time for family or intimate friends. In his dedications to Southampton in the two long poems, written in 1593 and 1594, the Bard does not use 'thee', rather addressing the earl as 'you'. The intimate anxiety for an heir is that of a father: in Sonnet 13 the poet wrote, 'You had a father, let your son say so'. When one regards the first seventeen sonnets as Neville's successful advice to his eldest son to marry and produce an heir, their mystery vanishes. Neville offers many reasons for his son to procreate, occasionally self-interested but almost always with high praise for his son's beauty, coupled with a warning of the dire certainty of decay with age, cured only by marriage and the procreation of another generation. Most of his reasons centre around the need for his beauty to reproduce itself. Nothing, needless to say, is ever said directly about how marriage to an heiress would benefit both of them and enrich the family. Neville however may have been hinting at this in Sonnet 13:

Who lets so fair a house fall to decay,
Which husbandry in honour might uphold
Against the stormy gusts of winter's day
And barren rage of death's eternal cold?
O none but unthrifts ...

Sonnet 4 is written in monetary metaphors and Neville certainly needed Elizabeth's dowry. By and large the poems are appeals to the son's high-mindedness and against his inevitable ageing without heirs. One source for these sonnets was Erasmus' advice to a young man to get married. Neville had two volumes of Erasmus in his library.[25] We speculate that Southampton may have advised Neville to write some of his extraordinary sonnets to convince his son to marry and that this may be implied in the dedication to Southampton as their 'onlie begetter'.

In 1609, for the first time in years, certainly since Neville had been ambassador to France in 1599, his financial situation appeared to have been about to improve. Through his eldest son's marriage to an heiress, his family's continuity as wealthy gentry appeared assured. Neville was pinning his financial expectations not merely on his son's marriage, but also on the success of the Virginia Company. Now Neville had reason to be in an optimistic mood, a fact reflected in the upbeat, facetious tone of the dedication. We contend that it was this mood, and the near-simultaneous occurrence of the wedding and the company launch, that caused Neville to commission the publication of *Shake-speares Sonnets* at this time.

Neville and Southampton in the Tower

The first section of the sonnets is followed by a sequence of verses which we suggest were written by Neville when he was a prisoner in the Tower from 1601 to 1603 alongside Southampton, roughly sonnets 25–37. A further sequence, from about 104 to 125, was written at the same time for the same reasons. These two closely related sequences are of considerable importance to the authorship question. Perhaps the most important thing to be said about them is that they are *not* addressed to the same man as are the first seventeen sonnets: they are addressed to Southampton, not to Neville's son. Many of these sonnets forgive the addressee for a serious wrong he had done to the poet, or bemoan the poet's current unfortunate state, or both. Posit Neville as the poet and Sonnet 25 makes complete sense, even to the last two lines, written when he could not 'remove nor be removèd' from his prison in the Tower.

> Let those who are in favour with their stars
> Of public honour and proud titles boast,
> Whilst I whom fortune of some triumph bars,
> Unlook'd for joy in what I honour most.
> Great princes' favourites their fair leaves spread
> But as the marigold at the sun's eye,
> And in themselves their pride lies burièd,
> For at a frown they in their glory die.
> The painful warrior famousèd for fight,
> After a thousand victories once foil'd,
> Is from the book of honour rasèd quite,
> And all the rest forgot for which he toiled:
> 　　Then happy I that love and am belovèd
> 　　Where I may not remove, nor be removèd.

This sonnet, like others in the same vein, written while Neville was in the Tower, combines self-pity at his degraded state and admiration for the executed Essex (the famous warrior). Sonnet 125 also seems to refer to the Earl of Essex. The words 'compound sweet' seem to suggest Essex's monopoly on sweet wines which he lost in 1600, an important financial loss that was a factor in his downfall. Essex and his circle were the 'pitiful thrivers' of the poem. There is also perhaps a reference to the Earl of Southampton as 'thou suborn'd informer' because Southampton had implicated Neville at his trial. Similarly, Sonnet 29 speaks of a time

> When in disgrace with Fortune and men's eyes,
> I all alone beweep my outcast state,
> And trouble deaf heaven with my bootless cries,
> And look upon myself and curse my fate …
> Yet in these thoughts myself almost despising,
> Haply I think on thee, and then my state
> … sings hymns at heaven's gate …

This combines Neville's self-pity with the restorative powers of his admiration for the imprisoned Southampton. (When was William Shakspere ever 'in disgrace with fortune and men's eyes', or was ever 'all alone' to 'bewail my outcast state'?)

Another example is Sonnet 33, which we propose refers to Neville's ambassadorship and the perception that he was a rising star of Elizabethan government, followed quickly by his imprisonment for treason:

Even so my sun one early morn did shine
With all triumphant splendour on my brow;
But out alack, he was but one hour mine,
The region cloud hath masked him from me now …

Sonnet 34 is an equally clear reference to Neville being promised high office by Essex and his supporters, including Southampton, and then being imprisoned as a traitor.

Why didst thou promise such a bounteous day,
And make me travel forth without my cloak,
To let base clouds o'ertake me in my way,
Hiding thy brav'ry in their rotten smoke? …
Though I repent, yet still I have the loss …

In Sonnet 35 Neville quickly forgives Southampton:

No more be grieved at that which thou hast done:
Roses have thorns, and silver fountains mud …

As we have seen, Southampton's surname, Wriothesley, was pronounced <u>Rosely</u>. In Sonnet 95 Neville tells of Southampton's shame, referring even more explicitly to his name:

How sweet and lovely dost thou make the shame
Which, like a canker in the fragrant rose,
Doth spot the beauty of thy budding name!

The final line of this sonnet uses the words 'ill vs'd' (1609 spelling). In his letter dated 8 December 1604, Neville wrote the words 'ill used'.[26]
   Neville returned to these themes in sonnets 104–125, for example in 110:

Alas 'tis true, I have gone here and there,
And made myself a motley to the view,
Gored mine own thoughts, sold cheap what is most dear,
Made old offences of affections new.
Most true it is that I have looked on truth
Askance and strangely …

Sonnet 111 similarly pleads:

O for my sake do you with Fortune chide,
The guilty goddess of my harmful deeds,
That did not better for my life provide
Than public means which public manners breeds.
Thence comes it that my name receives a brand …

This is about as clear a reference to Neville's life, a disgraced public and government figure, as one can expect in these verses. Again, Sonnet 112 states,

> Your love and pity doth th'impression fill
> Which vulgar scandal stamped upon my brow ...

Neville was fearful of public scandal and in 1601 pleaded in a letter to Robert Cecil, begging that he not be exposed to public scandal by his trial being publicised.

We saw in Chapter 8 that Sonnet 107 is one of the few which orthodox scholars generally agree can be dated precisely to 1603. With Sonnet 107 dated to 1603 we can date many of the second sequence of self-pitying sonnets (104–25) to near the end of Neville's term of imprisonment, around 1602–3. Another sonnet that can be dated from James I's coronation 1603 is number 125, in which Shakespeare wrote, 'Wer't aught to me I bore the canopy', referring to the role of the barons of the Cinque Ports carrying the canopy over the new king.[27] The sonnet has been dated to 1604. In the 1602–3 Tower notebook Neville annotated the text about coronation ritual in three places regarding carrying the canopy. One of these states, 'Barons 5. ports the canapie.' The third simply states, 'to cary the canapie' (see also Chapter 11).[28]

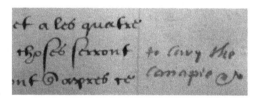

The Tower notebook, Worsley MSS 40.

In the sonnet Neville may have been using 'bearing the canopy' in a metaphorical sense. However, assuming that it was written in the Tower, he might also have meant it literally: that his degraded state made it impossible to participate in a high state occasion like a coronation.

Another of the sonnets in this sequence which appears to be directly relevant to the authorship question is 121, in which Neville comes close to removing the mask of secrecy:

> 'Tis better to be vile than vile esteemed,
> When not to be receives reproach of being, ...
> I may be straight though they themselves be bevel;
> By their rank thoughts my deed must not be shown,
>> Unless this general evil they maintain:
>> All men are bad, and in their badness reign.

We suggest that the first line contains both an obvious pun on Neville's name, as well as a close approximation to his family motto, 'Ne Vile Velis' ('Wishing nothing base'). If we are correct then only a Neville could write a sonnet based on an obvious pun on his name and family motto. The first line includes the name Neville in the words 'then vile' with just one letter missing (the 1609 spelling of 'than' is 'then' so the missing 'e' is just transposed by one space). In the original printing the third 'e' of 'receives' is just under the gap in 'n_vile', where the missing 'e' would be. When Neville is seen to be the author things fall into place and this contrasts starkly with the intractable puzzles that result from accepting William Shakspere from Stratford as the Bard.

Sonnets 135 and 136 pun on the word or name 'will'. This has been presumed to refer to William Shakspere's first name but it is also a play on will as penis or genitals. We suggest that Neville is here playing with and hinting at his own surname as well as boasting of his sexual prowess (by 1609 he had sired thirteen children).[29] Shakspere had only three children, the last, the twins, being born before he was twenty-one.[30] In the last three lines of Sonnet 135 Shakespeare repeats the words 'One will' which contain the name 'Nevvill'. The last line of Sonnet 136 contains the name Henry Nevvill: 'And then thou lovest me for my name is Will.'[31] Nowhere does the Bard play with or pun on the surname Shakespeare/Shakspere.

There are sonnets in *Romeo and Juliet* (dated 1591–5) and *Love's Labour's Lost* (1595–6), some of which were reprinted in *The Passionate Pilgrim* (1599). As previously stated some of the sonnets were certainly written before 1598, because they were known to Francis Meres who reported that they circulated 'among his private friends'. One of Neville's 'private friends' was Robert Killigrew who owned a copy of the second sonnet (Sloane MS 1792).[32] Robert Killigrew was Neville's wife's cousin. Robert's son, Thomas Killigrew, became a playwright. In 1669, a royal warrant gave the King's Players, the company established by Thomas Killigrew and Sir William Davenant, the exclusive right to perform twenty of Shakespeare's plays.[33] Robert Killigrew was a Member of Parliament and an investor in the Second Virginia Company and these roles would have led to contact with Neville even if they had not been related.

There have been some doubts that Sloane MS 1792 was Killigrew's. The volume is introduced by the words 'Robert Killigrew his booke witness by his Maiesties ape George Harison'. This is crossed out. Above it is a faint 'JA Christ Church' and one scholar speculated that this was a Jacob Aretius (or James Martius) from Christ Church College, Oxford. However, Killigrew himself attended Christ Church in 1591. There are two poems about Christ Church in the book. One, on folio 16, deals with a play about the fall of Wolsey and Henry VIII. It is reasonable to identify this as Shakespeare and Fletcher's *Henry VIII* because the poem quotes Wolsey's 'Ego et Rex meus', words spoken by Norfolk when he confronts the cardinal in the play:

> Then, that in all you writ to Rome, or else
> To foreign princes, 'Ego et Rex meus'
> Was still inscribed; in which you brought the king
> To be your servant. (3.2.315)

In another poem 'the usurping Richard ... the king of hate and therefore slave of fear' is said to be buried in Leicester (folio 30). The volume seems to be Robert's careful copying out of poems from other sources: the poems follow each other in neat, closely written pages. One poem is dated 26 August 1621 and the collection includes poems on the death of Elizabeth I (1603), James I (1625). If Killigrew was gathering into one little volume all the poems he had collected elsewhere then the original versions could date back at least as far as 1603. The copy of Shakespeare's second sonnet is interesting because it differs from the version printed in the 1609 edition. This may be because Killigrew was not an accurate scribe: he unnecessarily repeated the word 'like' in the fourth line (this word is not in the 1609 version). Alternatively it is possible that Killigrew's version of the second sonnet is an early version which the Bard revised before it was printed. The changes to the poem might be the result of Killigrew misreading the handwriting of a manuscript version (such as 'rotten weeds' instead of 'totter'd weed'). There are three minor corrections on the poem in a darker ink as if Killigrew later revised his copy. On folio 114 there is a version of William Basse's poem urging Spenser, Chaucer and Beaumont to make space for Shakespeare in their Westminster Abbey grave. On folio 74 there is a poem praising Sir Thomas Overbury and referring to his poisoning. After Overbury's death Killigrew came under suspicion of providing the poison because he had visited Overbury and supplied emetic medicines but he was exonerated. Neville was a friend of Overbury (see Chapter 11).[34]

Another manuscript copy of this popular second sonnet, dating from the 1630s, was owned by a Margaret Belasyse, but quite who this was is uncertain.[35] One Margaret Belasyse was the sister of Thomas Belasyse, Viscount Fauconberg (1627–1700). She was born in 1639. Her grandfather was Thomas Belasyse, 1st Baron and Viscount Fauconberg, (1577–1653). He was Neville's contemporary and a fellow Member of Parliament from 1597. His wife Barbara (*née* Cholmley) was descended from Cecily Neville, Duchess of York, who appears on stage in *Henry VI* and *Richard III*. Indeed the mitochondrial DNA from Barbara's descendants helped to confirm the identity of the recently discovered skeleton of Richard III.[36] Both copies of this sonnet can therefore be traced to people who had family connections with the Nevilles but no connection with William Shakspere from Stratford. The Killigrew and Belasyse manuscripts of the second sonnet are both Jacobean copies that have been dated to the 1620s. However, they may have been copied from a manuscript of the original sonnet rather than the 1609 printed version. If, for example, we take the second and third lines we can see they are identical but differ from the printed one.

1609 Printed version:
When fortie Winters shall beseige thy brow
And digge deep trenches in thy beauties field
Thy youthes proud livery so gaz'd on now …

Killigrew:
When forty winters shall besiege thy brow
And digge deep furrowes in that lovely field
Thy youth faire liverie soe accounted now …

Belasyse:
When threescore winters shall besiege thy brow
And trench deep furrows in y lovely field
Thy youths faire Liv'rie so accounted now …

Both the Killigrew and Belasyse versions use the words 'furrows', 'lovely', 'fair' and 'accounted'. This is evidence that two people who were related to Neville had access to an early variant of the second sonnet.

Neville's Use of Rare Vocabulary and Spellings in the Sonnets and in His Letters

In Neville's letters of 26 May 1599 and 4 June 1606, he used the word 'correspondence' which is unique to Sonnet 148.[37] On 9 April 1600, he wrote the word 'unperfitt' in a letter: 'unperfect' is to be found in Sonnet 23.[38] A month later, on 9 May 1600, he wrote 'memorial', which only occurs in Sonnet 74 and *Troilus and Cressida*.[39] In his letter of 21 June 1608, Neville used 'subsist' which is unique to Sonnet 122.[40] We cannot be sure of the date of the individual sonnets but we can be certain that Neville was using this vocabulary before the sonnets were published in 1609.

In his copy of *Leicester's Commonwealth* Neville made a marginal note about 'the tiranie of the Engli: state'. In the 1609 printing of Sonnet 115 this word is spelt 'tiranie'.

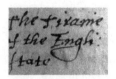

Worsley MSS 47, 6.

As we saw in Chapter 3, Neville made another note on 'a <u>tiranous</u> reuenge vpon a <u>tirante</u>'. In the 1609 printing of Sonnet 131 the spelling is '<u>tiranous</u>'. In sonnets 16 and 149 the spelling is '<u>tirant</u>'.

Another annotation in Neville's copy of *Leicester's Commonwealth* states, 'The Lo^rd(ship) of Denbigh a <u>great gift</u>'.

Worsley MSS 47: 27V.

In Sonnet 87 Shakespeare wrote: 'So thy <u>great guift</u>', spelling the word with a 'u' twice in the 1609 printing. Neville used the words, '<u>great Guifts</u>', in a letter dated 13 July 1599 with a 'u'.[41] The 1609 printing of Sonnet 122 also uses the spelling '<u>guift</u>'.

Neville used the word '<u>Unloked</u>' in a letter dated 1 November 1599.[42] In the 1609 printing of Sonnet 7 the spelling is '<u>Vnloked</u>'. Copying *Leicester's Commonwealth*, Neville used the spelling of 'pollicie':

Worsley MSS47, 42.

The same spelling is used in the 1609 printing of Sonnet 118 and in the first quarto edition of *Titus Andronicus* (1594, line 669).[43] Neville used the spelling 'made' instead of 'mad' in an annotation in *Leicester's Commonwealth*: 'Roland Howard and his made recorder'.

Worsley MSS 47, 22.

In the 1609 printing of Sonnet 129 lust is described as 'Made in pursuit', meaning 'Mad in pursuit'.[44] A few such similar spellings might be dismissed as coincidence but when there are as many as this they point towards Neville's authorship.

Numbers, Maths and Geometry

In the metaphors and numbering of the sonnets, Shakespeare demonstrates a familiarity with, and complex interest in, numbers. We noted in Chapter 3 how the Bard had played with numbers in *Love's Labour's Lost*, so this mathematical interest goes back to his early works. He also plays with the numbering of the poems as sonnets 7, 12 and 60 have to do with time (referring to days in a week, the twelve hours of a clock face and sixty minutes in an hour) and Sonnet 8 refers to music (the octave).

There are a total of 154 sonnets in the collection. This could have been the number the Bard happened to consider worth publishing or the number could have been deliberately chosen to have special significance. Knowing Neville had an interest in numbers we observe that 154 is 22 x 7. The value of Pi (π), by which we calculate the ratio of the circumference of a circle to its diameter, is 22 divided by 7. William Jones was the first to use the Greek letter π for this number in 1707. However, the number had been known since the time of the ancient Egyptian and Greek mathematicians. If there is some meaning inherent in Shakespeare's choice of 154 this number may represent a completed circle, an image of completion of the cycle of sonnets. We know that Neville had an interest in numbers and geometry. He had studied mathematics at Merton College, Oxford under his tutor Henry Savile. In the Merton library is a book about Ptolemy's celestial geometry which was donated by Neville and annotated by him in Latin and Greek.[45] One of the annotations, on page 49, reads, 'Theoreme per quod circumfentia colluguntur' which we translate as 'The Theorem by which circumferences may be calculated'. This note shows that Neville was aware of the geometry, as is confirmed by John Chamber's poem about Neville, in which he explicitly referred to his knowledge of Euclid (see Chapter 6). Neville's contemporary, Ludolph van Ceulen, spent years calculating the value of π. He published a twenty-decimal value in his 1596 book *Van den Circkel* (On the Circle) and in 1600 he was appointed the first professor of mathematics at Leiden University. He died in 1610.

Shakespeare used the words 'circumference' in *A Midsumer Night's Dream, King John* and *The Merry Wives of Windsor*, all works of the later 1590s. He used 'diameter' in *Hamlet* and 'circle' in eight plays from *Titus Andronicus* to *Antony and Cleopatra*. In *Henry V* (1599) the Duke of Burgundy advises the king on his wooing of Katherine:

Pardon the frankness of my mirth, if I answer you for that. If you would conjure in her, you must make a circle; if conjure up love in her in his true likeness, he must appear naked and blind. Can you blame her then, being a maid yet rosed over with the virgin crimson of modesty, if she deny the appearance of a naked blind boy in her naked seeing self? (5.2.287)

There are sexual puns here about the penis and vagina. The last sonnet, 154, is about Cupid (= Love, a blind boy). The erotic is essential to the fulfilment of love with the result of the creation of the next generation, which is a core subject of the sonnets. In Sonnet 7 the cycle of generation takes as its main image the sun (a circle). Sonnet 22 is about love and the cycle of life, including an image of a mirror (glass). Sonnet 77 is half way through the sequence of 154 poems. It includes a sundial (a circle, relating the sun and time) and a mirror. There is more to this number symbolism which is explored in detail by Leyland and Goding and in our appendix.[46]

Callaghan explained Shakespeare's interest in numbers thus: 'The sonnets demonstrate a thematic preoccupation with numbers of various kinds precisely because counting constitutes one of the essential elements of poetry. The poet's first task is to count out the metrical beat of the sonnet.'[47] Neville owned a copy of Horace's *Odes* and annotated a page which graphically depicts the rhythm of a poem.

Neville's notes (in Latin and Greek) on rhythm in Horace, Lib 1.17.

Horace's *Odes* were a source for Shakespeare's sonnets. For example, Sonnet 55 develops Horace's Ode 3.30. Neville annotated this sonnet in his copy. Further evidence of an interest in meter is in Neville's copy of Ovid's *Ars Amatoria* where one marginal annotation on the commentary points to a passage about meter in poetry and particularly pentameters.

There is evidence that Shakespeare knew Greek and used Greek literary models in his writing. The sonnet sequence ends with two strangely similar poems, 153 and 154 about Cupid. 'Both sonnets play on a conceit deriving from a six-line epigram by Marianus Scholasticus, a sixth century Byzantine poet.' The epigram was not translated at that time and 'Shakespeare's sonnets seem closer to the Greek original than any of the Latin or vernacular adaptations of it'.[48] Furthermore, these final two sonnets were written in a meter used by the Greek poet Anacreon. Neville assisted Henry Savile in his search for Greek and Byzantine manuscripts during their travels from 1578 to 1582 and, as we have seen, his library contained books in Greek which Neville annotated in Latin and Greek.

Once again we feel obliged to contrast Neville, who was educated to a high degree in mathematics, geometry and astronomy, and Latin and Greek, with William Shakspere from Stratford, for whom there is no evidence that he had any such knowledge.

A Lover's Complaint

After the sonnets, at the end of the little volume published in 1609, is a long poem of a woman's lament about being betrayed by her lover. It is to us, unfamiliar with the sixteenth-century convention of poetic complaint, a strange poem that has only reluctantly been accepted as having been written by Shakespeare.

The poem has been dated to the period when Neville was in the Tower, a time when he had reason to complain. We suggest that in using the metaphor of a woman who was seduced and betrayed by a faithless lover, Neville was working through his sense of betrayal by Southampton. The lover's 'complaint-cum-apology mingles dubious pleading with apparent confession'.[49] We have suggested that Sonnet 34 is Neville addressing Southampton. The sonnet echoes their situation and that expressed in *A Lover's Complaint*:

> For no man well of such a salve can speak
> That heals the wound, and cures not the disgrace:
> Nor can thy shame give physic to my grief;
> Though thou repent, yet I have still the loss:
> Th'offender's sorrow lends but weak relief
> To him that bears the strong offence's cross.
> > Ah! but those tears are pearl which thy love sheeds,
> > And they are rich and ransom all ill deeds.

Southampton, it seems, confessed his betrayal and wept. Writing of *A Lover's Complaint* Roe stated, 'Nothing is so seductive as the apparently sincere confession of past wrongs. Instead of heeding the warning, she imagines her task is to redeem him through love'.[50] The ending of *A Lover's Complaint* has a sense of bleakness and irrecoverable loss: the damage had been done. The poem fails to impress and, as Sonnet 34 says, although Southampton might regret his part in his downfall, Neville has had to cope with the consequent damage to his life, reputation, career, family and sense of self. Indeed, the poem contains the seeds of Neville's examination of what 'mole of nature', to quote Hamlet's view of tragedy, or to quote Neville in his 1601 confession, what *Imbecillitie and Weakness of my own Nature …*' (italics in the original), what element of his own make-up, was the source of his tragedy?[51] What was his responsibility in the debacle? The Bard worked through this in the great tragedies as his flawed heroes find that their faults inexorably lead to their downfall, however much others (witches, wicked villains and cruel daughters) may be blamed.

Neville's Inscription at the End of *A Lover's Complaint*

At the very end of the copy of *Shake-speares Sonnets* (1609) in the John Rylands Library, Manchester, someone has written a note after *A Lover's Complaint*. This suggests the presenter was giving the little volume as a gift to a friend.

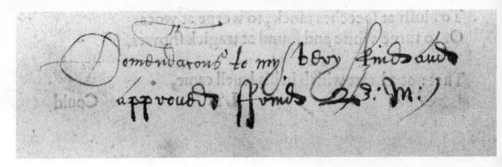

Comendacons to my very kind and approued ffrnid B: M:/ (John Rylands Library, © the University of Manchester.)

As a dedication it is written in neat, careful writing with a flourish appropriate to the occasion. We suggest that this could have been written by Neville. Ending a letter to Ralph Winwood, dated 21 June 1608, less than a year before the sonnets were published, he signed off saying, 'My affectionate <u>Commendations</u> and wishes of all good fortune and will ever be Your assured <u>Friend</u> to my best Ability, Henry Neville' (our emphasis underlined, we suspect the spelling in this printed 1725 edition of the letters had been modernised by Sawyer, the editor).[52] Of the many letters in *Winwood's Memorials* only Neville ended his letters with the word 'Commendations', although several other writers also used the formula 'assured friend'.[53] It is noteworthy that in all his uses of the word 'Commendations' Neville used a capital C, as in the inscription. Neville's father used the words 'my Hartie Comendacons' in a letter dating from the 1570s, employing a similar looping flourish above the word.[54]

Shakespeare used 'commendations' fourteen times in plays across the canon including 'commendations to my' which occurs in *Henry VI: Part I*. The word 'approved' is used nineteen times by the Bard, including 'approved friend' in *The Taming of the Shrew*.

The first word of the inscription, 'Comendacons', is spelt with a final 'cons' instead of 'tions'. This is consistent with Neville's use of the letter 'c' instead of 't' in many words in his writing, such as 'interpretacion', 'intencion', 'reputacion', 'approbacion' in his 1603–4 draft letter (in the Reading archives) and 'obligacion', 'mediacion' and 'preservacion' in his 1602 letter (at Hatfield House). As we saw in Chapter 8, the writer of Hand D spells the word 'addition' with a 'c': 'adicion'. The long, curving line with double intersecting lines over 'Comendacons' represents the missing 'i'. Neville used this identical form, ~ ,which curves upward in a horizontal 'S' shape, to indicate abbreviated letters in his copy of *Leicester's Commonwealth*, for example:

   'xmas', 'disposicōn' and 'tolleracōn' in Worsley MSS 47, 2, 7 and 9.

In the latter two we have the same use of 'con' instead of 'tion'. Though smaller, the form of the middle example above 'disposicon', where the central horizontal line curls back under the double vertical lines, and curls upwards at the other end, is identical to the flourish on the inscription. Neville continued to use these marks in letters.[55] The word 'Comendacons' ends with a rising s which has a backward hook at the top:

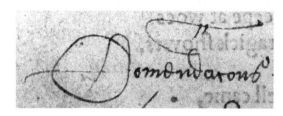

'Comendacons' in the inscription, 1609.

Examples of such a final rising letter 's' with a backward hook are to be found in Neville's letters:

'Commodities', 1601; 'perhaps' and 'this', 1613.

The word 'Commodities' here also starts with a capital letter C similar to, though smaller than, the one in the inscription.

   We note the 'v' of 'very' looks like a 'b'. We can compare the word 'very' here with the same word written in Neville's letter of 1603 and in his last extant letter of 16 July 1613:[56]

Inscription 1609, Neville's 1603 letter, and in his 1613 letter.

This shows the 'b'-like 'v' starts with a rising hook. Also the 'e' has the same form. The 'y' also sweeps backwards with a bulbous shape, most dramatically in the 1613 letter.

   The form of the 'k' in the word 'kind' can be compared with Neville's 'k's in his letter of 1601[57] and with Hand D:

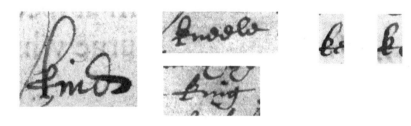

'kind' in the inscription; 'k' of 'kneele' and 'knig' in Hand D; Neville's letter 1601.

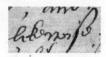

'likewise', 'make' and 'know' in Neville's 1613 letter. (Stowe 174 f 116, © British Library)

The 'k' of 'kind' in the inscription has a flat foot that can be seen in Hand D and in some of Neville's 'k's. None of the 'k's in the six extant Shakspere signatures have this flat foot. The 'k' has a bar across it that connects to the next letter in the word, and a loop above that reaches over the lower part of the 'k' as we can see in Neville's 1613 letter.

There are two spurred 'a's in the inscription: these straight spurs can be compared with those in Neville's 1601 letter:

 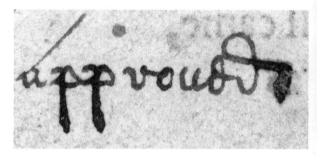

'and', 'approved' in the inscription, 1609. Four spurred 'a's: Neville's letter of 19th February 1601. 'and ordniary abuses may'.

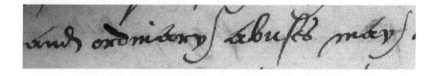

Note the 'd's on 'and' are virtually identical. We can also compare the 'd' on the first 'and' of Neville's letter with the 'd' on 'approved'. The 'y' on 'ordinary', with its backward sweep, can be compared with the 'y' s on 'my' and 'very' in the inscription.

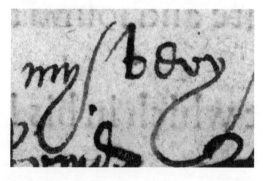

'my very' in the inscription, 1609.

Neville did not use such spurred 'a's in the rough drafts of his letters but he did so in the British Library copy of his 1601 letter which was a formal diplomatic letter to Robert Cecil, Secretary of State. We can see that in using them in this inscription he is formally addressing someone of rank.

The word 'ffrnid' (friend) is spelt in an unusual way in the inscription. This spelling is also to be seen in Neville's copy of *Leicester's Commonwealth* (Worsley MSS 47):

Above: 'frnid' and 'ffmid': Worsley MSS 47, front page, 46 and 6V.

Right: 'ffrnid' in the inscription, 1609.

The '8'-shaped form of the final 'd' in the second and third examples from Worsley MSS 47 matches the 'd' in the inscription. Neville used a double 'ff' in writing 'ffraunce' and 'fflaunders' in his copy of *Leicester's Commonwealth*:

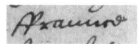 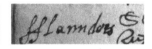

'ffraunce', 'fflaunders' and 'ffather' in Worsley MSS 47, 8V, 4V, 7.

The form here is again identical: the first 'f' is an arch connecting to the second 'f' which has a closed loop. This way of writing double 'ff' is consistent over a period of twenty-eight years (1585–1613). It is visible in Neville's 1603 letter when he wrote 'affected' and, in his 1613 letter, 'affection': again the first 'f' is an arch connecting to the second 'f' which has a closed loop. As the next example from Neville's copy of *Leicester's Commonwealth* shows, he did occasionally use a double 'f' for 'ffrnid':

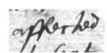 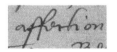 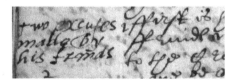

Above left and middle: 'affected' in Neville's 1603 letter and 'affection' in his 1613 letter

Above right: 'two excuses made by his frnids, ffirst is… ffrnid': Worsley MSS 47, 31V.

In a letter dating from the 1570s written by Neville's father (see chapters 3 and 8), he spells the word 'ffrind', so perhaps Neville picked up this spelling from him.[58] We can also compare this double 'ff' to the word 'offendor' in Hand D where we find the first 'f' is an arch connecting to the second 'f' which has a closed loop:

'offendor' in Hand D, *Sir Thomas More*: Hand D.

In all these double 'ff's, in Neville's manuscripts, Hand D and the inscription there is a horizontal bar connecting the two letters. Having checked the databases of LION and EEBO we can state that no other writer is recorded as having used the spellings of 'ffrnid', 'frnid' and 'frenid' between 1590 and 1624. The only example we have found is in Hand D:

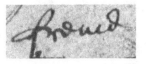

'frenid' or 'freind' in *Sir Thomas More*: Hand D.

The writer of the inscription used colons to abbreviate initials 'B:M:/' at the end:

B:M: in the inscription, 1609.

Neville used colons in his annotations of *Leicester's Commonwealth* (below right) and used forward slashes at the end of annotations, just as one is used after the date at the end of the inscription (below left):

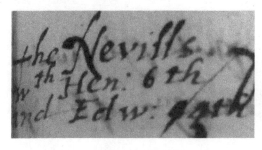 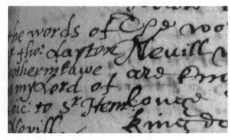

Left: 'the Nevills wth Hen: 6th and Edw: 4th', Worsley MSS 47, 36.

Right: 'my Lord of Leic: to Sr Hen: Nevill./', Worsley MSS 47, 32.

Beare, Worsley MSS 47, 8V.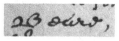

Neville's letters of 1603 and 1613.

We can also see that Neville used similar capital 'B's (on the words 'Beare', 'But' and 'Before') that look like the number 23 in his copy of *Leicester's Commonwealth* and in his letters of 1603 and 1613.

None of these however have the forward slash that seems to divide the letter 'B' into 2 and 3. Such a 'B' does occur in Hand D. Neville did use a downward slash in his flourishing capital 'B' in 1600:

Above: 'Bushell and Boeff': *Sir Thomas More:* Hand D, folio 8.

Right: Neville's capital 'B' in 'By Me' on his poem (see chapter 6).

We have found no match for the double 'pp' of 'approved' in Neville's writing. The examples we can find are sloping to the right, although the 'kepe' of the little poem written in Paris in 1600 is near perpendicular (see Chapter 6).

However when we look at the word 'appropriat' in Hand D we see both slanting and upright 'p's. Moreover, the form of the second upright 'p' is comparable to those of the inscription, except that it joins up with the following 'r'.

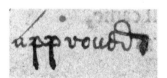  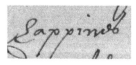

'approved' 1609 'kepe', 1600; 'happiness' 1613.

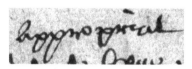

'appropriat' in *Sir Thomas More*: Hand D.

As we can see, Neville's handwriting varies and some small differences in style are not a reason to rule out his authorship of the inscription. The similarities are considerable but some of the matches between Neville's handwriting and the inscription occur because this was standard script, so it remains possible that the inscription was written by someone else. However, we have found no other example of handwriting that has so many matches, especially with the spelling of 'ffrnid'.[59] The inversion of 'in' into 'ni' is typical of Neville's habit of writing 'ni' in words like king (knig) and against (aganist) as can be seen in his copy of *Leicester's Commonwealth*, his letters, the NHMS, the annotated Hall and Hand D.[60]

The identity of 'B. M.' is uncertain: we cannot know whether these are initials or a cipher or simply stand for 'By Me'. (As we have seen, Neville wrote 'By me' after composing his little poem in Paris in 1600: see Chapter 6.) The form of 'B. M.' can be confused with the numbers 23.

Shake-speares Sonnets was only entered into the Stationers' Register on 20 May. It might be just coincidence that Neville was baptised on 20 May 1564, but it may also be that choosing that day in 1609 to register the sonnets felt auspicious. We have suggested they were published in order to coincide with the granting of the Charter of the Second London Virginia Company on 23 May 1609. It is possible that the capital B, which looks like 23, is, in fact, 23. This could only be 23 May: the M cannot stand for March because the sonnets were not registered until May. We suggest that this copy of the sonnets may be one inscribed three days after it was registered, on the very day of the Virginia Company launch. If so it would confirm our suggestion that Neville issued the sonnets to mark that launch. The most likely explanation for the handwritten inscription is that it was written by the author. Who else would send out a copy of this work on the day it was published?

David Ewald, who has researched the initials B. M., discovered there was a Member of Parliament called Barnard Michell who was also a subscriber to the Second London Virginia Company.[61] He was the only subscriber whose initials were B. M. The Michell family provided Parliament with several MPs in the sixteenth and seventeenth centuries and John Michell, member for Truro in 1563, married Jane Killigrew, daughter of John Killigrew. Her eldest brother was Henry Killigrew, Neville's father-in-law. It is possible, therefore, that Neville knew other members of the Michell family, including a fellow subscriber of the Virginia Company. Evidence for this is provided by a legacy of £60 to a James Michell in Neville's 1615 will.[62] Furthermore, in a document dated 1603, Neville made a note to send 'Mr Packer and Michell' to Shellingford.[63] Because we know that Packer was Neville's secretary we can reasonably surmise that Michell was a scribe or assistant secretary.

We are grateful to David Ewald who first asked whether this inscription was written by Neville. He had traced the history of the book back to Richard Farmer, a leading Shakespeare scholar, renowned book collector and Head Librarian of the Cambridge College Universities from 1778 to 1797. Being a keen student of Shakespeare, Farmer would have been eager to own the 1609 *Shake-speares Sonnets*. As the *ODNB* puts it, 'he more than once bought books for his personal library when he should have had the best interests of the university library at heart'.[64] George Spencer, 2nd Earl Spencer, Viscount Althorp (1758–1834), bought Farmer's book collection in 1798 and when it was eventually sold in 1892 it was bought for the John Rylands Library.[65] Spencer was a descendant of Neville through two of the latter's daughters, as well as a descendant of Southampton through his daughter Penelope Wriothesley Spencer.

Whether this volume of sonnets was given to Southampton or someone else by Neville, we suggest that the inscription represents the personal touch of the author in giving a newly printed copy to a friend. By qualifying the 'ffrnid' as 'approved', perhaps Neville was referring to the trials he and Southampton had passed through in the Tower, when they had proved their friendship through their shared suffering. However, it is impossible to be sure who the friend was and, given the letters Neville wrote to Winwood signing off with similar words, the book could have been sent to him, or perhaps to Bernard Michell, or another friend with the initials B. M.

The Tempest

There is an immediate connection between *Shake-speares Sonnets* and *The Tempest*. Neville had hoped that the Second London Virginia Company would restore his fortunes. However, it initially failed to make a profit, and, indeed, its early history was marked by misfortune. In June 1609, nine ships set out to settle Virginia under the Company's auspices. Neville had sold timber to the Virginia Company for building the ships that sailed to the New World. One of these, the *Sea Venture*, was wrecked at Bermuda and the lives of those on board apparently lost. Miraculously, after a year on the island, the ship's survivors managed to build two boats, sail to Jamestown, Virginia, and were then able to send word back to London of what had happened, causing a great sensation. The best-known account, written at the time, was by a survivor, William Strachey (1572–1621), who had been a passenger on the *Sea Venture* and who was acting as Secretary to the expedition.[66] Strachey sent back a lengthy description of the shipwreck and the subsequent salvation of the *Sea Venture's* crew and passengers. Dated 15 July 1610, it was addressed to 'an Excellent Lady' in England, generally believed to be Lady Smythe, the wife of Sir John Smythe, and it reached London in September 1610.

Because it was critical of the management of the Virginia Company, circulation of the letter was tightly restricted and it was not published until 1625, when it appeared as *A True Reportory of the Wrack and Redemption of Sir Thomas Gates* (Gates, who had been on board, was Governor of Virginia from 1611 to 1614). This document is known today as the 'Strachey letter'. In addition, several other works were immediately published in London about the shipwreck and the miraculous survival of those on board, especially Silvester Jourdain's *A Discovery of Virginia*, which appeared in October 1610, and *A True Declaration of the Estate of the Colonie in Virginia*, put together by the Virginia Company to refute 'scandalous reports' about itself and published in November 1610.[67] The importance of these works, and especially of the Strachey letter, lies in the fact that they were certainly used by the author of *The Tempest* throughout the play, in what Kathman has described as its many 'thematic, verbal, and plot correspondences'.[68] The earliest recorded performance of *The Tempest* was on 1 November 1611. Normally, the sources used by Shakespeare in his works are of interest only to specialist scholars, but in this case whether the Strachey letter was used in writing *The Tempest* is critical to the authorship question. First, if *The Tempest* was based on sources written in 1610 and which could not have appeared earlier, by definition the play must have been written by a man alive at that time. This would definitively rule out Edward de Vere, 17th Earl of Oxford, as the author of the play, as he died in 1604. For this reason, Oxfordians (those who believe that Oxford was Shakespeare) have waged a fierce campaign to discredit the identification of the Strachey letter and other works from 1610 as the sources for *The Tempest*. However, an unbiased assessment cannot leave the slightest doubt that they are wrong.[69] Secondly, and even more importantly, the fact that the Strachey letter was heavily restricted in its circulation, and remained unpublished until 1625, raises the central question of how others who have been put forward as the author of the canon managed to see it, copy out portions of it and use these in a play. If, in fact, William Shakspere from Stratford could not have secured access to the Strachey letter, then he could not have written *The Tempest*, and someone else, who must necessarily have had access to the letter, must have been the play's actual author.

The question of whether the Strachey letter was a necessary source for *The Tempest* has been addressed and answered in an important article by Barry R. Clarke.[70] Clarke noted the conclusion reached many years ago by the American scholar C. M. Gayley, that 'close verbal and literary coincidences between the play [*The Tempest*] and the [Strachey] letter are of such a kind as could not be accounted for by any mere conversation that Shakespeare may have had with Strachey'.[71] As Clarke pointed out, 'in other words, Shakespeare would have needed possession of the manuscript and a close inspection of verbal parallels confirms this'.[72]

This being so, the key questions are: could William Shakspere have gained access to the Strachey letter, and could Neville have had access to it? William Shakspere had no known connection of any kind with the Second London Virginia Company but is there any plausible way he could have managed to read and study it? Orthodox scholars have long attempted to provide an answer to this question, such as that set out by Frank Kermode in his Introduction to the second Arden edition of *The Tempest* (our emphasis is underlined):

> Shakespeare's knowledge of this unpublished work [the Strachey letter] makes it probable that he was deeply interested in the story. He was certainly acquainted with members of the Virginia Company ... Among these were Southampton and Pembroke, both of them financially interested in the plantation, and Shakespeare had friends in common with others of the Essex group similarly interested – Sir Robert Sidney, <u>Sir Henry Neville</u>, and Lord De La Warr, who was to be a governor of the colony. He also knew friends of Gates, who could have enabled him to meet Strachey, and almost certainly Sir Dudley Digges, ardent in the Virginian Cause, whose brother Leonard contributed memorial verses to the First Folio, and whose mother married Thomas Russell, the 'overseer' of Shakespeare's will. Both Dudley Digges and William Strachey contributed laudatory verses to Jonson's *Sejanus* in 1605, and Shakespeare acted in the play. Shakespeare's friend Heminge was at Digges's wedding, and signed as a witness. It seems likely that Shakespeare knew Digges, who may have procured Strachey's appointment as secretary [on board the *Sea-Venture*] in 1609, when Donne was a rival applicant. Leslie Hotson conjectures that Digges may have edited Strachey's confidential report on the state of Virginia, and produced the more cheerful *True Declaration*. There seems to have been opportunity for Shakespeare to see the unpublished report, or even to have met Strachey.[73]

Kermode's circular argument that because the Bard had to know the story he must have known the people that would have given him access to the Strachey letter does not convince because there is no evidence that William Shakspere knew any of the men named as associated with the Virginia Company, starting with Southampton and Pembroke.[74]

There are also more direct reasons for concluding that William Shakspere could *not* have read the Strachey letter. As Clarke pointed out, oaths of secrecy were administered by the Company from the beginning of the voyage of its ships.

> [N]ot only did oaths of secrecy restrict William Strachey, the Governor at Jamestown, and the entire Virginia Council in London from distributing or even discussing letters with outsiders, but Council members were collectively warned, before De La Warr set out for Virginia and before the [Strachey letter] was sent back to England, that actors were abusing the colony on the stage. There would also have been a political price to pay had the [Strachey letter], which exposed the weaknesses of the colony, gone beyond the safety of the Virginia Council and fallen into Spanish hands. So it is highly improbable that William Shakespeare, irrespective of the number of Council members he knew, could have gained access to the [Strachey letter] before *The Tempest* was performed at Whitehall in November 1611.[75]

There are also the very serious considerations about the logistics involved if one believes that William Shakspere read and copied out passages from the Strachey letter. Presumably Strachey sent a handwritten letter to Sir Thomas and Lady Smythe, who may have had a number of copies made by trusted scribes and clerks, sworn to secrecy. The notion that someone like Thomas Russell was able to take one of these closely guarded and strictly confidential copies of the letter, of which at most only a handful of duplicates would have existed, with him to Stratford-upon-Avon (the scenario hinted at by Kermode), three days' travel time from London, where he gave it to a known playwright to use in a play in breach of his own oath, beggars belief. Even more implausible is the notion that, although he had absolutely no connection with the Virginia Company, Shakspere from Stratford was allowed to read and copy out material from the letter in London, either at the offices of the company or at the home of Sir Thomas Smythe. Despite the fanciful conjectures there is no evidence that William Shakspere read and copied out material from the Strachey letter and there is no reason to suppose that its confidentiality had been so compromised. That being so and since *The Tempest* is heavily based on the Strachey letter, William from Stratford could not have written the play. Furthermore, because there is no doubt that the author of *The Tempest* wrote all of the other works in the Shakespearean canon (apart from those known to have been co-authored), the man from Stratford could not have written any of the other works attributed to him.

In contrast, Neville was a director of the Virginia Company and had just become a close relative by marriage to Sir Thomas and Lady Smythe. He was also an influential Member of Parliament, and, through his relationship with Sir Thomas Gresham and his work as an ambassador concerned with the difficulties of merchants (as is evident in many of his letters), he was connected with London's mercantile elite. Neville knew Strachey as they both attended the Mermaid Club. Neville could certainly have had immediate access to the Strachey letter, and writing a play like *The Tempest* fitted in well with his post-1600 experience of the dashed expectations of a man who, like Prospero, had been ruined years before and whose main concern now was the marriage of his daughter. *The Tempest* is generally seen as the Bard's farewell to the theatre (barring the last three plays co-authored with John Fletcher), which again fits in well (as always) with the chronology of Neville's life and its downward spiral at this point, the product of political and financial disappointment and ill health.

The themes of *The Tempest* fit Neville's psychological development. As Prospero he reflects on his betrayal, fall and struggle with his own anger and inner demon ('this thing of darkness I acknowledge mine'). He emerged into a new world, appreciating the wonder of life, forgiving enemies, achieving compassion and a higher philosophical standpoint from which he could contemplate the great globe itself dissolving. Scholars have noticed a concern with the dichotomous opposition of the noble and the vile. Caliban embodies the vile with the clowns Stephano and Trincolo. Caliban's vile race is 'opposed to the race *non vile* – the stock etymology of *nobile* ... Prospero expresses the qualities of the world of Art, of the *non vile*' (italics in the original).[76] The princes Sebastian and Antonio behave in ignoble, vile ways. Noble birth did not guarantee nobility. This reflects the Neville family motto 'Ne Vile Velis' and the Renaissance concern with virtue, a complex idea translated from the Latin word 'virtus', meaning the manly character qualities of courage, endurance and morality, 'closely related to the nature of the noble'.[77] John Chamber, George Carleton, Ben Jonson and John Davies all used the words 'virtus' and 'virtue' to describe Neville.[78]

Dr John Dee, the mathematician and magus, died in late 1608 or early 1609, just before the play was written. It is believed that Shakespeare may have modelled Prospero on Dee, whose magic included communicating with angels, just as Prospero talks with Ariel. One of Dee's spirits was called Anael. Neville was aware of Dee as is evident in an annotation in his copy of *Leicester's Commonwealth*:

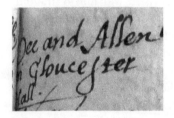

'Dee and Allen in Gloucester Hall', Worsley MSS 47, 27.

This annotation is documentary proof that Neville knew of Dr John Dee and took an interest in him. Dee was the leading mathematician of his day, a Renaissance man who combined practical science, such as navigation, with mystical Hermetic Neoplatonism. Shakespeare's last plays contain Neoplatonic elements in their poetry and plots. The above annotation also mentions Dr Thomas Allen, a mathematician, who went to Gloucester Hall in 1570 and lived there for the rest of his life (until 1632). His choice of Gloucester Hall was due to its being the habitation of great medieval mathematicians of the Benedictine Order. Furthermore, Allen had been trained in mathematics at Merton College, which Neville attended from around 1574 to 1577.[79] Given Neville's interest in mathematics, this annotation about Dee and Allen is not surprising. Indeed, Neville is likely to have known Allen because his own tutor, Henry Savile, was a friend and colleague.[80] Dee was travelling abroad from 1583 to 1589. Therefore Neville, annotating in 1584–5, must have been referring to a visit to Oxford by Dee before September 1583. In 1582, Neville had arrived back in England from his European travels with Savile (who surely would have gone back to Oxford on their return).[81]

Scholars have found traces of *commedia dell'arte* in Shakespeare's plays, including in *The Tempest*. There is no need to suppose the Bard learned about it from travellers who brought back accounts from Italy as Neville had been there and so would have had opportunity to see Harlequin and his comic crew.[82] The play focuses on Naples and Milan, the latter being in northern Italy. Neville may well have passed through Milan while on his travels in 1581 and 1582 (see Chapter 3). In his diplomatic letters, Neville reported on the politics of Italy, specifically referring to Milan, Naples, Genoa, Florence and Sicily in one letter of 24 April 1600.[83] He had crossed the Channel at least four times before he wrote *The Tempest* and so would have known about sea journeys and their hazards from personal experience. By contrast, there is no evidence that William Shakspere ever set foot on a ship, except, in all likelihood, for a rowing boat to cross the Thames.

In two letters, dated 15 November 1600 and 19 August 1604, Neville wrote the words 'open-eyed', which only occur in *The Tempest*.[84] In the First Folio it is spelt 'open-ey'd'. The hyphenated words 'open-eyed' were indeed rare at that time. The only other writer to use the hyphenated form with this spelling was Nicholas Breton in 1597.[85] In Neville's letter of 1604 he wrote 'open-eyed and ear'd'.[86] Shakespeare used the word 'ear'd' as 'prick-ear'd' in *Henry V* and 'flap-ear'd' in *The Taming of the Shrew*. Neville's use here in a letter of an apostrophe in 'ear'd', matches the First Folio spelling of 'open-ey'd'. In his letter of 11 March 1606 Neville used the word 'irreparable', which is unique to *The Tempest*. Neville therefore used this word up to five years before the Bard used it in the play.[87]

In the epilogue at the end of the play, Prospero, like Ariel, asks for his freedom. Neville had struggled to gain high office in the years 1610 to 1613 but by the time of his last extant letter of 16 July 1613 he had foregone further political ambition:[88]

Neville's letter of 16 July 1613.

I know the burden and weight of that place too well to desire to pull such a load upon me. And I am not apt to overvalue myself, neither do I place my happiness in greatness or titles, but rather in a <u>freedom</u> and contentment of mind, which is sooner found in a private life.

Prospero promises Ariel:

Shortly shall all my labours end, and thou
Shalt have the air at <u>freedom</u> … (4.1.264)

Although the letter postdates the early performances of the play, *The Tempest* was not printed until 1623, so it is not impossible that the epilogue was a later addition. In any case, the situation of Prospero seeking his rightful dukedom and freedom matches Neville's hopes for both high political office and the 'contentment of mind … found in a private life'. By 1614 the last plays, co-written with Fletcher, were on stage and Neville could indeed enjoy a peaceful retirement. He had just a year to live.

The Final Plays:
Co-Writing with John Fletcher
1612–1613

I've worn the garland of my honours long,
And would not leave it wither'd to thy brow,
But flourishing and green; worthy the man,
Who ... heirs my better glories.

Double Falshood, 1.1.5

Fletcher and Neville

John Fletcher worked with Shakespeare on three last plays: *Cardenio, Henry VIII* and *The Two Noble Kinsmen*. There are a number of links between Fletcher and Neville. Fletcher was born in 1579 in Rye, Sussex, not far from where Neville began working on his inherited iron foundry at Mayfield when he returned from his European travels in 1582. Richard Fletcher, the playwright's father, was present at the execution of Mary, Queen of Scots. Neville's father had been one of Mary's custodians in 1584 and 1585. Henry Neville, 6th Baron Bergavenny, one of the peers who sat in judgement on Mary, was Neville's father's cousin. Fletcher's uncle Giles (his guardian after his father's death in 1596) was, like Neville, caught up in the Essex rebellion. Francis Beaumont, John Fletcher and Neville were all members of the Mermaid Club. When *A King and No King* by Beaumont and Fletcher was first printed in 1619, Walkley's dedicatory epistle to Sir Henry Neville introduced the play (see Chapter 2).[1] *A King and No King* was first performed in 1611 in the same season as *The Tempest*. That year, Fletcher had also written *The Tamer Tamed*, the only contemporary sequel to a Shakespeare play (*The Taming of The Shrew*). Perhaps he was demonstrating his ability to the Bard. It was following this that Fletcher began to co-operate with Shakespeare and the plays they co-authored, *Cardenio, Henry VIII* and *Two Noble Kinsmen*, were written. Indeed, there are some textual echoes of *A King and No King* in *Double Falshood* (the extant version of *Cardenio*). *A King and No King* may have been offered to Neville by Fletcher, who was in effect saying, 'Look what I can write: now can we co-write, can I help you?' Or perhaps Neville saw the quality of the work and said, 'You can help me ...' If Neville was ill he may have needed help, or the ambitious younger playwright may have persuaded Neville to work with him (perhaps at the behest of the King's Men theatre company). The first scene of *Double Falshood* begins with an older man handing on to a younger man as he prepares for death. Duke Angelo uses a metaphor of a laurel wreath and the speech quoted at the start of this chapter could easily have been spoken by an older poet to a younger artistic heir.

The sequence of plays (with the earliest known performance or publication dates in brackets) is:

1611: *The Tempest* (1611, published 1623), *A King and No King* (1619)
1612: *Cardenio/Double Falshood* (Christmas 1612, 20 May and 8 June 1613)
1613: *Henry VIII* (29 June 1613)
1613: *Two Noble Kinsmen* (1634)

Also relevant to this sequence of dates is the fact that Fletcher's collaborator Beaumont retired to Kent in 1613, which coincides with the time when Fletcher had started to work with Shakespeare.

The History of Cardenio/Double Falshood

The first English translation of *Don Quixote*, completed by Thomas Shelton, was published in 1612. A section of Cervantes' masterpiece tells the story of Cardenio. For Christmas 1612 a play listed as *Cardenno* was performed at court. It was performed again on 8 June 1613 for the Ambassador of Savoy. In his letters as an ambassador Neville had referred to matters concerning Savoy. In 1653, Humphrey Moseley, a collector of play-manuscripts (who died in 1661), registered it as *The History of Cardenio* by Shakespeare and Fletcher.[2] This title was used by Shelton when he had translated the story.[3] Seventy-five years later, in 1728, a play, *Double Falshood*, was performed and published by Lewis Theobald. He claimed it was a version of a play by Shakespeare, based on three manuscript copies. Theobald stated that one copy of the script was given to him by an unknown 'Noble Person'. Theobald had business and property connections with the Nevilles which leads us to speculate that this 'Noble Person' was a member of the Neville family. Documents relating to business between Theobald and a branch of the Neville family still exist, and date from 1726–7, the very period before the performances of *Double Falshood* in 1728.[4] Theobald also took a lease on a property owned by the Nevilles in Yorkshire.

Because none of the three play manuscripts have survived (possibly lost in a fire at the Covent Garden Theatre Library), Theobald's claims have been treated with suspicion, some accusing him of perpetrating a forgery. A small amount of the play is by Theobald himself, who admitted that he had 'revised and adapted' the text. However, it has now been established beyond reasonable doubt that *Double Falshood* is the genuine remnant of *Cardenio*.[5] In recognition of this the play was performed by the Royal Shakespeare Company at Stratford-upon-Avon in 2011.

Evidence for Sir Henry Neville

Neville could read and speak Spanish; we know this because not only did he take part in negotiations with the Spanish while ambassador to France, but James I also considered him as a possible ambassador to Spain in 1604. There are also books in Spanish in Neville's library, including a book of Spanish plays by Lope de Vega dated 1607.

In 1606, two of Neville's friends, Dudley Carleton and John Chamberlain, shared a manuscript copy of an English translation of *Don Quixote*. On 21 December 1611, Arthur Throckmorton recorded in his diary that he had purchased 'a book of Don Quixote'. *Don Quixote* was published in 1612 so Arthur must have got hold of a pre-publication copy. Arthur had travelled through Europe with Neville in 1580 and 1581. When *Don Quixote* was published in 1612, Shelton wrote in the dedication that he had translated it five or six years earlier. Indeed, by 1609, Fletcher had written (with Beaumont) *The Coxcomb*, a play which some scholars believe takes one of its plots from *El Curioso Impertinente*, the same *Don Quixote* subplot that was used by Middleton in 1611 in *The Second Maiden's Tragedy*. If Fletcher and Neville's friends knew Cervantes' writings, it seems possible that Neville had also seen *Don Quixote* before the English edition was published.

Neville, Prince Henry and the Marriage of Princess Elizabeth

On 6 November 1612, James I's eldest son Henry, the Prince of Wales, the focus of hopes for a revival of chivalric and Elizabethan values, died suddenly, probably of typhoid, aged just eighteen. There was a national outpouring of grief. His funeral was on 7 December and his coffin stood in Westminster Abbey throughout the Christmas celebrations when *Cardenio* was first performed. Wilson suggested that the presence of a coffin on stage in the play is a reminder to the audience of the recent death of the prince.[6] This suggestion carries weight because the coffin does not feature in the Cervantes source and there is much talk of death and despair in the play. Henry's death resulted in the wedding of his sister Elizabeth to Frederick, the Elector Palatine, being postponed until 14 February. That Christmas at court, mourning mingled with laughter and Wilson suggested that this tragi-comic play caught the mood and was topical.[7]

The newly wed Elizabeth and Frederick 'left England on 25 April 1613, when they sailed from Margate for the Hague, there to be welcomed by the Palsgrave's maternal uncle, Maurice of Nassau'.[8] In a letter dated 25 June 1613, Turnbull wrote to Winwood that Frederick and his pregnant wife had safely arrived in 'Heydelbergh'. On 6 July, Turnbull wrote that Neville was in Brussels to see 'the Procession of the Sacrament of Miracles, the Princes and this Court in its Glory'.[9] It is not certain that Neville's visit to the Continent at this time was as part of the royal party but it seems possible, indeed likely.

Neville in the Text of *Double Falshood*

In the first scene there is mention of France, spies, and being owed money. Roderick says, 'He doth sollicit the return of gold' (1.1.37). Neville was owed £4,000 by Elizabeth I for when he was ambassador in Paris, a fortune in those days. Neville petitioned Robert Cecil in his 1603–4 draft letter for the repayment of the money he had had to pay out in expenses when ambassador, but to no avail.[10] He had gone to France to ask for the return of a loan that Elizabeth had made to Henry IV. In one of his diplomat letters (26 May 1599) he used the word 'sollicit' concerning the return of this loan, using the same spelling as in *Double Falshood*.[11] There is no mention of France in *Don Quixote*. In the play Roderick uses the word 'doth' saying, 'He doth sollicit'. Kukowski pointed out that Fletcher used 'does', whereas Shakespeare used 'doth'.[12] He concluded that Scene 1 of *Double Falshood* is the most likely of all the scenes to have been written by Shakespeare.

Double Falshood starts with a duke preparing for death and ends with an old man complaining of gout, which we know Neville suffered from because in a letter dated 1 November 1604 he wrote that he was 'in mych paine of the gout'.[13] As the play moves towards its denouement, Camillo, who can be seen as an alter ego for the aging Neville, says:

> Come what can come, I'll live a Month or two
> If the Gout please; curse my Physician once more,
> And then, —

> *Under this Stone*
> *Lies Sev'nty One.* (5.2.34)

This gravestone is cryptic: yes, on the surface it seems to state Camillo's age at the time he expects to die. But there is something playful about Camillo's headstone and it is intriguing that he does not suggest it would have a name on it. Why seventy-one? Brenda James suggested that this pointed to Sonnet 71, which is about the poet's death and burial:

> O if (I say) you look upon this verse,
> When I, perhaps, compounded am with clay,
> Do not so much as my poor name rehearse ...

In both play and sonnet the name of the deceased is absent. The space intended for Henry Neville's inscription on the Neville monument in St Lawrence's Church, Waltham St Lawrence, was left blank.[14]

In the play the duke is anxious about a younger son and the young man is called Henriquez, Spanish for 'son of Henry'. In 1609, Neville's son Henry was arrested for piracy and only got off the charge with Francis Bacon's help. It is little wonder then that in the first scene of this play, a scene which has definitely been attributed to the Bard, the father should be concerned about a wayward son. Roderick speaks of his brother's 'hot escapes of youth'. By 'hot escapes' we might presume he means exciting or dangerous escapades. Neville's son had escaped not only from violence but also from a very serious (indeed capital) charge. The young Henry had been studying in France. He was accused of theft by a French merchant naval captain, Jean Gandon, and received a serious head injury during a violent arrest.[15] This incident would have been in Neville's consciousness as he wrote a play about a wayward son. In Cervantes' text there are no trips to France, but that is where Julio has come from when the play starts.

Friendship, Trust, Betrayal and Forgiveness

Recent research into the consequences of psychological trauma has led to a greater appreciation of the lasting effects of sudden loss. Neville was at the height of his career when he was implicated in the Essex rebellion. He was not suspected until betrayed by his friend, Henry Wriothesley, Earl of Southampton. In the text of *Double Falshood* we find echoes of Neville's betrayal and imprisonment when Julio says:

> What a venomous World is this,
> When Commendations are the Baits to Ruin!
> All these good Words were Gyves and Fetters, Sir,
> To keep me bolted there: while the false Sender
> Play'd out the Game of Treach'ry. (4.1.35)

This speech recalls Neville's experience of the promises Essex made to him that he would become Secretary of State, promises which led him to prison (gyves, fetters, bolted). There is much in the play about friendship, trust and betrayal. The word 'friend' (or friendship) occurs thirty times in the play. The word 'trust' (or related words like 'distrust') occurs eighteen times. 'Betray' occurs seven times. The treachery of a friend is at the centre of the play as when Julio complains of Henriquez:

> Is there a treachery, like this in baseness
> Recorded anywhere? It is the deepest:
> None but itself can be its parallel
> And from a friend, professed! Friendship? Why 'tis
> A word for ever maimed; in human nature
> It was a thing the noblest. (3.1.15)

In this speech we find an echo of Neville's experience of his betrayal by Southampton. His friendship with the latter had survived and in 1611 (just a year before *Cardenio/ Double Falshood* was written) Southampton had advocated to James I that Neville become Secretary of State. Referring to Southampton's failure to win his friend high office, Henry Howard wrote in a letter that Neville was the earl's 'Dear Damon', thus linking them as an archetypal pair of friends in the friendship literature.[16] Significantly, the friendship of Julio and Henriquez also survives. However, the betrayal may have made Neville extremely cautious: Julio says, 'Trust no Friend: Keep thy Heart's Counsels close' (4.1.47).

The debacle of the Essex rebellion had done enormous damage to Neville's life and career. Violante, after the rape, laments:

> ... I am now become
> The Tomb of my own Honour: a dark Mansion,
> For Death alone to dwell in. I invite thee,
> Consuming Desolation, to this Temple,

Now fit to be thy Spoil: the ruin'd Fabrick,
Which cannot be repair'd, at once o'er-throw. (2.2.29)

This speech could have been spoken by the ruined Neville. Similarly Henriquez's words fit Neville when he says:

My Heart grows sick of Birth and empty Rank,
And I become a Villager in Wish. (1.3.23)

Eight years before he wrote *Cardenio*, Neville wrote in a letter to Winwood, dated 21 June 1605, 'I am out of my proper Orb when I enter into State Matters; I will therefore leave these Considerations to those to whom they apertain, and think of my husbandry in the Country.'[17]

The play, however, ends with the joy of reunion and the wayward son redeemed; Neville and his family must have felt just such joy when his own son returned safely home in 1609.

Henry VIII

Neville's father, Henry, and grandfather, Edward, both knew Henry VIII personally. Edward had been a fellow jouster, masquer and reveller with the king. Henry was a signatory of the old king's will. Neville made a special note of this testament in a marginal note (on the left side of the illustration below) in his copy of *Leicester's Commonwealth* in a discussion of what might bar Mary, Queen of Scots and her son James from the succession to Elizabeth I.

'K:H: 8ths testam^te', Worsley MSS 47, 45V.

The play *Henry VIII* is a complex exploration of the rise and fall of political figures, court politics and pageantry. When we posit Neville as one of the authors, its contemporary political meanings emerge into the light. It was on stage in 1613, but may have been written over a long period. Although a history play, the selection of the incidents from the king's long reign enabled the playwrights to obliquely comment on contemporary politics. It is possible that Neville chose to dramatise this reign because of a number of personal connections with Henry VIII, including the fact that he physically resembled the king. This similarity was noted in correspondence between James's I's favourite, Robert Carr, and Thomas Overbury who used the code name 'Similis' for Neville.[18]

Henry Neville also had a personal connection to Cranmer, who appears on stage in the play. The palace in Mayfield where Neville lived between 1582 and 1598 was an old monastic property which had belonged to Thomas Cranmer, the Archbishop of Canterbury. In 1545, he had turned it over to Henry VIII.[19] John Gresham purchased it from the king and upon the death of Sir Thomas Gresham, Elizabeth Gresham's uncle, it came into the Neville family. Elizabeth was Neville's mother. So Neville had lived in a house owned by an important figure in *Henry VIII*.

In the play, King Henry chooses the location for the hearing about the legality of his marriage to Katherine of Aragon:

The most convenient place that I can think of
For such receipt of learning is Blackfriars ... (2.2.138)

Henry Neville was baptised and grew up in Blackfriars, near the Office of the King's Revels. Neville's father asked permission for Richard Farrant to use part of the property to create the first Blackfriars Theatre for the child actors of the Chapel Royal.

The Nevilles On and Off Stage

Scholars agree that the first scene was written by Shakespeare. In that scene, George Neville appears on stage as Lord Abergavenny with Buckingham, his father-in-law. Norfolk describes the 1520 Field of the Cloth of Gold. Three members of the Neville family attended this glittering extravaganza, when the kings of France and England met to establish a brief peace treaty: Ralph Neville, 4th Earl of Westmoreland, George Neville, and his younger brother Sir Edward Neville, the last being Neville's grandfather.

Sir Edward Neville (1482–1538)

Edward Neville had been a close friend of Henry VIII. Edward, like his grandson, physically resembled Henry VIII and acted in court theatricals. Hall in his *Chronicle* reported Edward's part as the knight Valiaunt Desire in a theatrical pageant in 1510. 'Neville was not only a notable masquer. He was also an accomplished singer with a liking for merry songs. He possessed a talent for extempory verses, often of current topicality.'[20] At a banquet given by Cardinal Wolsey in 1527, Edward appeared wearing a mask and 'the cardinal was deceived, or pretended to be, in identifying Neville in his vizard as the king'.[21] A version of this incident occurs in the play *Henry VIII*. The playwrights distort the incident by removing Edward Neville but reprise the old story when, in Act 1, Scene 4, masked men enter a banquet at Cardinal Wolsey's house. One of them is the king in disguise but the cardinal guesses that the royal person is present. The source for this scene is George Cavendish's *Life of Cardinal Wolsey*, which was composed between 1554 and 1558, but it was not published during Shakespeare's lifetime. Scholars struggle to explain how either Shakespeare or Fletcher could have known or had access to the original manuscript. That Neville would have read a document that portrays his own grandfather is more likely. Sir Henry Wotton wrote about the masque scene in the play and the catastrophic consequences of the special effects, in a letter dated 2 July 1613:[22]

> I will entertain you at the present with what happened this week at the Bank's side. The King's players had a new play, called *All is True*, representing some principal pieces of the reign of Henry VIII, which was set forth with many extraordinary circumstances of pomp and majesty, even to the matting of the stage; the Knights of the Order with their Georges and garters, the Guards with their embroidered coats, and the like: sufficient in truth within a while to make greatness very familiar, if not ridiculous. Now, King Henry making a masque at the Cardinal Wolsey's house, and certain chambers being shot off at his entry, some of the paper, or other stuff, wherewith one of them was stopped, did light on the thatch, where being thought at first but an idle smoke, and their eyes more attentive to the show, it kindled inwardly, and ran round like a train, consuming within less than an hour the whole house to the very grounds.

If, as Wotton suggested, the pomp and ceremony in the play made such courtly ritual ridiculous to contemporaries, we can reflect that Neville had both documented interest in, and reasons to be satirical about, such royal dressing up.[23] Edward Neville was also present at the coronation of Anne Boleyn in 1532, so the Neville family would have had direct knowledge of the scene described and enacted in the play.[24]

The Tower Notebook

Neville made notes on coronation rituals from Richard II onwards while he was incarcerated in the Tower between 1602 and 1613. Brenda James identified the notebook as a source for the scene of Anne Boleyn's coronation in *Henry VIII*.[25] An example of this is the stage direction, 'Then under a canopy borne by four barons of the Cinque Ports, Anne the new Queen'. In the Tower notebook Neville annotated the text in three places about the Barons of the Cinque Ports carrying the canopy. One of these states, 'Barons 5 ports claym to Cary the Canapie on 4 Lances gilt staves. 4 men at a lance' (see also Chapter 10). George Neville, 5th Baron Bergavenny, who is on stage in the first scene of *Henry VIII*, was lord warden of the Cinque Ports. He officiated at the coronation of Anne Boleyn. His brother was Neville's grandfather.

Contemporary Politics in the Play

In the first scene of *Henry VIII*, George Neville complains about the enormous expense of the Field of the Cloth of Gold (1.1.80–85). James I was extravagant and had to return again and again to ask Parliament for more money. 'Neville hated excessive expenditure by the government and the burden it placed on the tax payer.'[26] The Field of the Cloth of Gold peace treaty was a failure. Neville was doubtful about James I's peacemaking with Spain, calling him 'Jacobus Pacificus' in a letter to Winwood in 1606 and saying, 'The kingdom generally wishes this peace broken.'[27] Complaining of the failure of the Field of the Cloth of Gold, Norfolk says:

> France hath flawed the league and hath attached
> Our merchants' goods at Bordeaux. (1.1.95)

As ambassador, and in the years following, Neville was much concerned about the difficulties of English merchants in France, as is evident in his letters (for example a letter dated 4 June 1606).[28] Furthermore, Neville knew about Henry VIII's international agreements with France, referring to the Treaty of Ardres (also known as the Treaty of Camp) in a letter dated 18 July 1599.

The play refracts contemporary political struggles through the historical power shifts of Henry VIII's court and the playwrights explore how the monarch can manage these.[29] After Salisbury's death in 1612, many people expected Neville to become the Secretary of State. On 14 May 1613, Henry Wotton stated that 'all men contemplate Sir Henry Nevil for the future secretary.'[30] In a letter dated 6 August 1613, Henry Wriothesley, the Earl of Southampton, expressed his confidence that Sir Henry Neville would become Secretary.[31] In the autumn of 1612, Neville had proposed that he and Ralph Winwood share the role of Secretary.[32] The only time the word 'secretary' occurs in the canon is in *Henry VIII*, where it is used five times, especially about new secretaries taking over the role. At least one of these uses occurs in a scene accepted as having been written by the Bard. Eventually, Winwood emerged as the Secretary. In *Henry VIII* a Dr. Pace, who had been the Secretary of State before Wolsey, was posted abroad by the cardinal who

> … fearing he would rise, he was so virtuous,
> Kept him a foreign man still; which so grieved him
> That he ran mad and died. (2.2.127)

Neville knew how maddening it was to be an ambassador. James I wanted to send Neville's friend and supporter, Thomas Overbury, as ambassador to Russia to remove him from court because he had fallen out of favour. Overbury turned the offer down and was consequently imprisoned in the Tower from 21 April 1613. We propose that Neville's concern for Overbury underlies the last play Shakespeare and Fletcher wrote, *The Two Noble Kinsmen*. Overbury and Neville both attended the Mermaid Club.

The Two Noble Kinsmen

This play was first published in 1634, its authorship identified on the front page of the quarto as 'written by the memorable Worthies of their time: {Mr John Fletcher, and Mr. William Shakspeare} Gent.' Based on 'The Knight's Tale' in Chaucer's *Canterbury Tales*, it had been written in 1613 and was presented on stage at the Blackfriars Theatre by the King's Men. Neville was related to Chaucer. No one has satisfactorily explained what this play refers to in contemporary life. With Neville as author, the politics behind the play become clear. Neville's last extant letters corroborate this by providing evidence on the play's contemporary context and meaning as well as clarifying when it was written.

Neville's Letter of 18 June 1613 and *The Two Noble Kinsmen*

Of 447 words to be found in Neville's letter of 18 June 1613, 144 words (32.2 per cent) occur in *The Two Noble Kinsmen*.[33] The high percentage of words used in the letter and this play, coupled with the large number of near misses (see below), suggest that the letter was written during the writing of the play, and if so this dates the writing of the play to the summer of 1613. The political background to the play suggests it was written between May and August 1613. Neville's letter of 18 June 1613 is the last of his letters in Winwood's *Memorials*.[34] (For the full text see the Addendum at the end of the chapter.)

In the letter Neville wrote (italics in the original, our emphasis underlined):

> The other great Busyness which filleth Mens Mouths now is *the Separation intended between myn Lord of Essex and his Lady; a Matter no less desired by my Lord and his Friends, then by her and hers; and yet I doubt there is scarce Matter enough confessed or proved to induce a Nullity in the Marriage, which is that which they both affect, because they desire to marry againe.*

In the play a school master laments their troupe of dancers has been let down by Cicely, the seamstress's daughter, who has not shown up:

> Our business is become a nullity
> Yea, and a woeful, and a piteous nullity. (3.5.51)

Neville used the word 'business' twice in the letter, including in the same sentence as the words, 'a nullity'. Neville had previously used the latter word in a letter dated 19 November 1599, referring to the French king's divorce.[35] This letter throws light on the politics behind *The Two Noble Kinsmen*. Neville wrote about the delays in his appointment as Secretary of State ('this long depending Busyness'). He reported that he had discovered that the Delay hath grown *upon two Suggestions secretly made to the King against me;* the one that I had some hand in the Matter wherewith Sir *Robert Maxwell* and Mr. *Whitlock* were charged, which is already cleared, the other, *that I have held continual Intelligence with Overbury since his Imprisonment: A matter so far from Truth, as I protest there never passed between us so much as a Message since his Commitment.*

Thomas Overbury had been sent to the Tower ostensibly for refusing to go as the king's ambassador to Moscow. However, his arrest also suited Robert Carr, Lord Rochester, who was in love with Lady Essex (*née* Frances Howard). At this time she was still married to Robert Devereux, the 3rd Earl of Essex. Overbury, fearing his displacement in Rochester's affections and the growing influence of the Catholic Howards at court, was opposed to this relationship between Rochester and Frances. As Neville states, the unhappy Essex couple were seeking 'a nullity' to free them from their loveless and unconsummated marriage. The occurrence therefore of the repeated words 'a nullity' in *The Two Noble Kinsmen* is topical, though they are carefully used in a comic line to avoid causing offence. The contemporary audience however would have spotted the allusion. The nullity of the Essex marriage was granted on 26 September 1613, Overbury having died on 14/15 September. We argue that the play was written before these events, while the nullity was still in question and Overbury alive.

Overbury was arrested and sent to the Tower on 21 April 1613. The next day, John Packer (who had been Neville's secretary and was now working for Rochester) wrote to Winwood of Overbury's arrest: 'That evening my Lord of Pembroke and Sir Henry Nevill were with him and so were againe this Morning; who have given him so good Advice that if he follow it, as I hope he will, all will be well with him, and no hurt to his Friend'.[36] John Chamberlain also wrote to Winwood, on 6 May 1613, about Overbury's refusal to go to Moscow and added that, 'the King apprehends the Busyness very earnestly, and hath caused Sir *Henry Nevill* to conferr with some of the Councill about it diverse times; wherein they say he showed great Sufficiency'.[37] On 10 June 1613 (just a week before Neville's letter), Chamberlain reported that 'two lame hexameter verses' had been found in Grey's Inn:

Curans, Lord Compton, Whitlocke, Overburie, Mansfield:
Nevill, Starchamber, Sutton, Scot, Baylie, divorcement.

We can see that the nullity or 'divorcement' was connected in the popular mind with Overbury and Neville.[38] Furthermore Henry Wriothesley's letter of 6 August 1613 confirmed these associations when he wrote of Overbury's situation, his own support for Neville's candidature for Secretary and the nullity of the Essex marriage.[39]

At the end of Worsley MSS 47, the notebook which includes Neville's copy of *Leicester's Commonwealth*, there is a handwritten copy of the report by George Abbott, the Archbishop of Canterbury to James I, on the divorce of Frances and the Earl of Essex, and His Majesty's response, dated 15 July 1613.[40] This is just one month after the letter we are examining. Another extant letter, written by Neville on 16 July 1613, the day after he wrote the notes in Worsley MSS 47, mentioned the nullity.[41] Neville, having been an ally of the 2nd Earl of Essex, was supportive of his son. Indeed, Neville was deeply involved in the annulment of Essex's marriage, as is clear in the papers from the subsequent trials following Overbury's death in which it is revealed that Neville had warned the Archbishop in July 1613 that Frances had 'a new husband ... readily provided for her'. He knew this from 'a speech of Overbury's once to me in that kind'.[42]

In 1611, Rochester, at Overbury's urging, had suggested to James I that he employ Neville in managing Parliament.[43] When Overbury realised that the king's dislike of him blocked his own ambition to be Secretary of State, he 'urged Rochester to persuade the King to give the job to their long-established political ally, Sir Henry Neville'.[44] Neville was also supported by the earls of Southampton and Pembroke. However, Overbury's arrogant behaviour alienated the king and this in effect tarnished Neville, whose candidacy for the Secretary of State Overbury had supported. Towards the end of 1612 Neville had written, 'There hath been much poison cast out of late unto the King both against him [Overbury] and me'.[45]

Neville's letters were written in June and July 1613. Overbury died in the Tower on the night of 14/15 September. If we are correct that *The Two Noble Kinsmen* refers to the events surrounding Overbury's arrest, he must still have been alive when the play was conceived because the play has scenes in prison and both prisoners leave prison: Arcite is released and Palamon escapes. The play is about compassion and release from prison, not about death in prison, although Arcite does die after his release. As an ex-ambassador who had repeatedly requested to come home, Neville would have understood Overbury's reluctance to go abroad. Overbury's arrest must have reminded Neville of his own period in the Tower with Henry Wriothesley, Earl of Southampton. A story about two friends imprisoned together would have resonated with Neville. The playwrights elaborate on the mutual dependence and affection of the two men during their imprisonment, which is not in Chaucer's original tale. As an ex-prisoner in the Tower, it is likely that Neville would have had compassion for Overbury and the word 'compassion' is used four times in the play (more than in any other Shakespeare play).

We suggest that the choice of Chaucer's 'The Knight's Tale' was deliberate: it enabled Neville to write a play about chivalry, compassion, imprisonment and the long struggle of a man in love to win his bride from another man. We suggest this reflects Rochester's struggle to win Frances from Essex. The two noble kinsmen, who begin as firm friends and become deadly rivals over a woman, may also be Overbury and Rochester. The play shows one of these men left in prison, just as Overbury was in prison at the time. Previous studies of the play have suggested that the political background to the play was the death of Prince Henry (in November 1612) and the marriage of Princess Elizabeth (in February 1613). Neville was close to the martial Henry who might be recalled in Arcite, the worshipper of Mars, who dies before he can be married. Neville was a supporter of the prince's revival of chivalric values which are celebrated in the play. This death and marriage, however, are more properly to be seen as behind the plot of *Cardenio/Double Falshood* which was probably staged during Christmas 1612 and was also performed in May and June 1613.

Conclusion

We have shown many connections between the final plays and the life and writings of Henry Neville. No one has ever, to our knowledge, shown such detailed evidence in support of any other potential author of the canon. There is, for example, no evidence at all that William from Stratford knew the sources, the people or the politics that he would have had to have known in order to write these plays. When Neville is accepted as the author, light is cast into previously uncertain areas and intractable questions are resolved.

A final piece of evidence is provided by the fact that there is a documented connection between Neville and the first printing of the folio. When the First Folio was finally printed it was dedicated to the Pembroke brothers, William and Philip Herbert. Neville knew William Herbert, as is evident from John Packer's letter of 22 April 1613 when he wrote to Winwood about 'My Lord Pembroke' (William Herbert 3rd Earl of Pembroke) meeting Neville when they were trying to help Overbury.

Addendum: Neville's Letter of 18 June 1613

Sir Henry Neville to Sir Ralph Winwood (italics in the original):

18th June 1613

Sir,

If my Letter comes later than you expected, let me be somewhat excused by the Slowness and Irresolution of our Proceedings. When I wrote last I had strong Presumptions that this long depending Busyness, wherein you have likewise an Interest, would be forthwith despatched, and I yet see no Cause much to doubt it; for I discover that the Delay hath grown *upon two Suggestions secretly made to the King against me;* the one that I had some hand in the Matter wherewith Sir *Robert Mansell* and Mr. *Whitlock* were charged, which is already cleared: the other, *that I have held continual Intelligence with* Overbury *since his Imprisonment: A matter so far from Truth, as I protest there never passed between us so much as a Message since his Commitment.* These impediments being removed, my Friends are confident the King will no longer deferr what he hath so long resolved. But to apply this to the Point wherein you required my Advice; I think you may do well to write to his Majestie to that Purpose which you mentioned in your Letter; yet with this Liberty and Power to be left to your Friends here, that is our Business be dispacht before your Letter comes, they may suppress it if they see Cause, and turn their Suit another way; but if they see it linger then to deliver it, and joyn their Mediation unto your Suite the sooner to effect it.

We are here busy in Consultation about the *Irish Busyness, willing enough to take a sharp Course to check this over Boldness of theirs, but for want of Means, inforced as I think to resolve upon a milder; But I fear it will be the* Via di Mezzo, *what will neither uphold our Reputation nor give them Satisfaction, and so leave us both without Awe or Love among them.* Those who are come over from them to the King have desired to Things of him; *That he will present himself when they are heard, and that they may be allowed Councill; both which he hath granted.*

The other great Busyness which filleth Mens Mouths now, is *the Separation intended between myn Lord of Essex and his Lady; a Matter no less desyred by my Lord and his Friends, then by her and hers; and yet I doubt there is scarce Matter enough confessed or proved to induce a Nullity in the Marriage, which is that which they both affect, because they desire to marry againe.* It will not be long ere we see some Issue in both. In the mean time I will take my leave, with Remembrance of my Love and Seruice to you, and remain &c.

HENRY NEVILLE

Single Words in Neville's letter Found in *The Two Noble Kinsmen*

Comes, than, somewhat, Proceedings, when, last, strong, long, Busyness, likewise, Interest, would, Cause, doubt, Delay, grown, two, against, some, hand, Sir, other, held, Intelligence, Since, *from*, Truth, never, impediments, Friends, Advice, write, well, Majestie, Purpose, yet, Liberty, Power, left, here, turn, Suit, another, way, deliver, sooner, effect, willing, even, Course, over, want, uphold, neither, our, Reputation, both, without, Love, among, Those, come, Things, present, himself, heard, granted, great, Mens, Mouths, myn, Lord, less, scarce, enough, induce, Marriage, affect, because, marry, againe, ere, Issue, remain.

Pairs of Words

that this, the one, the Matter, *so far*, between us, the King, no longer, so long, the Point, may do, before your, about the, *but for*, a sharp, I fear, give them, *when they*, leave us, The other, his Lady, a Nullity, desire to, take my, Seruice to.

Phrases of Three Words

I think you, to take a, so much as, the mean time.

Near Misses

There are a great many near misses in Neville's letter of words to be found in the play: 'our Proceeding' in *The Two Noble Kinsmen* instead of 'our Proceedings' in the letter; 'depend' in the play instead of 'depending' in the letter; 'in prison' in the play instead of 'imprisonment' in the letter; 'this business' in the play instead of 'this long depending Busyness'; 'confessors' instead of 'confessed'; 'despatch' instead of 'dispatched' or 'dispacht'; 'no such cause' instead of 'no cause'; 'discovered' instead of 'discover'; 'late' instead of 'later'; 'suggested' instead of 'suggestions'; 'secret/s' instead of 'secretly'; 'allow' instead of 'allowed'; 'commit/ted' instead of 'commitment'; 'charge' instead of 'charged'; 'clear' instead of 'cleared'; 'continually' instead of 'continual; 'appliance' instead of 'apply'; 'mention' instead of 'mentioned'; 'another's way' instead of 'another way'; 'bold/est/ly/er' instead of 'Boldness'; 'enforce' instead of 'inforced'; 'our ancient Reputation' instead of 'our Reputation'; 'desire' instead of 'desired'; 'things desire' instead of 'desired to Things'; 'fill'd' instead of 'filleth'; 'my Lord' instead of 'myn Lord'; 'approved' instead of 'proved'; 'I'th mean time' instead of 'In the mean time'.

Neville uses 'hath' three times in his letter. In disentangling what parts of *The Two Noble Kinsmen* were written by Shakespeare and which by Fletcher, it has been noticed by scholars that Shakespeare used 'hath' while Fletcher preferred the more modern 'has'.[46]

Double Falshood:

This letter's vocabulary is also related to that of *Double Falshood*. At least eighty-nine of the words in the letter occur in *Double Falshood* (21.3 per cent).

Single Words

Somewhat, Proceeding, Business, Interest, Wrote, Cause, Discover, Delay, grown, Suggestion, Against, Hand, already, Continual, Impediment, Truth, Never, Between,

Resolve, Wherein, Dispatch, Mention'd, Require/s, Advice, Purpose, Power, Letter, Another, Linger, Join, effect, Suit, Willing, Sharp, Course, over, Boldness, Means, Resolve, Satisfaction, Leave, Without, Love, Things, enough, scarce, marry, marriage, Service.

'Mention'd' only occurs in one other Shakespeare play, *Titus Andronicus*. Likewise 'mentioned' occurs just once, in *The Winter's Tale*.

Pairs of Words
The Matter, I protest, No longer, So long, I think, Your friends, Before your, To take, I fear, desire to.

Phrase of Three Words
For want of.

Near Misses
We find 'deliver'd' in the play instead of 'deliver' in the letter; 'Inforces' in the play instead of 'inforced' in the letter; 'Grant' in the play instead of 'granted' in the letter; 'Confess' and 'confessors' in the play instead of 'confessed' in the letter; 'Prove/s' in the play instead of 'proved' in the letter; 'to the Point' in the letter; 'to th' Point' in the play.

In the letter there is: 'no <u>Cause</u> much <u>to doubt</u> it' while in *Double Falshhood* there is the line: 'Some formal <u>Cause to</u> qualify my <u>Doubts</u>' (in a scene believed to have been written by Shakespeare: 1.1.31).

Henry VIII

There are 112 words found in the letter which are also to be found in *Henry VIII* (27 per cent).

Single Words
expected, somewhat, Proceedings, strong, long, Busyness, forthwith, Cause, doubt, Delay, grown, Suggestion, against, hand, Intelligence, already, charged, Continual, Truth, never, between, removed, Friends, confident, write, Majestie, Wherein, dispatch, required, Purpose, Liberty, Power, left, Suit, Letter, another, way, deliver, sooner, effect, willing, even, Course, over, Boldness, Means, want, our, Leave, without, Love, Things, present, himself, heard, council, granted, great, Mens, Mouths, Separation, mine, Lord, Lady, less, scarce, enough, induce, Marriage, affect, because, marry, againe, ere, Issue, remain, Service.

Pairs of Words
the Matter, his Imprisonment, between us, the King, so long, the Point, before your, a sharp, I fear, leave us, The other, desire to, Seruice to, to take, Your friends.

Phrases of Three Words
I think you, take my leave.

A near miss:
'I'll take my leave' in the play instead of 'I will take my leave' in the letter.

Henry Neville Was Shakespeare
Reviewing the Evidence

This is he;
Who hath upon him still that natural stamp:
It was wise nature's end in the donation,
To be his evidence now.

Cymbeline, 5.5.366

The Shakespeare authorship question is necessarily controversial, hard-fought and unsettling to those who cling to the comfort of the status quo. We have chosen to base our case strictly on evidence and contrasted the evidence for Henry Neville with the lack of evidence for others, especially for William Shakspere from Stratford. In many ways William Shakspere is the least likely authorship candidate but he is the man that most people have been told, since childhood, was the author.

Evidence

We have accumulated different classes of evidence. The sheer volume of all this evidence is now overwhelming. In marked contrast, those who believe the author was Shakspere from Stratford can offer very little such evidence and in some categories none at all. Neville's authorship is evidenced by his:

- social network;
- life experience, education and knowledge of specialist fields;
- interest in and connections with theatre;
- vocabulary in his letters;
- manuscripts and note books;
- library books, many of which contain relevant annotations;
- internal evidence of the plays and poems;
- psychology;
- cryptic clues and the need for secrecy.

We shall now review these classes of evidence.

Social Network

The author of the works of Shakespeare had to know the Earl of Southampton and a number of other significant figures including Francis Bacon. Henry Neville certainly knew both, and also knew many others who were significant for Shakespeare. Amongst these was the poet Philip Sidney who influenced the Bard and whom Neville knew personally, noting his name in italics in his copy of *Leicester's Commonwealth*.

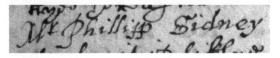 Worsley MSS 47, 10V.

Their fathers were close friends and Neville remained a lifelong friend of Robert Sidney, the poet's brother. Neville's home at Mayfield was just 15 miles from the Sidneys' house at Penhurst Place, so between 1582 and 1585, when Philip went to fight in the Netherlands, it is entirely possible that Neville would have visited Philip, Robert and their father Henry. Philip had positively referred to Neville in a letter to his brother during their earlier travels in Europe, so there is no doubt that they knew each other.

Neville met the Duke of Biron, upon whom Berowne in *Love's Labour's Lost* is based. Neville referred to Marshall Biron in a letter dated 24 April 1600. Neville may previously have encountered Biron when in France, during his earlier travels from 1578 to 1582. Sir Henry Killigrew, his father-in-law, had met Biron in 1591 when fighting in France under Essex. Neville would undoubtedly have met Biron when he came to England in 1598 as French ambassador because, that same year, Neville was chosen as English ambassador to France. Neville knew Antonio Perez, a model for Don Armado in *Love's Labour's Lost* (see Chapter 3). He met the ambassador to Barbary, el-Ouahed ben Messaoud, a possible model for Othello (see Chapter 7). He met Count Orsino at the time of *Twelfth Night* (see chapter 5). An annotation in Worsley MSS 47 suggests he knew Dr John Dee, a model for Prospero (see chapter 10). He also knew Thomas Overbury whose imprisonment, we suggest, underlies *The Two Noble Kinsmen* (see Chapter 11). Neville knew William Strachey, who wrote the letter that was the source for *The Tempest* (see Chapter 10). He knew Beaumont and Fletcher (see chapter 9). He knew William and Philip Herbert, the 3rd and 4th Earls of Pembroke, to whom the First Folio is dedicated (see Chapter 11). His portrait even hangs next to theirs at Audley End House.

Neville knew Walsingham, Essex, the Cecils and Elizabeth I. There are many other people relevant to the authorship question with whom Neville had documented contact. One such was George Carleton, who was Neville's vicar in Mayfield from 1589 to 1605. He eventually became Bishop of Chichester and married Neville's widow, Anne, in 1619. Among Neville's library books is a New Testament signed by 'G. Carleton' on its frontispiece. The book is annotated in Latin, Greek and Hebrew, though whether these notes are by Neville or Carleton it is difficult to tell. Carleton wrote a Latin poem that hinted that Neville was a poet and possibly writing tragedies for the stage (see Chapter 6).[1] In 1624, Carleton published a book, *A Thankfull Remembrance of God's Mercie*, about plots and assassination attempts during the reigns of Elizabeth I and James I. Neil MacGregor described Carleton's book as offering insight into Shakespeare's continual interest in threats to the body politic and the monarch's life as dramatised in his plays.[2] MacGregor was seemingly unaware that he was pointing to a text written by someone so close to the real Bard. We recall that it was Carleton's son-in-law, Thomas Vicars, who in 1628 hinted that the name Shakespeare was a pseudonym (see Chapter 2).

The evidence of Neville's social network is in sharp contrast with that of William Shakspere, for whom the evidence is that he appears to have known only actors, debtors and Stratford residents. The one significant figure he definitely knew was George Wilkins, the violent misogynist and brothel keeper who is believed to have written parts of *Pericles* (see Chapter 9).

Life Experience, Education and Knowledge of Specialist Fields

Throughout this book we have provided evidence of how Neville's life experience matched the trajectory and special interests of the Bard. He had travelled; experienced sea journeys; knew and was involved in the law; knew falconry and was a hunter; was a forester so knew about trees; had an iron foundry and manufactured cannon; was a courtier; his grandfather's execution and own experience of prison made him especially aware of the dangers of political life; he was a linguist able to read Shakespeare's sources in their original languages; he was a mathematician and astronomer; he suffered from gout, which made him lame; and complained of deafness.

Neville also clarifies the recurring question of whether Shakespeare was a secret Catholic. Neville was certainly Protestant. The plays *King John*, *Macbeth* and *Henry VIII*, written at the start, middle and end of his career, provide clear evidence that the Bard was Protestant. The strident anti-Catholic tone of *The Troublesome Raigne of John King of England* (probably the result of George Peele's hand in the writing of this original text) was toned down by the Bard when he revised the play that became his *King John*. Yet the king in the revised play would have been regarded as a heroic figure by the original audience when he, like Elizabeth I, says, 'Yet I alone, alone do me oppose against the pope and count his friends my foes' (3.1.96). Falconbridge, who we suggest is an alter ego for Neville, sneers at Pandolph as a 'thin halting legate' (perhaps with a pun on halting, i.e. limping, and leg/legate, 5.2.174). John is, however, humiliated by the papal legate and poisoned by a monk. Elizabeth I was excommunicated, labelled a bastard and threatened with assassination and this was explicitly sanctioned by the Catholic Church. Cardinals are particularly satirised by Shakespeare. The Catholic Cardinal Beaufort of Winchester is the villain of *Henry VI* (parts 1 and 2), murdering the good Duke of Gloucester and coming to a bad end himself: 'Beaufort's red sparkling eyes blab his heart's malice' (*Henry VI: Part II*, 3.1.154). The greedy, ambitious Cardinal Wolsey in *Henry VIII* is only treated sympathetically when he falls from power. From his letters and political acts we know Neville became especially anti-Catholic following the Gunpowder Plot. This fits with the porter in *Macbeth* who satirises the equivocation of the Jesuit Henry Garnet, whose *Treatise on Equivocation* advised Catholics to lie to Protestants to protect themselves from persecution, as God would know the truth in their hearts. Following this terrorist outrage, Neville served on fourteen parliamentary committees, devising measures against Catholics.[3] In *Henry VIII*, it is the Protestant Archbishop Cranmer who gives a rousing, visionary speech looking forward to James I's reign. Cranmer was later burnt at the stake by the Catholic Mary I. Furthermore, there is a covert attack on the Catholic Howard faction at James I's court implicit in *Henry VIII*. In the play the Surrey–Norfolk–Suffolk faction are members of the Howard family who supported Gardiner, another antagonistic Bishop of Winchester, against Cranmer. Shakespeare and Fletcher 'were hinting that the Howards were supporters of the Roman Catholic Church who, by implication, had tried to kill the whole royal family in the Gunpowder Plot of 1605. The faction opposing many of the Howard policies included Henry Neville and two parliamentary radicals, the Earl of Pembroke and … Neville's champion, the Earl of Southampton.'[4] Both these parliamentary radicals were Shakespeare's patrons: Southampton was a supporter of Neville's bid to become Secretary of State as well as the dedicatee of the two great poems and probably the sonnets; Pembroke and his brother were dedicatees of the First Folio.

It is significant that Shakespeare stopped writing when Neville died. William Shakspere lived a further year yet Shakespeare wrote nothing in that time, perhaps because the actual Bard was already dead.

Interest in and Connections with Theatre

There is evidence that William Shakspere was involved in theatre, certainly as a sharer in the Globe and also as an actor. His brother Edmund was named 'a player' at the time of his death. Ben Jonson listed 'Will. Shake-speare' as an actor on his published *Sejanus* in 1616 (see chapter 1). However no record of the parts he played nor any anecdote of his performances survives (whereas there are records of other actors).

Despite his secrecy, there is evidence that Neville had involvement in and connections with the theatre. Neville's grandfather took part in court theatricals. Neville's father was concerned with the establishment of the first Blackfriars theatre and took part in court entertainments. On the front page of the NHMS, which was owned by Neville, there is a list of plays which can, with some difficulty be made out:

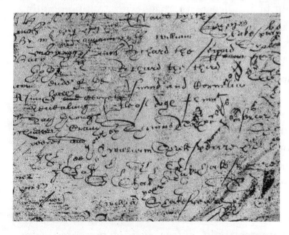

The Northumberland Manuscript. (By permission of the Archives of the Duke of Northumberland at Alnwick Castle, DNP: MS 525)

By Mr. ffrancis Bacon	William Rychard the second Rychard the third	Shakespeare Shakespear
Bacon end of the hall Asmund and Cornelia	Asmund and Cornelia[5]	Thomas
revealing day through every crany peepes and see	Ile of Dogs frmnt inferior plaiers by Thomas Nashe[6] William Shakespeare	Thom Thom Thomas

This confirms Neville's interest not only in Shakespeare but in a banned play by Nashe and Jonson. The reference to Nashe shows that Neville was aware of the satirist whom many scholars have suggested appears as the character Moth in *Love's Labour's Lost*.

Neville annotated books with references to the theatre and noted the classical Greek playwrights in his copy of Horace's *Epistles* (for more examples see Chapter 5). He annotated the page with the names of Sophocles, Thespis, Aeschylus and Plautus. He owned a copy of Plautus' plays (see Chapter 3).

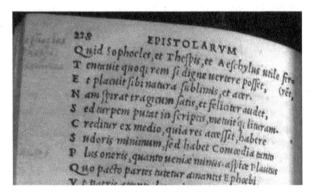

Horace, Epistles, book II. (Private collection)

This section of the *Epistles* is believed to be a source for *King Lear*.[7]

In 1603 the Earl of Southampton had dedicated his *Encomium* on Richard III to Neville (see Chapter 4). Beaumont and Fletcher gave Neville the manuscript of *A King and No King* (see Chapter 9). Neville used theatrical metaphors in his letters. Reflecting on Henry IV's actions in France, in 1600 Neville wrote that they were 'like to prove the first act of the tragedy …'[8] On 15 November 1600, Neville wrote to his secretary, Ralph Winwood, saying, 'The Earl of Essex is no actor in our triumphs.'[9] A fortnight later Winwood wrote to Neville about the wedding of Henry IV and Marie de Medici in Marseilles, writing that 'here are neither Excercises of Honor to entertain the Princes and Gentlemen, nor any Comedies or Tragedies, or publick Feasts to give Contentment to the Ladies; whereof at *Florence* there was Variety, full of many witty and worthy Conceits, whereof this Dialoge will give your Honor some kind of tast.'[10] This seems to be a reference to one of the earliest operas (which at first were called 'dialogues' because the term opera had not been coined): the *Dialogo di Giunone e Minerva* by Giovanni Battista Guarini (libretto) and Emilio de' Cavalieri (music). This work was the only major entertainment at the wedding titled 'a Dialogue', so it must be the work sent to Neville by Winwood.[11] There is a 1602 copy of Guarini's *Il Pastor Fido*, a Tragicommedia Pastorale, in Neville's library. As we saw in Chapter 11, Neville was in Brussels in 1613 to see 'the Procession of the Sacrament of Miracles, the Princes and this Court in its Glory'.[12] It seems he was an observer of pageantry just at the time that Shakespeare's *Henry VIII* was on stage with its rich scenes of pageantry.

There is hard evidence that Neville owned play scripts, made notes on theatres and used theatrical metaphors. There is evidence that he wrote plays in Chamber's Latin poem of 1599, which was addressed to Neville and included the words, 'Too little is your excellence seen by the common people of the Earth, were it not for the kindly company of the Muses who sing through you, granting you various arts: the refined Muse of Comedy giving you the eloquence to pour forth what you Will' (see Chapter 6). In 1603, Carleton's Latin dedication to Neville in his *Heroici Characteres* encouraged Neville with the words, 'Who would deny that these should not be further exalted on stage in Tragedy?'[13] Both John Chamber and George Carleton were saying that Neville was blessed by the Muses, suggesting he was a poet (which indeed he was, see Chapter 6). Ben Jonson also opened his poem addressed to Neville with the words, 'Who now calls on thee, NEVIL, is a Muse ...'[14] Given Jonson's capacity for writing cryptic verse with double meanings, this line could be read 'Nevil is a Muse', in other words, a poet. As the other leading dramatist of the Jacobean period, Jonson's praise for Neville is in stark contrast with his satirical attacks on the actor Shakspere. Neville, Fletcher, Beaumont and Jonson were members of the convivial Mermaid Club. Francis Beaumont wrote a verse letter about the Mermaid to Jonson in 1612, in which one line is *"Ne let* Sir Henry *count it vile"* (clearly a reference to Neville, punning on his family motto). Beaumont sent another verse letter to Jonson in 1615 in which he referred to Neville's funeral.[15] William Strachey, whose letter was a source for *The Tempest*, was also a member of the Mermaid Club. Another member was Hugh Holland who wrote a commendatory poem for the First Folio. Many have speculated that William Shakespeare, the writer, was a member of the Mermaid Club but there is no evidence that Shakspere from Stratford ever attended. With Neville identified as the Bard, this mystery vanishes because Shakespeare was indeed a member.

Perhaps the most significant development was Walsingham's creation of the theatre company, the Queen's Men. This occurred in 1583, the same year that Neville accompanied Walsingham on a diplomatic mission to Scotland. Walsingham and Philip Sidney realised that 'English history might be a wonderful resource for playwrights in the future, and unsurprisingly we find that the Queen's Men established the English history play in the popular theatre before other companies took it up'.[16] The Queen's Men were 'a deliberately political company in origin'.[17] It seems that Neville started playwriting for the Queen's Men. That he knew both Walsingham and Sidney put him in the right place at the right time. The early *Henry VI* trilogy was a huge creative achievement that features the Neville family rather more than the true history would fully justify. By contrast, no one has ever satisfactorily explained how William Shakspere from Stratford could arrive in London as a poor, unknown, uneducated man without connections, and immediately stage a massive three-part history play which, incidentally, featured none of his family nor indeed anyone from Stratford.

Shakespeare and Neville: Shared Sources and Rare Vocabulary

For many of Shakespeare's plays we can prove that Neville had access to the source books, many of which he annotated, revealing his interest in characters and stories that feature in the canon. That there is any such evidence after so many years is remarkable. Neville used the same rare vocabulary in his letters as the Bard used in the plays.

Hapax legomena are words that occur only once in a writer's works. They have been used by scholars to determine authorship.[18] In his letters Neville used many words that occur only once in Shakespeare's oeuvre (at a rate of approximately one every 100 words) and we are able to demonstrate this in the following table. In three cases, marked with an asterisk, have we used words that occur in two or more works. In one instance marked with a hash we note a plural in Neville's letter when there is a singular in Shakespeare's poem. Given that we have no Neville letters dated earlier than 1599 it is remarkable how many of these hapaxes date from the same year or were earlier than Shakespeare's usage. This shows that Neville had used this vocabulary before Shakespeare used it. In the table 'Hall' refers to the annotated Hall's *Chronicle* discovered by Alan Keen. We have also listed books that are to be found in Neville's extant library and whether these are annotated.

Shakespeare used Holinshed as a source for his history plays. Neville would have had access to the 1587 edition as his father-in-law was one of the editors but, because there is no extant volume of Holinshed in the Neville library, we have not listed it. Likewise, Neville had read Plutarch, quoting the story of Antigonus and his son Demetrius in his paper for James I (see Chapter 9) but there is no volume of Plutarch amongst Neville's extant books.

Play/Poem date	Book/source	Annotations in the text	Neville's life experience	Hapax/rare word in a Neville letter and in the play/poem[19]	Nevilles in the play[20]
All's Well 1604	Boccaccio's *Decameron*		N. went to Florence 1581	exempted: 8/12/1604	
Anthony and Cleo 1606–7	Tacitus, Ovid, Appian	√	N. in Rome 1581	maritime:[21] 3/1/1600	
As You Like It 1599–1600	*Diana Enamorada*: Montemayor		N. in France at the time	propositions: 9/4/1600	
Cardenio/ Double Falshood 1613			Neville read and spoke Spanish	presumptions: 18/6/1613	Henriquez (son of Henry)
Comedy of E. 1589–94	Plautus	√	N. read Latin	*inquisitive (twice): 28/12/1600	
Coriolanus 1607–8	Dionysius of Halicarnassus	√	N. in Rome 1581	pretext: 21/6/1608	
Cymbeline 1609–10	Boccaccio		N. worked on the Union of Scotland and England	procuring: 6/9/1599	

Edward III 1589–94	L/C; Tower Notebook; Ovid	√	N. went to Scotland 1583	imployd:[22] 26/5/1599	√
Hamlet 1600–01	Horace	√	N. in prison	questionable: 14/5/1600	
Hand D: S.T. More 1603–4			N. tried to procure a pardon	Pcure (procure) Pdon (pardon) both in L/C[23]	
Henry IV 1 & 2 1596–8	L/C; Tower Notebook; Hall	√	N., like Falstaff, had to muster men	1: peremptorily: 26/9/1599 2: *accommodated: 13/11/1600[24]	√
Henry V 1599	L/C, Tower notebook; Hall	√	N. in France 1578, 82 and 1599–1600	acknowledgement: 7/8/1599	√
Henry VI parts 1, 2, 3 1589–92	L/C; Tower notebook; Hall	√		1: sifted: 26/8/1599 2: obligations: 28/7/1599 3: Hollanders:[25] 16/9/1599	√ + Falconbridge
Henry VIII 1612–13	L/C; Tower notebook	√	N. aimed to become secretary[26]	privity: 19/8/1604	√ Neville was called 'Similis'[27]
Julius Caesar 1599	Tacitus, Appian	√ √	N. in Rome 1581	insisted: 26/9/1599	
King John 1596	L/C; Tower notebook	√	N. owned cannon foundary	foreigners:[28] 13/11/1599	Falconbridge
King Lear 1605–6			N. visited Dover	justification: 24/4/1600	
Love's L. L. 1594–6	9 books, see chapter 3	√	NHMS	congratulate: 5/10/1599	Falconbridge
Macbeth 1605–6		√	N. went to Scotland 1583	delinquents: 14/7/1599	
Measure for M. 1604			N. went to Vienna 1580	confiscation: 5/10/1599	
Merchant of Venice 1596–8			N. went to Venice 1581	discontinued: 26/5/1599	Falconbridge
Merry Wives of Windsor 1599			N. lived near Windsor	decipher: 27/6/1599	
Midsummer Night's D. 1595–6	Diana Enamorada: Montemayor			bashfulness: draft letter 1603–4[29]	
Much Ado About N. 1598–99				prohibit: 19/2/1601	
Othello 1602–3			N. went to Venice 1581	solicitation: 7/8/1599	

Pericles 1607–8		√	N. sailed overseas	reception: 28/8/1600	
Phoenix and Turtle 1601	Ovid; Tacitus	√		#obsequy:[30] 6/6/1599	
Rape of Lucrece 1593	Dionysius of Halicarnassus; Ovid's *Ars Amatoria*; Lydgate's *Fall of Princes*	√	NHMS	*uncontrolled:[31] 18/7/1599	
Richard II 1596	L/C; Tower notebook; Hall	√	NMHS	proportionable: 20/8/1599	√
Richard III 1592–3	L/C, Tower notebook	√	NHMS	definitively: 27/6/1599	√
Romeo and Juliet 1595–6	Petrarch		N. went to Verona 1581	prorogued: 28/7/1599	
Sonnets 1593–1609	Petrarch; the Tower notebook[32]	√	London Virginia Company Investor	148: correspondence: 26/5/1599	
Taming of the Shrew 1593–4	Ovid's *Ars Amatoria*; Aristotle *Ethics*		N. went to Padua in 1581	repaired: 26/5/1599	
Tempest 1610–11			N. had access to Strachey letter	irreparable: 11/3/1606	
Timon of Athens 1605			N. worried by debts	bankrupts, ardent: 8/12/1604	
Titus And. 1592–4	Ovid, L/C	√ stuprum		*Horace x 2:[33] 21/6/05	
Tr. & Cr. 1601–2				dependence: 24/9/1599	
Twelfth Night 1600			Winwood told N. of Orsino's arrival	recommended: 18/7/1599	
Two Gentlemen of Verona 1589–92	Ovid's *Ars Amatoria*; Boccaccio. *Diana Enamorada*: Montemayor	√	N. went to Verona 1581	disability: 13/7/1599	
Two Noble Kinsmen 1613			Two friends in prison: N. and H. W.	nullity: 18/6/13	
Venus + A. 1592	Ovid's *Ars Amatoria*	√		harken: 31/7/1602	
Winter's Tale 1610–11			N. went to Bohemia	cogitation: 13/11/1599	

Unlike Shakspere from Stratford, who left no letters, notebooks or manuscripts, Neville left a large number of manuscript documents. His copy of *Leicester's Commonwealth*, Worsley MSS 47, with its relevant annotations, has been shown to be a source for the history plays.[34] Similarly, Neville's Tower notebook of 1602 and 1603 shows him doing historical research that is relevant to the history plays. The Northumberland Manuscript is perhaps the single most important document linking Neville with William Shakespeare, the poet and playwright, and it dates from before that name appeared on any play. His annotations in numerous books that are sources for the plays are relevant to the plays' contents and show him researching literature before or at the time of writing the plays.

We have, throughout this book, shown how every play has some Neville connection. In contrast, there seems to be little or no evidential connection with William from Stratford. Until this point, we have neglected the poem *Venus and Adonis*. This was Shakespeare's first published work with the author's name printed in it. Published in 1593, the year of Neville's father's death, we suspect Neville took the risk to publish because he had no need to fear his father's displeasure nor any scandal that might distress the old man. In Neville's copy of Ovid's *Art of Love*, which Bate declared a source for *Venus and Adonis*, an annotator has underlined the name Adonis in the margin.[35]

Ovid's *Ars Amatoria* and *Remedia Amoris*, 3 verso.

Another book in Neville's library, *Amadis de Gaule*, dated 1574, is a recognised source for *Venus and Adonis*. A few marginal annotations show it that had been read. Several scholars have suggested a link between the poem and the great Renaissance painters of Italy, including Titian, whose painting of Venus and Adonis was on display at his home in Venice in the mid-1570s. Neville had been to Italy and visited Venice in 1581, so could have seen these paintings. Neville knew the Hoby family as his mother-in-law's sister, Elizabeth Cooke, married Thomas Hoby. In Neville's library at Audley End House there is a copy of Boccaccio's *Decameron*, dated 1555 and signed by Thomas Hoby. His brother, Philip Hoby, counted Titian amongst his friends.[36] The poem refers to the skills of a painter who 'would surpass the life' (stanza 47, line 289).

On page 181 of his 1546 volume of Dionysius of Halicarnassus on Roman history, Neville noted 'L. Tarquinius Sup_bus'.[37] Another annotation on page 136 again draws attention to 'L. Tarquinius'. This is Lucius Tarquinius Superbus who raped Lucrece. The argument at the start of *The Rape of Lucrece* opens with the words: 'Lucius Tarquinius, for his excessive pride surnamed Superbus'. Neville also made a note about 'Tarquinius Collatinus' who is named in the argument of *The Rape of Lucrece*, being Lucrece's husband (his full name was Lucius Tarquinius Collatinus, see Chapter 8). Thus we can see that Neville left some trace of the interest that led him to compose his two great poems. Unsurprisingly there is no such trace left by Shakspere from Stratford.

One final example of how Neville's letters anticipate Shakespeare's writing occurs in his 1603–4 draft letter when, appealing to Robert Cecil for financial assistance, Neville used a simile of a cripple waiting to be put into a healing pool.

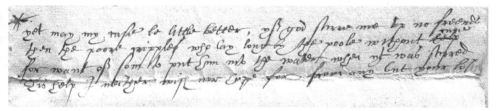

Neville's 1603–4 letter.

Neville wrote,

> yet may my case be little better, yf god stirre me up no freends then the poore cripple who lay long by the poole without [help] cure for want of som to put him into the water when it was stirred. This help I neither wish nor hope for from any but your Lo^rd(ship).

The word 'help' is deleted and '<u>cure</u>' substituted above.[38] We can compare this with the sonnets 153 and 154 in which the poet seeks a 'cure' in 'a seething bath', seeking 'help' in 'water', 'But found no <u>cure</u>'. The letter may even suggest an approximate date for the composition of these sonnets which show how love is the only cure for a 'sad distempered' poet. In 1603 Neville was released from prison back to his family, their love and forgiveness.

Psychology

All artists project aspects of themselves and their experience into their art. Shakespeare does this in ways we have been unable to fathom because we have been trying to find connections with the wrong man. With Henry Neville now identified as the real author, we can frequently see exactly what he was projecting into his plays. We have very little idea of what sort of man William from Stratford was. He was clearly litigious, pursuing people for small loans. He hoarded grain in a famine. He bought property. There is very little indication that he had the breadth of heart and soul that we find in the works of Shakespeare. Neville, on the other hand, psychologically matches what we might expect of the bard. We now offer three key examples of this:

1) The execution of Neville's grandfather.
2) His mother's death.
3) The trauma of his imprisonment (with the threat of execution and consequent terror) and his eventual release; the shame and separation from his family, and eventual joyous reunion).

Can we see these elements in the plays? The answer is yes, over and over again.

1) Transgenerational Issues: The Execution of Neville's Grandfather

The Comedy of Errors starts with the threat of an innocent man's execution. Of course, we see many executions in the history plays, in the Roman plays, in the romances and even here in a comedy the threat is never far away; indeed it hangs over the whole play until the very end. *Pericles* likewise begins with the heads of the executed princes who could not solve the riddle posed by Antiochus, and the threat that Pericles himself will be executed or assassinated for resolving the riddle. Both plays end in Ephesus (see Chapter 9), which, as we shall show in the next section, has a special resonance for Neville.

Sir Edward Neville (1485–1538) was executed in the Tower of London in 1538, aged fifty-four. Neville was in the Tower of London under threat of execution in 1601 when he was aged thirty-nine. He survived this and died in his fifties, aged between fifty-three and fifty-four. Both grandfather and grandson had suffered periods in the Tower and died in their early fifties. This suggests a pattern of death that Anne Schutzenberger wrote about in *The Ancestor Syndrome*, a book that describes the mechanisms of transgenerational processes that can mould people's lives.[39] Edward Neville was a masquer, a poet who improvised songs and verses, and took part in embassies to France and used disguise. Neville might then be seen to have what Shutzenberger called 'an invisible loyalty' to his grandfather, perhaps expressive of his own father's grief and anger at the loss of his father (he was eighteen years old when Sir Edward was executed and he lived until he was seventy-three).

An example of how this was projected into a play is to be found in *Henry VI: Part I* where a theme of transgenerational retribution on Henry VI for the original sin of his grandfather, Henry IV, in taking the throne from Richard II (and his murder), is developed. The Duke of Somerset, speaking to Richard Plantagenet (Richard <u>Neville</u>), shaming him, says:

> Was not thy father, Richard Earl of Cambridge,
> For treason executed in our late king's days?
> And, by his treason, stand'st not thou attainted,
> Corrupted, and exempt from ancient gentry?
> His trespass yet lives guilty in thy blood;
> And, till thou be restored, thou art a yeoman. (2.4.90)

To which Richard replies:

> My father was attached, not attainted,
> Condemn'd to die for treason, but no traitor. (2.4.96)

Later, referring to this incident, Richard asks Mortimer to explain to him the 'cause My father … lost his head' (2.5.54). Mortimer links it to the disputed succession to the throne and his own imprisonment as a rival claimant to the throne. He says, 'Methinks my father's execution was nothing less than bloody tyranny.' Mortimer warns Richard, 'With silence, nephew, be thou politic' (2.5.99). If Neville felt angry and politically critical of the execution of his grandfather as an act of tyranny, he knew he had to be politic and secret about his anger so he channelled it into the Shakespeare plays. In *Titus Andronicus*, Titus' grandson mourns his death:

> O grandsire, grandsire, e'en with all my heart
> Would I were dead, so thou did live again.
> O Lord, I cannot speak to him for weeping,
> My tears will choke me if I ope my mouth. (5.3.171)

Both *The Comedy of Errors* and *Pericles* end happily but they begin with the threat of execution which hung over Neville's own life and haunted his family history. Neville's father, grandfather and uncle were all close to the centre of power and involved politically in domestic and foreign affairs. This closeness to monarchs meant both privilege and vulnerability. It also meant a need for secrecy, for intelligence work, diplomacy and spying, and for the self-protection of anonymous authorship.

2) His Mother's Death

As we saw in Chapter 9, Neville's mother, Elizabeth, died in 1573, when he was about ten years old. The Bard knew a great deal about grief and its healing release. In *Henry VI: Part III*, King Lewis tells Margaret to 'tell thy grief it shall be eased' (3.3.19). In *Macbeth* Malcolm says:

> Give sorrow words: the grief that does not speak
> Whispers the o'er-fraught heart and bids it break. (4.3.209)

So vast is the material on grief in the works we will not list more examples. The word grief occurs 248 times in the canon; tears 320 times; sorrow 222; for comparison, rage occurs 135 times; angry 103; anger 59; guilty 84; guilt only 34. We find the word 'melancholy' occurs 72 times in the plays and often men are melancholic, sad without knowing why. To have lost a mother at age ten might predispose someone to bouts of depression especially round the anniversary of her death: the adult, not realising the anniversary was coming up, might feel low and not know why. Evidence that Neville's mother was still remembered at home exists in the inventory of Neville's father's property after his death in 1593 where the furniture of 'My Lady Gresham's Chamber' is listed twenty years after her death.[40] To grow up with such a shrine to his mother in the house would predispose a child to a longing for the lost loved one. Pericles asks:

> Why should this change of thoughts,
> The sad companion, dull-eyed melancholy,
> Be my so used a guest as not an hour,
> In the day's glorious walk, or peaceful night,
> The tomb where grief should sleep, can breed me quiet? (1.2.1)

Note here the occurrence of the word 'tomb' as if the writer knew the grief was due to a death. Pericles is finally reunited with the mother figure, Thaisa, whom he invites to be 'buried a second time within these arms', thus combining Eros and Thanatos in one action.[41]

It is possible that this boyhood loss is a reason for the special bond between Neville and Southampton. The young earl lost his father when he was nine years old: the compassion Neville would have felt for this boy, losing a parent at approximately the same age as he had done, may have made them especially close. They were of course imprisoned together in the Tower from 1601 to 1603.

Neville soon found himself with a stepmother. She was a formidable woman. Perhaps a hint of Neville's feelings about her are revealed in *The Troublesome Raigne of John* (the first version of *King John*):

A Mother though she were unnaturall,
Is better than the kindest Stepdame is ... (10.141)

Cymbeline also has a wicked stepmother on stage.

3) Neville's Imprisonment, the Threat of Execution and Eventual Release: The Shame and Separation from His Family and Eventual Joyous Reunion

Having been caught up in the Essex rebellion, Neville narrowly escaped from repeating his grandfather's fate – in 1538 he was imprisoned in the Tower of London and executed. Indeed, a number of Nevilles had spent time in the Tower, dating back to his distant relative Sir Thomas Faucomberge who was incarcerated there in 1378; Thomas Neville was in the Tower in 1415; Sir Humphrey Neville was imprisoned there in 1463, was released but later beheaded after a rebellion in 1469; George Neville, Archbishop of York, was in the Tower in 1471; another George Neville, 3rd Baron of Bergavenny, was imprisoned there in 1506; and Edmund Neville was committed to the Tower for twelve years from 1585 to 1597. This transgenerational pattern of imprisonment explains the repeatedly foreboding presence of the Tower of London in the history plays.

As we saw in Chapter 7, Caroline Spurgeon, in her classic analysis of Shakespeare's imagery, wrote that *Hamlet* and *Troilus and Cressida* show signs of having been written at the same time 'when the author was suffering from a disillusionment, revulsion and perturbation of nature, such as we feel nowhere else with such intensity'.[42] She also pointed out the distaste for poor quality food in *Troilus and Cressida*. At the time of writing this play, Neville was in the Tower of London, a place of disillusionment, revulsion and perturbation where one would not expect a gourmet menu. Such an experience, the ruin of his career, the execution of his admired friend Essex, indeed the threat of his own execution and the separation from his family, was demonstrably traumatic for Henry Neville, as is evident from his letters of the time.[43] Neville was ruined financially and politically by his imprisonment. He was regarded with furious contempt by his father-in-law who refused his own daughter refuge after Neville was exposed, until instructed to take her into his home by the government. This whole episode must have been deeply shaming to Neville. As we saw in Chapter 2, shame was a recurring theme in both Neville's life and Shakespeare's works. When Neville annotated his copy of Velutello's 1581 edition of Petrarch's poems he underlined the last three lines in the very first sonnet.

These three lines translated read:

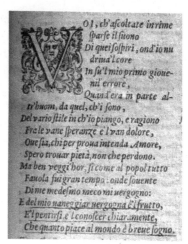

Velutello's 1581 edition of Petrarch, Sonnet 1. (Private collection)

And shame is the fruit of my vanities
And remorse, and the clearest knowledge
Of how the world's delight is a brief dream.

Petrarch was the original sonneteer whose poems were both inspiration and challenge: Shakespeare's sonnets both echo and react against the Petrarchan tradition.

After the catharsis of writing the tragedies a happier period ensued. We saw in Chapter 9 how the heroes of the romances are shamed men who are eventually forgiven and reunited with their surviving families. In plays written during this period, there is greater acceptance and patience: in *Pericles* the suffering king must go through the suffering, submit and accept. Looking at Marina he says, 'Thou dost look like Patience gazing on kings' graves and smiling extremity out of act' (5.1.128). Patience is used 184 times across the canon: eight times in *Pericles*. In *Othello* and *Troilus and Cressida*, the word occurs eleven and eight times respectively. *Othello* and *Troilus and Cressida* were written while Neville was in the Tower and patient acceptance of his life was required. *Othello*'s score of eleven is equalled in *Henry VIII*. At the time *Henry VIII* was written, Neville was waiting to hear whether he would be made Secretary of State. All he could do was be patient while the king made up his mind.

One reason for Neville being such a convincing candidate for the authorship of the Shakespeare plays is that psychologically he clearly 'fits' the stories, characters, imagery and underlying processes in the plays.

A Secret Writer: Cryptic Clues and the Need for Secrecy

Unlike Jonson, who trumpeted his identity and authorship, William from Stratford was remarkably reticent. If he had been the author this would have been decidedly odd, because he could have made money from his fame and commissions to write entertainments such as court masques. However Shakspere kept a low profile. Those in power must have known that the actor Shakspere was not the author Shakespeare, and this explains how he escaped the censure and imprisonment that other playwrights suffered when their plays were censored, banned or destroyed.

We note that there was a period of about ten years during which the Shakespeare plays were written and published anonymously: the earliest printings of plays that had been written between 1589 and 1592 were in 1594, but no play was acknowledged as by Shakespeare until 1598.[44] The first anonymous publications occurred just after Neville's father died: again perhaps he felt free to go into print now he could not embarrass his father. Eventually in 1598 the name Shakespeare appeared on the plays. Even allowing for the fact that playwrights were not often acknowledged on the title pages of quartos, this is a long time to withhold the identity of a writer. Indeed, if Shakespeare had begun writing plays in the mid-1580s, as Sams, Casson and Jolly have suggested, then this period of anonymity extended over thirteen years from 1585 to 1598.[45] We saw in Chapter 2 that Neville had reasons to keep his authorship secret and also that he placed cryptic clues that reveal his name and authorship in several places.

This book brings together some of the evidence that Neville was the playwright and poet known as Shakespeare. In science, a hypothesis is corroborated by evidence. The greater the evidence, the greater the probability the hypothesis is correct. In law, the weight of evidence for a case is weighed in the balance of probabilities which a jury decides. In both, when enough evidence accrues, evidence first becomes convincing and then compelling. We recognise that some of the evidence that we have presented is tentative and that weak pieces of evidence do not in themselves make a compelling case, but we are confident that most of what we have found is sufficiently strong to be convincing. A few scraps of evidence could be dismissed as coincidence, but an accumulating avalanche of evidence becomes convincing unless counter-evidence can be produced. One or two pieces of evidence might be dismissed, be erroneous or proved fallacious but when there are many sources of multi-dimensional evidence the case gathers strength. We believe the growing mass of evidence presented in this and other books supports Neville's authorship. More evidence is emerging as others study texts and find yet more links between Neville and the works of Shakespeare, so undoubtedly there will be more books to come. You, the jury, considering the evidence, will decide your verdict.

Appendix

Ring Composition in *Shake-speares Sonnets*

We are grateful to David Ewald for offering us the opportunity to publish his important discovery of chiastic forms in *Shake-speares Sonnets* and link this to Neville's authorship. Casson edited and revised this paper, so making further discoveries that confirm Ewald's work. A small section of this appendix appears in Chapter 10 but we have repeated the material here to ensure the integrity of this explanation. This discovery provides compelling evidence that the publication of the sonnets was carefully planned, not the result of a printer getting hold of the poems and pirating them.

Chiastic Form: Circular Structures in Classical Literature

Mary Douglas's book *Thinking in Circles, An Essay on Ring Composition* offers a new understanding of an archaic literary device. Ring composition, or chiastic structure, is defined by Douglas as 'a construction of parallelisms that must open a theme, develop it, and round it off by bringing the conclusion back to the beginning'.[1] To be more specific, she states,

> The minimum criterion for a ring composition is for the ending to join up with the beginning. A ring is a framing device. The linking up of starting point and end creates an envelope that contains everything between the opening phrases and the conclusion. The rule for closing the ring endows the work with unity ... It takes skill to compose a polished specimen. There has to be a well marked point at which the ring turns, preparatory to working back to the beginning, and the whole series of stanzas from the beginning to the middle should be in parallel with the other series going from the middle back to the start. Each section on the second side of the ring corresponds to a matching section on the first side. The form is well known. It is basically the chiastic structure, ABBA, or ABCBA, a form that pervades the Bible and other famous archaic texts. It comes in many sizes, from a few lines to a whole book enclosed in its macro-envelope, arranged throughout in intricately corresponding parallelisms.[2]

A ring composition is a disciplined, mirror-patterned form in which each stanza or section has its parallel pair. The members of a pair are placed on opposite sides of the ring, so that each faces the other and each indicates its pair by verbal correspondences. These two similar sections have been carefully matched so as to guide the range of interpretation. Another function is greatly to deepen the range of reference by playing on the double meanings of words. It is a form of literary play giving pleasure to the composer and the reader. Ring compositions, or chiastic structures, can be found in the Bible, the Qur'an, Homer's *Iliad* and *Odyssey, Gilgamesh, Beowulf*, Sidney's *Arcadia* and Milton's *Paradise Lost*.[3]

An example will show how complex a seemingly simple ring can be. We will start with the familiar story of the Garden of Eden, from the book of Genesis.[4] The more the story is familiar, the more the sense of surprise at the density of meaning that is packed into this form. The story seems to flow so smoothly that the underlying chiastic structure is unsuspected. It starts in an amorphous, misty, barren place that contrasts with the charming garden full of trees that God willed into being. The story begins before God had created man and woman (1:26–31). At first, there was no man to till the ground. God made a man from the earth, breathed life into him, and set him in a garden with four rivers in and around it (2:4–3:24). The concept of water channelled into rivers contrasts with the initial undifferentiated swampiness. The theme seems to be very simple in English, but there is punning play on the Hebrew word for a human being named Adam. The version we offer here is simplified in order to reveal the structure.

The Tragedy of Adam (Human Being) Formed from the Adamah (Soil)[5]

2:5 There was no *adam* to till the *adamah*.

2:7 God formed the *adam* from the dust of the *adamah*,

2:15 to guard and till the garden of Eden.

2:17 The *adam* was not to eat of the tree of knowledge.

2:21–24 To allay his loneliness God brought a partner out of the *adam*.

The *adam* is now *ish* and *ishshah*,[6] united in perfect harmony.

2:25 They are naked (*arumim*) and free from shame.

3:1–6 But the subtle (*arum*) serpent tempts them to disobey.

3:7–10 They become aware of their nakedness and feel shame.

3:16 Their harmony is spoilt: hereafter *ish* will dominate *ishshah*.

3:19 The *adam* must return to the *adamah* from which he was taken.

3:22 The *adam* may not eat of the tree of life.

3:23 The *adam* must till the *adamah* but with toil and sweat, no longer in Eden;

3:24 Eden now has a new guardian to keep the *adam* from the tree of life.

Note that the subject matter, the theme of return of Adam to the soil, is exemplified in the ring convention itself, the end returns to the beginning. Adam was made from the soil.

The effect also gives special emphasis to the pivotal central point. In the Eden story, this place is occupied by the intervention of the serpent. The serpent's malice is highlighted even more by the play on two words quite different in meaning but sounding very like each other, which come in adjacent verses (2:25 and 3:1).[7] These words refer respectively to the nakedness of the human pair and the slyness of the serpent. We note, however, that Hebrew has two words for 'naked': one is used in contexts of sexual activity, the other, '*arumim*', used in 2:25, always connotes vulnerability, such as that of children and other helpless persons. Such punning enables links to be made and such echoes, like mirror images, complete the ring.

Ring Compositions/Chiastic Structure in Shakespeare's Sonnets

Our aim here is to show how Shakespeare created three rings within the 154 sonnets published in 1609. We noticed first that there are 154 sonnets by Shakespeare and wondered whether this number had any significance. Why not 155 or 150, as a round number? Petrarch wrote 365 sonnets to denote the cycle of a year. 154 is 22 x 7. The value of Pi (π), by which we calculate the ratio of the circumference of a circle to its diameter, is 22 over 7. William Jones was the first to use the Greek letter π for this number in 1707. However, the number had been known since the time of the ancient Egyptian and Greek mathematicians. Was this simply a coincidence or is there some meaning inherent in Shakespeare's choice of 154? Does this number represent a completed circle, an image of completion of the cycle of sonnets? Shakespeare used the words 'circumference' in *A Midsummer Night's Dream, King John, The Merry Wives of Windsor*: all works of the later 1590s, 'diameter' in *Hamlet* and 'circle' in eight plays from *Titus Andronicus* to *Antony and Cleopatra*. In *Henry V* (1599) the Duke of Burgundy advises the king on his wooing of Katherine:

> Pardon the frankness of my mirth, if I answer you for that. If you would conjure in her, you must make a circle; if conjure up love in her in his true likeness, he must appear naked and blind. Can you blame her then, being a maid yet rosed over with the virgin crimson of modesty, if she deny the appearance of a naked blind boy in her naked seeing self? (5.2.287)

There are sexual puns here about the penis and vagina. The last two sonnets, 153 and 154, are about Cupid (Love, a blind boy contrasted with the mistress's eyes, in effect 'her seeing self'). Erotic, sexual attraction is essential to the fulfilment of love with the result of the creation of the next generation, which is a core subject of the sonnets. In Sonnet 7, the cycle of generation takes as its main image the sun (a circle). Sonnet 22 is about love and the cycle of life, including an image of a mirror (glass). Sonnet 77 is halfway through the whole sequence of 154 poems. It includes a sundial (a circle, relating the sun and time) and a mirror. Chiastic structures are circular, mirror structures. We will show how this greater circle of the whole sonnet sequence contains three inner ring compositions.

Neville studied mathematics at Merton College, Oxford under his tutor Henry Savile. In the Merton library is a book about Ptolemy's Celestial Geometry, which was donated by Neville and annotated by him in Latin and Greek.[8] One of the annotations, on page 49, reads, 'Theoreme per quod circumfentia colliguntur' which we translate as, 'The Theorem by which circumferences may be calculated.' This note shows that Neville was aware of the geometry and this is confirmed by John Chamber's 1600 poem on Neville which explicitly refers to his knowledge of Euclid (see Chapter 6). Neville's contemporary, Ludolph van Ceulen, spent years calculating the value of π. He published a twenty-decimal value in his 1596 book *Van den Circkel* (On the Circle). In 1600, he was appointed the first professor of mathematics at Leiden University. He died in 1610.

Helen Vendler, in her book *The Art of Shakespeare's Sonnets,* revealed her discovery of a literary device she called the 'Key Word Couplet Tie'. She found a purposeful intention by Shakespeare to verbally connect the beginning, middle and ending of a sonnet with highly significant words. She also noticed the use of antithetical chiastic form in Sonnet 29: 'With what I most enjoy contented least'.[9] Did Shakespeare utilise chiastic form on a larger sequential design? Did he know of and understand this archaic literary device observed in the great works of literature? He certainly knew the Bible, the *Iliad* and *Odyssey*. Engel has shown that Shakespeare did indeed use chiastic structures in his plays, particularly in *Pericles* and *The Two Noble Kinsmen*.[10] He also found chiastic elements in the poetry of the plays such as Richard II's 'I wasted time, and now doth time waste me' (5.5.49). Jolly also noticed the use of chiasmus in *Hamlet* when the queen promises:[11]

> If words be made of breath
> And breath of life, I have no life to breathe
> What thou hast said to me. (3.4.199)

Waugaman noted that 'Achilles' speech midway through *Troilus and Cressida* (3.3.103–11) is a beautiful chiasmus, enacting his words about our need to see ourselves mirrored in another person's image of us.[12] At the centre of the speech is "eye to eye", almost pallindromic in its symmetry. "This is not strange" is repeated in the first and last lines. Two words begin with "b" in the second line; two words end in its mirror image, "d" in the penultimate line'. The speech signals its chiastic nature by including the word 'mirror'd'.

We will now outline the three rings we have found in *Shake-speares Sonnets*.

The Three Rings

The three rings within the larger circle of the whole are sonnets 1–54, 55–98 and 99–154. The size of the three circles in the sonnets sequence are not quite equal: fifty-four, forty-three and fifty-five respectively. The central sonnets of each ring are 27–28, 77 and 126–27. We notice that it is only by dividing up the sonnets in this unequal way that the central point of the central ring is Sonnet 77: the very heart of the larger circle of the whole sequence.

The First Chiastic Structure: The Rose Ring (1–54)

Tracing the circuit of a ring composition we look for words, images and phrases that mirror each other on either side of the central turning point. It is essential that the first and last in the ring complement each other. We have found the following key words and images that match each other to create the ring (capitals and italics in the 1609 printing; spelling modernised).

Imagery	Sonnet	Number	Imagery
fairest, beauty's *Rose*, die, sweet, bud	1	54	beauty, Rose, fair/er, sweet, die, buds
sum, *Audit*	4	49	sum, audit
eye, sight, mortal, eyes	7	46	eye, mortal, sight, eyes
thou (x5), murd'rous, thought, my, me, thee	10	44	thought (x3), thou (x2), thee, kills me, my
minutes, truth and beauty	**14**	**41**	beauty (x3), years, truth
write, numbers,[13] Poet/Poet's, old, papers, meter, rhyme	17	38	Muse (x3), verse, paper, write, old, rhymers, numbers
compare, Sun and Moon, my love	21	35	Moon and Sun, compare, my love
books, more, read, writ, love	**23**	**32**	lines, more, pen, read, love
Image, bosom's, hanging, eyes, heart	24	31	bosom, hearts, eye, Hung, images
toil, repose, black night, day	27	28	rest, day (x4), night (x5), toil (x2), swart

→ **MIDPOINT TURN** ↑

We notice these verses match almost every third verse and, in two cases, 14–41 and 23–32, are mirror numbers. The first ring begins and ends with the poet using imagery of a <u>Rose</u> and <u>spring/summer</u> (the turning year) in making his case for eternalizing the fair youth's beauty by procreation or poetic creation. The midpoint turn is symbolised by day turning into night. The end of the first part is perhaps signalled by the word <u>expired</u> in Sonnet 27. Sonnet 28 opens with the words, 'How can I then <u>return</u>'. Both poems refer to the distance between the poet and his love, the first suggesting an imaginary journey/pilgrimage that he makes at night, the second complaining of the torture of being 'still farther off from thee'. The ring then has to be completed by a journey to its beginning, returning to the home of the beloved rose. (The form of the rose suggests a circle, as rose windows in cathedrals.) The mirror position of the turn in the circle is apparent in the reflective quality of the poet's thoughts and in his chiastic phrasing ('<u>but day by night and night by day</u>') and the image of day and night shaking hands (Sonnet 28). By adding the numbers of sonnets 27 and 28 we arrive at 55: the sonnet that starts the next ring.

The Second Chiastic Structure: The Looking Glass Ring (55–98)

According to Douglas, ring compositions are often preceded by a prologue and it appears that Sonnet 55 may have this function for the second ring. Douglas stated, 'There is generally an introductory section that states the theme and introduces the main characters. You can call it a prologue. It sets the stage, sometimes the time and the place. Usually its tone is bland and somewhat enigmatic. It tells of a dilemma that has to be faced, a command to be obeyed, or a doubt to be allayed. Above all, it is laid out so as to anticipate the midturn and the ending that will eventually respond to it.'

We first examine this prologue with Sonnet 55 (italics in the original; modernised spelling; with our emphasis underlined):

Not marble, nor the gilded <u>monuments</u>
Of princes shall <u>outlive</u> this pow'rful rhyme,
But you shall shine more bright in these contents
Than unswept stone, <u>besmeared with sluttish time</u>.
When wasteful <u>war</u> shall *Statues* overturn,
And broils root out the work of masonry,
Nor *Mars* his <u>sword</u>, nor <u>war's</u> quick fire shall burn:
The <u>living</u> record of your <u>memory</u>.
'Gainst death, and all ob<u>livious</u> enmity
Shall you pace forth, your praise shall still find room,
Even in the <u>eyes</u> of all <u>posterity</u>
That wear this world out to the ending doom.
So till the judgment that your self arise,
You <u>live</u> in this, and dwell in lovers' <u>eyes</u>.

Sonnet 55 is related to Sonnet 56, to the midpoint Sonnet 77 and to the ending Sonnet 98.

Imagery	Sonnet	Number	Imagery
war, sword, eyes, out-live, doom	55	56	force, edge,[14] sharpened, eyes, kill
monument, this powerful rhyme, time, memory, death, posterity	55	77	graves, Time's, eternity, memory, this book
Mars	55	98	*Saturn*

This prologue contains an essential element of Douglas's criteria for a prologue, in that it sets up the poet's desire to eternalise the fair youth's excellence for all posterity or at least until the world's ending doom. It also showcases a prime example of Vendler's Couplet Tie and Key Word (in all four units of the sonnet) in the following variations: Q1(2) – <u>outlive</u>, Q2(8) – <u>living</u>, Q3(9) – <u>oblivious</u> and C(14) – <u>live</u>, thus underlining the theme of the ring.

The second ring is a sonnet composition of forty-three parts (if we do not count the prologue as part of the ring). This cannot be divided into two, so that we find this odd number results in the pivot Sonnet 77 standing alone, itself a glass that mirrors the two sides of the ring. The midpoint is marked by the mirror Sonnet 77, 7 mirroring 7 in the number itself. Indeed the first seven lines of Sonnet 77 are mirrored by the last seven lines. The word 'glass' signifies a mirror and is repeated twice in the sonnet. Also repeated twice is the word 'dial', signifying the circuit of the sun and hours of the day. With graves and children we have the cycle of life and death. Another word repeated twice is 'memory'. Poems, the children of memory, reflect the past into the future. The rival ('Alien') poet first emerges, like a distorted mirror image of the writer, in the very next sonnet. We can also see more mirrorings: the images often are in reverse order in the mirrored pairs, such as 56–98, where the positions of winter and summer are reversed.

Imagery	Sonnet		Number	Imagery
spirit, *Int'rim*, Winter, Summer's	56	15	98	absent, spirit, summer's, Winter,
times/time, sovereign, absence	57		97	absence, time (x2), Lord's
revolution, days, praise	**59**		**95**	days, praise, turns to
Time doth transfix the flourish, nature's truth	60		94	nature's riches, summer's flower, it only live and die
self (x8), love (x2)	62		92	self, love (x3)
loss (x2), down razed, weep	64	16	90	loss (x2), overthrow, griefs, woe (x2)
forsworn, disgrac'd, disabled, ill	66	17	88	scorn, forsworn, weakness, attainted, injuries, wrong
cheek, dead, sepulchres	**68**		**86**	tomb, dead, countenance
beauty, praise (x2), thou alone	70		84	praise (x2), you alone, praises, beauteous
praise, true, love (x4), worth	72		82	worth, praise, love, true (x2)
memorial, earth (x2), dead, remembered	74		81	earth (x2), memory, death, monument
sweet, filching, steal, alone	75		79	alone, sweet, robs, stole
verse, pride, variation, I always write of you	76		78	verse, *Alien*, proud, thou art all my art
glass (x2), dial/dial's, waste, vacant leaves, book, graves, memory	← First seven lines	77	Last → seven lines	Time's, eternity, memory, look (x2) waste blanks, children, book

→ **Midpoint turn** ↑

Again there are two pairs whose numbers are mirrored: 59/95 and 68/86. The key words in the latter are also mirrored, being in reverse order. In 68–86 we find 'cheek', 'dead', 'sepulchre' mirrored by 'tomb', 'dead', 'countenance'. The sonnets 67 and 76, which are also mirror numbers, echo each other in having three 'Why?' questions.[18]

This ring contains a number of words that have been emphasised by being italicised. These italicised words occur at critical points in this ring: *Statues* (55), *Mars* (55), *Int'rim* (56), *Alien* (78), *Eve's* (93) and *Saturn* (98). *Statues*, in the prologue, introduces the theme of memorialising: by the poet (throughout), the youth (77) and the rival poet (78–86). Spelt *Intrim* in the 1609 edition (and modernised to int'rim to reduce the word interim to two syllables), *Int'rim* is at the very beginning of the ring which can be described as a central interim within the whole sequence of 154 sonnets. *Alien* in Sonnet 78 begins the rival poet sequence. *Eve's* in Sonnet 93 reminds us of the original dark lady of temptation and begins the sequence (93–96) in which the youth's shame is explored.

Mars and Saturn frame the whole Looking Glass Ring. The sequence begins with the myth of Mars and ends with the myth of Saturn: war and mortality. We hear of an emotional war within the poet, caused by physical separation from the beloved and the poetic assault by the rival poet. The poet contemplates his own mortality and what he leaves behind. Saturn was also the god of agriculture and he appears at the end of the sequence in a sonnet rich in flowers, their brief beauty harvested by the poet who is struggling to survive the winter of separation from the beloved.

Big-Bellied Sails and Pregnant Parentheses
Shakespeare appears to have created a purposeful relationship between the physical sail-like appearance of parentheses and the mental image of the sails in the following passages in *A Midsummer Night's Dream* and sonnets 80 and 86. In her response to Oberon asking her to give him the Indian boy, Titania replies:

… The fairy land buys not the child of me.
His mother was a votaress of my order:
And, in the spiced Indian air, by night,
Full often hath she gossip'd by my side,
And sat with me on Neptune's yellow sands,
Marking the embarked traders on the flood,
When we have laugh'd to see the <u>sails</u> conceive
And grow <u>big-bellied</u> with the wanton wind;
Which she, with pretty and with swimming gait
Following <u>(her womb then rich with my young squire)</u>
Would imitate, and <u>sail</u> upon the land,
To fetch me trifles, and return again,
As from a voyage, rich with merchandise.
But she, being mortal, of that boy did die;
And for her sake do I rear up her boy,
And for her sake I will not part with him.

In Sonnet 80 we find:

But since your worth <u>(wide as the ocean is)</u>
The humble as the proudest <u>sail</u> doth bear,
My saucy <u>bark</u> <u>(inferior far to his)</u>
On your broad main doth wilfully appear.
Your shallowest help will hold me up afloat,
Whilst he upon your soundless deep doth ride,
Or <u>(being wrecked)</u> I am a worthless <u>boat</u>,
He of tall building, and of goodly pride.
Then if he thrive and I be cast away,
The worst was this, my love was my decay.

And again in Sonnet 86 we see:

> Was it the proud full <u>sail</u> of his great verse,
> Bound for the prize of <u>(all too precious)</u> you,
> That did my ripe thoughts in my brain inhearse,
> Making their tomb the <u>womb</u> wherein they grew?

The words 'sail' and 'womb' only appear three times in the sonnets and there are forty-four pairs of parentheses in the sonnets. The fact that the sonnets contain 2,157 lines creates a very low level of probability that sonnets 80 and 86 would both contain a similar juxtaposition of sail/womb and parentheses to that created by Shakespeare in *A Midsummer Night's Dream*. We propose that these accentuations of parentheses by the author are a pointer to the determination of an intentional overall pattern of parentheses in *Shake-speares Sonnets* that reveal the next fifty-six-sonnet ring composition. The composition of the fifty-six-sonnet ring appears to be symbolically indicated by the overall structure of the author's usage of parentheses in the whole of the 154-sonnet sequence, specifically emphasised by the two blank pairs of parentheses at the end of Sonnet 126, the precise midpoint of the third ring (see diagram below). In order to discover a ring structure, Douglas suggested that 'one simple method is to start simply with a search for repeated formulae that make a pattern. It can start with words, rhymes, assonance, alliteration, and can show also in nonverbal markers, such as line endings, and punctuation marks, commas, full stops, or exclamation and question marks.'[19]

The midpoint isolation of Sonnet 126 in the sonnets 99–154 sequence is very evident in the following diagram: sonnets containing parentheses are in bold and bracketed.

1	2	3	4	5	6	**(7)**	8	9	10	11
12	13	14	15	**(16)**	**(17)**	18	19	20	21	22
23	24	25	**(26)**	**(27)**	**(28)**	**(29)**	**(30)**	**(31)**	32	33
34	35	36	37	38	39	40	41	42	**(43)**	44
45	**(46)**	47	48	**(49)**	**(50)**	**(51)**	52	53	54	55
56	**(57)**	**(58)**	59	60	61	**(62)**	63	64	65	**(66)**
67	68	**(69)**	70	**(71)**	**(72)**	73	74	75	76	77
78	**(79)**	**(80)**	**(81)**	82	**(83)**	84	**(85)**	**(86)**	87	88
(89)	90	91	92	93	94	**(95)**	96	97	**(98)**	99
100	101	102	103	104	105	106	107	108	109	110
111	112	113	114	115	116	117	118	119	120	121
122	123	124	125	**(126)**	127	128	129	130	131	132
133	134	135	136	137	138	139	140	141	142	143
144	145	146	147	148	149	150	151	152	153	154

Thus we can see that Shakespeare has signalled the presence of the third ring by its central sonnet being especially distinctive with its mysterious use of parentheses. Sonnet 98 is at the end of two rings which contained forty pairs of parentheses in thirty sonnets. The first ring contains fourteen sonnets with parentheses, the second ring contains sixteen sonnets with parentheses. There are just four pairs of parentheses in Sonnet 126, and no more in the entire final ring of sonnets 99–154, making a total of forty-four pairs in thirty-one sonnets.

The Third Chiastic Structure: The Hourglass Ring (99–154)

Using Sonnet 98 as a prologue links the second and third rings together. Saturn was the Roman God of sowing and harvesting as well as the turning point of the year, his festival being the Saturnalia when things were turned on their head, presaging the New Year (out with the old and in with the new). This sonnet moves from spring to summer and anticipates winter: the cycle of the year.

> From you have I been absent in the spring,
> When proud-pied April (<u>dressed in all his trim</u>)
> Hath put a spirit of youth in every thing:
> That heavy *Saturn* laughed and leapt with him.
> Yet nor the lays of birds, nor the sweet smell
> Of different <u>flowers</u> in odour and in hue,
> Could make me any summer's story tell:
> Or from their proud lap pluck them where they grew:
> Nor did I wonder at the <u>lily's</u> white,
> Nor praise the deep vermilion in the <u>rose,</u>
> They were but sweet, but figures of delight:
> Drawn after you, you pattern of all those.
> Yet seemed it winter still, and you away,
> As with your shadow I with these did play.

Sonnet 98 is related to Sonnet 99 through flowers, to midpoint Sonnet 126 through parentheses and italicised words, and to the ending sonnets 153–4 through Roman mythology: Saturn, Cupid and Diana. Saturn was the father of Jupiter; Jupiter was the father of Diana.

Imagery	Sonnet	Sonnet	Imagery
flowers, Lily's, Rose, sweet	98	99	sweet Lily, Roses, flowers
Parentheses and italics	98	126	Parentheses and italics
Saturn	98	153	*Cupid* (x2), *Dian(a)'s*
Saturn	98	154	Love-God, Nymphs

The third ring begins at Sonnet 99. This sonnet is unique in having fifteen instead of fourteen lines: perhaps the poet was signalling its special status as the start of the final ring. In Sonnet 99, the youth's many charms are absorbed by the thieving flowers. In Sonnet 126, the boy has grown to the height of his power, but is warned by the poet to be wary of Nature ('the sovereign mistress over wrack'), as she may surrender him to some undefined fate. Sonnet 126 is the turning point in this sequence where Nature, in Sonnet 127, loses her power to the Dark Lady, and, along with Time, is not referred to again as the poet turns his attention to this mysterious femme fatale. The sequence ends at Sonnet 154 when a boy (Cupid) becomes a victim of theft by a Dark (deceptive) Lady (Dyan's fairest votarist), who steals his love-charming brand in an attempt to quell its heat, absorbing it in a well, but the poet rekindles the flame in his mistress's eye (in the last line of sonnet 153), and the never-ending cycle of inspired love and attraction begins again. In Sonnet 100, *Satire* echoes *Saturn* in a sonnet about time and ageing. Time is an important theme in this ring, which at its heart has the hourglass shape created by the double parentheses of Sonnet 126 and the line, 'Time's fickle glass, his sickle, hour.' Sonnet 126 has twelve lines made up of six rhyming couplets, the numbers of which we can see in the number of the sonnet. This suggests the image of a clock face where the hour begins with the minute hand at 12, then sweeps downward to 6 at half-past the hour, before changing direction, and returning to the 12 at the end of the hour. This chiastic image is appropriate for this sonnet at the turning point in the ring, similar to the mirror image of 77.

Now we will explore the Hourglass Ring: _

Imagery	Sonnet	Number	Imagery
love's (x2), hand	99	154	love's (x2), hand
truth (x3), love, dumb	101	152	love (x2) truth (x2), blindness
love (x2), fair (x3), true (x3)	105	148	love (x2), fair, true (x3)
brain, divine, dust, dead	108	146	soul, divine, dross, dead
harmful deeds, pity (x3)	111	142	sin (x2), pity (x2), pitied
pity, ill, bad, world, dead	112	140	pity, deaths, ill (x2), world, bad
flattery (x2), true, bad, best, sin	114	138	truth (x2), lies (x2), best, false speaking, unjust, faults, flattered
wilfulness, prove	117	136	fulfil. *Will* (6), will fulfil, prove
losing ... win, spent	119	134	forfeit ... restore, lose, pays
befriends, hell, hard, crime, wounded bosoms, ransoms/ransom	120	133	wound, friend/friend's, harder, torment, bosom's, Prison, bail, Jail
vile (x2), false, deeds	121	131	false, deeds, slander
Time, present, past	123	129	Past (x2), before, behind
sweet, Nature, mistress, disgrace	126	127	Nature's, Sweet, disgrace, Mistress

→ **Midpoint turn** ↑

We can see links in the themes of these sonnets as well as in their vocabulary: as we have seen in Sonnet 99, the theft of the youth's charms by Nature is mirrored in Sonnet 154 and the theft of Cupid's arrow by a nymph. There are also contrasting pairs: Sonnet 101 invokes a Muse to praise a worthy boy, whereas Sonnet 152 regrets praise of an unworthy Lady. In Sonnet 103 the youth is too perfect for poet's justification; in Sonnet 150 the poet justifies the dark lady's imperfections. In Sonnet 117 the poet has 'hoisted sail to all the winds' in 'wilfulness'; in Sonnet 136, a *Will* sonnet, we find 'fill it <u>full</u> with <u>wills</u>'. This is subtly continued in Sonnet 118 where we find the word 'full', referring to over-eating which might make one 'ill', the poet attempting to prevent excessive attachment to the beloved. The paired Sonnet 135, however, counters this with excessive desire: the name *Will* occurring seven times ('Will' being a reference to the genitals). In sonnets 121, 122, 131 and 132 the poet sees good where others see bad. Other pairings have themes that mirror each other: in Sonnet 124 the poet qualifies his love for the youth, while in Sonnet 129 he qualifies his lust for the Dark Lady. In Sonnet 126 Nature is a threat to take away the youth's power; in Sonnet 127 the Dark Lady takes Nature's power.

Reflections on the Three Rings

Shakespeare's sonnets are peopled with three major characters: the fair youth, the rival poet and the dark lady. The fair youth is expounded upon in sonnets 1–126, the rival poet in sonnets 78–86 and the dark lady in sonnets 127–54. The rival poet sequence begins immediately following the midpoint turn (Sonnet 77) of the Looking Glass Ring and the dark lady sequence begins immediately following the midpoint turn (Sonnet 126) of the Hourglass Ring. There is a fourth character throughout the narrative, that being the poet of the sonnets, the person that keeps time, sows and harvests the characterisations of the other three and guides their entrances and exits. This circle of what is generally accepted to be two men, one youth and one woman happens to coincide with the only Roman gods present in the sonnets: *Mars, Saturn, Cupid* and *Diana*. The Looking Glass Circle begins with *Mars* and ends with *Saturn*; the Hourglass Circle begins with *Saturn* and ends with *Cupid* and *Diana*. The poet, describing himself as an older man, bears a resemblance to *Saturn* (keeping time). The rival poet can be compared to aggressive *Mars* (the proud full sail of his great verse bound for the prize, Sonnet 86); the dark lady to *Diana* (her heart eludes the speaker to the end) and the fair youth to *Cupid* (his eyes, like Cupid's bolts, continually piercing the speaker's heart).

Sonnets 77 and 126, the midpoint sonnets in the second and third rings, share the following words in common: 'Time's', 'minutes' and a 'glass' (a looking glass in sonnet 77 and an hourglass in Sonnet 126). A mirror reflects the self and the hourglass keeps its grains of sand in a chiastic format, where the first grains in are the last ones out and the last ones in are the first ones out. Time's minutes on a clock face are measured in a chiastic ring composition format as the minute hand begins at 12 and makes a complete sixty-minute revolution back to 12. Sonnet 77 also refers twice to a sundial on which the time is a shadow that follows the transit of the sun across the sky in a vast cosmic circle. In Sonnet 27, the central sonnet of the first ring, the time is night and the word 'shadow' occurs. Furthermore, midpoint turns of the second and third rings are underlined by the appearance of a new character in the sonnet sequence: at Sonnet 78 the rival poet, at Sonnet 127 the dark lady. These coincidences appear to substantiate the intentional character of the midpoint turns of the ring composition sequences. We have conducted checks on randomly selected sequences and, while some common significant words do occur in parallel sonnets, there are no significant beginning, ending and midpoint turns available in these random selections. These random checks provide evidence that what we have found is not the result of coincidence but of conscious design.

One consequence of this discovery is that we can now confirm that the first edition of *Shake-speares Sonnets* printed in 1609 was not a pirated edition brought out by a rogue publisher but was authorised, indeed carefully constructed, and published under the supervision of the poet. This confirms the work of Leyland and Goding who stated that the sonnets 'form a coherent whole'.[20] That Philip Sidney used chiastic forms, and these occur in classical sources, also points to Henry Neville's authorship because he knew Sidney, and was himself a classical scholar. Neville's knowledge of geometry and mathematics proves that he had an interest in numbers and circular forms. Given the weight of other evidence for Neville's authorship, we see the three rings in the sonnets are echoed by the three rings at the top left-hand corner of Neville's 1599 portrait at Audley End House and the three suns, the parhelion, that appear in Act 2, Scene 1 of *Henry VI: Part III*, to the three sons of Richard Plantagenet and Cecily Neville.[21] The three rings on the portrait are clearly stars and a reference to Neville's interest in astronomy; an interest Shakespeare also had as evident from the line in Sonnet 14 'I have astronomy'. While the occurrence of these astronomical circles might be dismissed as coincidence, we suggest they provide further evidence of a link between Neville, Shakespeare and the chiastic rings to be found in the sonnets.

Notes

Introduction

1. BBC website accessed 13 December 2014.
2. The books were removed from Neville's home at Billingbear in the nineteenth century. Billingbear burnt down in 1924.
3. Secretary script, italic and court hand.

Chapter 1

1. The best account of these anomalies is A. J. Pointon, *The Man Who Never Was Shakespeare: The Theft of Shakespeare's Identity* (2011). *The Spelling of Shakespeare's Name*, in John M. Shahan and Alexander Waugh, eds, *Shakespeare Beyond Doubt? Exposing an Industry in Denial* (2013), 14–28, is based upon chapters 1–3 of Pointon's book.
2. Performances at the royal palace at Greenwich on 26 and 28 December 1594 were paid for on 15 March 1595, to 'William Kempe, William Shakespeare & Richarde Burbage'. See Price, 2012, 31, for a discussion of this. In 1605, Augustine Phillips left 30 shillings in gold to his 'fellow William Shakespeare' in his will.
3. Pointon in Shahan and Waugh, op. cit., 27–8. See also F. E. Halliday, *A Shakespeare Companion* (Harmondsworth, 1964), 443–6.
4. Frank Davis, *Shakespeare's Six Accepted Signatures: A Comparison to Signatures of Other Actors and Writers of the Period*, in Shahan and Waugh, eds, ibid., 29–40. Park Honan, 'The Arden and Shakespeare Family Trees', in his *Shakespeare: A Life* (Oxford, 1999), 412–3.
5. The list of quartos with the name Shake-speare is created by consulting the title pages available on-line at: http://special-1.bl.uk/treasures/SiqDiscovery/ui/search.aspx accessed 15 February 2015.
6. James and Rubinstein, 2005, 205.
7. Honan, op. cit., *Shakespeare: A Life*, 43–5.
8. Steven Steinburg, in *I Come to Bury Shakespeare*, 2013, 200–11, points out that the curricula at English grammar schools in Shakspere's time varied considerably, with three (of four) grammar schools whose curricula are known to have been markedly less taxing and difficult than at St Bees School, which was used as the basis of T. W. Baldwin's well-known work, *Shakespeare's Smalle Latine and Lesse Greek* [sic] (1944), which is the basis of the notion that Stratford Grammar School had a remarkably comprehensive syllabus. We simply do not know the curriculum of the school in Shakspere's time.
9. Honan, op. cit., 44–5.

10. F. E. Halliday, op. cit., 141, and biographical information from the *Oxford Dictionary of National Biography (ODNB)*.
11. Cited in Ian Donaldson, Benjamin [Ben] Jonson (1572–1637), poet and playwright, *ODNB*.
12. ibid.
13. ibid. This was Sir Robert Cotton, 1st Baronet (1571–1631), described in his entry in the *ODNB* (by Stuart Handley) as an 'antiquary and politician'. In 1601, Cotton was commissioned by Henry Howard the younger, brother of the Duke of Norfolk, 'to write a tract demonstrating from precedent that the English ambassador to France, Sir Henry Neville, should take precedence over the envoy from Spain to Calais to discuss an Anglo-Spanish treaty'.
14. David M. Bergeron, Anthony Munday (1560–1633), playwright and translator, *ODNB*.
15. David Gunby, Cyril Tourneur (d. 1626), writer and soldier, *ODNB*.
16. Diana Price, *Shakespeare's Unorthodox Biography: New Evidence of an Authorship Problem* (Westport, Conn., 2012), 250–56. See also Stuart Gillespie, *Shakespeare's Books: A Dictionary of Shakespeare's Sources* (London, 2004).
17. Price, ibid., 254. Henry Neville's father was in Italy in 1554 as a Marian exile so might have bought a copy of the newly published *Il Pecorone* there.
18. Andrew Werth, Shakespeare's Lesse Greek, in *Report My Case Aright: The Shakespeare-Oxford Society, Fiftieth Anniversary Anthology, 1957–2007* (Yorkstown Heights, N.Y., 2007), 30–43. See also Martin Green, *Wriothesley's Roses* (Baltimore, 1993), 66–74.
19. David Kathman, Richard Field [Feild] (1561–1624), printer, *ODNB*.
20. David Kathman, *Shakespeare and Warwickshire*, in Paul Edmondson and Stanley Wells, eds, *Shakespeare Beyond Doubt: Evidence, Argument, Controversy* (Cambridge, 2013), 129.
21. Joseph Wright (1855–1930) had an academic career that was almost certainly unique at the time. His father was a poverty-stricken handloom weaver in a town near Bradford. Wright had no formal education in the conventional sense and began working at the age of six as a donkey boy, leading a donkey cart holding quarrymen's tools. He later attended night school, and, his extraordinary ability at languages being recognised, received a BA degree from London University and a doctorate from Heidelberg University. Most extraordinarily, Wright was appointed Professor of Comparative Philology at Oxford University in 1901, retiring in 1925. See Arnold Kellett, Joseph Wright (1855–1930), philologist and dialectologist, *ODNB*.
22. Ros Barber, *Shakespeare: The Evidence-The Authorship Question Clarified* (http://leanpub.com.shakespeare, 2014), 156.
23. Michael Egan in John M. Shahan and Alexander Waugh, eds, *Shakespeare Beyond Doubt? Exposing an Industry in Denial* (2013), 165.
24. Barber, op. cit., 156–205.
25. ibid., 191.
26. Egan, op. cit., citing A. J. Pointon, *The Man Who Was Never Shakespeare* (2001). See also Gary Goldstein, *Shakespeare's Native Tongue, DeVere Society Newsletter*, November 2009, available online.
27. Kathman, op. cit., 129.
28. Sidney Lee, *A Life of William Shakespeare* (London, 1899), 165–6.
29. Kathman, op. cit. To take another example, it has been suggested that the peculiar flow of the water under Clopton Bridge in Stratford-upon-Avon was being described by Shakespeare in *The Rape of Lucrece,* the Avon in flood there producing an eddy which forced the river to run backwards (Barber, op. cit., 146). But the parapets of the Clopton Bridge were raised significantly in 1696, and this phenomenon apparently long postdates Shakespeare. See Maurice Ribbans, *Clopton Bridge: A Short History of the Gateway to Stratford-upon-Avon* (Atlanta, Georgia., 2005), 13–14.
30. Richard Paul Roe, *The Shakespeare Guide to Italy: Retracing the Bard's Unknown Travels* (New York, 2011), 7–11.

31. Florio was born in London and lived as a child in an Italian-speaking Swiss town, but apparently never visited Italy itself. Desmond O'Connor, John Florio (1553–1625), author and teacher of Languages, *ODNB*.

32. Margaret Drabble, *Could the Plays Have Been Written By Someone Who Never Left England?* in Shahan and Waugh, eds, op. cit., 178.

33. See Ernesto Grillo, *Shakespeare and Italy* (Glasgow, 1949) and Naomi Magri, *Such Fruits Out of Italy: The Italian Renaissance in Shakespeare's Plays* (Buchholz, Germany, 2014). Dr. Magri's work notes that the author of the plays *must* have seen the paintings described in his plays as a first-hand eyewitness.

34. Alexander Waugh, *Keeping Shakespeare Out of Italy*, in Shahan and Waugh, eds, op. cit., 73.

35. Diana Price, *Shakespeare's Unorthodox Biography: New Evidence of an Authorship Problem*, 108–9.

36. F. E. Halliday, *A Shakespeare Companion* (Harmondsworth, 1964), 520.

37. ibid., 424.

38. Park Honan, Henry Wriothesley, 3rd Earl of Southampton (1573–1624), courtier and literary patron, *ODNB*; idem., *Shakespeare: A Life* (Oxford, 1999), 192.

39. Halliday, op. cit., 43.

40. *Brief Lives* was not published in any form until 1813, and not in full until the mid-twentieth century.

41. Halliday, op. cit., 42–3.

42. Honan, *Shakespeare*, op. cit., 61.

43. See Pointon, 2011, 79.

44. Price, op. cit., 112–160.

45. The best discussion of this topic is Richard F. Whalen, *The Stratford Bust: A Monumental Fraud*, in Shahan and Waugh, eds, op. cit., 136–51.

46. ibid., 137.

47. David Kathman, *Shakespeare and Warwickshire*, in Paul Edmondson and Stanley Wells, eds, *Shakespeare Beyond Doubt: Evidence, Argument, Controversy* (Cambridge, 2013), 131.

48. Tanya Cooper, *Searching For Shakespeare* (London, 2006), 51.

49. See Whalen, op. cit., 147–50 for a long list of such writers.

50. From http://en.wikipedia.org/wiki/Gerard_Johnson_(sculptor) accessed 28 January 2015.

51. ibid., 140.

52. ibid., 141.

53. ibid., 142–3. Greene was an important scholar of Shakspere's life who was the first to read the Stratford records for such events as Shakspere's baptism and was also the first non-contemporary to read his will, in 1747.

54. See Hanna Roisman, *Nestor the Good Counsellor*, *Classical Quarterly*, Vol. 55 (2006), 17–38.

55. Whalen, R. (2013), 139–40.

56. Pointer, 2011, 131, makes this point, suggesting that what he 'hath writ' would have meant a blank 'page'.

57. Line 3 in Sonnet 77.

58. See the many papers and book on this topic by Dean Simonton, e.g., *Genius and Creativity: Selected Papers* (Santa Barbara, 1997), and the discussion in Steven Steinburg, *I Come to Bury Shakespeare* (2013), 69–83.

59. Shakspere's daughter Susanna signed her name, as if copying it, on just one mortgage document over thirty years after her father's death. His other daughter, Judith, was certainly illiterate, using a mark instead of a signature on just one document in 1611.

Chapter 2

1. Rollett, 2015, 122.

2. ibid, Chapter 29.

3. Titherley, 1952.
4. Jowett, 2011, 352.
5. Rollett, 2015, in Chapter 8, suggested that Shakespeare's plays were revised by someone after Shakspere's death in preparation for the First Folio and that as Derby was alive he could have been responsible for these revisions.
6. Devised by John Casson in 2012.
7. 1613 is also the date of Neville's last extant letter.
8. James and Rubinstein, 2005, 163.
9. There are further links between Southampton and *Love's Labour's Lost* outlined by Woudhuysen who detected evidence of the rivalry between the Essex/Southampton grouping at court and Sir Walter Raleigh's School of Night. He also noted that Gervase Markham published a pamphlet in 1598 referring to a joke in *Love's Labour's Lost*. 'Markham was closely involved with the Earl of Southampton and the tract was published by William White, who was also responsible for the first quarto of the play' (Woudhuysen, 2001, 70, 78).
10. Sawyer, 1725, Vol 3, 467
11. Stopes, 1922, 362; Casson, 2009, 219.
12. Sawyer, 1725, Vol 3, 475
13. Titherley, 1952, 284.
14. See for example a comparison between Neville's trial statement of 1601 and 4 letters by Oxford in Bradbeer and Casson, 2015, Chapter 10.
15. Rollett, 2015, Chapter 27.
16. From the History of Parliament website: http://www.historyofparliamentonline.org/volume/1604-1629/member/neville-sir-henry-iii-1588-1629 (accessed 27/12/13)
17. See Williams, R. (2012) *Sweet Swan of Avon: Did a Woman Write Shakespeare?* Santa Fe, Wilton Circle Press.
18. For the full list of subscribers to the Second London Virginia Company see: http://www.learner.org/workshops/primarysources/virginia/docs/svc.html accessed 13/2/2015.
19. Bliss, 2004.
20. See Casson, 2010, 74–5.
21. See Bradbeer and Casson, 2015.
22. James and Rubinstein, 2005, 50.
23. Keen and Lubbock, 1954.
24. Worsley MSS 47 in the Lincoln Archives.
25. Keen and Lubbock, 1954, 127: Section on Henry IV, f.iv[a].
26. ibid, 148. Henry V, f.xlvi[b]. The Hall annotator here spells 'son' with a double 'nn': 'sonne'. The Annotator of Worsley MSS47 likewise writes 'sonne' and this is the preferred spelling in the First Folio: 'sonne' occuring 555 times, 'son' just 68 times (Crystal, 2008, 62).
27. ibid, 129. Henry IV, f.xii[a].
28. ibid, 147–9. Henry V, f.xliii[b], f.xlviii[a], f.l[b].
29. See Casson, 2010, Chapter 4.
30. See: http://collation.folger.edu/2012/03/spectral-imaging-of-shakespeares-seventh-signature/ accessed 13/2/2015.
31. Burgoyne, 1904, xvi.
32. The NHMS contains documents written in 1580, 1584, 1589, 1592, 1595, 1596 and lists *The Isle of Dogs*, a play written in 1597.
33. Burgoyne, 1904, xiv.
34. Before this date no play had been officially identified as by Shakespeare though *A Groatsworth of Wit* had hinted that *Henry VI: Part III* was by 'Shake-scene'.
35. Neville's great grandmother, Elizabeth Blount, may have met Erasmus as her cousin, William Blount, 4th Baron Mountjoy, was a scholar and student of Erasmus, and the man

responsible for bringing him to England (David Ewald personal communication, e-mail 22/2/13).

36. Bate, 2001, 9; 83; 87; 100.
37. See: http://en.wikipedia.org/wiki/Anthony_Fitzherbert accessed 27/6/12.
38. Casson, 2010, 167.
39. A recently discovered set of poems were signed 'W. Sh[K]R.' but this is believed to be in the hand of John Marston: see Peter Levi's (1988) New Verses by Shakespeare, London, Macmillan. The poems were for a wedding masque.
40. For a fuller list of all the Nevilles in the History plays see Bradbeer and Casson, 2015.
41. Bartholomew Keckermann's *Manduction to Theology*.
42. Manductio ad Artem Rhetoricam, first published in 1621.
43. Schurink, 2006, 73; see also: http://www.philological.bham.ac.uk/vicars/intro.html accessed 21/2/14. The full text of the passage is:

> Quo quidem in loco recenset ille poetas quosdam, quorum & numeros & laudavere sales nostri, & de quibus forsitan non immerito Anglia nostra gloriatur, Galfridum Chaucer, Edmundum Spencerum, Michael Draytonium, & Georgium Withersium Istis annumerandos censeo celebrem illum poetam qui à quassatione & hasta nomen habet, Ioan. Davisium & cognominem meum, poetam pium & doctum Ioan. Vicarsium. Ex quibus ego (neque enim affectum possum dissimulare plurimum semper sum delectatus Draytonio. Cuius libellum Heroic. Epsitolarum ad imitationem Ovidi: conscriptum, cum ego ante multos muliesiam annos perlegissem, taleis mihi assumpsi spiritus, ut Poeta repente prodirem, versusq istos, quos nunc subjicio, in laudem autoris protinus effutirem.

This has been copied from the 1628 volume in the British Library: BL11805.a.11. Our emphasis is underlined. Here below is a translation made available to us by L. S. Deas:

> In that place, indeed, that man lists certain poets, whose measures and wit our friends have praised, and about whom, perhaps not undeservedly, our England boasts: Geoffrey Chaucer, Edmund Spenser, Michael Drayton and George Wither. To be added to them, I consider, is that famous poet who from shaking and spear takes his name; John Davis and my namesake, the virtuous and learned John Vicars. Out of those (for I cannot hide my preference) I am charmed most by Drayton. His little book of Heroic Letters, composed in imitation of Ovid - when I read it through many years ago, I took such inspiration from it, that I immediately emerged as a poet, and forthwith blabbed out the very lines I now submit, to the praise of the author.

44. Nicholas van Maltzahn, Henry Neville (1620–94), politician and political writer, *ODNB*.
45. Casson, 2010, 34.
46. James and Rubinstein, 2005, 69. Neville was elected to Parliament in 1584. If he had been born in 1564, he would have been aged nineteen or twenty when elected. While there are precedents for election younger than twenty-one, it was more likely that he was twenty-two or twenty-three when first elected. If he was only thirteen in 1577, he was arguably too young to go on the European tour with Savile.
47. ibid, note 22, 315.
48. See Bradbeer and Casson, 2015, 10.
49. James, 2011, 91. The manuscript is in the library at Audley End House where Neville's books were moved from Billingbear in the nineteenth century.
50. Savile is said to have been appointed as Elizabeth I's resident in the Low Countries (the Netherlands) during this time.
51. See the Tower Notebook, 1602–3, Worsley MS 40 in the Lincoln Archives.
52. Duncan, 1974, 215: Kew National Archives, PRO/SP/14/43/22.

53. ibid, 224.
54. ibid, 230.
55. See James, 2011, 23–9.
56. Duncan, 1974, 270.
57. See Whitelocke's Liber Famelicus: http://archive.org/stream/liberfamelicus00camduoft#page/46/mode/2up accessed 24/2/2015.
58. Duncan, 1974, 275 referring to Whitelocke's Liber Famelicus. Neville sent Whitelocke a Christmas present of 'a side of a doe' in 1613 see: http://archive.org/stream/liberfamelicus00camduoft#page/32/mode/2up accessed 23/2/2015.
59. Showerman, 2013, 108.
60. Bradbeer and Casson, 2015, 186.
61. Goulding, 2004, *ODNB*
62. Duncan, 1974, 232: Kew Archives, PRO/SP/14/74:44.
63. Price, 2012, 276.
64. Bradbeer and Casson, 2015, 73.
65. *Ptolemiæi Astronomi*, dated 1538, about the Celestial Geometry of Ptolemy (32.A.4), is now in Merton College Library, Oxford.
66. William was born in 1596 in Mayfield, Kent. He went to Merton College, Oxford, in 1609, aged thirteen and was later a Fellow of Merton. He became a civil lawyer, rising to doctor in 1633, and was an Advocate of Doctors' Commons in 1634. He was appointed Chancellor of the Commissary Court of Chichester. He married Katherine Billingley in 1618. William died in 1640 and his will was proved in the Prerogative Court of Canterbury.
67. See Bradbeer and Casson, 2015.
68. See James and Rubinstein, 2005, xviii.
69. This is shown in a genealogical table in Sir E. K. Chambers' *William Shakespeare*.
70. Rubinstein, 2012, 146.
71. Worsley MSS 47, 36 and the copy in the Northumberland Manuscript (see Casson, 2010).
72. See Chapter 12 of Bradbeer and Casson, 2015.
73. Casson, 2009, 161.
74. Price, 2012, 225.
75. Whitt, 1932, 161.
76. Burgoyne, 1904, xvii.
77. ibid, 50. The letter is on folio 44–5 of the NHMS. The letter concerns the queen's proceedings towards Catholics and Protestants and explain these to a French recipient.
78. Sawyer, 1725, Vol 1, 229.
79. Spedding, 1890, Vol 2, 347: available online at: https://archive.org/stream/lettersandlifef04spedgoog#page/n362/mode/2up accessed 3/2/2015.
80. See Bradbeer and Casson, 2015, 197–8.
81. Milton, 2005, 59.
82. Bradbeer and Casson, 2015, Chapter 11.
83. See Whitelocke's *Liber Famelicus*: http://archive.org/stream/liberfamelicus00camduoft#page/46/mode/2up accessed 24/2/2015.
84. Fernie, 2002, 173.
85. ibid, 228.
86. We are grateful to Mark Bradbeer for this information: personal communication, email 1/3/2015.
87. *Venus and Adonis* was entered into the Stationers' Register on 18/4/1593. Richard Stonley bought a copy on 12 June 1593 (Schoenbaum, 1987, 176).
88. Casson, 2009.
89. ibid.
90. For a comprehensive list of the documentary references to William Shakspere see Pointon, 2011, 269.

Timeline

1. Plays including a character named Falconbridge (a Neville family name) are marked with *.
2. In both *King Lear* and *A Yorkshire Tragedy*, both of which fall into this period, the legitimacy of children is an important issue.
3. Overbury and Rochester codename Neville 'Similis' because he looked like Henry VIII (Somerset, 1997, 90). Sir Edward Neville, his grandfather, also looked like the king. The masque in *Henry VIII* is in at Wolsey's house.
4. The two signatures on the Blackfriars deed and mortgage are: 'William Shaksper' and 'Wm Shakspea'.
5. The three signatures on the will are: 'William Shackspere', 'Willm. Shakspere' and 'By me William Shakespeare': the last may be partly in a different hand, a legal clerk?

Chapter 3

1. Roe, 2011, 5.
2. Rowse, 1962, 90.
3. The canal to Milan had been completed in 1573, just eight years before Neville's visit: Roe, 2011, 47.
4. See the map in Roe, 2011, 34.
5. The other two plays are *King John* in which Cardinal Pandulph, the papal legate, is from Milan and *The Tempest*: Prospero was duke of Milan.
6. On 16 September 1581, Throckmorton reported in his diary that he had 'set out from the George in Venice and cam into the boote [boat] at 12 at night and saylled all the rest of the nyght.' Canterbury Cathedral Archives, Vol 1.
7. Grillo, 1949, quoted by Roe, 2011, xiv.
8. From http://en.wikipedia.org/wiki/Villa_di_Pratolino accessed 23/1/2015.
9. From http://en.wikipedia.org/wiki/Michel_de_Montaigne accessed 23/1/2015.
10. A translation is available by Donald Frame, 1983.
11. Goulding, R.D., (2004) Oxford Dictionary of National Biography.
12. Sawyer, 1725, Vol 1.
13. Roe 2011, xiii.
14. Sawyer, 1725, Vol 2, 78, 399
15. Woolfson, 1998, 138.
16. Levith, 1989, quoted by Roe, 2011, xiv.
17. Neville's Remembrances are dated 3 February 1602 so they may be actually 3 February 1603, due to the old style calendar in which the new year started at the end of March. They are at Berkshire Record Office: D/EN/F45/1–2.
18. Throckmorton was in Pisa in December, arrived at Genoa on 2 January 1582, travelled via Turin, then into France, through Orleans, arriving on 26 January in Paris and crossing the channel from Boulogne on 1 February. Arthur Throckmorton's diary, Canterbury Cathedral Archives, Vol 1.
19. On Saturday 10 September, 1580, Throckmorton recorded that 'Savelle, Robert Sydney, Henry Nevell … we lay at the golden goose' in Nuremburg.
20. Duncan, 1974, 16.
21. Spurgeon, 2001, 110.
22. Manuscript at Hatfield House.
23. Berkshire Records Office: D/EN/F43.
24. 'Arras counterpoints' are to be found in *The Taming of the Shrew* of 1594 (Act 2, Scene 1) but the other words are in the First Folio revised version.
25. Morris, 2004, 215, footnote.

26. Bate, 2001, 128, 159, 178.
27. ibid, 33.
28. ibid, 126.
29. 'Rhodope's pyramis' is mentioned in *Henry VI: Part I* (1.6.22): this pyramid is in Bulgaria: the ancient area of Thrace from whence Orpheus came.
30. Amphion.
31. Piscis here meaning fish, refers actually to a dolphin.
32. This translation is based on Moore's 1965 and Kline's 2001 versions with corrections by Casson.
33. Roe, 2011, 80, 83, 84.
34. {Inserts by the original author written above the line are in curled brackets.}
     This 1603/4 letter is D/EN F6/2/3, stored at the Berkshire Record Office, Reading.
35. Roe, 2011, 71.
36. Yong's translation was completed in 1583 but not published until 1598 in Brooks, 1990, lxiv.
37. This phrase means 'the new kingdom of Granada'. This was an entity in the Spanish possessions in the New World corresponding to present day Colombia and Venezuela (Mike Baynham, personal communication 8/9/14).
38. Sawyer, 1725, Vol 1, 127.
39. Duncan-Jones, 1991, 171; Casson, 2009, 49.
40. Foakes, 2005, xi.
41. White, 1980, 7.
42. Dorsch, 2004, 9.
43. Thompson and Taylor, 2006, 318.
44. Cambridge University Library: MSS Dd. 3. 63, on folio 50 verso. James and Rubinstein, 2005, 246.
45. Londre, 1997, 329.
46. Francis Bacon and France, notes by Peter Dawkins for Shakespeare Authorship Trust Conference 2014.
47. McQuain and Malless (1998) suggested that the word 'academe' is a Shakespeare coinage and that the Bard drew on ancient Greek for the word. Neville could read and write Greek and had books in Greek.
48. 'About the positive nurture and structure necessary for young French gentlemen.'
49. Neville's great-grandmother, Elizabeth Blount, may have met Erasmus as her cousin, William Blount, 4th Baron Mountjoy, was a scholar and student of Erasmus, and the man responsible for bringing him to England (David Ewald e-mail 22/2/13).
50. Woudhuysen, 2001, 224.
51. ibid, 194.
52. From: http://en.wikipedia.org/wiki/Antonio_P%C3%A9rez accessed 10/1/2015.
53. Ungerer, 1976, Vol 2, 388.
54. ibid, Vol 2, 219. Ungerer also speculated that Neville practised his Spanish with Perez, 229.
55. Sawyer, 1725, Vol 1, 121.
56. Ungerer, 1974, Vol 2, 267.
57. ibid, Vol 1, 259.
58. He sent copies to Southampton, Essex, William Cecil, Charles Blount, Robert Sidney, Henry Howard and Henry Wotton.
59. Marrapodi, 2007, 65–7.
60. Stopes, 1922, 128.
61. Armitage, Condren and Fitzmaurice, 2009, 104.
62. Rollett (2015) makes a case for William Stanley, 6th Earl of Derby, being Shakespeare and asserts that he may have witnessed the events in 1582 that lie behind the play but he was not in France in 1578, as Neville was.
63. Hunt, 1992, 2.

64. ibid.

65. Bate, 2006, 21.

66. Hadfield, 2005.

67. Peck, 183/*121*.

68. The volume is unmarked so we cannot know whether Neville read it. The shelf mark is (21. DD.6).

69. See Bradbeer and Casson, 2015.

70. Bate, 2006, 219.

71. Casson, 2010.

72. Peck, 100/*69*.

73. ibid, 75/*54*.

74. Henry IV fxxii[b], Keen and Lubbock, 1954, 130.

75. Casson, 2010, 74.

76. Sawyer, 1725, Vol 1, 161.

77. ibid, Vol 1, 21, 86, 98.

78. Stowe, 174, f.116, British Library.

79. Sir Henry Neville's letter is D/EZ138/1 at the Berkshire Records Office, Reading.

80. Laoutaris, 2014, 111–12.

81. See Casson, 2010, 213, 216.

82. Keen and Lubbock, 1954, 128.

83. Gibbons, 2004, 35.

84. After a period in France Charles Danvers returned to England and was caught up in the Essex rebellion. Neville met Danvers and the Earl of Southampton in the events that led up to the rebellion. For his part in the debacle Danvers was beheaded.

85. Gibbons, 2004, 31 note.

Chapter 4

1. The first quarto of *Henry VI: Part II* was titled *The First Part of the Contention betwixt the two famous Houses of Yorke and Lancaster with the death of the good Duke Humphrey* and published in 1594 in the anonymous period of Shakespeare's career.

2. This letter can be found in Burgoyne, 1904.

3. James and Rubinstein, 2005 and Casson, 2010.

4. See Pointon, 2011, for a clear exploration of this.

5. Readers who wish to read more detail about the Neville authorship of the history plays should consult Bradbeer and Casson, 2015.

6. James and Rubinstein, 2005, 60.

7. Bradbeer and Casson, 2015.

8. Worsley MSS 47 was discovered by Brenda James at the Lincoln Archives. In a major study Casson confirmed her conclusion that this manuscript was by Neville and was a source for the history plays. See: Casson, 2010, 32.

9. Bradbeer and Casson, 2015, 22–7.

10. Peck, 160/*107*.

11. ibid, 218, 220.

12. In *The Troublesome Raigne* Elinor says the will 'barres the way …' This spelling with the double 'r', as in Neville's annotations of Worsley MS 47, supports the suggestion that *TR* is an earlier version of *KJ* and that Neville was involved in the writing (see Bradbeer and Casson, 2015) and so this was Shakespeare's earliest history play, although it was revised later. In *The Troublesome Raigne* Arthur and his mother Constance repudiate this testament, suggesting it is a forgery by Elinor and not valid. We find just such an argument over Henry VIII's will in *Leicester's Commonwealth*. Indeed, one of the signatories of that

disputed testament was none other than Sir Henry Neville (Neville's father). This reference to Henry VIII's will is in a discussion about foreign birth being a bar to succession. The authors state that 'Arthur ... was declared ... lawful heir apparent ... though he were born in Bretaigne out of English allegiance' (Peck, 160/*107*).

13. Neville and his father were both royal foresters.
14. We are grateful to Hilary Elstone for making us aware of Ralph Neville in this context. See: http://en.wikipedia.org/wiki/Ralph_Neville accessed 8/4/15.
15. Bradbeer and Casson, 2015, 17–18. Other Nevilles hidden behind titles in the history plays are shown in Table 2, 20.
16. Worsley MSS 40 is in the Lincoln Archives.
17. Bradbeer and Casson, 2015, 19.
18. Sawyer, 1725, Vol 1, 51, 112.
19. Casson, 2010, 265.
20. From: http://routopedia.com/what-routes-are-right-for-me/about-mayfield/mayfield-gunfoundry/ accessed 8/7/15. We are grateful to David Ewald who pointed this out to us.
21. See Bradbeer and Casson, 2015, 22.
22. Here we see a clear example of Neville's tendency to write 'Knig' instead of 'King'.
23. Globe Theatre programme note for their 2015 production of *King John*, page 4.
24. Peck, 91.
25. Keen and Lubbock, 1954, 128.
26. D/EN F6/2/3, stored at the Berkshire Record Office, Reading.
27. HERE LYETH BURYED Sʳ HENRY NEVILL KNIGHT. DESCENDED OF THE NEVILLS BARONS OF ABERGAVENNY WHO WERE A BRANCHE OF THE HOWSE OF WESTMORELANDE.
28. Sawyer, 1725, Vol 1, 89.
29. Casson, 2010, 77–8.
30. Peck, 179/*118*.
31. In *King Lear*, 5.3.18.
32. Peck, 188/*124*.
33. ibid, 188/*124*.
34. Warren, 2003, 29.
35. Peck, 124.
36. ibid, 151/*101*.
37. Casson, 2010, 97.
38. Bradbeer and Casson, 2015, 112.
39. Duncan, 1974, 209.
40. Bradbeer and Casson, 2015, 113.
41. Gillespie, 2004, 265.
42. It has been dated to *c.* 1600 by previous scholars. However, Casson found it was written on paper watermarked 1603: the date is very clear on the last sheet but the same watermark can be seen on the dedication page and folios 3 and 15.
43. Additional MS 29307.
44. Sydney Papers, ed. Collins, 1746, ii. 132.
45. Kincaid, 1977, v–vi.
46. See Bradbeer and Casson, 2015, 190.
47. The word 'statistes' might be understood as statesmen, state employees or politicians: those who run the modern state as opposed to the hereditary nobility, the traditional powers in the land.
48. Casson, 2010.
49. Whitt, 1932, 161.
50. See Bradbeer and Casson, 2015, 178.
51. Stopes, 1922, 313.

52. Green, 1993.
53. Bradbrook, 2005, 94.
54. Laoutaris, 2014, Family Tree of Elizabeth Russell at the front of the book.
55. Prior, 1993, 261.
56. British Library, Lansdowne MSS: Number 65 item 64.
57. Melchiori, 1998, 58.
58. James and Rubinstein, 2005, 83 and available on line at http://www.philological.bham. ac.uk/eedes/
59. Melchiori, 1998, 58, 104, 138.
60. ibid, 58; 138.
61. Tillyard, 1944, 121–1 quoted by Sams, 1996, 165.
62. Mortimer, 2008, 353, 375.
63. Keen and Lubbock, 1954, 127.
64. Nicholls and Williams, 2011, 125.

Chapter 5

1. See Chapter 4, note 4.
2. Keen and Lubbock, 1954, 137.
3. For more examples of this pro-Neville bias see Bradbeer and Casson, 2015.
4. Scoufos, 1079, 129.
5. Humfreys, 1966, 129, footnote.
6. Bradbeer and Casson, 2015, 59.
7. In the first quarto of *Richard II* the same spelling is used.
8. See Casson, 2010, 65–72.
9. Crystal, 2008, 62.
10. The abbreviated name 'Hen:' is down inside the binding, impossible to photograph but clear enough for a careful reader to see.
11. Peck, 178/*117*.
12. Keen and Lubbock, 1954, 130–1.
13. ibid, 135.
14. ibid, 130.
15. James and Rubinstein, 2005, 120.
16. William from Stratford's father, John Shakspere, did not die until 1601.
17. Bradbeer and Casson, 2015, 66.
18. Keen and Lubbock, 1954, 135.
19. ibid, 135.
20. See Bradbeer and Casson, 2015, 60.
21. James, 2011, 150.
22. Scoufos, 1979, 131.
23. James, 2011, 153: Sawyer, 1725, Vol 1, 229.
24. Sawyer, 1725, Vol 1, 88.
25. ibid, 93.
26. ibid, 115.
27. ibid, 121.
28. Bradbeer and Casson, 2015, 69–71.
29. Sawyer, 1725, Vol 1.
30. ibid, 38.
31. Though not named, there is an allusion to James I in *Henry VIII* (5.4.41–54).
32. Sawyer, 1725, Vol 1, 274.
33. ibid, 82.

34. ibid, 84.
35. ibid, 92.
36. ibid, 102 and 156.
37. See Bradbeer and Casson, 2015, 82–8.
38. Keen and Lubbock, 1954, 137.
39. 'Exposition' is used by the Bard in *Henry IV: Part II* (4.2.7) and four other plays.
40. It is spelt 'Salicke' in the 1600 quarto.
41. Keen and Lubbock, 1954, 136.
42. Casson, 2010, 37, 76, 73–94.
43. Donaldson, 2011, 87.
44. On 10 May 1600 he referred to Cuffe in a letter to Cecil (State Papers at the National Archives, Kew, SP 78/44/110).
45. Translation: 'Services are welcome so long as it seems possible to requite them: when that stage is left far behind, the return is hatred instead of gratitude.'
46. Daniell, 1998, 369, 330.
47. See http://en.wikipedia.org/wiki/Quintus_Antistius_Labeo accessed 6/9/14
48. See Bradbeer and Casson, 2015, 21.
49. Brooks, 1990, xxxiv.
50. Sawyer, 1725, Vol 1, 34.
51. ibid, 74.
52. ibid, 161.
53. Wine, 1973, 82. The word also occurs in *Arden of Faversham* which Casson, 2009, suggested was an early play by Neville.
54. Berkshire Record Office: D/EN/L2/1.
55. Cairncross, 1976.
56. Sawyer, 1725, Vol 1, 101.
57. The First Folio spelling in *The Winter's Tale* is 'Seue'night'.
58. Sawyer, 1725, Vol 1, 55.
59. ibid, 104.
60. ibid, 123.
61. ibid, 141.
62. Ashridge is near Neville's former estate in Mayfield, Sussex: James and Rubinstein, 2005, 324.
63. James and Rubinstein, 2005, 131.
64. British Library: MS Mus. 1591.
65. Though referred to as both a duke and a count Orsino is specifically called 'Count Orsino' in 1.5.101; 3.1.102; and 3.4.336.
66. James and Rubinstein, 2005, 132.
67. Sawyer, 1725, Vol 1, 292.
68. ibid, 267.
69. ibid, 274.
70. McClure, 1939, 51, 63.
71. The names Sebastian and Antonio recur as villainous courtiers in *The Tempest* in a way that points to Neville's family motto (see Chapter 10).
72. There are two copies of this letter: one is a draft which is complete and stored at the National Archives, Kew, PRO 30/50/2 folio 104. The copy that was posted was burnt at the edges in a fire at Ashburnham House, 23 October 1731 and so is incomplete. It is to be found in the British Library, Cotton Manuscripts, Caligula EX folio 21 (see Casson, 2010, appendix 8). In the full version of this one letter Neville used ten words that occur only in one play, amounting to 1.29 per cent of the total 772 words. This is a high percentage indeed when compared with ten of his letters, dated between 1599 and 1613, which have percentages between 0.71 per cent and 1.29 per cent. (The average percentage in all ten

letters is just 0.98 per cent.) These rare words range from the earliest to the last plays. The words are: 'Rochester' in *Henry IV: Part I* (1.2.125); 'acknowledgment' in *Henry V* (4.8.120); 'prejudicial' in *Henry VI: Part III* (1.1.144: the speaker is Richard Neville); 'inconvenience' in *Henry VI* part 1 (1.4.14); 'clothiers' in *Henry VIII* (1.2.32); 'recommend' in *Coriolanus* (2.2.150); 'viciousness' in *Antony and Cleopatra* (3.13.112); 'prohibit' in *Much Ado About Nothing* (5.1.320); 'congratulate' in *Love's Labours' Lost* (5.1.81); 'presenting' in *The Merchant of Venice* (2.9.55).

Chapter 6

1. William Green, *Shakespeare's Merry Wives of Windsor* (Princeton, N. J., 1962), 17–18, citing two antiquarian works about Windsor by Robert Tighe and James Edward Davis (1858) and by T. Eustace Harwood (1929). Green's valuable work is unduly neglected.
2. Olwen Hedley, *Windsor Castle* (London, 1994), 92.
3. ibid., 93.
4. ibid. Sadly we have not been able to trace this manuscript.
5. In the inventory of Sir Henry Neville, who died in 1593, there is a list of his cattle including 'twelve kyne whereof one with a calf' (Berkshire Record Office: D/EN/F43).
6. Windsor: see http://en.wikipedia.org/wiki/Windsor,_Berkshire accessed 7/2/2015. See also John Stoughton, *Windsor: A History and Description of the Castle and the Town* (London, 1862). The first regular coach service between London and Windsor only began in 1673. (P. H. Ditchfield and William Page, eds, *Victoria County History: A History of Berkshire, Volume 3*, London, 1923).
7. Green, *op. cit.*, 42. Alice-Lyle Scoufos, in her *Shakespeare's Topological Satire* (Athens, Ohio, 1979), 212, notes that William Dethicke, Garter King of Arms at the time, stated that 'the Queene begunne service' at the Garter Knights' Installation ceremony on 6 June 1599. As with the 1597 Installation, there is no evidence that Elizabeth was there more than a day or two, and no evidence that any play was performed on this occasion. Moreover, according to T.W. Craik in his Introduction to the Oxford edition of *The Merry Wives*, 'she was not present at the installation' in 1599. (T.W. Craik, ed., 1990, 10.)
8. Similarly, neither of the two best-known alternative candidates to have written Shakespeare's works, Edward De Vere, 17th Earl of Oxford and Sir Francis Bacon, had any close connections with Windsor or Berkshire; neither was a Knight of the Garter. De Vere hired rooms in Windsor from 1569 to 1570 when he was recovering from an illness, but this was thirty years before *The Merry Wives* was written; he had no known subsequent links with the town. See Mark Anderson, *Shakespeare By Another Name: The Biography of Edward De Vere, Earl of Oxford, The Man Who Was Shakespeare* (New York, 2005), 40.
9. From 1589 to 1597 Neville was MP for Mid-Sussex, and from 1597 to 1601 was MP for Liskeard in Cornwall. Alan Harding, Henry Neville (1562–1615), in W. Hasler, ed., *The History of Parliament: The House of Commons, 1558–1603* (London, 1981), available online at: http://www.historyofparliamentonline.org/volume/1604-1629/member/neville-sir-henry-i-1564-1615 accessed 7/2/2015.
10. Ramon Jiménez in Shahan and Waugh, 2013, 167.
11. Binfield – The Centre of Windsor Forest, in Royal Berkshire History, available online at: http://www.berkshirehistory.com/villages/binfield.html accessed 7/2/2015.
12. Sawyer, 1725, Vol 3.
13. The three documents in the Berkshire Record Office, Reading are: D/EN/O30: an order for felling oaks for use at Windsor Castle, 1582; D/EN/012/19: a letter from Lord Howard of Effingham re: house in Windsor Castle; D/EN/Z3: a petition to HN from Richard Hinde, linen draper of Newbury, for help of Sir Henry Savile in persuading the Dean and Canons of St George's Chapel, Windsor, to grant a renewal of a lease, *c*. 1603. The catalogue

is available online at: http://www.berkshireenclosure.org.uk/CalmView/Overview.
aspx?s=Henry+Neville accessed 7/2/2015.

14. *Ptolemiæi Astronomi*, 32.A.4
15. 21.DD.6
16. Duncan, 1974, 79, 84–5.
17. ibid., 76
18. Berkshire Record Office: D/EN/F43. The words 'bucking tubs' are to be found in *Locrine* which was first published in 1594 as by 'W.S.' but may date back as far as 1585 (Casson, 2009, 100). In the play Strumbo is a happy cobbler whose first speech is a comic tour de force. Strumbo speaks of his tears as plenteous as 'the water runneth from the buckingtubs' (1.3.11). He describes himself as: 'a gentleman of good fame and name, majestical, in parrel comely, in gate portly ... a proper tall, young man of a handsome life ...' (1.2). This sounds like a self-portrait of Neville, who, in 1587, was aged twenty-five or twenty-six. The word 'portly' occurs just 7 times in the canon, two of which are used by Falstaff to describe himself: firstly in *Henry IV* part 1, as 'A goodly portly man,' (2.4.416); in *The Merry Wives of Windsor* he speaks of 'my portly belly' (1.3.59). As he composes a love letter to Dorothy, Strumbo says, 'I will dite an aliquant love-pistle' (1.3.28). Gooch (1981, 59) suggested this was a pun on a Spanish wine from Alicante and the word 'eloquent'. This very same pun is used in *The Merry Wives of Windsor* by Mistress Quickly, when she is talking to Falstaff about courtiers sending love letters to Mistress Page: 'in such alligant terms, and in such wine and sugar ...' (2.2.65). The link with wine is made immediately. Strumbo tells his servant Trompart to 'carry this letter to Mistress Dorothy' (1.3.64). In *Merry Wives* Falstaff also writes love letters. He tells Nim to 'bear thou this letter to Mistress Page;' and instructs Pistol 'and thou this to Mistress Ford' (1.3.69). Just as Falstaff here has an interest in two wives, so Strumbo has two wives in *Locrine*. Strumbo speaks of 'the little god, nay the desparate god Cuprit' (1.3.14), while Falstaff evokes 'Cupid a child' (*Merry Wives*: 5.5.28). Falstaff calls Quickly, 'my good she-Mercury' (*Merry Wives of Windsor* 2.2.76). Humber calls Strumbo, 'Mercury in clownish shape' (4.3.75).

 If *Locrine* was written ten years before Falstaff appeared we can see here the younger version of that great mountain of a character! It seems impossible that Shakespeare would copy so many of the words and mannerisms of a minor comic character in an anonymous play: Strumbo is like Falstaff because he is the idea of such a character germinating in the Bard's imagination. The latest possible date for *Locrine* is 1594–5, when it was published. The earliest date for the Falstaff plays (*Henry IV: Part I* and *Part II* and *The Merry Wives of Windsor*) is 1596.

19. This theory derives from Leslie Hotson, *Shakespeare versus Shallow* (London, 1931).
20. Elizabeth Schafer, The Date of the *Merry Wives of Windsor*, *Notes & Queries* 236, n.s. 38 (1991), 57–60, cited in Lukas Erne, *Shakespeare As Literary Dramatist* (Cambridge, 2013), 110.
21. In Melchiori's excellent Introduction to the third Arden edition of the play (2000, 12).
22. ibid., 22. On the other hand, as David Lindley has pointed out, 'Shakespeare, after all, unlike Beaumont, Chapman, or Jonson, never - as far as we know - provided the text for an entertainment at court.' David Lindley, Blackfriars, Music and Masque: Theatrical Contexts of the Last Plays, in Catherine M. S. Alexander, ed., *The Cambridge Companion to Shakespeare's Last Plays* (Cambridge, 2009), 39.
23. Sawyer, 1725, Vol 1, 51.
24. ibid. Vol 1, 83.
25. ibid. Vol 1, 121; 160.
26. ibid. Vol 1, 26.
27. James, 2008, 66.
28. Melchiori, 2000, 148, note.
29. The use of italics for *Will* is in the 1609 printing.

30. See: http://en.wikipedia.org/wiki/William_Garrard accessed 7/2/2015. William had a brother Francis and his name appears on the frontispiece of a volume of Erasmus' *Adagiorum Chiliades* at Audley End.
31. Sawyer, 1725, Vol 1, 160.
32. ibid, Vol 1, 183.
33. Melchiori, 2000, 26, note.
34. John Chamber's Latin poem to Henry Neville: 1599

> EIVSDEM.
> AD ILLVSTRISS. VIRVM
> DOMINVM HENRICVM NE-
> uillum Sereniss. Reginæ Elizabethæ ad
> Galliarum Regem legatum.
> ET *genus & proauos numeros licet ordine lòngo*
>   *Principis ut pateant atria celsa tibi.*
> *Nil tamen in tantâ fortunâ tanta meretur,*
>   *Quam virtutis honos, ingenijque decus.*
> *Quo tua cuncta regis, quo tanta negotia tractas,*
>   *Quo fugiens terras sydera lœtus adis.*
> *Sydera lœtus adis, vbi te tua plurima virtus*
>   *Æternans superis afferit ante diem.*
> *Et superasse parum terras, vulgúmque videris,*
>   *Te nisi musarum personet alma cohors,*
> *Musa dedit varias artes, dedit ore rotundo*
>   *Fundere quœ Velles, culta Thalia tibi.*
> *Te docet Euclides, fontes elementáque pandens,*
>   *Téque Pelusiachus ducit ad astra senex.*
> *Nec sic contentus, manes, cinerémque sepultum*
>   *Barlaami Monachi sollicitare soles.*
> *Non ego iam quantum memoro, quotiésque rogasti*
>   *Illius vt prœlo subdere scripta velim.*
> *En igitur tandem Monachi tibi scripta, typorum*
>   *Verbere, iam doctum docta referre sonum.*
> *Quod nisi Savillus prior hac in laude fuisset,*
>   *Deberet Barlaam iam sua λύτρα tibi.*
> *Námque tuis monitis pariter, paritérque rogatu*
>   *Musa viri superest, quœ peritura fuit.*

     We have modernised all Elizabethan long ∫ into s; have mostly modernised u into v, though some v must be u (as in 'ut').

35. Chamber named this Muse as Thalia.
36. 'Ore rotundo' literally means 'from a round mouth'. Here there is an echo of Horace: 'Graiis dedit ore rotundo Musa loqui', from *De Arte Poetica* 323–4.
37. John Chamber used the word 'Velles', the imperfect subjunctive. The 'Velis' in 'Ne Vile Velis', Neville's family motto, is present subjunctive, a polite imperative: 'May you wish'.
38. Ptolemy, the astronomer, lived in Alexandria, at the mouth of the Nile. The Pelusiac was the Eastern most branch of the Nile Delta and the city of Pelusium was at its mouth. The Pelusia was a festival in honour of Isis celebrating the Nile flooding. Neville owned a book on Ptolemaic celestial geometry (dated 1538) which is in the library of Merton College Oxford (32.A.4). It is annotated by Neville in Latin and Greek.

39. Carleton referred to 'Illa quidem maioribus attolenda cothurnis' which we translated as 'Who would deny that these should not be further exalted on stage in Tragedy?'. For the relevant text of Carleton's poem see Bradbeer and Casson, 2015, 176–7.

40. Bradbeer and Casson, 2015, 177.

41. We are grateful to L. S. Deas for this translation which is from E. C. Wickham's 1903 volume.

42. William Oldys (1696–1761) claimed to have heard and recorded the 'bitter Ballad' written by Shakespeare against Lucy from a 'very aged gentleman' who lived at Stratford and died around 1700. It begins 'A parliement member, a justice of peace, At home a poor scare-crowe, at London an asse …' How this 'aged gentleman' (who could not have been born much before 1610) came to know and precisely remember the 'bitter Ballad', allegedly written about twenty-five years before he was born, is unclear.

43. S. M. Thorpe, Sir Thomas Lucy (before 1532–1600), in Hasler, ed., *The History of Parliament, op. cit.* There are a number of errors in this passage, such as that Aubrey first set down the story. The wording used in the play (at 1.1.4) is 'in the County of Gloucester' not 'come from Gloucestershire'.

44. 'A Star Chamber Prosecution for Deer Stealing By a Sir Thomas Lucy', in *Notes & Queries* (series 3) xii (September 7, 1867), 181–2.

45. Schoenbaum, 1987, 198.

46. Hotson, *Shakespeare versus Shallow, op. cit.*, 29. This is the same work in which Hotson proposed the 1597 Garter Installation as the play's première.

47. 'William Gardiner (1531–97)' in Hasler, ed., *op. cit.*

48. ibid: 'Liskeard Borough'.

49. ibid: 'Helston Borough' and 'Lostwithiel Borough'.

50. Armstrong, 1963, 170.

Chapter 7

1. On Essex, see Robert Lacey, *Robert, Earl of Essex: An Elizabethan Icarus* (London, 1971); Paul E. J. Hammer, *The Polarisation of Elizabethan Politics: The Political Career of Robert Devereux, 2nd Earl of Essex, 1585–1597* (Cambridge, 1999); Alexandra Gajda, *The Earl of Essex and Late Elizabethan Political Culture* (Oxford, 2012). See also Paul E. J. Hammer, 'Robert Devereux, 2nd Earl of Essex (1565–1601), soldier and courtier,' in the *ODNB*. The classic work which introduced Essex to many was Lytton Strachey, *Elizabeth and Essex: A Tragic History* (London, 1928).

2. Duncan, 1974, 166; Spedding, 1890, Vol 2, 348

3. See Paul E. J. Hammer, 'Henry Cuffe (1562/3–1601), classical scholar and secretary to the Earl of Essex,' *ODNB*.

4. ibid.

5. Owen Lowe Duncan, 'The Political Career of Sir Henry Neville: An Elizabethan Gentleman at the Court of James I,' unpublished doctoral dissertation, Ohio State University (1974), 151.

6. Spedding, 1890, Vol 2, 345 and Duncan, 1974, 162. Duncan thought the reference by Neville to the 'back gate' suggested a clandestine meeting with Neville being especially secretive. This would suggest he was like one of the conspirators in *Julius Caesar*. However it is not possible now to determine for sure what the reference to the back gate means and where it was: on the Strand, onto the river Thames or into a side street, possibly Milford Lane, see: http://mapco.net/london/1677arundelhouse.htm (accessed 20/7/2015).

7. ibid., 162–3.

8. ibid., 167–9.

9. It has been argued that this performance was actually of a work by Sir John Hayward, *The First Part of the Life and Raigne of King Henry IV,* (1599) which also deals with Richard II.

But Hayward's was a prose work, not a play. As Sir E. K. Chambers argued convincingly, this must have been a performance of Shakespeare's *Richard II,* since it was given by the Lord Chamberlain's Men. The request was not initially well-received because 'it was so old and out of use' that it could not readily be put on. But while *Richard II* dates from 1595, Hayward's prose work was written only in 1599. (It was, however, dedicated to Essex.) Claims by the queen that *Richard II* was performed forty times seem highly dubious, given the limited time frame. After Essex's rebellion, when members of the Lord Chamberlain's Men - but *not* Shakspere himself - were questioned by the authorities, none was arrested, presumably because they were simply following instructions. The play was not regarded as seditious in and of itself, since it had been performed many times before. (See E. K. Chambers, *William Shakespeare: A Study of Facts and Problems, Volume I* (Oxford, 1930), 354–5.

10.   Duncan, op. cit., 173–4.

11.   ibid., 173.

12.   ibid.

13.   Ernest Dowden (1843–1913), an Irish Protestant, was Professor of English Literature at Trinity College, Dublin. His unusually perceptive and pioneering studies of Shakespeare deserve renewed attention.

14.   Dowden, Shakspere, op. cit., 280.

15.   ibid.

16.   An important neglected work by Robert Boies Sharpe, *The Real War of the Theaters: Shakespeare's Fellows in Rivalry With the Admiral's Men, 1594–1603* (Boston, Mass., 1935) argued that the two main acting companies, the Lord Chamberlain's Men and the Lord Admiral's Men, had identifiable political allegiances, the former – Shakespeare's company – supporting Essex, the latter supporting Cecil and the 'Establishment'. If this view is accurate, Neville must have used his long-standing connection with the Lord Chamberlain's Men to strengthen his ties with the Essex circle, and had all the more reason to keep his identity a secret. The Lord Admiral's Men was under the patronage of Charles Howard, Earl of Nottingham (1536–1624), who commanded the English fleet which defeated the Spanish Armada. It was headed by Edward Alleyn, and put on plays by Marlowe, Heywood, and Jonson among others, and was just as prestigious as the Lord Chamberlain's Men.

17.   See Park Honan, *Shakespeare: A Life* (Oxford, 1999), 169–95.

18.   Neither the Earl of Oxford nor Sir Francis Bacon, the two leading alternative Authorship candidates, had any reason to be adversely affected by Essex's execution, let alone in a clearly traumatic way, as both were his strong opponents. Bacon was one of the prosecuting barristers against Essex at his trial, while Oxford was the foreman of the jury of peers in the House of Lords which tried Essex and Southampton, and condemned both to death. In the case of Oxford there is the additional consideration that Oxfordians do not believe that the accepted chronology of Shakespeare's plays is accurate, and that *Hamlet* was actually written many years earlier. As things stand, Oxfordians have no coherent alternative chronology which accounts either for the demonstrable evolution of Shakespeare's works in general or the author's traumatic response to Essex's rebellion and its failure in particular. Some Oxfordians have argued that Southampton was Oxford's son by Queen Elizabeth which is patently absurd.

19.   Mark Nicholls and Penny Williams, 'Sir Walter Raleigh (1554–1618), courtier,' *ODNB.*

20.   ibid.

21.   See: http://en.wikipedia.org/wiki/Charles,_Duke_of_Orl%C3%A9ans accessed 15/10/2014

22.   In Thomas Nashe's prefatory Epistle to Robert Greene's *Menaphon.*

23.   Jolly, 2014.

24.   ibid, 162.

25.   *Hamlet and the Scottish Succession,* Cambridge University Press, 1921: Lilian Winstanley (1875–1960) was a senior lecturer in English Literature at the University College of

Wales–Aberystwyth (now the University of Aberystwyth). Her book, it should be noted, was published by Cambridge University Press. This section of her work drew in part on an older work by Edward Abbott (1838–1926), *Bacon and Essex* (1877). Abbott, a true polymath, is best-known as the author of *Flatland* (1884), the famous mathematical fantasy about a two-dimensional world. He was headmaster of the City of London School, the well-known public school. His best-known pupil was Herbert Asquith, the future Prime Minister. Another product of his school at that time was Sir Sidney Lee (1859–1926), the second editor of the *Dictionary of National Biography,* who wrote the *DNB*'s entry on William Shakespeare.

26. These words are not in the first quarto version, so Jolly's suggestion that this was an earlier version revised by Shakespeare in 1600–1 confirms the validity of Winstanley's observation. The words are in the 1604 second quarto which must therefore be Shakespeare-Neville's revision of 1601.

27. Although every recent standard edition of *Hamlet* discusses the date it was written, not one mentions this parallel. Bradbeer and Casson (2015) show there are also connections between Essex's final speech and that made by Buckingham in *Henry VIII*.

28. The first quarto was recorded in the Stationers' Register on 26 July 1602, the entry in the Register stating that 'it was lately acted by the Lord Chamberlain his servants' and it was printed in 1603. Bringing the first version out before the revised version may have been aimed at capitalising on the early version and ensuring the revision was not seen to be too obviously referring to Essex. When the revised version (Q2) did finally appear in print, in 1604, James I was safely settled on the throne and Neville released from prison. Q2 was further revised for the First Folio.

29. See Ann Thompson and Neil Taylor, Introduction to the third Arden edition of *Hamlet* (London, 2006), 47–59.

30. The story of Amleth was first told in a work *Historia Danica* by Saxo Grammaticus (*c.* 1150–*c.* 1206). The earliest translation into English was in 1894. Saxo was Belleforest's source for the tale and it is clear that Shakespeare relied on Belleforest.

31. See Jolly, 2014, 184.

32. A second theme highlighted by Winstanley is the parallel with the Scottish succession crisis under Darnley and Mary, Queen of Scots, as well as its suggestion that it is also about the succession to the throne by James VI of Scotland after Queen Elizabeth – hence the title of her work. In light of what we now know of who wrote it and why, these parallels seem less clear and central, if they exist at all. It seems very doubtful that Neville had anything but the Earl of Essex's rebellion in mind when writing *Hamlet,* given the fact that he had just been imprisoned for taking part in it.

33. Winstanley, *op. cit.,* 139.

34. ibid., 140.

35. ibid., 142.

36. ibid., 145.

37. Bradbeer and Casson, 2015, 72.

38. Winstanley, 153–4.

39. ibid., 154. As a leading Court official and friend of Essex and his inner circle, Neville might well have been able to read this letter, or been told of its contents, perhaps via Sir Henry Killegrew, Cuffe, Southampton or Robert Cecil. It is inconceivable that William Shakspere could have been privy to a letter from these sources, which he must have necessarily have read between May 1600 and mid-1601.

40. These words only appear in the First Folio version: perhaps it was only after his release that Neville was able to add the references to prison. This is in line with trauma studies which show that it is only after a traumatic period is over that a person can reflect on their experience.

41. Spurgeon, 2001, 121, 318, 133.

42. ibid, chart VII, at the end of the book.
43. ibid, 131.
44. Sawyer, 1725, Vol 2, 17.
45. From: http://en.wikipedia.org/wiki/Tade%C3%A1%C5%A1_H%C3%A1ljek accessed 7/2/2015.
46. Goulding, (2004) *ODNB*.
47. Armitage, Condren & Fitzmaurice, 2009, 145.
48. ibid, 147.
49. See Bradbeer and Casson, 2015, Chapter 10, for a full analysis.
50. Sawyer, 1725, Vol 1, 183.
51. James, 2008, 213.
52. James, 2011, 302 and note 224.
53. Jost, 2012.
54. James and Rubinstein, 2005, 164.
55. See Bradbeer and Casson, 2015, Chapter 10.
56. The poem is signed by 'William Shake-speare', perhaps because Neville, by using the mysterious hyphen, wanted to hint the name was a pseudonym, given his status as a state prisoner. See Boris Borukhov, 'R. Chester's *Loves Martyr* and the Hyphenated Shakespeare', *Notes and Queries*, Volume 58 (2) 2011, 258–260. (Of course Borukhov regards the Stratford man as the poem's author.) Borukhov argues persuasively that the signature 'Shake-speare' was authorial, that is, that it was signed by the author himself as a hyphenated name. He does not address the question of why the Stratford man would sign his own name in this bizarre manner. If he regarded the poem as dangerously controversial just after Essex's rebellion, surely he would have published it anonymously.
57. See John Roe, in his Introduction to *The Poems* [of Shakespeare] (Cambridge Shakespeare, updated edition, 2006), 41.
58. Richard McCoy, 'Loves Martyrs: Shakespeare's *Phoenix and the Turtle* and the Sacrificial Sonnets', in Claire McEachern and Debra Shugar, eds, *Religion and Culture in Renaissance England* (Cambridge, 1997), cited in Roe, 1998, 77.
59. Roe, 1998, 53.
60. ibid., 43.
61. 'Salusbury, Sir John (*c.* 1565–1612) of Lleweni, Denbighshire', in W. Hasler, ed., *The History of Parliament: The House of Commons, 1558–1601* (London, 1981), online. (Salusbury was an MP from 1601 to 1604.) Although the 1601 date for his knighthood has been questioned, it is the year stated in this authoritative source. See also his briefer entry in A. D. Carr, 'The Salusbury family (*c.* 1454–*c.* 1684), gentry', in the *ODNB*, which gives the same date for his knighthood and states that he 'was knighted as a result' of his anti-Essex activity.
62. He was certainly not the Robert Chester of Royston, Hertfordshire suggested by Grosart and by a number of recent commentators. See Boris Borukhov, 'Was the Author of *Loves Martyr* Chester of Royston?' *Notes and Queries*, Volume 56 (1) 2009, 77–81.
63. See Carleton Brown, Poems By Sir John Salusbury and Robert Chester (London 1913).
64. Roe, 1998, *op. cit.*, 44, n.4. Another theory is that Shakspere had once worked for the acting company of Lord Strange, later Lord Derby, the real father of Salusbury's wife, and thus Shakspere would have had some contact with Salusbury's family. Sir John Salusbury had matriculated at Jesus College, Oxford in 1581 (aged fourteen) and so could have met Neville at the University as the latter returned from his travels in Europe in 1582.
65. Roe, 1998, 48–50.
66. The third Arden edition is dated 1999.
67. E. A. J. Honigmann, 'Appendix I: Date', in *Othello* (third Arden edition, London, 2003). Jonathan Bate and Eric Rasmussen, eds, *William Shakespeare: Complete Works* (London, 2007), 2,085, argue for 1604 as the date when the play was written, noting that it apparently uses Knolles's *Historie of the Turkes*, published in late 1603, as a source, but point out (ibid.) that 'some scholars argue for a slightly earlier date'. 1604 is possible, perhaps revised by

Neville shortly after he left the Tower, although an earlier date is consistent with what we now know. The earliest known performance of the play (as *The Moor of Venis*) was in November 1604. It was not entered into the Stationers' Register until 1621, after which it was published in quarto form in 1622.

68. A. C. Bradley, *Shakespearean Tragedy: Lectures on Hamlet, Othello, King Lear, Macbeth* (London, 1905), 175.
69. Hammer, *ODNB*
70. Spedding, 1890, Vol 2, 344.
71. Honigmann, Introduction, op. cit., 33.
72. ibid., 50–2
73. Hammer, 'Henry Cuffe', *ODNB*, op. cit.
74. Cuffe's book was written in manuscript form in 1600, but only published posthumously in 1607. If Shakspere had written *Othello* in 1602, he could not have read the published work, and it is plainly most unlikely that he would have read Cuffe's work in manuscript or have had any real knowledge of his intimate character. There is no evidence that the two men ever met whereas we know Neville met Cuffe many times.
75. Honigmann, *op. cit.*, 368.
76. Ben Jonson's *Masque of Blackness*, 1605, also used blackness as a metaphor.
77. Roe, R., 2011, 166.
78. Sawyer, 1725, Vol 1, 93, 118, 124, 126.
79. Honigmann, 2003, 2.
80. Ambassage (not embassage) is the spelling used in the first 1609 printing of Sonnet 26.
81. Sawyer, 1725, Vol 1, 250.
82. Honigmann, 2003, 3.
83. James, 2011, 17.
84. Spedding, 1890, Vol 2, 346.
85. See: http://www.historyofparliamentonline.org/volume/1604-1629/member/lewknor-sir-edward-ii-1587-1618 accessed 11/10/2014.
86. Duncan, 1974, 233.
87. James and Rubinstein, 2005, 336.
88. On the following pages of the Henry IV section, f.xi[a/b]; f.xii[a/b]; f.xvi[a/b]; f.xvii[a/b].
89. Casson, 2010, 92.
90. Sawyer, 1725, Vol 1, 77.
91. ibid, Vol 1, 84, 232.
92. ibid, Vol 1, 168.
93. D/EN F6/2/3, stored at the Berkshire Record Office, Reading.
94. Sawyer, 1725, Vol 2, 35. Neville's sister Katherin Doyle wrote to him on 30 January 1599 (1600) inviting him to visit her in Norfolk but saying, 'I fear the gout will be so troublesome unto you that you will not undertake so longe a journy': Berkshire Record Office: D/EN/F6/2.
95. See: http://en.wikipedia.org/wiki/Othello#Date_and_text accessed 20/7/11.
96. In the First Folio (1623) the word is 'mamm'ring' while in the Second Quarto (1630, 43) it becomes 'mam'ring'.
97. Duncan, 1974, 193.
98. Bate, 2001, 131.
99. Palmer, 1982, 65.
100. ibid, 71.
101. Spurgeon, 2001, 323.
102. Sawyer, 1725, Vol 1, 232.
103. MSS at Hatfield House Library, Salisbury Collection.
104. Palmer, 1982, 312.
105. According to his biography, see: http://www.historyofparliamentonline.org/volume/1604-1629/member/neville-sir-henry-i-1564-1615 accessed 12/10/2014.

Chapter 8

1. From *Englandes Mourning Garment* (recorded in the Stationers' Register on 25 April 1603), cited in Chambers, *William Shakespeare*, Volume 2, 189. It appears that Chettle, the alleged author of *Greene's Groatsworth of Wit* of 1592, did not know the real identity of William Shakespeare in 1603. Chettle – about whom surprisingly little is known – wrote for the Lord Admiral's Men, and had no known connection with the Lord Chamberlain's Men. His date of death is unknown, and he was described as 'sweating and blowing, by reason of his fatnes'. (Emma Smith, Chettle, Henry (d. 1603x7 [*sic*]), printer and playwright, *ODNB*, online).
2. Daugherty, 2010, 45.
3. Cited in Charlotte Carmichael Stopes, *The Life of Henry, Third Earl of Southampton, Shakespeare's Patron* (Cambridge, 1922), 259–60.
4. Duncan, op. cit., 189.
5. Park Honan, Wriothesley, Henry, 3rd Earl of Southampton (1573–1624), courtier and literary patron, *ODNB*, online. The farming of customs on sweet wines allowed Southampton to hire someone to collect import duties on sweet wines, with most of the revenues coming to him.
6. ibid.
7. N. W. Bawcutt, Introduction to *Measure for Measure* (Oxford Shakespeare, Oxford, 1991), 2.
8. Sawyer, 1725, Vol 2, 17.
9. Bawcutt, op. cit., 1.
10. The term 'problem play' was first applied to these works by Frederick S. Boas in his *Shakespeare and His Predecessors* (London, 1896).
11. Brian Gibbons, Introduction to the New Cambridge Shakespeare (Cambridge, 1991), 2.
12. John Masefield, *William Shakespeare* (London, 1912), 176.
13. Rosalind Miles, *The Problem of Measure for Measure* (London, 1976), 125.
14. ibid., 13–14.
15. Halliday, *Shakespeare Companion,* op. cit., 444.
16. Sawyer, 1725, Vol 2, 35.
17. ibid, Vol 1, 130.
18. Lever, 1989, xxxi.
19. Sawyer, 1725, Vol 2, 25.
20. McClure, 1939.
21. James and Rubinstein, 2005, 165–9.
22. James, 2008, 347.
23. Stanley Wells and Gary Taylor, William Shakespeare: *A Textual Companion*, originally Oxford University Press, 1987; reprinted by W. W. Norton, New York, 1997.
24. Bate and Rasmussen, op. cit., 587.
25. Salisbury MSS, 1910, 268.
26. The pairs of words 'hath made' and 'made me' occur separately (not 'hath made me' in one phrase).
27. Neville wrote, 'So as I have not only sold mine owne land, but made over my freends, to satisfy her Matie presuming that so solemne an agreement, would have bin as sure for me as for other in the like kinde now till I have <u>my pardon</u>, I can neither give my freends any recompence for the land which they have made over for me, nor receave mony for the land I have sold of mine owne.' (Our emphasis underlined.)
28. This letter is probably to Robert Cecil.
29. The other two being *Love's Labour's Lost* and *Titus Andronicus*.
30. Literature Online database.
31. These include reverence, importune, fully, freely, express, speech, conscience, witness, offence, proceedings, deserved, entertain, knowledge, inclined, presence, poverty, vice,

especially, fault, whatsoever, grown, requiring, bestowed, implore, modesty, hopeful, somewhat, difficulties, approbation, recompense, licence, likewise, enriched, acknowledge, disposition, boldness, imposed, granted, better, state, body, enriched, keeping, favours, service, means, desires, satisfied, content, charge, gracious, restrained, testimonies, stir, poor, without, help, cure, water, power, suffer, continue, conceive, example, respect, public, bonds, merit, hereafter, honest, mind, humbly, pardon, commandment, assured, liking, comfort and 'Compound with', 'mine own', 'this instant'.

32. Snyder, 1998, 20.
33. Wells and Taylor, op. cit., 126–7.
34. Alexander Leggatt, Introduction to *All's Well That Ends Well* (Updated edition, New Cambridge Shakespeare, Cambridge, 2003), 11.
35. ibid., 10.
36. G. K. Hunter, ed., *All's Well That Ends Well* (Arden edition, London, 1967), xxiii and xxv. A date of 1604–5 is also supported by Susan Snyder (p. 24) in the Oxford (1998) edition of the play.
37. Halliday, *Shakespeare Companion*, op. cit., 29.
38. Hunter, op. cit., xxv.
39. Roe, 2011, 189–215.
40. Woolfson, 1998, 130.
41. Sawyer, 1725, Vol 1, 175.
42. ibid, Vol 2, 35.
43. The manuscript is in the British Library: Harley MS 7368.
44. Simpson (1820–76) was an Anglican clergyman who then became a Roman Catholic and a magazine editor; he was convinced that Shakespeare was a secret Catholic. The provenance of the *Sir Thomas More* manuscript before 1728 is unknown. It was first published in 1844, before the identification of Hand D with Shakespeare was made.
45. Edward Maude Thompson, *Shakespeare's Handwriting: A Study* (Oxford, 1916), 200.
46. The other contributors to the volume were W. W. Greg, J. Dover Wilson, and R. W. Chambers, all leading Shakespeare scholars.
47. See Casson, 2009.
48. T. H. Howard-Hill, ed., *Shakespeare and Sir Thomas More: Essays on the Play and Its Shakespearean Interest* (Cambridge, 1989), which contains essays by eight scholars; John Jowett, ed., *Sir Thomas More* (third Arden edition, London, 2011).
49. Crystal, 2008, 38.
50. See the discussion of this matter in Gary Taylor, *The Date and Auspices of the Additions to Sir Thomas More,* in Howard-Hill, ibid., 101–30. Taylor suggests that the 1603 version of the play was actually a revival by the King's Men of the old Lord Admiral's Men's play. Some scholars also believe that the portion of the play written by Hand C may also have been composed by Shakespeare, although written out by a scribe.
51. The NHMS is available online and in Burgoyne, F. J. (1904) Collotype Facsimile and Type Transcript of An Elizabethan Manuscript preserved at Alnwick Castle, Northumberland, London, Longmans, Green and Co.
52. The letter was written to Robert Cecil on 19 February 1601 (the very day of the Earl of Essex's trial and the day after Augustyne Phillypps was interrogated about the performance of *Richard II* before the rebellion) when Neville was at Rochester on his way back to his ambassadorship in France (see Casson 2010, 265–7). It is in the Cotton Manuscripts, Caligula EX folio 21, at The British Library. It was damaged in a fire in 1731 so some of the text is missing. However, Casson discovered a draft copy of the letter which is complete amongst Neville's diplomatic papers in the National Archives at Kew (PRO 30/50/2 folio104), enabling him to reconstruct the whole letter.
53. This letter was written to Robert Cecil on 31 July 1602, while Neville was imprisoned in the Tower of London. This is in the collection of manuscripts of the Marquis of Salisbury at Hatfield House (Salisbury MSS, 1910, 268).

54. Neville's letter of 1603-4 is an undated draft to be found in a collection of Neville papers catalogued as D/EN F6/2/3, stored at the Berkshire Record Office, Reading.
55. Dawson, 1990, 128.
56. Berkshire Record Office: D/EZ/138/1.
57. Melchiori, 1998, 175.
58. Crystal, 2008, 35.
59. Casson, 2010, 90.
60. see Casson, 2010, 87-91.
61. Weis, 2010, 56.
62. 'Imbecility' only occurs in *Troilus and Cressida* (1602).
63. 'Privity' is unique to *Henry VIII* (1613).
64. 'Disability' is unique to *The Two Gentlemen of Verona* (1590? but not printed until 1623).
65. Sawyer, 1725, Vol 1, 89, 254, 287.
66. Yelverton XXXIX, MS 48035, f.41V, British Library.
67. Casson, 2010, 85.
68. Sawyer, 1725, Vol 1, 20.
69. Stowe, 174, f.116, British Library.
70. See Casson, 2010, 65-72.
71. We are grateful to Dr. Andrea Clarke Curator of Early Modern Historical Manuscripts at the British Library for confirming this in an email received 5/10/11.
72. Jowett, 2011, 363, note 5.
73. Sawyer, 1725, Vol 1, 176 and 177.
74. See Casson, 2010, 167.
75. R. A. Foakes, Introduction to *King Lear* (third Arden edition, London, 1997), 92.
76. N. M. Fuidge: Ansley [Anslowe], Brian (d. 1604), of Kidbrooke and Lee, Kent, in W. Hasler, ed., *The History of Parliament: The House of Commons, 1588-1603* (London, 1981), online. The will of Annesley (the name as given in that document) was probated for a second time in the Prerogative Court of Canterbury on 3 December 1604. The references to this entry and its quotations are all to official records, especially those of the Court of Wards. Ansley had two surviving daughters; a third daughter, Audrey, had died in 1591.
77. John Ferris and Rosemary Sgroi, Hervey [Harvey], Sir William I (c. 1565-1642) of Soberton, Hants. and The Strand, Westminster; later of Kidbrooke, Kent, in Andrew Thrush and John Ferris, eds, *The History of Parliament: The House of Commons, 1604-1629* (Cambridge, 2010), online. In this entry, his wife is referred to as Cordelia. This man should not, of course, be confused with Sir William Harvey, who discovered the circulation of blood.
78. ibid.
79. See also Bradbeer and Casson, 2015, 64.
80. Foakes, op. cit., 92.
81. Simon Adams, 'Sir Robert Dudley (1574-1649), mariner and landowner,' *ODNB*, online.
82. ibid.
83. ibid.
84. M. R. P. [*sic*],Sidney, Robert (1563-1626), of Penshurst, Kent, in Hasler, ed., *The History of Parliament*, op. cit.
85. ibid.
86. Alan Harding, Sir Henry Neville II (c. 1575-1641) of Birling, Kent, in Hasler, op. cit.
87. M. R. P., Sir Robert Sidney, op. cit.
88. Gloucester and his two sons, Edgar and Edmund, are a reprise of the two Falconbridge brothers, Robert and Philip, legitimate and bastard, in *King John* but as these two names occur in *The Troublesome Raigne* perhaps this use of the Sidney brothers' names is merely a coincidence.
89. Sawyer, 1725, Vol 2, 35.

90. It might be noted that if these two incidents were used in writing the play, as appears likely, this eliminates the Earl of Oxford as a possible Authorship candidate, since he died in June 1604.
91. Foakes, op. cit., 91–2.
92. Sawyer, 1725, Vol 2, 216.
93. ibid, 411.
94. He may have passed through Dover in 1578 on setting out on his European tour with Savile and again in 1582 on their return.
95. Wells and Taylor, op. cit., 128–9.
96. ibid., 128.
97. ibid.
98. ibid.
99. Abergavenny, Marquesses of, *Burke's Peerage* (1999 edition) available on-line. The 'mormaers' were territorial magnates, the equivalents of Earls in England. See also Nick Aitchison, *Macbeth: Man and Myth* (Stroud, 1999), 17–19.
100. Iain Wright, Gwinne, Matthew, physician and playwright, 1558–1627, *ODNB*, online, citing Anthony Nixon's *Oxford Triumph* (1605).
101. ibid.
102. ibid. Gwinne wrote plays for performance at Oxford, not by the London theatre companies. St John's College, Oxford, which Gwinne attended, had a strong tradition of theatrical performances. It is not too far-fetched to speculate that this may have influenced the young Neville. It might also be noted that, if the 1605 pageant was a formative influence on the writing of *Macbeth*, its author could not have been the 17th Earl of Oxford, who died in June 1604.
103. Davies, 2010, 134.
104. Clark, 1981, 177.
105. Thomas, 2014, 150.
106. Clark, 1981, 119.
107. Swayer, 1725, Vol 1, 249.
108. ibid, Vol 1, 271.
109. Sawyer, the editor of the letters, translated these code numbers to identify what they mean. Neville's letters contain other examples.
110. Sawyer, 1725, Vol 1, 274.
111. Clark, 1981, 14–18, 181, 187.
112. Casson, 2010, 83–4.
113. All other references between 1611 and 1624 are to Tygresse, Tigers (the plural) and spell 'Hyrcan' with a 'y'.
114. Brooke, 1998, 158.
115. In the 1595, 1600 and 1619 quartos of *Henry VI* part 3 'Hycania' is spelt 'Arcadia'.
116. Anthony B. Dawson and Gretchen E. Minton, eds, *Timon of Athens* (third Arden edition, London, 2008), 12.
117. Wells and Taylor, op. cit., 128.
118. H. J. Oliver, ed., Introduction to *Timon of Athens* (Second Arden edition, London, 1963), xli.; E. K. Chambers, *William Shakespeare*, Volume One, op. cit., 483.
119. Jowett, 2004, 20 footnote.
120. Oliver, 1963,. Xiii–xiv.
121. Wells and Taylor, op. cit., 127.
122. ibid.
123. Andrew Thrush, Sir Henry Neville I (1564 [*sic*]–1615) of Billingbear, Waltham St Lawrence, Berks., and Tothill Street, Westminster in Andrew Thrush and John Ferris, eds, *The History of Parliament: The House of Commons, 1604–1629* (Cambridge, 2010), online.
124. Halliday, *Shakespeare Companion*, op. cit., 444–5.

125. Dixon Wecter, *The Purpose of Timon of Athens, Publications of the Modern Language Association* (1928), cited in Oliver, Introduction, op. cit., xxiii.

126. ibid. The exclamation mark is in the original.

127. Wecter claimed (p. 707) that the parallel between Timon and Essex was 'so transparent … that the play was mutilated shortly after its composition when a contemporary event, the trouble over Samuel Daniel's *Philotus,* demonstrated that a public vindication of Essex would still be politically offensive'. Wecter's neglected article also presents many parallels between Timon and Essex.

128. Jowett, 2004, 7.

129. These include: Points, shortly, Hostile, Laws, Customs, likewise, Justice, hereafter, Trade, sufficient, Companies, common, purchase, Purposes, particular, Carriage, Reputation, Credit, Quantity, furnish, abandon, your Busyness, proceeded, Affection, remain, Assured.

130. Wells and Taylor, op. cit., 129–30.

131. Bate and Rasmussen, op. cit., 2,161.

132. John Wilders, Introduction to *Antony and Cleopatra* (third Arden edition, London, 1995), 74.

133. Michael Neill, *William Shakespeare – The Tragedy of Antony and Cleopatra* (Oxford, 1994), 22.

134. F. E. Halliday, *Shakespeare Companion,* op. cit., 33.

135. Neill, op. cit., 8, n. 1, citing Bullough, Volume 5 (London, 1964), 216–17.

136. ibid.

137. ibid., and John Gouws, ed., *The Prose Works of Fulke Greville, Lord Brooke* (Oxford, 1986), 93. Helen Morris, Queen Elizabeth I 'Shadowed' in Cleopatra, *Huntington Library Quarterly,* Volume 32, No. 3 (1969), 272. See also Keith Rinehart, Shakespeare's Cleopatra and Elizabeth's England, *Shakespeare Quarterly,* Volume 23, No. 1 (1972), 81–6. According to Gouws's entry on Greville in the *ODNB,* he 'took the … precaution of destroying all copies of his play *Antony and Cleopatra*' during 1599–1601. (John Gouws, Fulke Greville, 1st Baron Brooke of Beauchamps Court (1554–1628), courtier and author, online.)

138. *Huntington Library Quarterly,* 1969.

139. Morris, ibid., 272 ff.

140. Luke MacMahon, Sir Henry Killigrew (1525x28[sic]–1603), diplomat, *ODNB,* online.

141. We are grateful to John O'Donnell who noticed this passage: 'I have been enforced to defer my Answers thus long, because that in the chief and mayne Points of them, namely the Negotiations you have had with *the* Venetian *and* Florentine *Ambassadors; the Queen* hath been very irresolute how to proceed. Partly from a Diffidence, that *the Great Duke's* and the *Segniory* of *Venice's* good Affection, *will extend no further then to Words and Wishes,* and an Unwillingness thereupon, to discover any Indigence with no hope of Fruit; *and partly upon an innate and inveterate Humor, to desire things till they be offered, and then to neglect them.* I do not doubt but in the end, any good Offers that shall come from that side will be willingly embraced; but till we see some liklyhood, *we are loath to discover our selves to need any body.*' Sawyer, 1725, Vol 1, 270.

142. Marcellus is a name that also occurs in *Hamlet.*

143. See Casson, 2009, 24–6; 39; 210–14.

144. Bate, 2001, 203–5.

145. Gillespie, 2004, 266.

146. Sawyer, 1725, Vol 1, 45.

147. ibid, Vol 1, 94

148. ibid, Vol 1, 101

149. ibid, Vol 1, 101

150. ibid, Vol 1, 111

151. ibid, Vol 1, 101

152. ibid, Vol 1, 125

153. ibid, Vol 1, 136

154. ibid, Vol 1, 141
155. ibid, Vol 1, 159
156. ibid, Vol 1, 182
157. ibid, Vol 2, 78
158. Bate and Rasmussen, op. cit., 1,539.
159. Wells and Taylor, op. cit., 131.
160. ibid.
161. Halliday, *Shakespeare Companion,* 116.
162. Lee Bliss, *Introduction to Coriolanus* (New Cambridge Shakespeare, Cambridge, 2000), 10–17. For Camden's knowledge of Neville's confession see James and Rubinstein, 2005, 267.
163. ibid., 33–7.
164. ibid., 36. He notes that Coriolanus (like Essex) was charged with treason, although this charge was not to be found in Plutarch's account of the life of Coriolanus.
165. It has also been suggested that the character of Coriolanus was based in part on Sir Walter Raleigh, who had been imprisoned in the Tower in 1603 (see Bliss, ibid., 37–40). Neville had no real connections with Raleigh, while, of course, his association with Essex and his rebellion was a seminal event in his life.
166. Bliss, ibid., 27–33.
167. Duncan, ibid., 214.
168. Duncan, op. cit., 67 and 220–75. See also Clayton Roberts, *Schemes and Undertakings: A Study of English Politics in the Seventeenth Century* (Ohio State University Press, 1985).
169. E. Kuhl, Shakespeare and the Founders of America: *The Tempest, Philological Quarterly* XLI (1962), 145.
170. Bliss, op. cit., 28, n. 5. citing Richard Wilson, *Will Power: Essays on Shakespearean Authority* (Chicago, 1993), Chapter 4, 88–125.
171. 'M. A. P.' [*sic*], Warwickshire, in Hasler, ed., *History of Parliament,* op. cit.
172. Wilson, op. cit., 104. Greville was again elected as MP for Warwickshire in 1621, many years later, but did not sit in Parliament between 1604, when the 1601 Parliament was dissolved, and 1621. (P. W. Hasler, Fulke Greville (1554–1628) of Beauchamp Court, Alcester, Warks., in Hasler, ed., ibid.
173. Paul Honeyball, Warwickshire, in Andrew Thrush and John Ferris, eds, *History of Parliament,* op. cit. Greville had been returned at the previous five general elections.
174. Andrew Thrush, Greville, Sir Edward (1566–1634) of Milcote, Warks., later of Pishobury, Herts., and Fulham, Mdx, in ibid.
175. Bliss, op. cit., 17.
176. ibid. It should be noted that there were similar disturbances over enclosure in the eighteenth and nineteenth centuries. Many historians believe that enclosures resulted in more jobs for agricultural labourers, not fewer.
177. Bliss, op. cit., 25.
178. Halliday, Shakespeare Companion, 444.
179. ibid., 525.
180. Park Honan, *Shakespeare: A Life* (Oxford, 1999), 390.
181. Parker, 1998, 18.
182. Sawyer, 1725, Vol 1, 34.
183. ibid, Vol 1, 85, 147.
184. ibid, Vol 1, 93.
185. ibid, Vol 1, 106
186. ibid, Vol 1, 111.
187. ibid, Vol 1, 164.
188. ibid, Vol 2, 35.
189. ibid, Vol 2, 411.
190. ibid, Vol 1, 55, 94.

Chapter 9

1. Warren, 2004, 17.
2. Casson, 2009, chapter 2.
3. Warren, 2004, 92.
4. ibid, 17.
5. See James, 2011, 34.
6. J. M. S. Tomkins 'Why Pericles?', an article in RES (Review of English Studies) 3, 1952, 315–24 referenced by Warren, 2003, 16.
7. Sawyer, 1725, Vol 2, 411.
8. Neville's birth date is discussed in Chapter 2. This is also discussed in James and Rubinstein, 2005, 69 and Bradbeer and Casson 2015, 215.
9. James and Rubinstein, 2005, 315.
10. Gossett, 2004, 56.
11. See Prior, 1972.
12. Casson, 2009, Chapter 6.
13. Warren, 1998, 64.
14. Sawyer, 1725, Vol 2, 77.
15. In *Cymbeline* Guiderius says, 'I have <u>sent</u> Cloten's clotpoll <u>down</u> the stream.' (4.2.); in *Henry VIII* Queen Katharine says, 'there have been commissions <u>sent down</u> among 'em' (1.2.).
16. Fields, 2006, 35.
17. Sawyer, 1725, Vol 2, 198.
18. We agree with the Oxford editor (Warren, 1998) that it is likely that the original name for the character was Innogen (= innocent) not Imogen.
19. Sawyer, 1725, Vol 2, 35 and 37.
20. Warren, 1998, 62.
21. Sawyer, 1725, Vol 2, 216.
22. This letter is listed (on page 31) in a catalogue of letters to Ralph Winwood published in 1899 by Eyre and Spottiswoode, (under Her Majesty's Stationery Office), in a Report on the Manuscripts of the Duke of Buccleuch and Queensberry, preserved at Montagu House, Whitehall, vol.1 (now in the British Library). Many of these letters were not printed in Sawyer (1725). This volume was referenced by Brenda James in the first Journal of Neville Studies, 2008, page 79.
23. Salisbury, 1906, 268. For analysis of the vocabulary in this sentence see Bradbeer & Casson, 2015, 31–2.
24. Sawyer, 1725, Vol 1, 50.
25. ibid: Vol 1, 92; 103.
26. ibid: Vol 1, 101.
27. ibid: Vol 1, 111.
28. ibid: Vol 1, 123.
29. ibid: Vol 1, 149.
30. ibid: Vol 1, 163.
31. ibid: Vol 1, 230.
32. ibid: Vol 1, 287.
33. Her first husband was Sir Robert Doyley who died in 1577. Her second husband was Sir Henry Neville. She married Sir William Peryman in 1595, two years after Sir Henry Neville had died.
34. Wotton was back in England in 1611. In 1614 he commented on Shakespeare and Fletcher's *Henry VIII* (Orgel, 1996, 15).
35. Falk, 2014, 202.
36. ibid: 202.
37. James, 2011, 237.

38. Warren, 1998, 20.
39. Gesner, 1907, 113.
40. Warren, 1998, 27.
41. Nosworthy, 1969, xxv.
42. Both were baptised at Waltham St Lawrence Church: the first on 25 November 1593; the second on 17 November 1605.
43. Berkshire Record Office: D/EN/F6/1/4.
44. This marriage settlement, JER/WA/35/6, is held at the Public Records Office of Newport in the Isle of Wight. It is jointly signed by Neville and his oldest son, Henry Neville. It is to our knowledge unique in providing both their signatures on one document, thus enabling us to compare them. Two other documents, JER/WA/35/7 and JER/WA/35/9, show Neville involved in land transactions with Richard Worsley with regards to the manor of Appuldurcham.
45. Orgel, 1996, 13–14.
46. Much of this paragraph is taken from the Parliamentary biography of Neville available online: http://www.historyofparliamentonline.org/volume/1604-1629/member/neville-sir-henry-i-1564-1615 accessed 27/12/14.
47. Orgel, 1996, 267.
48. Roe, 2011, 251.
49. Casson, 2009, 54.
50. In *Leicester's Commonwealth* (1584) Robert Dudley, the Earl of Leicester, is referred to as such directly: 'my Lord of Leicester (whom you call the Bearwhelp)' (Peck, 2006, 73/53). This bear image is further developed in the document:
    'my Lord of Leicester is very well known to have no title to the crown himself, either by descent in blood, alliance, or otherways ... he will play the Bear when he cometh to dividing of the prey and will snatch the best part to himself.' (Peck, 2006, 127/86) Robert Dudley was not only linked with a bear by the authors of *Leicester's Commonwealth*. In 1573 Dudley gave Elizabeth I 'a fan of white feathers set in a gold handle decorated with emeralds, diamonds and rubies, on each side a white bear and two pearls hanging a lion ramping with a white bear at his feet.' Dudley had received a gift of 'white bears' from the Muscovy Company in 1571 (Haynes, 1987, 100). In *Mucedorus* Segasto says to Mouse: Thou talkest of wonders, to tell me of white bears. But, sirra, didst thou ever see any such? (1.4.39) Mouse replies, 'No, faith, I never saw any such, but I remember my father's words: he bade me take heed I was not caught with a white bear' (1.4.42) (Casson, 2009, 55–6).
51. Bate and Rasmussen et al, 2013, 505–6.
52. James, 2011, 24, 34, 335.
53. ibid, 34.
54. Rubinstein and James, 2005, 78.
55. It was the manor of the Anthony Browne, 1st Viscount Montagu, whose wife gave birth to twins: Mary and Anthony Browne. Mary was Southampton's mother.
56. Green, 1993, 179.
57. Chamberlain's letter is to Ralph Winwood, dated 10 August 1612: 'Sir *Harry Nevill* and his Lady took a Journey this Day se'nnight toward the Isle of *Wight* and so into *Somersetshire* to see his Daughters; making account to be almost a Month abroad.' Sawyer, 1725, Vol 3, 385.
58. ibid, Vol 1, 77.
59. ibid: Vol 1, 88.
60. ibid: Vol 1, 102.
61. ibid: Vol 1, 106.
62. ibid: Vol 1, 155.
63. ibid: Vol 1, 178.
64. ibid: Vol 1, 184.

65. Marapodi, 2007, 9.
66. Lyne, 2006 accessed on line from www.thefreelibrary.com, 9/2/2015.
67. ibid: Vol 3, 407.

Chapter 10

1. 'Tho. Thorpe entred for his copie under the handes of master Wilson and master Lownes Wardenes a booke called Shakespeares sonnettesvjd.' is the entry in the Stationers' Register of 20 May 1609. From: http://en.wikipedia.org/wiki/Shakespeare's_sonnets accessd 31/10/2014.
2. 'Time the devourer' is the theme of Sonnet 19, memory and monuments being core issues of some later sonnets (e.g., 55 and 81).
3. An edition (in modern typeface) of *A Good Speed to Virginia* is available online at Google Books. This quote is from 19-10 of the Google Book edition. The similarity of Gray's introduction to the sonnets' dedication was first noticed by the late Robert Brasil, a pro-Oxfordian researcher, in his online blog '1609 Chronology' of 24 April 1609, then mentioned in Katherine Chiljan's *Shakespeare Suppressed: The Uncensored Truth About Shakespeare and His Works* (San Francisco, 2011), 314, another pro-Oxfordian work. So far as we are aware, Gray's pamphlet is not mentioned or discussed in any mainstream, scholarly edition of the sonnets.
4. The site is now occupied by No. 1 Poultry in the Cordwainer Ward of the City of London.
5. David Kathman, 'Thorpe [Thorp], Thomas (1571/2–1625?), bookseller,' in the *ODNB*, online. In contrast to Kathman's biographical entry, F.E. Halliday, in *A Shakespeare Companion* (Harmondsworth, 1964), 494, states that 'Thorpe's first registration was in 1604, of Marston's *Malcontent*' later than the 1603 date for the East India Company pamphlets given in the *ODNB* entry. Kathman's entry on Thorpe notes that he published *A Discovery of the New World*, a translation by John Healey of (Revd) John Hall's *Mundus Alter et Idem*. This is not a travel book, and is not about the 'New World' but a satirical description of London, said to have influenced *Gulliver's Travels*, in which the ship *Fantasia* visits the lands of Crapulia, Vivoginia, Moronia, and Lavernia in the southern seas.
6. As with Shakspere and Thorpe, neither Eld, Aspley, nor Wright were 'adventurers' who invested in the London Virginia Company.
7. One such copy is at the John Rylands Library, Deansgate, Manchester, UK.
8. John M. Rollett, 'Secrets of the Dedication to Shakespeare's Sonnets' in Richard Malim, ed., *Great Oxford* (Tunbridge Wells, 2004), 253–6, which had previously been published in *The Oxfordian*, Volume II, October 1999, 60–75. Needless to say, our present work disagrees fundamentally with the assertion that the Earl of Oxford wrote Shakespeare's work.
9. The price, 5*d*, (five old pence) is handwritten on the first page of the John Rylands Library Manchester copy. Robert Giroux, *The Book Known As Q: A Consideration of Shakespeare's Sonnets* (New York, 1983), 4.
10. See Figure 2, page 5 in Edmondson and Wells, 2004.
11. Many other theories have been offered as to who 'Mr. W. H.' might be. The most plausible is William Herbert, 3rd Earl of Pembroke (1580–1630), to whom the First Folio was jointly dedicated (along with his brother Philip, Earl of Montgomery). But there is no evidence that Shakspere had any dealings with him. (Shakspere may have been a member of Pembroke's Men, an acting company, before joining the Lord Chamberlain's Men in 1594, but this company belonged to the third earl's father, Henry Herbert, 2nd Earl, who died in 1601.) The First Folio was almost certainly dedicated to Pembroke and his brother because Pembroke was Lord Chamberlain (from 1615–25) and his brother was expected to succeed him. Nor would Thorpe conceivably have addressed a powerful earl as 'Mr. W. H.', or in less than obsequious language. Another favoured possibility is that 'Mr. W. H.' followed

by 'all happinesse' suggests that the dedicatee was a Mr. W. Hall. A man of that (obviously common) name was apparently a London printer at that time, but there is no evidence to conclude that he was the Sonnet's 'onlie begetter' or had any known connection with Shakspere or Neville. A further theory, put forward at length in Leslie Hotson's *Mr. W. H.* (London, 1964) is that 'Mr. W. H.' was one William Hatcliffe of Hatcliffe, Lincolnshire (1568–1631), who was 'Lord of Misrule' at the Gray's Inn celebrations of 1587–8. There is nothing – absolutely nothing – to connect Hatcliffe with Shakespeare or the sonnets apart from his initials. When *A Comedy of Errors* was apparently premièred at a similar celebration at Gray's Inn on 28 December 1594, its 'Lord of Misrule' was not Hatcliffe but a Henry Helme. According to Hotson, Hatcliffe, for no apparent reason, travelled from Lincolnshire to London in 1609 to have the sonnets published by Thorpe. In its 328 pages, Hotson does not provide one scrap of real evidence that Hatcliffe was 'Mr. W. H.' Another man suggested as 'Mr. W. H.' is Sir William Hervey (or Harvey, *c.*1565–1649), Southampton's stepfather, who had married his widowed mother in 1597, an MP who was later created Lord Hervey. But as Southampton was still alive in 1609 (he died in 1624), he was presumably the owner of the sonnets, not his stepfather, who had no *locus standi* in the matter.

12. See Leyland and Goding, 2015. David Ewald has also done groundbreaking research on the sonnets (personal communications).
13. Sawyer, 1725, Vol 2, 199.
14. We are grateful to David Ewald for pointing out to us the match between the number of this sonnet and Wriothesley's age: twenty.
15. From Neville's Parliamentary biography: see http://www.historyofparliamentonline.org/volume/1604-1629/member/neville-sir-henry-i-1564-1615 accessed 7/11/2014
16. He later received a knighthood and was also known as Sir Henry Neville (1588–1629).
17. The surname can be spelt Smythe or Smith: Neville himself used the latter spelling.
18. Duncan, 1974, 215, quoting a document in the National Archives, Kew, PRO/SP/12/43/22.
19. See Peter Lefevre and Andrew Thrush, 'Sir John Smythe (1557–1608) of Westenhanger near Hythe, Kent', in Andrew Thrush and John Ferris, eds, *The History of Parliament: The House of Commons 1604–1629* (Cambridge 2010), online, and M. R. P. [*sic*], 'Sir John Smythe I (1557–1608) of Westenhanger, Kent', in W. Hasler, ed., *The History of Parliament: The House of Commons 1558–1604* (London, 1981), online. The latter entry described him as 'one of the richest men in Kent'. His only son later became Lord Strangford. For the £3,000 dowry, see 'Sir Henry Neville I (1564–1615)' in Thrush and Ferris, ibid. This account of Neville's life states that he was born in 1564, but he was born between December 1561 and December 1562, almost certainly in 1562.
20. Peter Lefevre, 'Sir Thomas Smythe (*c.* 1558–1625) of Philpot Lane, London and Bounds Place, Bidborough, Kent', in Thrush and Ferris, eds, ibid., and M. R. P., 'Sir Thomas Smythe', in Hasler, ibid. He also shared with Neville that fact that a relative had founded a public school: his grandfather had founded Tonbridge School. See also Basil Morgan, 'Smythe [Smith], Sir Thomas (*c.*1558–1625), Merchant' in the *Oxford Dictionary of National Biography,* online.
21. The three letters are in Sawyer, 1725, Vol 2, 35, 198, 399; the letters dated 1 November 1604; 11 March 1605; 12 May 1608.
22. Sawyer, 1725, Vol 2, 198
23. Leslie Hotson, *Mr. W. H.* (London, 1964), 136, citing C. S. Lewis, *English Literature in the Sixteenth Century* (Oxford, 1954), 503.
24. See Park Honan, 'Wriothesley, Henry, 3rd Earl of Southampton (1573–1624), courtier and literary patron', in the *ODNB,* online.
25. These were the 1558 *Adagiorum* and the 1591 *Colloquiorum*. See Muir, 1979, 36, about the use of Erasmus in the sonnets.
26. Sawyer, 1725, Vol 2, 38

27. Since William Shakspere had as much chance of 'bearing the canopy' at high state occasions as becoming Mikado of Japan (he had trouble obtaining a Coat of Arms and recognition as a gentleman, let alone being made a peer or knight), it is difficult to see why he would express himself in this way. On the impossibility that Shakspere might have 'bor[ne] the canopy' at any state occasion whatever, see John M. Rollett, 'Shakespeare's Sonnet 125: Who Bore the Canopy?', *Notes and Queries,* Volume 60 (3) (2013), 438–41.

28. The formal writing on the left of the image is possibly by Neville's secretary John Packer, while the annotation in the margin is by Neville himself.

29. The son who died as the couple travelled to France was unnamed. Neville and Anne had fifteen children in all, two daughters being born in 1610.

30. It is quite possible, given his lengthy periods of residence by himself in London, perhaps almost inevitable, that William Shakspere contracted venereal disease and become infertile at a young age. Many commentators, especially since the 1960s, see the sonnets as expressing the author's homosexuality or bisexuality. It is easy to see why. There is nothing in the known facts of Shakspere's life to suggest homosexuality, and none of the apocryphal stories about his life suggests this. It is possible that, in his two years in the Tower alongside Southampton, Neville developed homosexual desires, as some men do in prison. Given the male friendship cult of the time (evident in *The Two Gentlemen of Verona* and *The Two Noble Kinsmen*) it is more likely that heterosexual men wrote about other males they admired in this way, without this homoeroticism being translated into sexual activity.

31. We are grateful to David Ewald for pointing this out to us.

32. The manuscript is now in the British Library: Sloane MS 1792, f.45r.

33. Casson, 2010, 34.

34. Somerset, 1997, 342: see Chapter 11.

35. Add. MS 10309, in the British Library.

36. From http://en.wikipedia.org/wiki/Henry_Cholmley_(died_1616) accessed 30/10/2014.

37. Sawyer, 1725, Vol 1, 29; Vol 2, 216

38. ibid, Vol 1, 168

39. ibid, Vol 1, 182

40. ibid, Vol 2, 411

41. ibid, Vol 1, 65

42. ibid, Vol 1, 126

43. Malone Society Reprint, 2002.

44. Casson, 2010, 201.

45. Merton College Library shelf mark: 32.A.4.

46. Leyland and Goding, their new book is published by Leanpub and see their website: www.leylandandgoding.com

47. Callaghan, D. (2007) *Shakespeare's Sonnets*, Oxford, Blackwell

48. Duncan-Jones, 2005, 422.

49. Roe, 1998, 65.

50. ibid, 65, 69.

51. Neville repeated the phrase 'imbecillyty of my nature' in his draft letter of 1603–4 (in the Reading archives).

52. Sawyer, 1725, Vol 2, 411.

53. Neville used 'commendations' in a number of letters from 1600 onwards, for example: 23 January 1601 'I end with hearty Commendations from my self and all your Friends,' (Sawyer, 1725, Vol 1, 290); 29 January 1601 'And so with my very hearty Commendations, I commit you to God &c. Your very loving Friend,' (Sawyer, 1725, Vol 1, 292); 4 June 1606: 'I will conclude with my affectionate Commendations and best wishes unto yourself and Mrs. Winwood, and so take my leave Your very assured Friend to dispose of' (Sawyer, 1725, Vol 2, 216).

54. Sir Henry Neville's letter is D/EZ138/1 at the Berkshire Records Office, Reading.

55. For example see James and Rubinstein, 2005, Figure 5.

56. Stowe 174 f 116, © British Library.
57. Cotton Manuscripts, Caligula EX folio 21 © British Library.
58. Berkshire Record Office: D/EZ/138/1.
59. Titherley, 1952, 283, showed that William Stanley, another authorship candidate, used the spelling 'ffrend'.
60. See Casson, 2010, 65–72.
61. An alternative spelling of his name is Bernard Mitchell. He was MP for Weymouth and Melcombe Regis from 1610 replacing Robert White who was ill. He was a merchant trading in Europe. See: http://www.historyofparliamentonline.org/volume/1604-1629/member/michell-barnard-1647 accessed 3/4/15.
62. James was in some position in the household as the will qualifies the bequest with the words 'yf he serve me at the tyme of my deathe'. A copy of the will is at the National Archives, Kew, London: PROB 11/126/63.
63. The document is D/EN/F45/1-2 in the Reading Archives of the Berkshire Records Office. It is dated March 1602 which under the old calender would have been March 1603, just before Neville was released from the Tower. The document is a list of Remembrances, notes shows Neville managing his estates and planning what needs to be arranged. Shellingford was a manor bought by Neville in 1598. It was later owned by the Packer family.
64. Sherbo, 1992.
65. From: http://en.wikipedia.org/wiki/George_Spencer,_2nd_Earl_Spencer accessed 3/11/2014
66. Strachey had previously been Secretary to the Levant Company and had been to Turkey.
67. David Kathman, 'Dating *The Tempest*', shakespeareauthorship.com, online.
68. ibid.
69. To summarise briefly this debate: J. Thomas Looney, the originator of the Oxfordian theory, agreed that *The Tempest* was written in 1610–11, but claimed that its actual author was not the man (Oxford) who wrote the other works of Shakespeare. Today, most Oxfordians claim that a lost, anonymous play called *The Tragedy of the Spanish Maze,* which was performed at Court in February 1605 along with plays by Shakespeare (and others) was actually *The Tempest*, these performances being a posthumous tribute to Oxford, who had died the previous year. Since *The Tempest* has nothing to do with Spain, is classified in the First Folio as a Comedy, not a Tragedy, and has an entirely different title, readers can draw their own conclusions. They also claim that the Strachey Letter could not have reached England in time to be read and used in a play written in 1611, and may not have been available until it was published in 1625. There is no doubt that they are wrong, and that the Letter had reached the London Virginia Company in time to be read by its directors, including Neville. The case for Oxford has been set out, among other places, in Roger A. Stritmatter and Lynn Kositsky, *On the Date, Source, and Design of Shakespeare's The Tempest* (Jefferson, N. C., 2013). For responses to this viewpoint, see Alden T. Vaughan, 'William Strachey's 'True Reportory' and Shakespeare: A Closer Look at the Evidence', *Shakespeare Quarterly* 59 (2008), 245–77; Tom Reedy, 'Dating William Strachey's 'A True Reportory of the Wrack and Redemption of Sir Thomas Gates': A Comparative Textual Analysis', *Review of English Studies* 251 (2010), 529–52; and Kathman, ibid.
70. Barry R. Clarke, 'The Virginia Company and *The Tempest*', *Journal of Drama Studies* 5 (July 2011), 13–27. This article is important in showing, with new evidence, that the play is based on the Strachey Letter.
71. C. M. Gayley, Shakespeare and the Founders of Liberty in America (New York, 1917), 75.
72. Clarke, op. cit., 19.
73. Frank Kermode, Introduction to *The Tempest* (second Arden edition, originally London, 1954; reprinted London 1994), xxvii–xxviii.
74. Dudley and Leonard Digges, it might be noted, were the grandsons of Ursula Neville, the cousin of Sir Edward Neville, Sir Henry's grandfather, and were thus fairly close blood relatives of Sir Henry.

75. Clarke, op. cit., 21.
76. Kermode, 1990, xlvii, note 2 and li.
77. Kermode, 1990, xliv, liii.
78. See Bradbeer and Casson, 2015, chapter 11.
79. Foster, 1981, 103, 127.
80. ibid, 109, 112.
81. Casson, 2010, 61.
82. Kermode, 1990, lzvii.
83. Sawyer, 1725, Vol 1, 175
84. ibid, Vol 1, 274 and Vol 2, 25
85. In his *Wits conference betwixt a scholar and an angler*. According to the LION and EEBO databases other writers used the spellings 'open eied' with, and mostly without, a hyphen.
86. Sawyer, 1725, Vol 2, 25
87. ibid, Vol 2, 198
88. In the British Library Manuscripts: Stowe 174 f 116.

Chapter 11

1. In 1622 T. Walkley published the first quarto of *Othello*. He wrote a short epistle in which he stated the writer was dead.
2. Salerno, 2000, 16.
3. Freehafer, 1969, 502.
4. East Riding of Yorkshire Archives and Records Service: EASTOFT FAMILY OF EASTOFT Catalogue Ref. ref. DDBE/20/25 - date: 8 Mar 1726, Reference: DBE/21/3 – Account of debts of Francis Estofte, esquire Creation dates: 18 Jun 1726 Sent by Lewis Theobald to Madam Neville at 29 Gloucester Street (All this number relates to the list at DDBE/27/37) Also ref. DDBE/20/25–ref. DDBE/20/28 date: 29 April 1727.
5. Casson, 2009; Hammond, 2010. See also Boyd and Pennebaker, 2015.
6. Wilson, 2004, 242.
7. ibid, 232.
8. Yates, 2004, 9.
9. Sawyer, 1725, Vol 3, 467
10. D/EN F6/2/3, stored at the Berkshire Record Office, Reading.
11. Sawyer, 1725, Vol I, 32
12. Kukowski, 1991, 88.
13. Sawyer, 1725, Vol 2, 35
14. Casson, 2009, 221.
15. James and Rubinstein, 2005, 249.
16. ibid, 246, 341.
17. ibid, Vol 2, 77
18. Somerset, 1997, 90.
19. Duncan, 1974, 66.
20. Hawkyard, 2004, 489.
21. ibid, 489.
22. Life and Letters of Sir Henry Wotton, Vol 2, 32–3. Smith, L. (1907) Oxford, Clarendon Press. https://archive.org/stream/lifeandletterss00wottgoog#page/n37/mode/2up accessed 14/1/2015.
23. We recall that on 6 July 1613 Turnbull wrote that Neville was in Brussels to see 'the Procession of the Sacrament of Miracles, the Princes and this Court in its Glory'.
24. Duncan, 1974, 5.
25. James and Rubinstein, 2005, 44, 218–221.

26. Duncan, 1975, 201.
27. ibid, 201.
28. Sawyer, 1725, Vol 2, 217.
29. See Bradbeer and Casson, 2015, Chapter 8.
30. Sawyer, 1725, Vol 2, 24. Wotton was a rival for the role and Neville wrote that Wotton's Savoy embassy had not helped his bid: see Vol 1, 125.
31. Stopes, 1922, 363.
32. Duncan, 1974, 243.
33. There are 113 words found in the letter which are also to be found in *Henry VIII* (27 per cent). The letter includes the word '<u>irresolute</u>' which Shakespeare only used once, in *Henry VIII* (in a scene believed by scholars to have been written by Shakespeare: 1.2.209). There are eighty-nine words found in the letter which are also to be found in *Double Falshood* (21.3 per cent). This lower figure may possibly reflect the fact that the text of *Double Falshood* has definitely been cut by the editor/s of the original *Cardenio*, or simply that as it is the earliest of the three final collaborative plays it is more remote from the letter. However the letter does contain the word '<u>presumptions</u>' which is uniquely to be found in *Double Falshood* (in a speech believed by Oliphant to be by Shakespeare: 3.2.11).
34. Sawyer, 1725, Vol 3, 462.
35. ibid, Vol 1, 131.
36. ibid, Vol 3, 448.
37. McClure, 1939, 448.
38. ibid, 459.
39. Sawyer, 1725, Vol 3, 275: Southampton's letters states … 'the Busyness of which we desire so much to hear the Conclusion, is still in Suspense. The Difficulty alledged, is the not having as then the accommodated the Matter of Sir *Thomas Overbury*, which may times bred Disturbance, and *hindred the Performance of the Resolution taken; and it is in vaine to hope for any good issue of the other until that be settled*, which I think to be done long ere this after this Manner; that upon *his submission he shall have leave to travail, with the private Intimation not to return until his Majesties Pleasure be further known.* And so much adoe there hath been to keepe him from a publique Censure of Banishment and loss of Office, *such a rooted Hatred lyeth in the King's Heart towards him*; and that Blocke being now removed, I find the same Confidence that I left touching Sir *Henry Neville*; which I shall be as glad of as any, but (as I wrote before) this often deferring hath made me doubtfull. Of the Nullity I see you have heard as much as I can write … the King coming to my House imposeth a Necessity at this time upon me of returning …' Here Southampton refers to 'waiting for a wind' as he is writing to Winwood from the continent and was waiting for a sailing across the channel.
40. Worsley MSS 47 in the Lincoln archives: see Casson, 2010. That Neville made these notes on the divorce at the end of this notebooks is evidence that he kept his copy of *Leicester's Commonwealth* close at hand over thirty years.
41. In Stowe 174, folio 116, British Library.
42. Somerset, 1997, 128.
43. ibid, 66.
44. ibid, 91.
45. ibid, 92.
46. Hammond, 2010, 99.

Chapter 12

1. See also Chapter 11 in Bradbeer and Casson, 2015.
2. MacGregor, 2014, Chapter 11.

3. Duncan, 1974, 203.
4. Bradbeer and Casson, 2015, 138.
5. *Asmund and Cornelia* is an unknown work. It is not entirely clear whether this is by Bacon, Nashe or Shakespeare but the logic of its position in the list is that this is an unknown work by William Shakespeare. It is listed twice: immediately below *Richard III* by Shakespeare and immediately above a quotation from *The Rape of Lucrece*: 'revealing day through every crany peepes and see …' which is a misquotation of stanza 156. The name Cornelia occurs twice in *Titus Andronicus* (4.1.12; 4.2.143) but these are two different women: one the mother of the Gracchi (as a mother dedicated to her sons), the other a midwife. The name Asmund is an invention with no precedent in Roman history or myth. Asmund is a Norse name. The English equivalent is Osmund. 'Asmath' is a fiend evoked by Margaret Jourdain in *Henry VI: Part II* (1.4.23), though this First Folio spelling may be a mis-reading of Elizabethan secretary script for 'Asmode(us)' (Warren, 2003, 144). Only in one other place is Lucrece associated with Cornelia: in a funerary poem by 'W. Har.' who is believed to be William Hervey, Baron of Kidbrooke and Ross. Published in 1594 it predates the NHMS and refers to *The Rape of Lucrece*:

> You that haue writ of chaste Lucretia,
> Whose death was witness to her spotelsse life:
> Or pen'd the praise of sad Cornelia,
> Whose blamelesse name hath made her fame so rife,
> As noble Pompey's most renowned wife …

It is not clear here if 'you' refers to just one writer or to two different poets but Ocham's razor would suggest one poet and the NHMS reference to *Asmund and Cornelia*, immediately adjacent to a quotation from *The Rape of Lucrece*, identifies that poet as Shakespeare. In 1598, Hervey married Mary, daughter of Anthony Browne, 1st Viscount Montagu and the widow of Henry Wriothesley, 2nd Earl of Southampton, and of Thomas Heneage. Mary was therefore the mother of the Henry Wriothesley to whom *The Rape of Lucrece* had been dedicated. Hervey was in that circle and a supporter of Essex. After Mary died, Hervey married Cordella, daughter of Brian Annesley in 1608. Due to her struggle with his sisters over her senile father, 1603–4, Cordella has been seen as a model for Cordelia (*King Lear* was written in this period, the earliest recorded performance being in 1606). Neville was 'in an excellent position to know of the Annesley case' (see Chapter 8 and James and Rubinstein, 2005, 175). The name 'Haruey' occurs in the first Quarto of *Henry IV: Part I* and Bevington (2008, 5) suggested this was because Shakespeare knew Southampton's stepfather. 'Haruey' is listed as one of the robbers on Gadshill (later the name was changed to Peto). Bevington suggested this satirical naming of Hervey as a thief was due to Southampton's unhappiness with his stepfather.

The other contemporary person associated with Cornelia was Elizabeth Hoby, née Cooke, Neville's wife's aunt. Walter Haddon wrote a poem after Thomas Hoby's death in 1566 that compared Elizabeth to Cornelia Metella, Pompey's wife. Haddon was with Anthony Browne, 1st Viscount Montagu, in Bruges between 1565 and 1566 so it is possible that Hervey (who as we have seen married Browne's daughter) was referring to Haddon as the poet who 'pen'd the praise of sad Cornelia'. Hervey could have been referring to Thomas Kyd, as the year before the NHMS, in 1595, Kyd had published *Pompey the Great, his fair Cornelia's Tragedy*, an English translation of a French poem by Robert Garnier (which may have circulated in manuscript before being printed). This however makes no mention of Asmund and in any case was published after Hervey's poem. It is possible that Shakespeare may have written a poem or play based on Kyd's translation, adding a new character called Asmund. Whatever the nature of *Asmund and Cornelia*, Neville, in the NHMS, seems to have special knowledge of Shakespeare's work matched by no one else at the time.

6. Thomas Nashe dedicated *The Unfortunate Traveller* to The Earl of Southampton in 1593. 'It is evident from this dedication that Nashe knew of Shakespeare's dedication to Southampton when he wrote it' (Stopes, 1922, 57). It is possible that Southampton's bailiff, Richard Nash, was a relative to the satirist (Stopes, 1922, 55). Nashe wrote *The Choice of Valentines* which he also dedicated to Southampton and in which he referred to Ovid, perhaps also meaning Shakespeare. There are clear connections between Neville and Southampton and the NHMS is evidence of a connection between Neville and Nashe.

7. Gillespie, 2004, 265.

8. Duncan, 1974, 126 and Sawyer, 1725, Vol 1, 183.

9. Sawyer, 1725, Vol 1, 274.

10. The latter is dated 29 November 1600: Sawyer, 1725, Vol 1, 267.

11. We are grateful to John O'Donnell for clarifying the identity of this opera.

12. Sawyer, 1725, Vol 3, 467

13. Bradbeer and Casson, 2015, 177.

14. James and Rubinstein, 2005, 57.

15. Bradbeer and Casson, 2015, 140. See also Rubinstein, 2012, 146.

16. Haynes, 2004, 76.

17. McMillan, 1987, 59: see also Bradbeer & Casson, 2015, 184.

18. In the 1920s N. Harrison used hapaxes to determine the authorship of St Paul's Epistles. See: https://en.wikipedia.org/wiki/Hapax_legomenon, accessed 26 August 2015.

19. The dates listed in this table are formatted under the English system: 1/5/1599 = 1 May 1599.

20. For a full list of Nevilles in the History Plays see Bradbeer and Casson, 2015.

21. Other hapaxes in *Antony and Cleopatra* to be found in Neville's letters include: 'forborne': 6 June 1599 (Sawyer, 1725, Vol 1, 45); 'president': 6 September 1599 (Ibid, Vol 1, 101); 'persisted': 9 May 1600 (Ibid, Vol 1, 182); 'contestation': 2/11/1600 (Ibid, Vol 1, 271). Just before Shakespeare wrote *Antony and Cleopatra* Neville used the word 'entangled' in his letter dated 21 June 1605, (Ibid, Vol 2, 77) which only occurs in *A&C* and *Coriolanus*.

22. 'Employed' is a hapax in *As You Like It*: the spelling used in the First Folio is 'employed'. The spelling in the quarto of *Edward III* is 'imployd'. Neville's spelling in his letter is 'imployed'.

23. Neither 'procure' nor 'pardon' are hapaxes but these abbreviated spellings are found in Hand D and Neville's copy of Leicester's Commonwealth, Worsley MSS 47.

24. 'Accommodated' is to be found also in *Cymbeline* (5.3.32). The word 'accommodate' is unique to *King Lear* (4.6.81).

25. Spoken by Warwick, Richard Neville, in *Henry VI: Part III*: 4.8.2. The hapax 'prejudicial', which also occurs in *Henry VI: Part III*: 1.1.144, (also spoken by Richard Neville) is to be found in Neville's letter of 1 August 1599 (Sawyer, 1725, Vol 1, 83, spelt 'prejudiciall') and in his draft letter of 19 February 1601 (National Archives, Kew, PRO 30/50/2 folio 104).

26. The word 'secretary' is only used in *Henry VIII* (five times) about men who are gaining or losing power.

27. 'Similis' meaning he looked like Henry VIII: see Chapter 11.

28. Spelt 'Forreyners' in the First Folio; Neville spelt the word 'forayners': both with a 'y'.

29. Probably written to Robert Cecil: D/EN F6/2/3, stored at the Berkshire Record Office, Reading.

30. In his letter Neville used the word 'obsequies'. Shakespeare used this plural 6 times from his earliest (*Henry VI: Part II* and *Part III*) to his later plays (*Cymbeline*). The word is used in *Hamlet*, written just a year or so after this letter, at about the same time the Bard used the singular word 'obsequy' as *The Phoenix and the Turtle*.

31. Shakespeare only used 'uncontrolled' in the two long poems, *The Rape of Lucrece* and *Venus and Adonis*. He used 'uncontroll'd' only in *Richard II*. In his letter Neville spells the word 'uncontrolled'.

32. 'Cary the canapie': Sonnet 125, see Chapter 10.

33. Horace is also referred to in *Love's Labour's Lost* and quoted in other plays such as *Henry V*. It is therefore not a true hapax being mentioned twice in *Titus Andronicus* and once in *Love's Labour's Lost*.

34. See James and Rubinstein, 2005; Casson, 2010; Bradbeer and Casson, 2015.
35. Bate, 2001, 24, 50.
36. See Laoutaris, 2014, 30.
37. See Bradbeer and Casson, 2015, 147 for a photograph of this annotation.
38. The 1603/4 Neville letter is D/EN F6/2/3, stored at the Berkshire Record Office, Reading. The letter is undated but must date to soon after his release sometime in 1603–4.
39. Schutzenberger, 1998.
40. Berkshire Records Office: D/EN/F43. It has been suggested that this Lady Gresham was Neville's maternal grandmother. We have found no evidence to settle the question of whose room this was for certain.
41. Gossett, 2004, 152.
42. Spurgeon, 1958, 320.
43. These are preserved in the Cecil papers at Hatfield House.
44. In 1594 the following plays were printed anonymously: *Titus Andronicus, Henry VI: Part II, The Taming of the Shrew*.
45. See Sams, 1986; Casson, 2009; Jolly, 2014.

Appendix

1. Douglas, 2007, x.
2. ibid, 1–2.
3. See Engel (2009).
4. Cassuto, 1997, identified this as one of the little rings of which Genesis is composed.
5. The tragedy of Adam (human being) formed by the adamah (soil). Courtesy of Robert Murray, cited by Douglas (2007). Shakespeare likewise puns on soul and soil.
6. 'Ish' means male and 'ishshah' female.
7. Chapter divisions are medieval, not original to the Hebrew Bible.
8. Merton Library Catalogue number: 32.A.4.
9. See Vendler, 1999, 29.
10. Engel, 2009.
11. Jolly, 2014, 49.
12. R. M. Waugaman, M.D. personal communication with David Ewald.
13. Numbers refer to the measurement of meter in verse.
14. In Sonnet 56 the sword's, or appetite's, edge is blunter or sharpened. In sonnet 95, at the other end of this ring, we also find the image of the knife that 'ill used doth lose his edge.'
15. Both Sonnet 56 and 98 describe the effects of being separated from his love.
16. Both Sonnet 64 and 90 are about the loss of the loved one.
17. The theme of these two sonnets, 66 and 68, might be summed up as 'Bearing all wrongs for love'. They point especially to Neville who was disgraced, attainted (a legal term in treason cases) and captive after the Essex rebellion.
18. We are grateful to Bruce Leyland for pointing this out to us: see Leyland & Goding, 2015.
19. Douglas, 2007, 102.
20. Leyland and Goding, 2015, Chapter 4, 47.
21. James and Rubinstein, 2005, 260.

Bibliography

Abbott, E., *Bacon and Essex* (London: Seeley, Jackson & Halliday, 1877)

Aitchison, N., *Macbeth: Man and Myth* (Stroud: Sutton Publishing, 1999)

Alexander, C. M. S., (ed.), *The Cambridge Companion to Shakespeare's Last Plays* (Cambridge: Cambridge University Press, 2009)

Anderson, M. *Shakespeare By Another Name: The Biography of Edward De Vere, Earl of Oxford, The Man Who Was Shakespeare* (New York: Gotham Books, Penguin, 2005)

Armitage, D., Condren, C. & Fitzmaurice, A. *Shakespeare and Early Modern Political Thought* (Cambridge, UK: Cambridge University Press, 2009)

Armstrong, E. A., *Shakespeare's Imagination* (Lincoln/London: University of Nebraska Press, 1963)

Atkinson, D. F., *The Source of Two Gentlemen of Verona* (University of North Carolina Press: Studies in Philology, Vol 41, No 2, 223–34, 1944)

Baldwin, T. W., *Shakespeare's Smalle Latine and Lesse Greek* (Urbana: University of Illinois Press, 1944)

Barber, B., *Shakespeare: The Evidence - The Authorship Question Clarified* (http://leanpub.com. shakespeare, 2014)

Bate, J., *Shakespeare and Ovid* (Oxford: Clarendon Paperbacks, Oxford University Press, 2001)

Bate, J., *Titus Andronicus* (London: The Arden Shakespeare, Thomson Learning, 2006)

Bate, J. & Rasmussen, E., (eds), *William Shakespeare: Complete Works* (London: Palgrave Macmillan, 2007)

Bate, J., Ramussen, E., Sewell, J. & Sharpe W., *William Shakespeare & Others: Collaborative Plays* (Basingstoke, Hampshire: Royal Shakespeare Company, Palgrave Macmillan, 2013)

Bawcutt, N. W., *Measure for Measure* (Oxford: The Oxford Shakespeare, Oxford University Press, 2008)

Bevington, D., *Henry IV Part One* (Oxford: The Oxford Shakespeare, Oxford World's Classics, Oxford University Press, 2008)

Bliss, L., *Coriolanus* (Cambridge: New Cambridge Shakespeare, Cambridge University Press, 2000)

Bliss, L., (ed.), *A King and No King by Francis Beaumont and John Fletcher* (Manchester: Manchester University Press, 2004)

Boas, F. S., *Shakespeare and His Predecessors* (London: John Murray, 1896)

Borukhov, B., 'Was the Author of Loves Martyr Chester of Royston?' (*Notes and Queries,* Volume 56 (1), 2009)

Borukhov, B. R., *Chester's Loves Martyr and the Hyphenated Shakespeare* (*Notes and Queries,* Volume 58 (2), 2011)

Boyd, R. L. and Pennebaker J. W., *Did Shakespeare Write Double Falsehood? Identifying Individuals by Creating Psychological Signatures with Text Analysis* (Article in Psychological, ScienceOnlineFirst, Sage, 2015)

Bradbeer, M. and Casson J., *Sir Henry Neville, Alias William Shakespeare|: Authorship Evidence in the History Plays* (Jefferson, North Carolina: MacFarland, 2015)

Bradbrook, M. C., *Shakespeare* (Abingdon: Routledge, 2005)

Bradley, A. C., *Shakespearean Tragedy: Lectures on Hamlet, Othello, King Lear, Macbeth* (London: Macmillan, 1905)

Brooke, N., *Macbeth* (Oxford: The Oxford Shakespeare, Oxford World's Classics, Oxford University Press, 1998)

Brooks, H. F., *A Midsummer Night's Dream* (London: The Arden Shakespeare, Methuen, 1990)

Brown, C., *Poems By Sir John Salusbury and Robert Chester* (London: Early English Text Society, by K. Paul, Trench, Trübner & Co, 1913)

Bruce, J., (ed.), *Liber Famelicus of Sir James Whitelocke* (London: The Camden Society, available on line: http://archive.org/stream/liberfamelicus00camduoft#page/n3/mode/2up accessed 24/2/2015], 1858)

Burgoyne, F. J., *Collotype Facsimile and Type Transcript of An Elizabethan Manuscript preserved at Alnwick Castle, Northumberland* (London: Longmans, Green and Co., 1904)

Cairncross, A. S., *Shakespeare and Ariosto, Much Ado About Nothing, King Lear and Othello* (Chicago: Renaissance Quarterly Vol 29, No 2, p 178–82, University of Chicago Press, 1976)

Callaghan, D., *Shakespeare's Sonnets,* (Oxford: Blackwell, 2007)

Casson, J., *Enter Pursued by a Bear, The Unknown Plays of Shakespeare-Neville* (Bognor Regis: Music for Strings, 2009, republished from Tatcham, Berkshire: Dolman Scott, 2010).

Casson, J., *Much Ado About Noting, Henry Neville and Shakespeare's Secret Source* (Tatcham, Berkshire: Dolman Scott, 2010)

Cassuto, U., From Noah to Abraham (Jerusalem: Magnes Press, 1997)

Chambers, E. K., *William Shakespeare, A Study of Facts and Problems, Volume II* (Oxford: Clarendon Press, 1966)

Clark, A. M., *Murder under Trust, The Topical Macbeth and other Jacobean Matters* (Edinburgh: Scottish Academic Press, 1981)

Clarke, B. R, *The Virginia Company and The Tempest, Journal of Drama Studies* 5 13-27 (University of Pennsylvania: July 2011)

Collins, A., (ed.), *Sydney Papers in Letters and Memorials of State, from the reign of Queen Mary to that of Charles II* (London: T. Osbourne, 1746)

Cooper, T., *Searching For Shakespeare* (London: Exhibition Guide, National Portrait Gallery, 2006)

Craik, T. W., (ed.), *The Merry Wives of Windsor* (Oxford: Oxford University Press, 1990)

Crystal, D., *Think On My Words, Exploring Shakespeare's Language* (Cambridge: Cambridge University Press, 2008)

Daniell, D., *Julius Caesar* (London: Thomson Learning, The Arden Shakespeare, 2005)

Daugherty, L., *William Shakespeare, Richard Barnfield, and the sixth Earl of Derby*, (Amherst, New York: Cambria Press, 2010)

Davies, J. D., *Blood of Kings, The Stuarts, the Ruthvens and the Gowrie Conspiracy* (Hersham, Surrey: Ian Allan Publishing, 2010)

Dawson, G., *Shakespeare's Handwriting*, Shakespeare Survey 42 (Cambridge: Cambridge University Press, 1990)

Dawson, A. B. and Minton, G. E., (eds.), *Timon of Athens* (London: Cengage Learning, The Arden Shakespeare, 2008)

Ditchfield, H. and Page, W., (eds.), *Victoria County History: A History of Berkshire, Volume 3* (London: *Victoria County History*, 1923)

Donaldson, I., *Ben Jonson A Life* (Oxford: Oxford University Press, 2011)

Dorsch, T. S., *The Comedy of Errors* (Cambridge: The New Cambridge Shakespeare, Cambridge University Press, 2004)

Douglas, M., *Thinking in Circles, An Essay on Ring Composition* (New Haven and London: Yale University Press, 2007)

Dowden, E., *Shakspere: A Critical Study of His Mind and Art* (Cambridge: Cambridge University Press, 1875)

Duncan, O. L., *The Political Career of Sir Henry Neville* (unpublished PhD Thesis: Ohio State University, 1974)

Duncan-Jones, K., *Sir Philip Sidney, Courtier Poet* (London: Hamish Hamilton, 1991)

Duncan-Jones, K., *Shakespeare's Sonnets* (London: Thomson Learning, The Arden Shakespeare, 2005)

Edmondson, and Wells, S., *Shakespeare's Sonnets* (Oxford: Oxford University Press, 2004)

Edmondson, and Wells, S., (eds), *Shakespeare Beyond Doubt: Evidence, Argument, Controversy* (Cambridge: Cambridge University Press, 2013)

Engel, W. E., *Chiastic Design in English Literature from Sidney to Shakespeare*, (Farnham, Surrey: Ashgate Publishing Ltd., 2009)

Erne, L., *Shakespeare As Literary Dramatist* (Cambridge: Cambridge University Press, 2013)

Falk, D., *The Science of Shakespeare, A New Look at the Playwright's Universe* (New York: Thomas Dunne Books, 2014)

Fernie, E., *Shame in Shakespeare* (London: Routledge, 2002)

Fields, B., *Players: The Mysterious Identity of William Shakespeare* (Stroud, Gloucestershire: Sutton Publishing, 2006)

Foakes, R. A., *King Lear* (London: Thomas Nelson & Sons Ltd, The Arden Shakespeare, 1997)

Foakes, R. A., *The Comedy of Errors* (London: Thomson Learning, The Arden Shakespeare, 2005)

Foster, M., *Gloucester Hall and the Survival of Catholicism* (Oxoniensia 46, Oxfordshire Architectural and Historical Society, 1981)

Frame, D. M., *Montaigne's Travel Journal* (San Francisco: North Point Press, 1983)

Freehafer, J., *Cardenio, by Shakespeare and Fletcher* (P. M. L. A., 501–13, 1969)

Gajda, A., *The Earl of Essex and Late Elizabethan Political Culture* (Oxford: Oxford University Press, 2012)

Gayley, C. M., *Shakespeare and the Founders of Liberty in America* (New York: The Macmillan Company, 1917)

Gesner, C., *Shakespeare & the Greek Romance, A Study of Origins* (Lexington: University Press of Kentucky, 1970)

Gibbons, B., *Measure for Measure* (Cambridge: New Cambridge Shakespeare, Cambridge University Press, 1991)

Gibbons, B., *Romeo and Juliet* (London: Thomson Learning, The Arden Shakespeare, 2004)

Gillespie, S., *Shakespeare's Books: A Dictionary of Shakespeare's Sources* (London: Athlone Press, 2004)

Giroux, R., *The Book Known As Q: A Consideration of Shakespeare's Sonnets* (New York: Vintage Books, 1983)

Given-Wilson, C. and Curtles, A., *The Royal Bastards of Medieval England* (London: Routledge & Kegan Paul, 1984)

Gooch, J. L., *The Lamentable Tragedy of Locrine: A Critical Edition* (New York: Garland Publishing Inc., Garland English Texts No. 7, 1981)

Gossett, S., *Pericles* (London: Thomson Learning, The Arden Shakespeare, 2004)

Goulding, R. D., *Savile, Sir Henry (1549–1622)* (Oxford: Oxford Dictionary of National Biography, 2004)

Gouws, J., (ed.), *The Prose Works of Fulke Greville, Lord Brooke* (Oxford: Clarendon Press, 1986)

Green, W., *Shakespeare's Merry Wives of Windsor* (Princeton, N.J.: Princeton University Press, 1962)

Green, M., *Wriothesley's Roses in Shakespeare's Sonnets, Poems and Plays* (Baltimore, Maryland: Clevedon Books, 1993)

Hadfield, A., *Shakespeare and Republicanism* (Cambridge: Cambridge University Press, 2005)

Halliday, E. F., *A Shakespeare Companion 1564–1964* (London: Gerald Duckworth, 1964)

Hammer, E. J., *The Polarisation of Elizabethan Politics: The Political Career of Robert Devereux, 2nd Earl of Essex, 1585–1597* (Cambridge: Cambridge University Press, 1999)

Hammond, B., *Double Falsehood* (London: Methuen Drama, The Arden Shakespeare, 2010)

Harding, A., *Henry Neville (1562–1615)* in W. Hasler, ed., *The History of Parliament: The House of Commons, 1558–1603* (London: 1981), available online.

Hasler, W., (ed.), *The History of Parliament: The House of Commons, 1558–1603*, London: 1981) available online.

Haynes, A., *Walsingham, Elizabethan Spymaster and Statesman* (Stroud, Gloucestershire: The History Press, 2004)

Hawkyard, A., *The biography of Sir Edward Neville* (Oxford: Oxford Dictionary of National Biography, Vol 40, 490, 2004)

Hedley, O., *Windsor Castle* (London: Robert Hale, 1994)

Honan, *Shakespeare: A Life, The Arden and Shakespeare Family Trees* (New York: Oxford University Press, 1999)

Honigmann, A. J., *Othello* (London: Thomson Learning, The Arden Shakespeare, 2003)

Hotson, L., *Shakespeare versus Shallow* (London: Nonesuch Press, 1931)

Howard-Hill, T. H., (ed.), *Shakespeare and Sir Thomas More: Essays on the Play and Its Shakespearean Interest* (Cambridge: Cambridge University Press, 1989)

Humfreys, A. R., *Henry IV Part II*, (London: Methuen, The Arden Shakespeare, 1966)

Hunt, M., *The double figure of Elizabeth in Love's Labour's Lost*, (Essays in Literature, Chicago: Western Illinois University, 1992)

Hunter, G. K., *All's Well That Ends Well* (London: Methuen & Co. Ltd., The Arden Shakespeare, 1967)

James, B. and Rubinstein, W. D., *The Truth Will Out: Unmasking The Real Shakespeare* (Harlow: Pearson Longman, 2005)

James, B., *Henry Neville and the Shakespeare Code* (Bognor Regis: Music for Strings, 2008)

James, B., *Understanding the Invisible Shakespeare* (Bognor Regis: Cranesmere Press, 2011)

Jolly, M., *The First Two Quartos of Hamlet* (Jefferson, North Carolina: McFarland & Company Inc., 2014)

Jowett, J., *Timon of Athens* (Oxford: The Oxford Shakespeare, Oxford University Press, 2004)

Jowett, J., *Sir Thomas More* (London: Methuen Drama, The Arden Shakespeare, 2011)

Jost, J. S., *Hamlet's Horatio as an allusion to Horace's Odes* (Notes and Queries, Oxford University Press, 9 January 2012)

Kathman, D., *Dating The Tempest*, online at: shakespeareauthorship.com

Keen, A. and Lubbock, R., *The Annotator* (London: Putman, 1954)

Kermode, F., *The Tempest* (London: Routledge, The Arden Shakespeare 1990)

Kincaid, A. N., *The Encomium of Richard III by Sir William Cornwallis the Younger*, (London: Turner & Devereux, 1977)

Kuhl, E., *Shakespeare and the Founders of America: The Tempest,* (Iowa: University of Iowa, *Philological Quarterly* XLI, 1962)

Kukowski, S., *The Hand of John Fletcher in Double Falshood* (Cambridge: Shakespeare Survey 43 The Tempest and After, edited by Stanley Wells, Cambridge University Press, 1991)

Lacey, R., *Robert, Earl of Essex: An Elizabethan Icarus* (London: Weidenfeld & Nicholson, 1971)

Laoutaris, C., *Shakespeare and the Countess, the Battle that gave birth to the Globe* (London: Fig Tree, an imprint of Penguin Books, 2014)

Lee, S., *A Life of William Shakespeare* (London: Smith, Elder & Co., 1899)

Leggatt, A. *All's Well That Ends Well* (Cambridge: Cambridge University Press, New Cambridge Shakespeare, 2004)

Lever, J. W., *Measure for Measure* (London: Routledge, the Arden Shakespeare, 1989)

Levi, *New Verses by Shakespeare* (London: Macmillan, 1988)

Levith, M., *Shakespeare's Italian Settings and Plays* (New York: St Martin's Press, 1989)

Leyland, B. and Goding J., *Shakespeare, Sir Henry Neville and the Sonnets Decrypted*, e-book from Leanpub, 2015)

Lindley, D., *Blackfriars, Music and Masque: Theatrical Contexts of the Last Plays*, in Alexander, C. M. S., (ed.), *The Cambridge Companion to Shakespeare's Last Plays* (Cambridge: Cambridge University Press, 2009)

Londre, F. H., (ed.), *Love's Labour's Lost Critical Essays* (Kansas City: University of Missouri, Garland Shakespeare Criticism, 1997)

Lyne, R., *English Guarini: recognition and reception*, New Hall Cambridge: Gale, Cengage Learning, 2006) accessed online from www.thefreelibrary.com, 9 February 2015.

MacGregor, N., *Shakespeare's Restless World: an Unexpected History in Twenty Objects* (London: Penguin Books, 2014)

Magri, N., *Such Fruits Out of Italy: The Italian Renaissance in Shakespeare's Plays* (Buchholz, Germany: Laugwitz Verlag, 2014)

Marrapodi, M., (ed.), *Italian Culture in the Drama of Shakespeare and His Contemporaries: rewriting, remaking, refashioning Anglo-Italian Renaissance Studies* (Aldershot, Hants, UK: Ashgate Publishing Limited, 2007)

Masefield, J., *William Shakespeare* (London: T. Butterworth, 1912)

McClure, N. E., (ed.), *The Letters of John Chamberlain, Two Volumes* (Philadelphia: The American Philosophical Society, 1939)

McCoy, R., *Loves Martyrs: Shakespeare's Phoenix and the Turtle and the Sacrificial Sonnets* (in McEachern & Shugar 1997)

McEachern, C. and Shugar, D., (eds.), *Religion and Culture in Renaissance England* (Cambridge: Cambridge University Press, 1997)

McMillan, S., *The Elizabethan Theatre and the Book of Sir Thomas More* (Ithaca, N.Y.: Cornell University Press, 1987)

McQuain, J. and Malless, S., *Coined by Shakespeare: Words and Meanings First Penned by the Bard* (Springfield, Massachusetts: Merriam-Webster Inc., 1998)

Melchiori, G., *King Edward III* (Cambridge: Cambridge University Press, The New Cambridge Shakespeare, 1998)

Melchiori, G., *The Merry Wives of Windsor* (London: Thomson Learning, Arden Shakespeare, 2000)

Michell, J., *Who Wrote Shakespeare?* (London: Thames & Hudson, 2000)

Miles, R., *The Problem of Measure for Measure: A Historical Investigation* (London: Vision, 1976)

Milton, A., *The British Delegation and the Synod of Dort (1618–1619)* (Woodbridge, Suffolk, UK: Boydell Press, Church of England, Record Society, 2005)

Morris, B, *The Taming of The Shrew* (London: Thomson Learning, The Arden Shakespeare, 2004)

Morris, H., *Queen Elizabeth 'Shadowed' in Cleopatra* (San Marino: *Huntington Library Publications, Huntington Library Quarterly*, 1969)

Mortimer, I., *The Perfect King: The Life of Edward III, Father of the English Nation*, (London: Vintage Books, 2008)

Muir, K., *Shakespeare's Sonnets* (London: George Allen & Unwin, 1979)

Neill, M., *The Tragedy of Anthony and Cleopatra* (Oxford: Oxford University Press, The Oxford Shakespeare, 1994)

Nicholls, M. and Williams,, *Sir Walter Raleigh in Life and Legend* (London: Continuum International Publishing Group, 2011)

Nosworthy, J. M., *Cymbeline* (London: Methuen Drama, The Arden Shakespeare, 1969)

Oliver, H.J., (ed.), *Timon of Athens* (London: Methuen & Co. Ltd., The Arden Shakespeare, 1963)

Orgel, S., *The Winter's Tale* (Oxford: Oxford University Press, The Oxford Shakespeare, 1996)

ODNB: Oxford Dictionary of National Biography available on line

Palmer, K., *Troilus and Cressida* (London: Methuen & Co., The Arden Shakespeare, 1982)

Parker, R. B., *Coriolanus* (Oxford: Oxford University Press, The Oxford Shakespeare, 1998)

Peck, D. C., *Leicester's Commonwealth, The Copy of a Letter Written by a Master of Art of Cambridge (1584) and Related Documents* (London: Ohio University Press, 1985)

Peck, D. C., (ed.), *Leicester's Commonwealth, The Copy of a Letter Written by a Master of Art of Cambridge (1584) and Related Documents (*Athens, Ohio: Ohio University Press, Reprinted in PDF format, 2006: http://www.dpeck.info/write/leic-comm.pdf, **2006**) – We have used both Peck's (1985) published text and the internet download. We have therefore referred to the page numbers as Peck (65/48), putting the book page number first, followed by the internet text page number in italics

Pointon, A. J., *The Man who was Never Shakespeare: The Theft of Shakespeare's Identity* (Tunbridge Wells, Kent: Parapress, 2011)

Pollard, A. W., *Shakespeare's Hand in the Play of Sir Thomas More* (Cambridge: Cambridge University Press, 1923)

Price, D., *Shakespeare's Unorthodox Biography: New Evidence of an Authorship Problem* (Westport, CT: Greenwood Publishing Group [republished in paperback with revisions in 2012 by shakespeare-authorship.com] 2001)

Prior, R., *The Life of George Wilkins* (Cambridge: Cambridge University Press, Shakespeare Survey 25, 1972)

Reedy, T., *Dating William Strachey's 'A True Reportory of the Wrack and Redemption of Sir Thomas Gates: A Comparative Textual Analysis*, (Oxford: The *Review of English Studies* 251, 529–52, Oxford Journals, 2010)

Ribbans, M., *Clopton Bridge: A Short History of the Gateway to Stratford-upon-Avon* (Atlanta, Ga.: RFP, 2005)

Rinehart, K., *Shakespeare's Cleopatra and Elizabeth's England* (Washington D.C.: Folger Shakespeare Library, *Shakespeare Quarterly*, Volume 23, No. 1, 1972)

Roberts, C., *Schemes and Undertakings: A Study of English Politics in the Seventeenth Century* (Columbus: Ohio State University Press, 1985)

Roe, J., *The Poems* (Cambridge: Cambridge University Press, The New Cambridge Shakespeare, 1998)

Roe, R., *The Shakespeare Guide to Italy* (London: Harper Perennial, 2011)

Roisman, H. *Nestor the Good Counsellor*, *Classical Quarterly*, Vol. 55, 17–38, (Cambridge: Cambridge University Press, 2006),

Rollett, J., *The Dedication to Shakespeare's Sonnets* (The Elizabethan Review, vol. 5, no. 2, Autumn, 93–106, 1997)

Rollett, J., *Secrets of the Dedication to Shakespeare's Sonnets* (The Oxfordian Volume II, (October, 60–75, 1999)

Rowse, A. L., *Raleigh and the Throckmortons* (London: Macmillan, 1962)

Rubinstein, W. D., *Who Wrote Shakespeare's Plays?* (Stroud: Gloucestershire: Amberley Publishing, 2012)

Salerno, H., *Double Falshood Shakespeare's Cardenio: A Study of a 'Lost' Play* (New Jersey, USA: Xlibris Corporation, 2000)

Salisbury, *Calendar of Manuscripts of the Marquis of Salisbury at Hatfield House* (Dublin: HMSO, Volume XI, 1906)

Sams, E., *Shakespeare's Edmund Ironside: The Lost Play* (Aldershot, Hants: Wildwood House, 1986)

Sams, E., *Shakespeare's Edward III: An early play restored to the canon* (London: Yale University Press, 1996)

Sawyer, E., *Memorials of State in the Reigns of Q. Elizabeth and K. James I Collected from the Original Papers of the Right Honourable Sir Ralph Winwood*, 3 Volumes, (London: T. Ward, 1725)

Schafer, E., *The Date of the Merry Wives of Windsor* (Oxford: Notes and Queries, Oxford University Press, 38(1), 57–60, 1991)

Schurink, F., *An Unnoticed Early Reference to Shakespeare* (Oxford: Notes and Queries, Oxford University Press, March, 2006)

Schoenbaum, S., *William Shakespeare, A Compact Documentary Life* (Oxford: Oxford University Press, 1987)

Schutzenberger, A., *The Ancestor Syndrome* (London: Routledge, 1998)

Scoufus, A-L., *Shakespeare's Typological Satire: A study of the Falstaff-Oldcastle Problem* (Athens, Ohio: Ohio University Press, 1979)

Shahan, J. and Waugh, A., *Shakespeare Beyond Doubt? Exposing and Industry in Denial* (Tamarac, FL: Llumina Press, 2013)

Sharpe, R. B., *The Real War of the Theaters: Shakespeare's Fellows in Rivalry With the Admiral's Men, 1594–1603* (Boston, Mass: D. C. Heath, 1935)

Sherbo, A., *Richard Farmer, master of Emmanuel College, Cambridge: a forgotten Shakespearean* (Oxford: *ODNB*, 1992) available from: http://www.oxforddnb.com/view/article/9169?docPos=1 accessed 3/11/14

Showerman, E., *How did Shakespeare Learn the Art of Medicine*, Chapter 9 in Shahan, J. M. and Waugh A., 2013.

Simonton, D., *Genius and Creativity: Selected Papers* (Greenwich, CT: Ablex Publishing, 1997)

Smith, L., *Life and Letters of Sir Henry Wotton*, 2 Vols (Oxford: Clarendon Press, 1907)

Snyder, S., *All's Well That Ends Well* (Oxford: The Oxford Shakespeare, Oxford University Press, 1993/1998)

Somerset, A., *Unnatural Murder: Poison at the Court of James I* (London: Weidenfeld & Nicolson, 1997)

Spedding, J., *The Life and Letters of Francis Bacon* (London: Longmans, Green, and Co., 1890)

Spurgeon, C., *Shakespeare's Imagery and what it tells us* (Cambridge: Cambridge University Press, 2001)

Steinburg, S., *I Come to Bury Shakspere* (Café Padre Publishing, 2013)

Stopes, C., *The Third Earl of Southampton* (Cambridge: Cambridge University Press, 1922)

Stoughton, J., *Windsor: A History and Description of the Castle and the Town* (London: Ward & Co., 1862)

Strachey, L., *Elizabeth and Essex: A Tragic History* (London: Chatto & Windus, 1928)

Stritmatter, R. A. & Kositsky, L. *On the Date, Source, and Design of Shakespeare's The Tempest* (Jefferson, N.C.: MacFarland, 2013).

Thomas, A., *Shakespeare, Dissent and the Cold War, Defiant Will* (Houndmills, Basingstoke: Palgrave Macmillan, 2014)

Thompson, A. and Taylor, N., *Hamlet* (London: Thomson Learning, The Arden Shakespeare, 2006)

Thompson, E. M., *Shakespeare's Handwriting: A Study* (Oxford: Clarendon, 1916)

Tillyard, E., *Shakespeare's History Plays* (London: Chatto and Windus, 1944)

Titherley, A. W., *Shakespeare's Identity: William Stanley, 6th Earl of Derby* (Winchester: Warren & Son Ltd, The Wykeham Press, 1952)

Ungerer, G., *A Spaniard in Elizabethan England: The Correspondence of Antonio Perez's Exile*, 2 Vols (London: Tamesis Books Limited, 1976)

Vaughan, A. T., *William Strachey's 'True Reportory' and Shakespeare: A Closer Look at the Evidence*, *Shakespeare Quarterly* 59, 245–77 (Washington D.C.: Folger Shakespeare Library, 2008)

Vendler, H., *The Art of Shakespeare's Sonnets* (London: The Belknap Press of Harvard University Press, 1999)

Vickers, B., *Shakespeare, Co-Author* (Oxford: Oxford University Press, 2004)

Warren, R., *Cymbeline* (Oxford: Oxford University Press, The Oxford Shakespeare, 1998)

Warren, R., *Henry VI Part Two* (Oxford: Oxford University Press, The Oxford Shakespeare, 2003)

Warren, R., *Pericles* (Oxford: Oxford University Press, The Oxford Shakespeare, 2004)

Wecter, D., *The Purpose of Timon of Athens, Publications of the Modern Language Association* (PMLA) Volume 43, Issue 3, September, 701–21, 1928) (available at JSTOR)

Weis, R., *King Lear, A Parallel Text, Second Edition*, (Harlow: Longman Pearson, 2010)

Wells, S. & Taylor, G., *William Shakespeare: A Textual Companion* (Oxford: Oxford University Press, [reprinted by W.W. Norton, New York, 1997] 1987)

Werth, A., *Shakespeare's Lesse Greek*, in *Report My Case Aright* (Yorkstown Heights, N.Y.: The Shakespeare-Oxford Society, Fiftieth Anniversary Anthology, 1957–2007 2007)

West, D., *Shakespeare's Sonnets, With A New Commentary* (London: Duckworth Overlook, 2007)

White, D. J., *Richard Edwards' Damon and Pitias, A Critical Old-Spelling Edition* (New York: Garland Publishing Inc., 1980)

Whitt, B., *New Light on Sir William Cornwallis, The Essayist* (Oxford: Oxford University Press, The Review of English Studies (R.E.S.) Vol 8, No. 30, April 1932) available from www.res.oxfordjournals.org.

Wickham, E. C., *Horace for English Readers: Being a Translation of the Poems of Quintus Horatius Flaccus into English Prose* (Oxford: Clarendon Press, 1903)

Wilders, J., *Antony and Cleopatra* (London: A & C Black Publishers, Ltd., The Arden Shakespeare, 1995)

Williams, R., *Sweet Swan of Avon: Did a Woman write Shakespeare?* (Santa Fe: Wilton Circle Press, 2012)

Wilson, R., *Will Power: Essays on Shakespearean Authority* (Chicago: Wayne State University Press, 1993)

Wilson, R., *Secret Shakespeare, Studies in theatre, religion and resistance* (Manchester: Manchester University Press, 2004)

Wine, M. L., (ed.), *The Tragedy of Master Arden of Faversham* (London: Methuen & Co. Ltd., The Revel Plays, 1973)

Winstanley, L., *Hamlet and the Scottish Succession* (Cambridge: Cambridge University Press, 1921)

Woudhuysen, H. R., *Love's Labour's Lost* (London: Thomson Learning, The Arden Shakespeare, 2001)

Woolfson, J., *Padua and the Tudors: English Students in Italy, 1485–1603* (Cambridge: James Clarke & Co Ltd., 1998)

Yates, F., *The Rosicrucian Enlightenment* (London: Routledge Classics, 2004)

Index

About the Authors

John Casson is a retired psychotherapist who has completed thirty years' practice as a dramatherapist and psychodrama psychotherapist. He lives near Bolton in Lancashire. He is the author of three academic books on Henry Neville as Shakespeare: *Enter Pursued by a Bear* and *Much Ado About Nothing*, both published by Dolman Scott; and, with Mark Bradbeer, *Sir Henry Neville, Alias William Shakespeare: Authorship Evidence in the History Plays*, published by McFarland.

William Rubinstein was a professor of History at the University of Wales, Aberyswyth and had previously been professor of History at Deakin University in Victoria, Australia. He now lives in Melbourne, Australia, and is currently adjunct professor at Monash University. His previous book, *Who Wrote Shakespeare's Plays?* is also published by Amberley.